Ancient Mediterranean Incarceration

Ancient Mediterranean Incarceration

Matthew D. C. Larsen and Mark Letteney

UNIVERSITY OF CALIFORNIA PRESS

Please visit the Ancient Mediterranean Incarceration companion website at www.historyofincarceration.com to access the data underlying this book.

University of California Press
Oakland, California

Suggested citation: Larsen, M. D. C. and Letteney, M. *Ancient Mediterranean Incarceration*. Oakland: University of California Press, 2025. DOI: https://doi.org/10.1525/luminos.239

Cataloging-in-Publication Data is on file at the Library of Congress.

ISBN 978–0-520–42260-5 (cloth)
ISBN 978–0-520–38722-5 (pbk.)
ISBN 978–0-520–38723-2 (ebook)

GPSR Authorized Representative: Easy Access System Europe, Mustamäe tee 50, 10621 Tallinn, Estonia, gpsr.requests@easproject.com

33 32 31 30 29 28 27 26 25
10 9 8 7 6 5 4 3 2 1

CONTENTS

List of Illustrations   *vii*
Preface   *ix*
List of Abbreviations   *xv*

Introduction   *1*

PART ONE. IDEALS AND SPACES

  1. Incarceration and the Law   *19*

  2. Spaces of Incarceration   *45*

PART TWO. EXPERIENCES AND PERCEPTIONS

  3. Experiences of Incarceration   *91*

  4. Ancient Mediterranean Prison Societies   *123*

  5. Prison Management   *154*

Afterword: The Prison's Antiquity   *197*
  Wendy Warren
Acknowledgments   *203*
References   *205*
Source Index   *221*
Subject Index   *229*

ILLUSTRATIONS

1. The Tullian Prison   47
2. Civic prison of Cosa   49
3. Reconstructed elevation of curia and east tribunal in the old forum at Ulpia Traiana Sarmizegetusa   51
4. Cuicul civic prison complex   53
5. Military prison at Lambaesis   57
6. Amphitheater of Carales with Gladiator Prison and Prison for the Condemned   60
7. Gladiator Prison within the Carales amphitheater   60
8. Second phase of the incarcerated and enslaved workers quarters at Simitthus   62
9. Late Roman prison at Corinth   67
10. Inscribed wall in the Prison for the Condemned at Carales   69
11. Early Christian prison graffito   71
12. Temple complex at Sufetula   77
13. Sufetula, forum baseplan   78
14. Sufetula, proposed civic prison underneath the central temple   79
15. Mosaic of the Captives   137
16. Fresco of Pero and Micon   140
17. Roman terracotta plaque   145
18. Sixteen lead figurines depicting prisoners   146
19. Mosaic of the Damnati   148
20. Relief of a triumphing emperor   150

viii   ILLUSTRATIONS

21. P. Mich. Mchl. 5   *159*
22. P. Tebt. 2.290   *162*
23. P. Cair. Zen. 3.59492   *166*
24. Script comparison of P. Mich. 1.87 and P. Cair. Zen. 3.59492   *167*
25. William Hogarth, *The Gaols Committee of the House of Commons*   *202*

PREFACE

This book offers an account of spaces, experiences, and ideologies of incarceration in the ancient Mediterranean basin, focusing primarily on sources dating between 300 BCE and 600 CE. We argue that incarceration was prevalent across this geographic and temporal span and that sources point overwhelmingly to prisons and practices of incarceration as an integral part of the social, economic, and political life of ancient Mediterranean societies. By "Mediterranean," we mean communities and regimes that hold a "middle sea" in common—who look to the Mediterranean as a central node through which cultural, economic, and social currents flow. Our data include the following: literary sources prescribing an idealized carceral order and accounts of prisons and those inside; carceral facilities known through archaeological investigation; documentary evidence from and about prisoners, including letters, bail receipts, tax receipts, and orders for arrest; and visual depictions of captives and spaces of incarceration. We aim to demonstrate that the prison is not a modern, medieval, or even late ancient invention, despite widespread and persistent claims to the contrary.

Our method is to foreground voices of incarcerated people and their experience of carceral facilities through documentary, archaeological, and visual sources, and to use that material to reframe our reading of literary sources—especially legal materials. This approach has dictated the contours of our archive: We begin around 300 BCE with the earliest significant corpus of documentary sources on papyrus, and we end with the emergence of new empires, structures of governance, and dominant languages across the Mediterranean around 600 CE, as the late antique world lumbered into the Middle Ages, a period in the history of the prison whose long roots Julia Hillner (2015) has thoroughly traced and that Guy Geltner (2008) has investigated marvelously with respect to the Italian city-states. Likewise, J. Nicholas

Reid (2022) has recently subjected ancient Mesopotamian sources to detailed analysis, yielding useful new insights about the earliest written materials depicting prisoners, prisons, and the administration of state punishment, and Marcus Folch (2026) is completing a significant cultural and literary history of ancient Mediterranean incarceration beginning with the earliest Greek literary evidence.

While other scholars have investigated ancient Mediterranean carceral ideals and practices from a variety of angles, our analysis bridges a gap in the field by allotting archaeological and documentary evidence as much analytical weight as literary materials. To give a sense of evidentiary asymmetry in classic works on the ancient prison, we should consider this small but telling datum: in December 1997, sixteen of the leading voices on the study of ancient incarceration met in Strasbourg, publishing their proceedings as a book in 1999 titled *Carcer: Prison et privation de liberté dans l'Antiquité classique* (Carcer: prison and the deprivation of liberty in classical antiquity). The collection's index of ancient sources includes thirteen pages of literary materials, while documentary sources comprise just shy of a page and a half. Privileging the experiences of prisoners as seen in documentary materials alongside the ideology of their captors brings much-needed evidentiary parity, which, we argue, suggests somewhat different conclusions about the nature and place of incarceration in ancient Mediterranean societies. With this book, we especially aim to decenter legal ideals as the premier source for the status and function of incarceration in the ancient world and to recenter prisons and carceral practices in scholarly imaginations of ancient life. We hope to demonstrate that attending closely to archaeological and documentary sources offers a different picture than what emerges primarily from literary materials.

As we discuss below in detail, our archive is irreparably lumpy: the overwhelming majority of documentary sources are preserved in Egypt, for instance, while archaeological, literary, and visual materials span the Mediterranean basin, however unevenly. Legal materials, for their part, shed more light on the third century CE and beyond than they enlighten earlier periods. Patterns of scholarly interest and publication also inflect the availability of evidence: Ptolemaic, Roman, and Byzantine materials have received the most sustained scholarly interest; as such, they are better represented than the few sources that survive from marginalized communities and away from imperial metropoles.

This book makes a different argument from those that have come before within the field of carceral studies, yet it builds on a trend in ancient history that contends the prison has a history not of two centuries but of two millennia at least, and doubtless much longer. In fact, if it is origins that we are after, then we should probably say that the jail—defined as a separate purpose-built facility intended solely to detain people before trial—is an invention of Late Antiquity, while the prison's roots plunge deeper into history than our surviving data attests. These are strong claims that invert a common sense in carceral studies; at this point, they are merely assertions disputing a century-old consensus, but we are not the first ancient historians to raise this challenge. Nevertheless, as we demonstrate in our analysis and document across the corpus of materials related to ancient incarceration, sources attesting the prison's long history are abundant. Taking them seriously—both individually and as a corpus—must change our historical framework. While ultimately there may prove to be no lessons to learn from antiquity about a more just carceral system, we hope that from a new framework, new historical consciousness may arise around contemporary practices of incarceration. More than anything else, this material points to the extraordinary durability of carceral structures across time, and their fundamental imbrication with issues of class, ethnicity, gender, and imperialism. Even so, seeing this material gives us an opportunity to learn something about our own choices, aided by what Hans-Georg Gadamer (2013) called "the hermeneutic significance of temporal distance" (291–99). These sources help us to see that choices to incarcerate, including how, whom, where, and why to cage people, are just that—choices encoding an ideology of punishment that, in the absence of critical examination, we might mistake as obvious, natural, innocent, or without real alternative.

Our analysis is built on data collected over the course of nine years, including dozens of visits to sites of ancient incarceration, hundreds of inscriptions, papyri, and ostraca translated anew (and not a few for the first time), and literary and visual sources selected, excerpted, and mobilized to contextualize the material remains of carceral practices. A wide variety of sources underlie our analysis, and we survey them throughout. Even so, this is not a sourcebook. It is a synthetic account that offers new data and arguments, especially regarding incarceration as a practice, as an institution, and as a system of social control. With this book we hope to offer an arena in which to ask new questions about the nature and scope of the prison's history, to open a number of new lines of inquiry, and to offer a few moments of provocation. Nevertheless, our analysis is hardly comprehensive. It is neither the first nor the final word on any of the topics covered—just as we build on the work of previous scholars, we hope that this book will serve as a resource for others going forward.

Most of the data are available in an open access database at historyofIncarceration.com. Source citations throughout this book include a database ID comprising two parts: a letter indicating the type of evidence—D (Documentary), A (Archaeological), V (Visual), or L (Literary)—and a number indicating the specific source within that category. The sequence of sources was determined by sheer happenstance. Thus, a source labeled A34 is the thirty-fourth archaeological source listed in the database, while D183 is the 183rd documentary source. In-text citations indicate the relevant publication information, database ID, and date. We encourage readers to visit the database to explore the evidence in full, to interact with three-dimensional models of archaeological materials, and to read commentaries that we have written for each source.

This book aims to speak to more than one audience. As ancient historians, we hope that the book aids colleagues studying the ancient world by offering a fresh perspective on what we argue was a central feature of many ancient Mediterranean societies. We also hope that the work will be useful to scholars in the field of carceral studies and to those with a general interest in the history of incarceration. To the degree it is possible to speak to a general readership interested in the question of incarceration without compromising academic rigor, we have tried to do so. Because of our broad intended audience, citations to scholarly debates and secondary sources are judicious, indicating direct interlocutors or important interventions with which our analysis interacts. Our citations should not be interpreted as reflecting the breadth of scholarship available on any particular source or question. A more comprehensive bibliography of relevant sources is available in the companion database, which we hope will serve scholars, public policy workers, and the interested public alike as a resource.

A brief word about what we mean by incarceration: our approach invokes a number of overlapping terms in critical prison studies. A prison is a physical place where incarceration happens, though incarceration occurs in facilities that are not formally prisons. "Prison systems" indicate larger networks of practice—political, social, economic, and so on—that intersect, support, and are implicated with the institution of incarceration as a critical node. Courts, for instance, are part of the prison system, but they are not prisons; nor are they the only system that interacts with the prison. "Incarceration" refers to a constellation of practices that involve confinement of human bodies for perceived deviance: legal, social, political, economic, or otherwise. For us, then, incarceration includes confinement in a civic prison as a result of legal proceedings, but it is not limited to that one form. Incarceration also includes other systems in which someone with power enforces involuntary confinement of another human for perceived deviance within a physical space. We argue below that any clean bifurcation between people condemned to hard labor and "prisoners" is a distinction without a substantive difference; in practice, both were incarcerated. The relevant data supports this capacious definition—ancient sources often use the same terminology for both penal laborers and people confined in civic prisons, as we detail below. Over the course of this book we also employ the common distinction between a jail, which indicates a purpose built structure intended for detention before sentencing, and prison, a space intended to hold people after conviction, as one part of their punishment.

The following chapters distinguish between spaces, experiences, and ideologies of incarceration, building on Henri Lefebvre's (1974) spatial trichotomy comprising lived spaces, perceived spaces, and conceived spaces, each of which offers a different epistemic perspective. By "ideology of incarceration," we do not mean to signal that our analysis is a form of ideological criticism. Rather, we mean something more generic: how incarceration was conceived of working, most often by people *outside* the cage. This framework allows us to consider archaeological and documentary evidence as a way of foregrounding lived experiences of incarcerated persons (lived and perceived spaces), and to keep them conceptually separate from various depictions of the prison (conceived spaces) as presented in literary materials, including in the law.

Finally, at a number of points we allude to modern carceral practices. It is important to note that when doing so, we do not intend to draw a direct comparison or to suggest that ancient and modern practices are identical, or even genealogically related. Rather, we make these comparisons because insights from the field of carceral studies can, at times, provide a fresh lens on the ancient data and can help us formulate new and fruitful questions. Conversely, a number of contemporary carceral practices widely considered to be uniquely modern have, in fact, been in evidence since antiquity. It is productive to understand earlier instances of such practices, and when relevant comparanda appear, we will occasionally note them.

In 2014–15, the artist Titus Kaphar produced a series of paintings called *The Jerome Project*, each inspired by his experience of searching prisoner databases for records relating to the incarceration of his own father, Jerome. Kaphar found ninety-seven men who shared his father's name and went about interviewing many of them, investigating their histories, and producing portraits that are part mugshot, part Byzantine icon. To our eyes, the icons evoke another stylistic category: they look like painted memorials to departed women and men who lived in Egypt's Fayum oasis during the Roman period, a type of artifact now widespread in museum collections whose piercing, veristic eyes often evoke a presence to viewers even today, some two millennia later. Kaphar dipped many of his portraits in tar, the image obscured in proportion to the amount of time its subject spent behind bars.

We chose *Jerome II* for our cover because in Kaphar's portraits the past burdens the present, surrounding and framing it. He does not ask after the logic or processes that underlie or seek to justify these men's incarceration. Time, tar, and prison silence these Jeromes, stripping them of individuality and humanity. Kaphar's art requires the viewer to hold these men's gaze—whatever is left of it—and confront the desire to look away or to forget these men whom society has segregated and silenced. The portraits are a provocation, "a pondering of whose lived experiences we consider, whose we forget, and whose we erase" (Kaphar 2023). We began to frame this book amid conversations with Kaphar in New Haven from 2012–2017. Our approach to the ancient world parallels Titus's insistence on attending to overlooked people in the contemporary moment.

We are ancient historians, though we concede that we do not solely look backward: we are also invested in a more just future. The prison is not a recent invention, nor are prisons, prison systems, or practices of incarceration. Claims to the contrary are too easy—bordering on facile—one-liners, often deployed by well-meaning people who wish for a world without prisons. We also desire a world without prisons, and so we aim to take a fresh look at the deep prehistory of a contemporary society that posits, in the words of Ruth Wilson Gilmore (2007), "cages as a catchall solutions to social problems" (2).

AE	*L'Année Épigraphique.* 1888–.
ANF	Roberts, Alexander, and James Donaldson, eds. 1885–87. *The Ante-Nicene Fathers: Translations of the Writings of the Fathers Down to A.D. 325.* Charles Scribner's Sons.
APIS	The Advanced Papyrological Information System. Edited by Bagnall, Gagos, and Oates. Hosted at Papyri.info, accessed December 3, 2024, http://www.papyri.info.
BGU	*Aegyptische Urkunden aus den Königlichen Museen zu Berlin: Griechische Urkunden.* 1895–.
BKU	*Aegyptische Urkunden aus den Königlichen Museen zu Berlin: Koptische Urkunden.* 1895–.
BM	British Museum (London).
BnF	Bibliothèque nationale de France (Paris).
CI	Frier, Bruce W., ed. 2016. *The Codex of Justinian: A New Annotated Translation, with Parallel Latin and Greek Text Based on a Translation by Justice Fred H. Blume.* Cambridge University Press. Translations made with reference to this volume.
CIL	*Corpus Inscriptionum Latinarum.* 1893–. Berlin-Brandenburgische Akademie der Wissenschaften.
CIIP	*Corpus Inscriptionum Iudaeae/Palaestinae.* 2011–. De Gruyter.

CLE   *Carmina Latina Epigraphica.* 1895–.
C. Pap. Lat.   Cavenaile, Robert, ed. 1958. *Corpus Papyrorum Latinarum.* Harrassowitz.
CPR   *Corpus Papyrorum Raineri.* 1895–.
CTh, Sirmondian, NTh. Mommsen, Theodor, and Paul Meyer. 1905. *Theodosiani libri XVI cum Constitutionibus Sirmondianis: et Leges novellae ad Theodosianum pertinentes.* 2 vols. Weidmanns. Translations made with reference to Pharr, Clyde. 1952. *The Theodosian Code and Novels, and the Sirmondian Constitutions.* Princeton University Press.
D   Mommsen, Theodor, and Paul Krüger, eds. 1870. *Digesta Iustiniani Augusti.* Weidmanns. Translations made with reference to Watson, Alan. 1998. *The Digest of Justinian.* 4 vols. University of Pennsylvania Press.
FIRA²   Riccobono, Salvatore, Giovanni Baviera, Contardo Ferrini, Giuseppe Furlani, and Vincenzo Arangio-Ruiz, eds. 1968. *Fontes Iuris Romani Antejustiniani.* Vol. 2. S. A. G. Barbèra.
IG   *Inscriptiones Graecae.* 1873–. Berlin-Brandenburgische Akademie der Wissenschaften.
IGLSyr   *Inscriptions grecques et latines de la Syrie.* 1929–.
ILAlg   *Inscriptions latines de l'Algérie.* 1922–.
KMW   Kunsthistorisches Museum Wien (Vienna)
LCL   *Loeb Classical Library.* Harvard University Press. 1911–.
LSJ   Liddell, Henry George, and Robert Scott. 1996. *A Greek-English Lexicon.* 9th ed. Clarendon Press.
MET   Metropolitan Museum of Art (New York)
MV   Musei Vaticani (Vatican Museums, Vatican City)
Nov. Just.   Schöll, Rudolf, and Wilhelm Kroll, eds. 1954. *Corpus iuris civilis.* Vol.3, *Novellae.* Weidmanns.
O. Wilcken   Wilcken, Ulrich, ed. 1899. *Griechische Ostraka aus Aegypten und Nubien.* 2 vols. Gieseke & Devrient.
OGIS   Dittenberger, Willhelm, ed. 1903–5. *Orientis graeci inscriptiones selectae.* 2 vols. S. Hirzel.
P. Bagnall   Ast, Rodney, Hélène Cuvigny, and Todd Hickey, eds. 2013. *Papyrological Texts in Honor of Roger S. Bagnall.* American Society of Papyrologists.
P. Cair. Masp.   Jean Maspero, ed. 1911–16. *Papyrus grecs d'époque byzantine, Catalogue général des antiquités*

	égyptiennes du Musée du Caire. 3 vols. Institut français d'archéologie orientale.
P. Cair. Zen.	C. C. Edgar, ed. 1925–40. *Zenon Papyri, Catalogue général des antiquités égyptiennes du Musée du Caire.* 5 vols. Institut français d'archéologie orientale.
P. Col.	Columbia Papyri. 1929–.
P. Coll. Youtie	Hanson, Ann Ellis, ed. 1976. *Collectanea Papyrologica: Texts Published in Honor of H. C. Youtie.* Papyrologische Texte und Abhandlungen, vols. 19–20. Habelt.
P. Enteux.	Guéraud, Octave, ed. 1931–32. Ἐντεύξεις: *Requêtes et plaintes adressées au Roi d'Égypte au IIIe siècle avant J.-C.* Institut français d'archéologie orientale.
P. Fam. Tebt.	van Groningen, Bernhard Abraham, ed. 1950. *A Family-Archive from Tebtunis (P. Fam. Tebt.).* Papyrologica Lugduno-Batava 6. Brill.
P. Fay.	Grenfell, Bernard P., and Arthur S. Hunt, eds. *Fayûm Towns and Their Papyri.* Egypt Exploration Fund, Graeco-Roman Memoirs 3. Egyptian Exploration Society.
P. Hib.	*The Hibeh Papyri.* 1906–55. 2 vols. Egypt Exploration Society.
P. Lond.	*Greek Papyri in the British Museum.* 1893–.
P. Mich.	*Michigan Papyri.* 1931–.
P. Mich. Mchl.	Michael, E. M. 1966. "A Critical Edition of Select Michigan Papyri." PhD diss., University of Michigan.
P. Oslo	*Papyri Osloenses.* 1925–36. 3 vols. Det Norske Videnskaps-Akademi.
P. Oxy.	*The Oxyrhynchus Papyri.* 1898–. Egypt Exploration Society.
P. Petr.	*The Flinders Petrie Papyri.* 1891–1905. 3 vols. Royal Irish Academy.
P. Petr. Kleon	van Beek, Bart, ed. 2017. *The Archive of the Architektones Kleon and Theodoros.* Collectanea Hellenistica 7. Peeters.
P. Polit. Jud.	Maresch, Klaus, and James M. S. Cowey, eds. 2001. *Urkunden des Politeuma der Juden von Herakleopolis (144/3–133/2 v. Chr.).* Abhandlungen der Nordrhein-Westfälischen Akademie der

	Wissenschaften. Sonderreihe Papyrologica Coloniensia 29. Westdeutscher Verlag.
P. Princ.	*Papyri in the Princeton University Collections.* 1931–42. 3 vols.
P. Ryl.	*Catalogue of the Greek and Latin Papyri in the John Rylands Library, Manchester.* 1911–52. 4 vols. Manchester University Press.
P. Sorb.	*Papyrus de la Sorbonne.* 1966–2011. 3 vols.
P. Strasb.	*Griechische Papyrus der Kaiserlichen Universitäts- und Landes-bibliothek zu Strassburg.* 1912–.
P. Tarich.	Armoni, Charikleia A., ed. 2013. *Das Archiv der Taricheuten Amenneus und Onnophris aus Tanis.* Abhandlungen der Nordrhein-Westfälischen Akademie der Wissenschaften und der Künste. Sonderreihe der Abhandlungen Papyrologica Coloniensia 37. Ferdinand Schöningh.
P. Tebt.	*The Tebtunis Papyri.* 1902–.
P. Wash. Univ.	*Washington University Papyri.* 1890–1990. 2. vols.
P. Yale	*Yale Papyri in the Beinecke Rare Book and Manuscript Library.* 1967–2021. 4 vols
PSI	*Papiri greci e latini. (Pubblicazioni della Società Italiana per la ricerca dei papiri greci e latini in Egitto).* 1912–.
RIC	*Roman Imperial Coinage.* 1923–94. 13 vols.
RIU	*Die römischen Inschriften Ungarns.* 1972–.
SB	*Sammelbuch griechischer Urkunden aus Aegypten.* 1915–.
SEG	*Supplementum Epigraphicum Graecum.* 1923–.
Stud. Pal.	C. Wessely, ed. 1901–24. *Studien zur Palaeographie und Papyruskunde.* Von Avenarius.
O. Did.	Cuvigny, Hélène, ed. 2012. *Didymoi: une garnison romaine dans le désert oriental d'Égypte.* Vol. 2. Praesidia du désert de Bérénice 4. Institut français d'archéologie orientale.
O. Mon.	Epiph. Crum, Walter E., ed. 1926. *The Monastery of Epiphanius at Thebes Part II: Coptic Ostraca and Papyri.* Vol. 2. Publications of the Metropolitan Museum of Art Egyptian Expedition 4. Metropolitan Museum of Art.
O. Petr. Mus.	Funghi, M. Serena, Gabriella Messeri Savorelli, and Cornelia Römer, eds. 2012. *Ostraca greci e bilingui del Petrie Museum of Egyptian*

	Archaeology. Papyrologica Florentina 42. Gonnelli.
OGIS	Dittenberger, Wilhelm, ed. 1903–5. *Orientis graeci inscriptiones selectae*. 2 vols. S. Hirzel.
UPZ	Wilcken, Ulrich, ed. 1927–57. *Urkunden der Ptolemäerzeit (ältere Funde)*. 2 vols. De Gruyter.

Introduction

The Ancient Prison in Historiography

The Italian architect Carlo Bonucci was appointed director of excavations at Pompeii in 1824, and for a quarter century he oversaw the first glimpses of a city buried under volcanic ash seventeen centuries prior. Three years into his appointment, Bonucci (1827) published a description of ongoing efforts, including a riveting, if impressionistic, account of excavations of the ancient city's civic forum, "the most noble and magnificent district of Pompeii" (149). Pompeii's forum—its social, commercial, religious, and governmental center—boasted all the amenities Bonucci knew to be typical of Roman cities. Excavators had uncovered meeting spaces for social clubs, an imposing temple to Jupiter within which archaeologists identified the city's treasury and, in the shadow of the temple on the western edge of the forum, with a small, dark entry to an underground space, "we caught a glimpse of the prison which began to be unearthed, and whose exceedingly narrow doors were equipped with iron bars. There were discovered chambers without light, well secured and vaulted. In them lay the bones of skeletons, those struck by the inundation which accompanied the eruption of 79" (151). Fifty years later, the German archaeologist Johannes Overbeck (1875) reiterated Bonucci's interpretation, finding just off the forum "the building in which one recognizes the prison, which according to [the ancient architect] Vitruvius is due a place on the forum. The discovery of some vaulted rooms without windows and some skeletons in them has greatly strengthened this assumption" (68). Following what was prescribed in an ancient architectural handbook, nineteenth-century excavators knew the civic prison to be a necessary and regular feature of any Roman city; following the evidence they saw on the ground, they identified one such facility in the corner of Pompeii's forum.

Another 1875 publication, however, offered an alternative identification of the space as a civic treasury, and by the turn of the twentieth century the identification of the site as a prison had fallen out of vogue (Fiorelli 1875, 251). In 1899, the German archaeologist August Mau suggested that the space was in fact a treasury servicing (unconnected) municipal offices above (91), and by 1918, Albert W. Van Buren, librarian at the American Academy in Rome, offered an overview of excavations and the state of scholarly interpretation, saying only that the space is "usually explained as municipal treasury offices with treasure vaults beneath." (73–74). Nineteenth-century archaeologists thought they had found Pompeii's civic prison; by the early twentieth century, it had disappeared again.

What happened? What change precipitated the disappearance of the civic prison of Pompeii from the archaeological record, and in its stead the arrival of two civic treasuries located some fifteen meters apart? A full accounting of the historical currents on which shifting identifications drift is beyond the scope of this book, and the answer is surely not monocausal. We point to one trend as influential: increasing availability of works of classical jurisprudence, newly edited and analyzed by architects of the budding discipline that we now call classics. No scholar has been more responsible for vanishing prisons from the imagined classical world than Theodor Mommsen, editor of late ancient works of Roman law and author, in 1899, of *Römisches Strafrecht* (Roman criminal law), to this day the most influential study on the topic and one progenitor of the now ubiquitous claim that Romans did not use prisons for punishment, but solely in a custodial function as a holding facility on the way to punishment in the form of death, exile, or labor outside the city. If municipal prisons were intended exclusively for temporary pretrial or presentencing custody, and incarceration was a marginal aspect of the judicial process as a whole, then the presence of a prison at the heart of cities like Pompeii was harder to explain, and easier to explain away.

Mommsen built his conviction about the absence of punitive incarceration in the Roman world on two cornerstones—one piece of ancient evidence, and one ideal as to the nature of true "punishment." His evidentiary support is an opinion from a jurist named Ulpian, to whom we return below. As we discuss in chapter 1, Roman jurists are legal scholars, commentators, and imperial advisors. Early in the third century CE, Ulpian wrote a work titled *On the Duty of the Proconsul*— a handbook of sorts, delineating how Ulpian believed provincial administrators ought to behave. In it, he claimed that "Governors are in the habit of condemning people to be kept in prison or that they might be kept in chains, but they ought not do this, for punishments of this type are forbidden; the prison should be used to confine men, and not for their punishment" (*D* 48.19.8.9, L120 [early-third century CE]). Governors do use prison for punishment, Ulpian claims, but they ought not to, as he felt such uses were a form of judicial abuse.

Mommsen (1899) finally turns squarely to the question of punishments in the fifth and final book of *Römisches Strafrecht*, opening the analysis with his guiding ideal. "Punishment [*Strafe*] is the evil [*Übel*] inflicted upon a person in retaliation [*in Vergeltung*] for a crime committed by him, according to a statutory or customary legal norm, through a governmental sentence [*staatliches Urtheil*]. Without a governmental sentence in respect to a specific person there is no punishment . . . A sentence imposed not according to a statutory norm, but rather because of capriciousness of the magistrate, is not a punishment in the legal sense" (897). According to Mommsen, penal incarceration did not exist in Rome because *true* penal sentences must be prescribed according to legal ideals and implemented by judges as precise recompense for defined crimes. If Ulpian is right that prison penalties were unlawful, then definitionally any use of the prison for punishment was an arbitrary sanction imposed by a judge, and arbitrary sanctions are definitionally not "punishment." Andrea Lovato (1994) goes further, claiming that penal incarceration as defined by Mommsen did not occur "in any system and at any historical moment" before the early modern period (88). Alberto De Simoni (2022) sums up the argument: "If we accept Mommsen's framework, we reach two interesting conclusions. On the one hand, imprisonment as a penalty did not exist at any point in Roman criminal law since it does not meet the requirement to be qualified as such. On the other, historical instances of imprisonment become deviations from the rule and therefore lose their relevance because they carry the label of something that should not exist" (36). Mommsen's argument involves a version of the no true Scotsman fallacy—no true Roman would employ the prison as a penalty, and aberrations simply prove the rule.

Lovato (1994) was among the first to point out a fundamental flaw in Mommsen's coercive/punitive dichotomy, showing that already in the Roman republic judges imposed even coercive imprisonment with a genuinely punitive function, however infrequently (so he argues) (80–83, 87–88). For all its nuance and rigor, his book *Il carcere nel diritto penale romano: dai Severi a Giustiniano* (The prison in Roman criminal law: from the Severans to Justinian) has been occasionally misunderstood as claiming either that penal incarceration was technically illegal and materially rare, or that it was technically lawful but remained uncommon. Other legal historians take a more definitive approach, like Yann Rivière, author of two important books on the topic: *Le cachot et les fers: détention et coercition à Rome* (2004a) (The dungeon and the irons: detention and coercion at Rome) and *Histoire du droit pénal romain: de Romulus à Justinien* (2021) (History of Roman criminal law: from Romulus to Justinian). Riviére's (2021) updated analysis restates Mommsen's conclusion: "in Roman penal law, incarceration never had the function of penal confinement, defined for a limited-term or in perpetuity, and it was solely through the negligence of judges or procedural delays that detainees awaiting trial could be held within the walls of a cell" (409). Instances of punitive prison sentences were aberrations stemming from governmental officials' coercive power (*coercitio*) and not from their legal mandate (*iurisdictio*), even when that coercive power included legitimate punitive aims. Riviére's claim would perhaps be defensible if by "incarceration" he means strictly penal sentences in civic prisons. As we discuss below, however, the Romans he invokes considered convict labor part of the punitive carceral system.

We return to this specific argument about penal incarceration and legal ideology in chapter 1. For now it will suffice to say that among historians, the ancient prison's marginality is nearly dogmatic—a question asked and answered, and an interpretive tool of broad application. For instance, the ancient Roman historian Livy recorded that in the second century BCE, the politician Lucius Scipio's enemies intended to "lock [him] up in a prison among nighttime thieves and bandits, to have him expire in the dark lower prison." J. C. Yardley's 2018 translation for the Loeb Classical Library includes a note of objection: "This is a gross exaggeration. Lucius's imprisonment would be temporary, lasting only until the fine was paid or guarantors found" (200n262). In this instance, we argue, a received orthodoxy has framed the evidence in a way that obscures it.

As Alexander Nogrady put it succinctly in 2011, in the Roman world "there was no such thing as a prison sentence to be served in prison; prisons were used solely to hold suspects in custody until they were sentenced and, if necessary, until the death penalty that had been imposed was carried out" (389). In the same volume, Romina Schiavone (2011) claimed, "imprisonment as a punishment did not yet exist in the Roman Empire" (236). Examples of such canonical statements could be multiplied here, but will not be. A historiographic dogma had taken shape in Mommsen's wake: the notion that "Romans did not use prisons for punishment" has become a handy slogan for historians, widely repeated by specialists and assumed as a bedrock principle by generalists and historians of later periods.

As we hinted earlier, the field of classical archaeology often responds to scholarship on the history and literature of antiquity, and the case of the prison has been no exception. In his overview of "Political Spaces in Late Antiquity," Luke Lavan (2007) writes, "Of prisons we know little. We have no securely identified architectural evidence" (121). In something of a narrative two-step, historians have in turn looked to archaeology—itself reflecting previous historical analysis—and found their conclusions more or less confirmed. Julia Hillner (2015) uses very similar language to Lavan, asserting, "archaeologically, we know very little about late Roman prison, or Roman prisons more generally, and this may be due to the often improvised nature of legal imprisonment in a variety of public spaces. For example, there is some evidence from late antique Egypt that unused temples were used as prison" (125; she is referring here to P. Oxy. 17.2154; D18 [fourth century CE], on which more below). Likewise, Kristina Sessa (2018), in her book *Daily Life in Late Antiquity*, offers this reflection: "Most of the time, prisons were used to detain people accused of crimes before the court appearance, or, in the case of debtors, to hold them until they rendered payment. The Romans thus did not construct prisons as distinct spaces, as we do today. Instead, they relied on preexisting buildings, typically private homes, to incarcerate men and women" (144). Sessa is of course correct that private spaces and temporary facilities were sometimes employed as ad hoc prisons, but the notion that the Romans did not purpose-build carceral facilities is simply incorrect, as chapter 2 demonstrates in detail.

Even so, the hermeneutic circle is not entirely closed; over the years a number of archaeologists working on ancient Hellenistic and Roman sites have identified a wide variety of carceral facilities—importantly at Rome, Cosa (Italy), Messene (Greece), Djemila (Algeria), Tiberias (Israel), and Sarmizegetusa (Romania), as we detail below. Unfortunately, sites like these have been seen as peculiar rather than regular, and interpreted as jails rather than prisons. In other words, archaeologically attested carceral spaces have been categorized as exceptions to the norm rather than challenges to it. With this book, we join a scholarly movement aspiring to change that.

In other instances historical dogma has overshadowed even careful studies that might have upset the scholarly consensus, like Jens-Uwe Krause's (1996) magisterial social history of prison ideals and practices in *Gefängnisse im römischen Reich* (Incarceration in the Roman Empire). Krause's analysis is rich and thorough, and it is one of the few studies that might have changed the conversation among historians of the Roman Empire, analyzing as it does a broad swath of documentary evidence for incarceration alongside literary materials. His study nevertheless begins—on its very first page—with a reiteration of Mommsen's creed. "In its modern form the prison owes its existence to the late eighteenth century; in medieval and early modern Europe, imprisonment was the exception. The prison housed defendants pending judgment and convicts pending execution of the sentence. Corporal punishment was dominant. In principle, in antiquity the prison was also used for pretrial detention and execution detention" (1). Despite his survey of an impressive range of evidence unknown in the late nineteenth century, Krause ultimately did not veer far from Mommsen's position.

Outside the realms of classics, ancient history, and archaeology, the notion that ancient Mediterranean prisons were marginal relies largely on two other academic celebrities. Émile Durkheim published the first part of "Deux lois de l'évolution pénale" ("Two laws of penal evolution") in 1899—the same year as Mommsen's *Roman Criminal Law*—and came to a similar conclusion that Mommsen came to about antiquity. Quoting Wilhelm Rein's (1844) *Das Criminalrecht der Römer von Romulus bis auf Justinianus* (Roman criminal justice from Romulus until Justinian), Durkheim begins from the premise that across Mediterranean antiquity, "Prison . . . was originally no more than a place for preventive detention. Later it became a means of punishment. However, it was rarely used, except for slaves, soldiers and actors" (79). The idea of a marginalized premodern prison held disciplinary sway for decades, but it was in 1975 when the notion of the Roman state without penal, limited term, or reformatory incarceration jumped from the academic disciplines of history and anthropology to the pages of a mass market trade paperback, written by one of the most important and influential public intellectuals of the twentieth century: Michel Foucault.

Surveiller et punir: naissance de la prison (1975) was a watershed in the historical study of the prison, receiving quick translation and appearing by 1977 in English under the title *Discipline and Punish: The Birth of the Prison*. Foucault analyzed the coconstituted modern carceral state and carceral subject-of-state. Writing in the wave of a decades-long scholarly tradition that saw the prison in antiquity as used solely for pretrial detention and postconviction segregation until proper punishment could be meted out (typically on the body of the convicted), he saw in antiquity a radical alternative to modern society. So, while throughout the twentieth century Mommsen and others had argued that prison was not (or *should not be*) used as a form of punishment in the ancient world, in 1975 Foucault took the next step of claiming that the modern prison system was born in the early modern period, though its roots could be traced back to medieval monastic confinement.

Foucault has dictated the terms of engagement for scholars of incarceration, not only for historians of the modern period but also historians of the more distant past. Julia Hillner's 2015 book, *Prison, Punishment and Penance in Late Antiquity*, makes a case, as the title suggests, for how concepts of penance and punishment intermingle with ideas and practices of confinement across Late Antiquity. Her book investigates the "long-term genesis of the sixth century Roman legal penalty of forced monastic confinement," showing how a complex web of competing, preexisting legal and punitive discourses help to contextualize the landmark reforms of Justinian in 542 and 556 CE, in which "the penalty of confinement in a monastery was introduced to public law" (ii, 1–4, 12, 314–16; cf. Hillner 2007, 205–37). By "long-term genesis," Hillner refers to ideas stretching back centuries to classical Athens in Plato's dream of Magnesia, with its three prisons, including the "Reformatory" (33–38). She argues that Plato's idea of punishment as reform was then refracted in Roman imperial discourse through ideas of education, as well as late antique Christian principles of punishment, to finally find expression in late Roman legal theory of forced monastic confinement (45–88). Shifting punitive uses of confinement and exile in the later Roman Empire prepared the ground for late ancient monastic confinement, Hillner argues, before which Roman emperors "were anxious to reduce the function of the public prison" and so "limit the number of prisons" (120–21; see also 139–40).

Readers of Foucault's landmark study will recognize immediately that Hillner's argument operates within a Foucauldian frame, even if she disagrees with his chronology. While Foucault "saw [the modern prison penalty's] origin in the ordering of time, space and activities in the medieval monastery," Hillner objects that Foucault had "overlooked the late antique phenomenon of monastic confinement," and demonstrates that the legal theory and practice of monastic confinement undermines Foucault's view of "monasteries as homogeneous communities of spiritual volunteers" (348–49). For Hillner, the modern prison penalty should not be traced back to the medieval monastery but to late antique monastic confinement: "sixth century monastic confinement demonstrates that not only an idea but also the practice of educative punishment—punishment that aimed not only at the body but also the 'soul', through segregation, surveillance and discipline of behaviour—existed in Western society over a thousand years prior to the introduction of the modern prison penalty" (348). Punishing the soul; surveillance; discipline; segregation; punishment—these are all Foucauldian terms.

Our argument is not that Mommsen single-handedly caused prisons to disappear, or that Foucault believed the prison was invented out of whole cloth. Rather, it is that Mommsen's argument about the marginal role of Roman prisons was so influential that for the better part of the twentieth century, prisons fell off most historical and archaeological maps. The impact of Foucault's work was similarly determinative for scholars of carceral studies, such that the field has been defined as an almost entirely modern field of study, in practice even if not in theory. We object not to their intentions but to their impacts.

It is difficult to overstate the impact of Foucault's analysis, and the reification that his book imposed on its underlying historical claims. When Didier Fassin (2017) opened his *Prison Worlds: An Ethnography of the Carceral Tradition* with the assertion "Prison is a recent invention," he was able to do so because of an orthodoxy in the field of critical prison studies traceable, ineluctably, to Foucault (14). Foucault was not the first to construct a premodernity with marginal prisons, but his account remains the most broadly influential, and it set a course in which the overwhelming majority of histories assume that before the early modern period, there is no true prison to be found (Moran and Morin 2015). Summarizing her own account of the prison's history for the *Oxford Research Encyclopedia of Criminology and Criminal Justice*, sociologist and prison historian Ashley T. Rubin offered a concise definition of the prison and an absolute timeline for its emergence.

> Prisons are government-sanctioned facilities designed for the long-term confinement of adults as punishment for serious offenses. This definition of prisons . . . emerged relatively late in human history. For most of Western history, incarceration played a minor role in punishment and was often reserved for elites or political offenders; however, it was rarely considered a punishment in its own right for most offenders. The notion of the prison as a place of punishment emerged gradually, according to most accounts, over the 17th through 19th centuries. (2018, 1)

We aim to show that such accounts are historically incorrect, but we maintain that their authors are not historiographically culpable; for more than a century, scholars have handed down as fact a set of arguments well established as the historical state-of-the-art. Reading widely in carceral history, one gets a sense that more than his arguments, Foucault's subtitle, *The Birth of the Prison*, has framed what it means to study the carceral history in the subsequent half-century.

Thus, the influential *Oxford History of the Prison* begins its analysis with "The prisons of the ancient world have disappeared" (Peters 1995, 3). In a strict sense, the sentiment gets at something true: modern scholarship has obstructed our attention to ancient incarceration. But rumors of the prison's absence say more about how the history of incarceration has been understood than about the sources on offer; in this standard reference book of the field, eighteen of the four hundred pages are devoted to prisons before the medieval period, and even they analyze only selected literary sources from Greece, Rome, Byzantium, and the Bible. Rather than indicating the breadth of available data, this selection represents an historiographical tradition that sees the prison as a novel and peculiar legacy of the West. The volume, however, was released in 1995, on the eve of a new wave of research into the prison's ancient roots.

Our impulse to search for the ancient prison beyond legal sources is not new; we are indebted to a large number of scholars who have thought critically, carefully, and expansively about the place of the prison in the ancient Mediterranean for some thirty years already, beginning with Krause's (1996) groundbreaking volume mentioned above, along with two colloquia held in Strasbourg in 1997 and 2000 that produced volumes of great learning on portions of the ancient carceral regime from classical Greece to the European Middle Ages (Bertrand-Dagenbach et al. 1999, 2005). The early 2000s saw a burst of interest in ancient incarceration lead by Spanish scholars like Sofía Torallas Tovar (2003) and Inmaculada Pérez Martín (2003b), whose edited volume *Castigo y reclusión en el mundo antiguo* (Punishment and confinement in the ancient world) brought together fourteen scholars to work on the topics of punishment and carcerality, and in the same year Pilar Pavón Torrejón's exquisite *La cárcel y el encarcelamiento en el mundo romano* (The prison and incarceration in the Roman world) introduced a rich array of archaeological data to a conversation that had largely occurred, theretofore, in the realms of literary and documentary materials. A second wave of scholarship has brought further texture and grand new insights to the field, beginning with two excellent studies from 2015: Julia Hillner's *Prison, Punishment, and Penance in Late Antiquity* and José Luis Zamora Manzano's *La administración penitenciaria en el derecho romano* (Penitentiary administration in Roman law). More recently still, J. Nicholas Reid has contributed important analysis of the ancient Mesopotamian evidence, while Marcus Folch and Jacob Abolafia have analyzed the classical Athenian evidence anew (Reid 2022; Folch 2021a,b,c; Abolafia 2021, 2024).

We build on each of these studies below, which together demonstrate that reports of the prison's birth have been greatly exaggerated. In fact, it is not clear that "the prison" is the kind of institution that could have a birthday to mark, or an origin to uncover. As such, the aim of this book is not to find the seeds of the prison or their earliest stages of germination, but rather to show that across the Mediterranean basin beginning with the earliest documentary sources available on papyrus, prisons and practices of incarceration already existed within a sophisticated system of social control and economic exploitation throughout the timespan of our study. We are left to wonder if a search for the "birth of the prison" may prove a fool's errand; perhaps the problem with debate over the prison's origin is not that it is too difficult to locate but that points of origin are legion.

It is important not to mince words: we do not mean simply that carceral facilities did exist across the ancient Mediterranean basin, and that they were used occasionally to detain people on a temporary basis. Rather, we argue that prisons existed as an integrated penal institution, and that the institution boasted a great majority of the facets that historians have, until recently, seen as novel to modernity. Historians are not liable for repeating a long-established orthodoxy about the birth of the prison, and we do not intend to censure colleagues from whom we have learned a great deal. However, in the case of an institution so central and insidious, camouflaged and rife as the prison, it is urgent to get the history right, and the data that ancient historians have assembled, translated, modeled, and synthesized over the past thirty years offer a remarkably different picture than the one that carceral historians have inherited.

As we argue at length below, in various contexts across Mediterranean antiquity, prisons—both civic prisons and other sites of formal imprisonment—were sometimes intended as spaces of punishment for deviance, and they were often experienced that way. We find explicit evidence for instances of limited-term sentences of incarceration, even at times with the further intention of reforming the offending person. We see evidence of remarkable disparities in carceral victimization, with indigenous and indigent people bearing the brunt of a carceral society that relied on bodily inputs to serve economic needs of the state. We find evidence of long-term solitary confinement, punitive food rations, a bureaucratic system for placing and keeping people in penal detention, and we witness a comprehensive legal theory of punishment promulgated by emperors who state in no uncertain terms that "the prison is for punishment. The prison is for guilty people" (*CTh* 11.7.3, L35 [320 CE]). And we find archaeological evidence for purpose-built carceral facilities over a vast stretch of space and time, along with evidence for their widespread use. We find, in other words, The Prison. Put differently, we cannot find any reasonable way, based on our data, to avoid the conclusion that "the notion of the prison" as defined by Rubin (2018) existed already in antiquity (1).

Our analysis begins with the earliest significant corpus of documentary sources for incarceration: papyri from Egypt of the early Ptolemaic period. Prior to these papyri, the overwhelming majority of relevant Mediterranean evidence is literary—often political treatises and dramatic materials of the fifth and fourth centuries BCE, such as those written by Demosthenes, Lysias, Plato, Thucydides, and Xenophon. Similarly to the Roman evidence, these classical Greek sources have most often been read to indicate the use of state prisons solely for pretrial detention, even though the speeches of many Athenian legal advocates note incarceration as one of the formal punishments available as sentences for those convicted of crimes—this much was demonstrated by Danielle Allen (1997) in a now classic article that similarly sought to overturn a nineteenth-century dogma according to which penal incarceration was not a legal punishment for citizens of Athens in the classical period, nor was it used.

Recent work by Marcus Folch and Jacob Abolafia explores the use of incarceration as a tool for political leverage in Greek literary materials of the classical period. As Abolafia (2024) indicates, there are only two classical Athenian authors who "wrote in any sustained way about incarceration, and the paucity of such evidence has fed the scholarly confusion over the prevalence and importance of incarceration in Athens" (28). The archive, in other words, only gives access to a thin sliver of carceral ideologies or practices. Folch (2021a) likewise contends that, while the Athenian prison was likely used as part of a broader legal system, the authors of our extant literary sources did not consider such functions to be particularly noteworthy, nor did they think or write in legal categories that are the legacy of late Roman jurisprudence (344–46). "Custodial, coercive, and punitive imprisonment was uninteresting to fifth- and fourth-century historians and orators. For Athenians and non-Athenian authors living in classical Athens, the prison became important when it ceased to be procedural and was enlisted within democratic and antidemocratic conflict" (513). Abolafia's work confirms Folch's (2021a,b) insights, and shows that when historical analysis is restricted largely to literary materials from elite authors, the prison appears only in glimpses constructed by political thinkers extrapolating (sometimes) from common practices to idealized and rhetorical systems. For the most part, such sources are all that we have from classical Athens, and they are necessarily far removed from the voices of traders and wage laborers captured in the papyri because their aim was never to enlighten the prison's nonpolitical functions. Nevertheless, we argue that these earlier literary sources point in a similar direction as later documentary materials, and we agree with Allen, Folch, and Abolafia that a portrait of an elite prison in classical Greek literature is an artifact of the archive more than a reflection of common practices. Different kinds of sources do not just give us different information; they give us different kinds of knowledge. The literary sources from classical Athens were simply not interested in most of the prison's use, function, or history; nor are they particularly useful for answering such questions.

Today, there is an urgent need to rethink what prisons are for, if indeed they should be for anything at all. Part of that reimagination must involve grappling with the long and ugly tail of the prison's history, and to do so we will need to engage an archive of sources that speak to the prison in all its guises, not just its legal intention or political function. This is a central aim of our book.

INCARCERATION IN HISTORY

The earliest sources for the use of punitive, coercive, and custodial incarceration happen also to be among the earliest written sources extant anywhere in the world—ancient Mesopotamian materials like a small clay tablet from the twenty-second century BCE that records the names of three laborers from the city of Ur (Tell el-Muqayyar, Iraq) who were incarcerated on a particular day, and thus should not be paid a wage. "Kitušlu the son of Gemegišbare; Luzah the son of Imta; EnDU the son of Lugalen. Total: 3 workers. They did not go out, they are dwelling in prison" (British Museum 88538 [twenty-second century BCE]; trans. Reid 2022, 41–42). A Sumerian Hymn to Nungal, composed sometime in the early second millennium BCE and surviving in over fifty copies, speaks of a "river ordeal"—a judicial process after which the innocent are released and the guilty are returned to prison as punishment. As Tikva Simone Frymer (1977) points out, "There does not seem to be any doubt that these hymns reflect an actual juridical situation: That in Sumer of the late Neo Sumerian period the temple of Nippur played an important role in the judicial system, serving as a site for the river-ordeal, and providing prison facilities for those convicted by such (and probably other) trials" (89).

Already by 300 BCE, a highly developed vocabulary was available in both Greek and Latin to describe diverse types of prison and practices of incarceration. The terms are a constellation—often overlapping and in more than a few cases interchangeable, even within a single source. In Greek, a civic prison is typically called a *desmōtērion* while *fulakē* serves as a more general term, often interchangeable with other terms like *eirgmos* and *heirktē* (Riaño Rufilanchas 2003, 77–79). Regional variation is visible, as for instance in Sicily where writers often use the Latin term *karkaron* even when writing in Greek. Some technical terms like *froura* lead double lives—occasionally used to denote a military prison specifically, but other times employed as a general term for a prison (Pavón Torrejón 2003b, 29–31). Jargon and colloquialisms are common, too: Jaime Curbera (2018) lists twenty terms in ancient Greek, and we shall see that many prisons received hyperlocal monikers. Coptic terminology largely reflects the Greek, with a few unique phrases noted by Sofía Torallas Tovar (1999) and, as we have argued elsewhere, some specialized terms in Greek (like *aichmalōtos*) and Latin (like signa/*sikne*) became generalized in Coptic. Terminology in Latin is somewhat more circumscribed, with *carcer* used to denote a wide variety of prison facilities; often terms are used to denote the status of imprisoned people rather than their place of incarceration, words like *vincula* and *custodia*, both of which are widely interchangeable with *carcer* (Pavón Torrejón 2003b, 74–79; Rodríguez Martín 2003, 182–85; Zamora Manzano 2015, 25). Peter Garnsey (1970) notes that *custodia* has a particularly wide range of applications: "It covers the various ways in which a defendant might be held in custody before the trial or the execution of sentence. It stands for the imprisonment that is an act of *coercitio* by a magistrate. It refers to methods of punishment after sentence has been passed" (147).

Adjectives could also be used to differentiate prison spaces—for instance, by specifying a civic prison as *carcer publicus* or a military prison as *carcer castrensis*. In imitation of Rome's civic prison, the terms *tullianum* and *robus* came to indicate the lower, darker parts of a prison, while the lighter, outer parts of the prison are called *vestibula*. In time, yet more creative terminology developed—like the use of *signa*, a noun denoting military standards that came to indicate instead a prison that stood nearby or underneath a legion's temple where they held their standards (Livy, *From the Founding of the City* 38.5 [early first century CE], Calpurnius Flaccus, *Declamations* 4, L46 [second century CE]). The Latin term *signa* appears also in Coptic (*sikne*) as a general term for a prison, and even in Arabic as *sijn*, which is still in contemporary use (Letteney and Larsen 2021, 84–85, 98–102; Crum 1926, 201n8). As today, the ubiquity of incarceration spawned a variegated and sophisticated constellation of terms, each with their own nuance: *prison; jail; lockup; slammer; clink; big house; inside; supermax; tank; brig; SHU.*

The data are quite clear on this one fact, as simple as it is unsettling and, we argue here, undeniable: carceral practices were ubiquitous in the ancient Mediterranean world and an inescapable part of society. Most city dwellers of classical and Hellenistic Greece, in the Ptolemaic kingdom of Egypt, the Roman Republic and Empire, and well into the Byzantine period in the eastern Mediterranean knew that their own town had a prison that was designed as a part of the built environment of the city and used to confine deviant people. They would have known precisely how to walk from their home to the civic prison, and in their mind's eye, they could envision its dirty, barred window, guarded door, and the poor souls suffering inside. Some would have glanced inside as they walked down the city's main street and found tired eyes set in sullied faces looking back at them through the window. Or they had heard prisoners' voices, smelled the stench of their quarters, and watched them transported through the city center on their way to trial, to a prison camp out of town, to beg for food or money, or to be executed and disposed of. In the words of Alain Chauvot (1999a), "The [ancient Roman] prison was an unthinkable presence in the heart of the city, a fixed instrument and a tool with a variety of functions, capable of evolving and adapting; in a word, an historical object among the others, neither more or less banal than the others, at the same time like a brutal emptiness, sucking in and canceling all goodness and dignity. If its study requires from the historian all the necessary learnedness, it is also a measurement of the distances and the proximities that [the historian] maintains with the structures of the ancient world" (224). Most ancient city- dwellers must have known that some mid-sized towns like Oxyrhynchus and Pompeii actually had more than one carceral facility, that larger cities contained several, with people incarcerated not only in civic prisons but also gladiator barracks, amphitheaters, *praetoria*, bakeries, and private villas, and that myriads more sat incarcerated far from urban centers in work camp prisons, toiling alongside enslaved laborers and animals on behalf of the state to bake bread, extract stone, ore, minerals, or to serve those who did.

Our argument is that across the ancient Mediterranean basin, prison systems were just that: a system woven into the fabric of nearly every aspect of public life, not just the legal sphere. By paying close attention to the architecture, documentation, and visual representation of this system, we can begin to trace its contours. Doing so, we find proof of the prison system as a state-taxed, state-funded institution that was perceived to provide a public good. It cannot have been lost on Roman taxpayers of the second century CE that their receipt included line items for prison maintenance and prison staff salaries, recorded next to other taxes of a similar sort: those for road and waterworks maintenance, public safety, and a dozen other publicly funded and explicitly enumerated services, including housing for soldiers and care for the poor (SB 24.16185, D68 [151 CE]). Prisons were weight-bearing beams of societal infrastructure—it would be hard to account for production of metals and food, or maintenance of roads and water supplies, without practices of incarceration. Some historians have found it difficult to imagine a prison *system* in the ancient world. We argue that the available data suggest essentially the opposite: it is impossible to imagine the ancient Mediterranean without one.

This system impacted larger societal institutions, of course, but it also inflected the lives of individuals, families, and communities in profound ways. Residents in Ptolemaic Philadelphia (Kom el-Kharaba el-Kebir, Egypt) may have heard a plea from Phaneisis, recently incarcerated far from home, and left to beg for food to keep him alive until his family has time to arrive (P. Cair. Zen. 3.59519, D134 [263–226 BCE]). In the Idumean City of Maresha (Beit Guvrin, Israel), locals may have heard the pleas of Zebatus, who was held for three years in a place he calls "the Punishments" and was close to death as a result of his incarceration (CIIP 4.3.3689, D170 [probably second century BCE]). Maybe Theodorus's neighbors heard about his happy ending: after he served a twenty-two month sentence for sexual deviance, the west Anatolian man walked out of prison alive. Many of them would at least have seen the stele recording his story (SEG 38.1237, D167 [235–36 CE]). And perhaps residents saw a new law in Thamugadi (Timgad, Algeria) promulgated around 360 CE and posted at the city center, indicating that locals incarcerated in the public prison should be fed at public expense (CIL 8.17897, D171 [361–63 CE]).

Individuals were surrounded by the system in more mundane ways. Whether they knew it or not, every time a Roman walked over a floor in a public building covered in the coveted Numidian yellow marble, they walked on the fruits of carceral labor: on stone extracted by prisoners in the city of Simitthus (Chemtou, Tunisia; A13). Roman citizens receiving free bread from politicians had the capacity to see that their food was often produced by convicts sent to labor in public bakeries. Spectators at public games in Carales (Cagliari, Italy) could easily learn that their city's amphitheater was equipped with two prisons: one for gladiators and another for their human victims (Gladiator Prison, A33; Prison for the Condemned, A24). It may not have escaped the notice of a native Latin speaker that such places were called *carceres*: the same name given to cages that held animals at the edges of the amphitheater. All were being held in preparation for public execution.

We argue over the course of this book that the ancient economy, the food system, public entertainment, travel networks, architecture, the sensory experience of walking through a city—all of it—was supported by the bodies of the imprisoned, caught in a system built to punish them for deviance and, at times, to exploit their bodies as a public good in recompense for bad behavior. Of course this is a metaphor, but it is not only a metaphor. As we will see, the courthouses where law was practiced were often structurally supported by the pillars and vaults of the prison underneath. There is a haunting sense in which the prison upheld ancient Mediterranean society.

The Mediterranean world was no stranger to practices of incarceration that were at once violent and banal, and inequitable in ways familiar in our contemporary moment. Today gleaming courthouses send men, women, and children to dilapidated warehouses for deviant humans, with certain groups disproportionately targeted for incarceration. The ancient system's noble garb similarly veiled a nasty underbelly. Legislators and lawyers calmly debated the uses of incarceration, sparing a rare word on the violence inherent in practices they prescribed. As is often the case, men who made laws concerning ideal prison functions rarely faced the consequences of their legislation. This simple fact places a profound demand on historians, reminding us that the intention of incarceration often has little to do with its effects, and that to mistake prescriptive laws with descriptive practices is to live in the fantasyland of an elite who have always been the prison's proprietors, and rarely its victims. It is hardly novel to suggest that elites were unlikely to suffer the worst excesses of their punitive apparatus. Nevertheless, ancient legislators were often more forthright than their modern counterparts about the discriminatory practices inherent within systems that they built and perpetuated; many created a legal system that explicitly targeted socially and economically vulnerable groups for more regular and strenuous carceral penalties than their socially elite counterparts (Garnsey 1970, 153–80).

The view from the lawcourt above must be counterbalanced, and perhaps upended, by the view from inside the prison below. In the Roman context, legal reformers debated whether the prison ought to be used as a form of punishment, as we detail below (p. 21–33). Their occasional disagreement over aims is almost wholly distinct, on the one hand, from practices on the ground in provincial prisons hundreds and sometimes thousands of kilometers away, and, on the other hand, from experiences of incarceration as punishment expressed in documents produced by and for the prison's victims. For the incarcerated individuals attested in our data, who toiled in prison camps or wasted away in civic facilities for months and years on the verge of death, the intentions of theorists and legislators had long since faded from view as material to understanding their plight. We are lucky to have such prisoners' letters, graffiti, court testimony, and bail receipts, and our approach is to listen when they tell us what prisons were like and what incarceration was, asking after their experience at least as much as we ask after the intentions of their captors. Such data about experience of incarceration has too often been regarded as somehow less real than the opinions and ideals of legislators as a historical source of penal incarceration; from our point of view, their experience is *at least as real*, and maybe more so.

Furthermore, historical study of the experiences of ancient prisoners have often been unnecessarily anecdotal, viewed through the lens of a few figureheads who came to have canonical status among subsequent interpreters: Socrates, Paul the Apostle, or Boethius, just to name a few (Allen 1997; Schellenberg 2021; Relihan 2007). Even if we could gather a list of names comprising *all* prisoners from a certain period known to historical sources, such a list would not represent more than a small fraction of the total prison population. The vast sea of incarcerated individuals will inevitably remain nameless, lost to the historian. The task is not futile, however, and to the degree we can recover the voices of prisoners from the past, we feel obliged to do so. We ought to allow prisoners to be privileged informants—admitting their experience of incarceration into the historical record as a valid form of inquiry and reversing, in some small way, the indelible taint of criminality that disqualifies carceral subjects as "knowers" of the system that binds them (Jones 2023, xxxii). Prisoner experiences are part of history, even as they are subjugated knowledges: "historical contents that have been buried or masked in functional coherences or formal systematizations . . . a whole series of knowledges that have been disqualified as nonconceptual knowledges, as insufficiently elaborated knowledges: naive knowledges, hierarchically inferior knowledges, knowledges that are below the required level of erudition or scientificity" (Foucault 2003, 7). As Michelle Daniel Jones (2023) writes in *Who Would Believe a Prisoner?*: "We are here to counter the dominant narratives, to expand the canon of knowers and knowledge, and to rewrite history justly" (xxxix). As historical facts, prisoner experiences ought to be part of any rigorous history of the prison.

Prison practices can be submitted to historical analysis; and, while legal and political historians often prefer to view carceral practices as secondary and subsequent to intellectual trends, the assertion is never obviously true; in at least some instances it is demonstrably false. For instance, Guy Geltner (2008) has shown at length that medieval lawmakers "mostly abhorred" penal incarceration, and yet it was commonly imposed by judges with the result that "in the case of punitive imprisonment in the Middle Ages, legislation lagged behind practice, and both departed from contemporary, mainstream penal thought" (44). Jacob Abolafia (2024) has recently asserted that "In the case of the prison, the idea precedes the institution" (1). Geltner's study shows that, in the case of medieval Italy, precisely the opposite was true. We hope to make a similar case, at least as regards the relationship between Roman law and Roman carceral practice. If theory does not always predate or motivate practice, then to grasp one is not to understand the other. And, importantly, understanding practices and experiences of incarceration is to understand something significant, and perhaps controlling, about the history of the prison. They offer a glimpse at a true genealogy of the prison, in Foucault's (2003) words, "this coupling together of scholarly erudition and local memories, which allows us to constitute a historical knowledge of struggles and to make use of that knowledge in contemporary tactics" (8).

Privileging prisoner experiences alongside juristic ideals, we find that the history of the prison is not a handbook that offers more just models or answers to pressing moral questions of today. The task, however, might present a mirror: one that we can hold up to contemporary society and offer a glimpse of ourselves from the foreign vantage point of the past, in which we are able to see which aspects of our carceral society are novel and which are bound up in longer histories. We stand better able to perceive that aspects of our justice system that seemed unique to us at first blush are not unique at all, and that policies that seem obvious and even natural are in fact choices encoding historically peculiar ideologies of punishment.

When deployed as a mirror, prison history better positions us—both historians and those involved in public policy—to work at shaping a kind of society that perhaps has not yet existed: a world without the violence of prison. The notion may sound grandiose or even impossible, but we mean it seriously. Homo sapiens forges new futures all the time. Why not now?

PART ONE

Ideals and Spaces

1

Incarceration and the Law

Documentary sources show that carceral facilities were used under public and private regimes for a variety of purposes: sometimes prisons were used to hold defendants prior to their trial, and again briefly after trial before they could receive another form of punishment; sometimes prisons were employed to coerce repayment of publicly or privately held debts, or in hopes of deterring deviant behavior in a wider civic population; sometimes prisons were used to neutralize political enemies, or as forms of torture and execution in and of themselves, where people were sent to waste away before their bodies were discarded. And sometimes people were placed into carceral facilities as a form of punishment, even for a limited-term sentence. From a purely legal perspective, some of these uses of the prison were clearly permissible, and some were contested. Some were abuses, and some were unquestionably sanctioned. All, however, were carceral practices, whose stunning variety we investigate as they appear on a continuum from limited-term incarceration in public prisons to sentences of carceral convict labor.

Because we intend the voices of the incarcerated to have the final word, it seems fair to let the lawyers and judges have the opening statement. If the notion of an ancient world in which prisons were marginal were not so widespread, we might have begun our analysis elsewhere; however, our study will prove more effective if we first demonstrate that surviving legal materials do permit punitive incarceration as part of legal procedure, and that varieties of incarceration were a widely available legal sanction, at least within the Roman legal tradition of the imperial period. So, we begin there, with an overview of previous work where legal historians have argued for the widespread use of prison facilities and for the possibility of legal, penal incarceration, before we turn in chapter 2 to discussing spaces where incarceration took place and, in the remainder of the book, to investigating lived experiences and social perceptions of the prison.

Compared to documentary and literary sources, legal sources on incarceration are somewhat scant. Nevertheless, a number do remain, mostly as collected in late antique compilations of Roman law—compilations that are useful because, for the majority of our period, Roman law was operative across the Mediterranean basin as one of many legal frameworks and eventually as the dominant framework for nearly all inhabitants of the region. It is, of course, a flawed historiography to reduce the history of incarceration to theoretical debates and expressions of law. Much of the carceral apparatus existed beyond the realm of courts, judges, advocates, and laws. Even so, as Robert Gordon (1984) argued in a classic treatment of the relationship between elite sources of legal disputation and law as practiced, the writing of judges and jurists "are among the richest artifacts of a society's legal consciousness. Because they are the most rationalized and elaborated legal products, you'll find in them an exceptionally refined and concentrated version of legal consciousness" (120). At the same time, influence flows both ways: sometimes elite prescriptions trickle down in "vulgarized forms" as popular practices, and sometimes juristic sources "represent simply an elaborated, purified, and formalized version of a consciousness whose primary producers are to be found all over the society" (121). So, what do squarely legal sources say about how incarceration *ought* to function in an ideal world?

Roman legal materials are dynamic and diverse. Juristic sources from the likes of Paul, Ulpian, and Modestinus are rather uncontroversially idealized texts, while laws preserved in the late Roman codes are more akin to statute law—idealizing still, but differently so. At base, legal sources of all stripes present a spectrum of carceral practices, including limited-term or perpetual sentences in public prisons, condemnation to hard labor in or adjacent to carceral facilities meant to house convict laborers, imprisonment in public or private facilities intended to coerce debt collection, and temporary incarceration en route to other forms of punishment—sometimes temporary incarceration before execution within a civic prison, and sometimes transfer to another prison to await punishment of a different sort. All these practices are carceral. Above all, legal sources dispute and disagree about the precise ideal shape of this carceral constellation, and there are possible readings of some sources that may imply penal incarceration in particular was outlawed in the Roman Empire. Other elite normative sources claim that penal incarceration is not only acceptable but in fact preferable. As a purely legal matter, we find a diversity of idealized practices, but we join a growing number of scholars to advocate that they trend in one direction: the notion that penal incarceration was materially common and legally acceptable at several points in the various, evolving Roman legal systems. We wait until chapters 3 and 4 to discuss how the prison was often experienced as punishment and how such ideologies proliferated through society; here we argue that jurists and emperors often intended and used carceral facilities as such.

We make this distinction because it is one thing to argue that incarcerated people understood their imprisonment as punishment, another thing to suggest that some administrators misused incarceration as punishment, and yet another to determine that lawyers, legal theorists, and administrators intended incarceration as punishment. In the following section, we deal primarily with legal sources, intending to isolate the contours of a Roman theoretical discourse on the relationship between incarceration and law. We hope to demonstrate that when Constantine legislated "The prison is for punishment. The prison is for guilty people," he meant what he said, while also tapping into a long tradition of officials who legislated and implemented penal incarceration, even while some jurists disagreed and reformers protested the practice (*CTh* 11.7.3, L35 [320 CE]).

JURISTS, JUDGES, AND EMPERORS ON PUNITIVE INCARCERATION

The role of jurists is difficult to delineate in contemporary terms: they were legal scholars, commentators, and advisors to the imperial apparatus. While jurists and emperors were both interested in law, their relationship with it was fundamentally different. Roman emperors were a source of law, while (before the late antique period) jurists were interpreters of it. Members of a third category—enforcers of the law, in the person of governors, judges, and court officials—in some cases show keen awareness of the pronouncements of emperors and opinions of jurists, but in many instances they were either not up to date on the legal theory or did not feel beholden to it in their own practices.

The contention that incarceration was at times intended as a legal punishment is at odds with trends in understanding Roman law since at least the late nineteenth century. As discussed in the introduction, Yann Rivière (2021) is only the most recent in a long line of scholars to reiterate the now traditional view, so we will engage his account and his conclusion: "incarceration never had the function of penal confinement, defined for a limited-term or in perpetuity, and it was solely through the negligence of judges or procedural delays that detainees awaiting trial could be held within the walls of a cell" (409). Words like *never* and *solely* paint an idealized picture in broad strokes. In Rivière's estimation, the conclusion constitutes an essential historical fact, though after dismissing the need to provide evidence supporting such a widely repeated claim, he relents, offering the same two pieces of evidence mustered most everywhere else: Ulpian's comment that governors ought not to use prisons for punishment, and the jurist's discussion of doubled sentences for people who escape from condemnation to public works.

The problem, here and elsewhere, is that none of this evidence says what it has been often interpreted to mean. Before Ulpian prescribed his ideal state, in which incarceration is not used for punishment, he described the world as he knew it in practice: "Governors are in the habit of condemning people to be kept in prison or that they might be kept in chains, but they ought not do this, for punishments of this type are forbidden . . . [*Solent praesides in carcere continendos damnare aut ut in vinculis contineantur: sed id eos facere non oportet. Nam huiusmodi poenae interdictae sunt . . .*]" (D 48.19.8.9, L120 [early third century CE]).

Now, jurists use normative language like "but they ought not do this" (*sed id eos facere non oportet*) in a number of different ways that occasionally conflict. Sometimes *oportet* means "the legal rule ought to be X," while other times it means "as an ethical matter, we ought to do X," "the legal rule should properly be X," "it is illegal for the judge to do X," and, in some cases, "X is not suitably effective." Given the number of legal sources that prescribe penal incarceration in some variety, and given its apparent widespread use—both according to the documentary record, literary sources, and according to Ulpian himself in this very passage—we find it most compelling to translate Ulpian's Latin with either of two possibilities, rendering it as follows: "Governors are in the habit of condemning people to be kept in prison or that they might be kept in chains, but [as an ethical matter/ the law should normatively declare that] *they ought not to do this, for punishments of this type are forbidden*; the prison should be used to confine men, and not for their punishment" (D 48.19.8.9, L120 [early third century CE]). Not all texts can or should be read against the grain, but this opinion invites such an interpretation.

There has even been a recherché grammatical discussion in the literature suggesting various emendations to Ulpian's text, on the theory that the Latin manuscript must be corrupt and that some words (*aut*) should be deleted, while others (*perpetuis*) ought to be supplied. What Ulpian *actually* wrote, it has been proposed, speaks to his distaste for governors keeping prisoners permanently in chains, and does not indicate a prohibition on penal incarceration tout court (Lovato 1994, 133–39; Rivière 1999, 58–59; Hillner 2015, 136). The arguments are complex and contested, and they would warrant detailed analysis if Ulpian's passage were the only legal source that speaks to the ubiquity or acceptability of penal incarceration. As we show below, however, scholars have been in the habit of taking Ulpian's distaste for the common use of penal incarceration as the locus classicus for the discussion about penal incarceration in Roman law, but they ought not do so. Penal incarceration appears regularly in legal sources, and while the specific reading of Ulpian's legal opinion is contested, its effect is not; whatever the particular aim of Ulpian's displeasure was, he speaks squarely to the fact that legal ideals had frustratingly little impact on penal practices in the Severan era, or that his opinion was in the great minority. If we wanted strictly to understand the internal ideal world of Roman law, then a long digression would be warranted (cf. Rodrígeuz Martín 2003, 175–92; Zamora Manzano 2015, 72–94). But our aims are different, so we must press on.

Rivière's other piece of evidence is this: Ulpian claims that in cases where people escape from condemnation to public works, their sentence is doubled. He clarifies, however, that the entire sentence is not doubled "from the time when [the convict] was arrested and imprisoned," but rather that only the time remaining on their sentence should be doubled upon escape (*duplicato tempore damnari solet: sed duplicare eum id temporis oportet*) (D 48.19.8.7, L120 [early third century CE]). In this case, Ulpian distinguishes between people who are condemned to public works and people who are condemned to civic prisons, speaking only to the former category. It is crucial to remember, however, that a variety of legal punishments were available to Roman judges. Just as Ulpian claims that it is customary to use prisons as punishment, though he saw the practice as distasteful, he claims that it is customary to double sentences for escapees. The availability of condemnation to public works does not preclude condemnation to civic prisons, and in reality both were explicitly conceived of as carceral facilities within a larger punitive system.

Dozens of legal sources speak to the widespread use of prisons for punishment, while other literary materials help to contextualize Ulpian's concerns. In the late first century BCE, Cicero employed common knowledge and language for uses of prisons, and the types of people inside them, in service of a larger principle: "For in this connection we do not need to discuss cut-throats, poisoners, forgers of wills, thieves, and embezzlers of public money, who should be worn out not by lectures and discussions of philosophers, but by chains and prison walls" (*On Duties* 3.18; L225 [46–43 BCE]). Centuries later from the court of Constantine, Eusebius complained that Christians had been condemned to the entire gamut of acceptable legal penalties: some fought gladiators and beasts, some were castrated and sent to the mines, and others were submitted to tortures and then "cast into prison" (*Martyrs of Palestine* 7.4, L54 [early fourth century CE]; cf. Tertullian, *Apology* 44–45, L262 [197 CE]; Eusebius, *Theophania* 5.28, L154 [ca. 324 CE]).

Ulpian did not rule out the use of public incarceration as a form of public reprove, either—in his treatise *On the Edict* he approves of it (or at least in his gloss of the edict he reports that the pretor reserves the option to use the prison) as an *animadversio*—a chastisement for deviance, in this case for a man who brings a knife to a dice fight and may be punished with either a fine, a term in the stone quarries, or one in the public prison (*in vincula publica*) (D 11.5.1.4, L116 [early third century CE]). Even if one wants to avoid translating *vincula publica* as "public/municipal prison," it remains unavoidable that Ulpian viewed some kind of public incarceration as a formal legal punishment. For us, the exact location need not be the civic prison alone; as we discuss at length in chapter 2, attempting to delineate neatly between penal incarceration in a civic prison and penal incarceration in a facility for convict laborers seems to miss the forest for the trees. What matters for our discussion here is the use of incarceration as one of the formal penalties available to judges.

If Ulpian's criticisms are the best evidence that can be mustered from the legal corpus against the legal use of penal incarceration (and they are), we must at least countenance the conclusion that penal incarceration was simply legal, prevalent, and commonly accepted throughout parts of the Roman world. This argument, while controversial, is hardly novel—Peter Garnsey made it already at length in 1970, concluding "Ulpian disapproved, but nevertheless *vincula* or *vincula publica* appears as a punishment alongside *relegatio, exilium, deportatio, opus publicum*, and the money fine. The governors, in employing imprisonment as a penalty, could be said to have shown a fuller understanding of the direction in which the penal system was evolving" (149–50). Or, elsewhere: "The Severan jurist Ulpian complained of the 'custom' of governors of sentencing condemned men to prison . . . But judges evidently took a less purist stance, and [in the imperial period] imprisonment became a regular alternative to penalties such as exile, the fine, and public labor" (Garnsey 1968, 152). In other words, prisons were one of the tools in the evolving Roman legal toolbox.

It is important to note that penal incarceration was not invented by Romans of the high and late empire. Already in 353 BCE, Demosthenes discussed incarceration as a formal "bodily" punishment (as opposed to a financial punishment) that the law courts could impose as a sentence to someone convicted of crimes—one with the effect of blocking the wealthy elite from avoiding carceral punishment by paying a fine while the poor endured prison (*Against Timocrates* 24.146 and 151, L27 [353 BCE]; Allen 1997, 124–25, 132; Folch 2021b, 508). It appears in republican Rome, as well: in a classic article comparing various accounts of the Catilinarian conspiracy of the mid-first century CE, Werner Eisenhut (1972) argues, "the facts allow for no other conclusion: during the period of Cicero's consulship, incarceration was a viable punishment so common that Caesar could propose it as a legal alternative to execution. The senators . . . and the writers who report on the Senate session evidently agreed with this view" (1972, 272).

Two Greek inscriptions of a Roman edict dated to 68 CE from Tiberius Julius Alexander (prefect of Egypt from 66–69 CE) on debt imprisonment specified the legal use of prisons for holding debtors and indicate that the only person who should be detained in a public prison is someone who is a "criminal." (This law perhaps overturns a provision of the Twelve Tables, which likely permitted debt imprisonment in public facilities.) In it, the governor declares that debtors to the state ought to be kept in the local treasury prison (*praktoreion*) "so that the extraction of debt may be from the property, rather than from the bodies"—apparently the *praktoreion* was less onerous than the civic prison. By way of explanation what 'extracting a debt from the bodies' would entail, the prefect elucidates that only criminals (*kakourgoi*) should be held in the civic prison (*eis fulakēn*) (Temple of Hibis 2.4, D177 [68 CE]; OGIS 669, D185 [68 CE]). These carceral facilities retained their Ptolemaic titles even under Roman administration, and their use remained intact as places of bodily punishment. And, importantly, debt incarceration itself had a punitive function, even when sentences were served in prisons reserved for financial offenders.

Disarticulating debt incarceration from incarceration for perceived criminality is quintessentially modern and reductive, as is a clean distinction between coercive, custodial, and penal control. A generation ago Richard Ireland (1987) showed that the tripartite theoretical division between custodial, punitive, and coercive imprisonment that is near-axiomatic in modern penology does not hold in medieval English legal ideology *or* practice, where defaulting on debt constituted a social offense itself deserving of punishment, and where penal incarceration was intended as a deterrent against breach of contract; to understand debt imprisonment as strictly coercive is to dramatically misunderstand the social world of medieval England. The same approach and potential problems extends also to the ancient Mediterranean. Hillner employs this now-standard taxonomy, with the added caveat that "the penal landscape of the Roman world was more complex than these previous models allow." More than questioning the utility of applying modern models to the ancient world, Hillner suggests that "forms of imprisonment understood as 'reformative' had their place in this landscape" (2015, 1–2, cf. 14–15, 113–16).

Nevertheless, when applying modern penal theories to antiquity, it is often hard to square the circle. Such categories can mislead as much as they reveal; for instance, we agree with Zamora Manzano (2015, 22), Garnsey (1970, 149–50), and others that even custodial and coercive control was a de facto penal sanction in the Roman legal imaginary. Ulpian himself admits as much in book 7 of *On the Duty of the Proconsul*, commending the imperially sanctioned practice of placing insane individuals in the prison in order to constrain their behavior, noting the double-effect of even "purely custodial" incarceration in cases where murderers falsely claim insanity as a defense. Anyone claiming insanity should be incarcerated, "such that if he was faking, he is punished, and if he is insane, he is confined in the prison" (*ut si simulasset, plecteretur, si fueret, in carcere contineretur*) (D 1.18.13.1; L287 [early third century CE]; Pavón Torrejón 2000: 202).

In a series of studies beginning in 1994, Andrea Lovato has published what is still the most sophisticated analysis of the prison's place in Roman penal ideology, making his analysis worth briefly discussing here. Lovato (1999) shows convincingly that at least by the period of the late Roman republic, the oft-cited delineation between a judge's jurisdictional power and his coercive power had collapsed, and that even the coercive use of civic prisons had punitive aims and functions (50–51; Zamora Manzano 2015, 29). He also showed how the advent of a new legal regime under the *cognitio* process changed the legal framework under which carceral sentences were imposed and allowed for greater judicial discretion in sentencing, even though neither changed the Roman punitive regime in its broad outlines (Lovato 1994, 88–89). Our point of departure is indebted to Lovato, who showed that it constitutes a historical failure to extract a general rule about the nonexistence of a prison sentence from Ulpian's famous comment, and further that according to Roman law, the civic prison was only one part of a multifaceted punitive regime which included prisons of other types (2).

Instead of letting Ulpian's ideals dictate our analysis, we too have decided to take a different tack: letting pronouncements of rulers before and after Ulpian's time guide our understanding of Roman law. Throughout this evidence, from Julius Caesar to Constantine and beyond, we find clear evidence of carceral control as a *poena*—a punishment meted out to avenge a legal or social violation. The vast corpus of Roman legal materials has a number of distinct throughlines on this topic. First, jurists discuss incarceration regularly, and emperors legislate about it; its use was a staple of successive Roman legal systems. Second, while some jurists found penal incarceration distasteful, others express no compunction about imprisoning people as punishment after conviction. While not unanimously agreed on as an ideal practice, it is undeniable that the prison was a tool used by some administrators for maintaining civil order and sanctioning people for perceived deviance. Third, both in the older formulary and imperial *cognitio* procedures, a wide range of sentences were available to judges, including permanent or time-bound banishments, permanent or time-bound condemnation to prison, public works, and mines, and death by starvation, strangulation, sword, or spectacle.

Condemnation to the mines in particular was a topic of perennial interest to jurists, but we should be careful not to assume that the level of juristic interest in the status and plight of imprisoned workers reflects the proportion of people punished in this way. (Roman jurists were also intrigued by the legal liability of dogs and their owners; it is an interesting juristic conundrum, but we should not assume that interest on the part of legal professionals reflects ancient legal dockets heavy with canine torts. Justinian's compilers apparently needed more information on mines than on other punishments, and thus excerpted that material more heavily.) Fourth, people serving sentences of convict labor were still caught up in the larger punitive carceral system—they were often considered as a type of prisoner: for instance, when Seneca the Younger calls the mines at Sicily a "natural prison" (*nativus carcer*) (*On Consolation* 17.4, L94 [37–41 CE]). Archaeological sources like the incarcerated workers quarters at Simitthus, too, suggest that these spaces functioned as permanent and purpose-built prisons with intentional design elements allowing for separation of prisoners of different types (Simitthus Workers' Prison, A13). Documentary evidence further demonstrates that, in some cases, a majority of convicts condemned to the mines were in fact not laboring underground but were restrained inside a carceral facility for long stretches of time during their sentence—they were in prison, awaiting their turn to work. We return to each of these points below (p. 125–127).

Jurists and emperors at times even prescribed sentences of incarceration for a limited term, mainly for lower social status offenders: a practice that is hard to make sense of apart from the intention of incarceration as punishment for deviance. Writing in the late second century, Papinian discussed a rescript of Marcus

Aurelius and Lucius Verus some forty years earlier on the topic of limited-term, penal incarceration. The law immediately concerns slaves who had been sentenced to limited-term imprisonment by a judge, and addresses the question of whether they could receive an inheritance after their sentence was served. "The imperial brothers wrote in a rescript that slaves condemned to temporary imprisonment [*servos in temporaria vincula damnatos*] may obtain their freedom and an inheritance or legacy when they have served their time [*postquam tempus expleverint*], given the fact that the period of restraint which results from a legal sentence satisfies the punishment [*consequi quia temporaria coercitio, quae descendit ex sententia, poenae est abolitio*]" (D 48.19.33, L41 [161–69 CE]). It is important to remember that the subjects of this rescript were *already* slaves; the text speaks to their limited-term incarceration as a punishment for deviant behavior, not to restraint in chains related particularly to their enslaved status. Most importantly, the logic of the passage relies on a broader theory of carceral practice: the reason that a slave's capacity to inherit is returned to him after his period in chains is that "the period of restraint satisfies the punishment." Not only was limited-term penal incarceration under discussion in this imperial pronouncement from the mid-second century CE, but it invokes a broader legal principle that time incarcerated can be calibrated to deviance and act to satisfy the need for punishment. We return to this point in chapter three.

A rescript of Hadrian discussed by Callistratus in the third century CE speaks both to limited-term penal incarceration and to sentencing enhancements reminiscent of more recent American carceral practice, in which subsequent misconduct can render one punishment into another, harsher option. In the early second century CE, Hadrian ordered that in cases where convicts escape or otherwise fail to fulfill the terms of their punishment, "a certain gradation should be observed with reference to prisoners—namely, that those who were sentenced for a certain period of time [*in tempus damnati*] should be sentenced for life [*in perpetuum damnati erant*)]" (D 48.19.28.14, L122 [117–38 CE]). Some have attempted to explain away the limited-term, penal aspect of this rescript by restricting its application solely to free men condemned to public works, and not, as it says, people under carceral control (*ita . . . in custodiis*). Such harmonization is possible, and Hervé Huntzinger (2005) offers precisely such a solution on analogy with Ulpian's opinion on doubling of public slave sentences from a century later, likely before Callistratus wrote (24). It is hardly the only solution, however, and suffers from two defects: (1) It is not what the text *says*, which instead refers to people condemned to hard labor simply as prisoners; and (2) Ulpian himself attests both disagreement between jurists and, famously, between legal ideals and practiced realities.

In the second book of his *On the Duty of the Proconsul*, Ulpian laid out his ideal procedure for someone facing an accusation. There are four options: they are "to be admitted to the prison" (*in carcerem recipienda*), "delivered to a soldier" (*an militi tradenda*), or "committed to the care of their sureties, or to that of themselves" (*fideiussoribus committenda vel etiam sibi*) (D 48.3.1, L105 [early third century CE]). What Ulpian intends, then, is a system of pretrial custodial incarceration with allowances for bail—either cash bail or bail on the recognizance of the accused, both of which are amply attested in the documentary record. Some laws, like *CTh* 9.1.7 and 9.1.18, from the middle and latter parts of the fourth century respectively, record imperial pronouncements that incarcerated people should be tried within a month (*CTh* 9.1.7, L89 [338CE]; *CTh* 9.1.18, L290 [396 CE]). A law of 423 CE further explicates the bail system, though it claims to simply restate "the rules long ago made for criminal cases." These timeworn rules indicate that accused people should generally not be incarcerated simply by virtue of accusation, but that certain serious crimes require both accuser and accused to be incarcerated, with the conditions of their custody "taking into account their rank" (*dignitatis*)—which is to say that high-ranking people are not to be incarcerated in public prisons, an invocation of the Roman class-based caste system long since instituted by the fifth century (*CI* 9.2.17.0, L5 [423 CE]; cf. D 48.19.9.11; Harries 1999, 139–42).

Earlier jurists like Venuleius Saturninus, working in a somewhat different legal system, likewise prescribe that people should be incarcerated after they confess until they are sentenced (D 48.3.5, L107 [early third century CE]). Importantly, none of the laws say that the sentence cannot be further incarceration, only that they should be sentenced in a reasonable time, and Saturninus similarly speaks only to preconviction detention without indicating the range of possible punishments. A set of opinions forged in the name of the famous jurist Paul, probably sometime in the late third century, details available punishments for crimes of varying severity: people convicted of the most serious crimes may incur beheading, crucifixion, and immolation as punishment; deportation, condemnation to the mines, or gladiatorial combat for less severe crimes; and for the lowest level of infractions options include banishment, condemnation to public works, and incarceration (*vincula*) (*Sententia Pauli* 5.17.2, FIRA², 405 [late third century CE]).

Labeling it as a "less purist stance," Garnsey (1968) notes that for some jurists "imprisonment became a regular alternative to penalties such as exile, the fine, and public labor" (152). Already in the mid-second century CE, the emperor Antoninus Pius had written to the people of Antioch that someone accused of a serious crime should not be released on bail, "but should suffer this same penalty of imprisonment before his punishment [*verum hanc ipsam carceris poenam ante supplicium sustinere*]" (D 48.3.3, L106). So linked were the prison and punishment that Roman legal theory provided for both pre- and postconviction penal incarceration, and one punishment was not exclusive of another—one could be "punished" with incarceration before undergoing another form of punishment. But again, the fact that another form of punishment was possible does not negate the penal aspect of incarceration itself—or, indeed, its use as a sanction in and of itself.

The emperor Constantine says as much in a number of reformatory laws promulgated in 320 and the years following. In *Theodosian Code* 11.7.3 he legislated that tax debtors should not be incarcerated or suffer any other type of bodily harm by the legal apparatus. Constantine's justification for the law offers another glimpse into a carceral logic of the early fourth century, in the context of a dramatic reorganization of Roman legal bureaucracy. He specifies that prisons are not intended for tax debtors, but for a different type of persons: convicts. "The prison is for punishment; the prison is for guilty people [*carcer poenalium, carcer hominum noxiorum est*]" (*CTh* 11.7.3, L35 [320 CE]). If we were to frame our understanding of Constantine's legislation as bound by Ulpian's distaste for punitive uses of incarceration nearly a century prior, or the notion that prisons are ideally custodial and not part of the punitive apparatus, then we could find a way to explain away Constantine's rather clear invocation of prisons as a place for the punishment of convicts. Still, we argue that the two men's status is relevant: Constantine was an emperor, Ulpian was a jurist. If we add to this the fact that Ulpian explicitly says that prisons were regularly used as punishment in his own day, it becomes hard to read Constantine's statement to say anything other than its plain meaning. If, as Lovato argues, laws such as these reflect a desire for stricter sentencing guidelines that were previously lacking in the *cognitio* procedure, the point is doubly made—punitive sentencing to prison was perhaps previously one possible outcome, only later to become a standardized regime (1994). Another set of reforms appear in a Constantinian law from the same year. At issue is the plight of defendants awaiting trial of any kind and the danger inherent in prolonged carceral detention. Such defendants as these ought to be kept in salubrious conditions, in loose-fitting chains, and with access to light (at least during the day). The law offers its own justification, as well: "The idea is that he does not perish from the punishments of prison [*ne poenis carceris perimatur*], which is regarded as pitiable for the innocent, but not sufficiently severe for the guilty" (*CTh* 9.3.1, L133 [320/1 CE]).

Constantine's legislation on the subject is something of a thorn in the side of Lovato's analysis. In his commentary on the law, Lovato (1994) admits that "the term *poenae carceris* [punishment by imprisonment] appears in the law: we have already noted that this is an expression used inappropriately" (183). The phrase does appear several times, so on what grounds does Lovato accuse the emperor of using the expression "punishment of imprisonment" inappropriately? Lovato agrees that Ulpian's distaste for penal incarceration is not the proper context in which to understand Constantine's discussion of penal incarceration, and he offers instead a novel reading of Constantine's reformatory justification that death on account of the squalid conditions is "a fate which is considered pitiable for the innocent but not severe enough for the guilty." In Lovato's estimation, the "punishment of imprisonment" is poor wording because the prison is intended here with a "preventative function"—that is, to hold prisoners until trial, given that "the establishment of the accused's innocence is a point of arrival, not departure" (182). Thus, the law indicates that imprisonment *itself* is not severe enough for the guilty—that "a punishment of this kind would have been insufficient"—and thus the prison cannot have been used as punishment at all (183–84). This is a possible reading of Constantine's law, but it is hardly the most compelling one. In addition to providing a subtle interpretive sleight of hand, Lovato's comment fails to acknowledge the awful torture of imprisonment—tortures that the law in question explicitly aims to mitigate. Even so, if the concern is about people dying in prison, the law does not necessarily speak for or against the use of penal incarceration.

In Lovato's estimation, Constantine was prone to legislative mistakes. Six years later, when promulgating yet another law discussing the use of penal incarceration, the emperor was responsible for "another improper use of the term *punishment*" (185). The law reads,

> If any person should be apprehended in that kind of infraction or crime that appears to deserve the confinement of prison and the squalor of custody, and if after a hearing before the public records the commission of the crime should be established, he shall sustain the penalty of imprisonment, and thus somewhat later he shall be led forth and heard before the public records. For thus a reminder of the crime committed shall be made under public attestation, so to speak, so that when judges rage excessively, it may appear that certain restraints and moderation have been employed. (*CTh* 9.3.2, L172 [326 CE])

The law indicates the order of operations for a person suspected of a "infraction or crime [*culpa vel crimine*]" that appears to warrant incarceration after their guilt has been established in the public record. Interestingly, the emperor indicates precisely that there are a variety of infractions that deserve incarceration (while pointedly refusing to distinguish between "infractions" and "crimes"), and after conviction people guilty of such deviance "shall bear the penalty of imprisonment [*poenam carceris sustineat*]." In the broader context of the law it is clear that Constantine intends the prison to be used only in criminal cases, sparing debtors to the state from a variety of physical and social sanctions by implementing a looser military custody while limiting the use of carceral punishment to convicted criminals (Rivière 2004b, 209–10). His son Constantius prescribed a somewhat more expansive policy, legislating in 349 CE that public prisons should be used both for nonpunitive custody before trial, and for postconviction punishment. "Prisons shall hold the scoundrels when they are convicted [*sceleratos convictosque carceres teneant*], tortures shall tear them apart, the avenging sword shall do away with them. Thus, in this way, the freedom of the habitually lawless will be prevented" (*CTh* 2.1.1, L34 [349 CE]). Lest we think that the listed punishments—prison, tortures, and death—are intended to be sequential rather than prison as a punishment in and of itself, an early sixth-century jurist in the West added an interpretation, noting that even people working on imperial estates are subject to whichever punishment is demanded by their guilt, including prison, torture, and death. "Should any of the Emperor's own slaves or tenant farmers be involved in any criminality, [judges should] arrest and punish them, just as their guilt demands—the same as if they were private persons" (*CTh* 2.1.1.Int). Both this fourth-century law and its sixth-century gloss present prison as one penal option out of many available to judges, no matter the identity of the defendant. This is the way that the emperors Gratian, Valentinian II, and Theodosius I understood the status quo, as well; fifty years after Constantine's legislation, they reiterated that: "Before he is convicted, no one should be chained in prison" (*CTh* 9.2.3 L90 [380 CE]). Confinement *after* conviction, it seems—and even confinement in life-threatening chains—was both acceptable and normal. Were these people still in custodial custody, on the way to punishment, or was custody part of their punishment itself? Commentators disagree, as we have shown. What is clear, though, is that prolonged postconviction incarceration was nevertheless common, and deadly in itself.

In fact, in the early fifth century the emperors Honorius and Theodosius II spoke to the possibility that people who had been sentenced to some form of exile were instead punished with serving that time in a prison, either by accident or as a result of judicial abuse. In such cases, they decree that the prisoner should be

> absolved from further punishment, released from their chains, freed from custody [*solutos poena vinculisque laxatos custodia liberari*], and have no fear of the miseries of exile afterwards. Let it suffice that they have atoned once for all through the sufferings of immeasurable tortures, so that those persons who have been long deprived of the breath of our common air and the sight of light and who, confined within a narrow space, have been burdened with the weight of chains shall not be compelled to sustain also the punishment of exile [*exilii poenam sustinere*]. (*CTh* 9.40.22, L96 [414 CE])

Importantly, time spent "in chains" (*vinculis*), and "custody" (*custodia*) are forms of incarceration, a codified legal penalty that the law places alongside exile. As a penalty, however, incarceration was so much more severe that someone who was sentenced to exile and instead served that time in prison was to be immediately absolved of further penalties. Here we see both location of bondage and extent of time carefully calibrated as related forms of punishment that respond both to the nature of the crime and the status of its perpetrator.

Across six centuries, then, Roman legal sources regularly prescribed incarceration as a sanctioned form of punishment, including incarceration for a limited term. Reflection on Ulpian's distaste for incarceration, as well as on the distinction between incarceration and sentencing on the part of jurists like Venuleius Saturninus and emperors like Antoninus Pius, has led modern historians to understand that Roman incarceration was purely custodial, that custody was kept until punishment was rendered, and that the punishment rendered was never further incarceration.

Such an assumption, however, involves three fundamental errors. First, it is to assume that jurists like Ulpian speak descriptively rather than prescriptively, an assumption that is undercut by scores of documentary and literary sources, and by the fuller context of Ulpian's own comment. Roman jurists often presented a vision of an idealized judicial system, not a reflection of the system as practiced. However, when they speak explicitly of the system as practiced, they point to penal incarceration as a norm; Ulpian admits that "governors are in the habit of condemning people to be kept in prison or that they might be kept in chains" (D 48.19.8.9, L120 [early third century CE]). As Hillner (2015) points out, "even a positivist reading of Ulpian's passage as a prohibition of the prison penalty would suggest that provincial governors applied it in their sentencing practice. The nearly proverbial status in literary texts ranging from the late republic to late antiquity seems to confirm the widespread use of punitive imprisonment during the empire" (136). While "no true Roman" ought to do so, apparently lots of Romans did exactly this. Second, it is an error to assume that jurists like Ulpian were speaking authoritatively rather than offering opinions about what the law means and how it should work. Jurists' opinions could be influential, but they were not socially powerful in the way that we understand a law to be today, or in the way that an imperial constitution was in Ulpian's day. The third historical error is to read a text like that of Venuleius Saturninus, who says that people who confess should be incarcerated "until sentence is passed on him," to mean that incarceration itself was not an available sentence (D 48.3.5, L107 [early third century CE]). This source speaks to the use of custodial incarceration in antiquity but it does not suggest that custody was the only reason for relegating someone to prison. Saturninus wrote about the topic of pretrial bail, not about whether penal incarceration was an available form of sentencing. We show below that prisoners regularly described and experienced their incarceration as a punishment, and documentary sources attest to prisoners released from incarceration and other forms of punishment after serving a time-limited sentence.

Legal sources also stress that penal sentences were often intended to be limited in term. Callistratus wrote in the early third century CE, "In the mandates given by the emperors to provincial governors it is provided that no one is to be condemned to permanent chains/imprisonment [*perpetuis vinculis damnetur*], and the deified Hadrian also wrote a rescript to this effect" (D 48.19.35, L42). The rescript, and Callistratus's description of the various mandates that he has seen, implies precisely that further limited-term imprisonment is at least theoretically acceptable, and that only *permanent* incarceration was outlawed—though even Hadrian's rescripts are inconsistent on the permissibility of permanent sentences, as discussed below (D 48.19.28.14, L122 [117–38 CE]). Of course, documentary and literary sources show that permanent—or at least indefinite and prolonged—incarceration was commonly practiced, again pointing to the fissure between legal theory and social practice (cf. Quintus Curtius, *History of Alexander* 7.1–10, L188 [41–54 CE]). We return for the moment, however, to legal theory.

VARIETIES OF PUNITIVE INCARCERATION: CONDEMNATION TO HARD LABOR

Condemnation to unpaid convict labor is prevalent in Roman legal sources and was predominantly categorized as an aspect of the larger system of penal incarceration, a framing that documentary and literary sources largely corroborate (Huntzinger 2005). Penal mine service existed in two interlocking but formally distinct categories: those condemned to the mines with heavy chains (*ad metallum*) and those condemned to a lesser service of mine labor with lighter chains (*ad opus metalli*) (D 48.19.8.6, L120 [early third century CE]). Mine service was a peculiar aspect of the Roman carceral system, and jurists were most interested in the intellectual problems that these statuses presented. While Hillner (2015) categorizes condemnation to hard labor as a "special form of exile," legal sources characterize penal labor as a form of carceral control, reserved for low status offenders and related to but legally distinct from enslavement (199–211; Larsen 2019). For Millar (1984), a clear bifurcation between imprisonment and condemnation to the mines is merited: "Imprisonment therefore was not (in principle) a recognised long-term penalty ... *Opus publicum*, however, clearly was a regular custodial penalty, frequently referred to in legal sources" (132–33). It is worth pausing to question the utility of such a clean distinction and ask if it is more useful to frame the discussion differently. In our view, a "custodial penalty" is, if nothing else, a carceral practice; mines and mining complexes were functional prisons even though they were not identical to imprisonment in a municipal facility. Jurists and emperors were creative in their sentences of condemnation to hard labor, including one of Constantine's political rivals who was condemned to work, fettered, in an imperial weaving establishment in Carthage (*CTh* 4.6.3, L135 [336 CE]), while a law of the mid-fourth century condemns people convicted of lesser crimes to work in the bakeries of Rome (*CTh* 9.40.5, L95 [364 CE]). In discussing not just the prison but also the broader legal ideologies carceral practices, we incorporate sentencing to hard labor into our analysis of incarceration, including sentences sending convicts to mines, quarries, bakeries, brothels, and other public works—places where people were sent as prisoners to perform unpaid labor on behalf of the state or its contracted partners.

Convict labor was employed beyond resource extraction, especially in the condemnation of prisoners to serve a punitive limited-term carceral sentences in public works, a fate typically reserved for lower-status individuals (Pavón Torrejón 2003b, 188–92). A rescript of Antoninus Pius on the topic of people who steal goods from sinking ships is illustrative of a widely implemented practice of differential punishments, varying in the Roman Republic according to citizenship status, and by the high empire and throughout late antiquity, rigidly according to social class (Cardascia 1950). The emperor prescribes that, after being convicted, higher-status free people should be "beaten with clubs and banished for three years, or if they are of the lower classes, condemn them to public works (*opus publicum*) for the same period [that is, for a three-year sentence]" (D 47.9.4.1, L170 [mid–second century CE]). Enslaved people convicted of this crime, the emperor clarifies, should be flogged and then sent to the mines. Here the time and location are clearly specified, with both unapologetically calibrated to the social status of the convicted. Ulpian proposed that people who had been condemned to public works (*opus publicum*), only to escape, should have the times of their sentences doubled as further punishment (D 48.19.8.7, L120 [early third century CE]). Likewise, if the escapee had originally been condemned to ten years of labor, his sentence should be extended to life, or alternatively changed to a different, harsher sentence: condemnation to the mines.

For sake of scope we keep our focus on incarceration, yet recent works like Douglas Blackmon's *Slavery by Another Name* (2008) and Michelle Alexander's *The New Jim Crow* (2010) challenge the desire and the utility of drawing clean lines between the categories of enslavement and incarceration. It is worth clarifying that legal sources disambiguate enslaved people from those who are legally incarcerated. Writing in the late third century, the Roman jurist Hermogenian clarified the idealized legal status of even free people condemned to mine service. He claims that "Those condemned to the mines [*damnati . . . in metallum*], as also to the service of the mineworkers, are made into slaves, that is, 'penal slaves'" (D 48.19.36, L161). Hermogenian's syntax makes clear that both men (mineworkers) and women (who were condemned "to the service of mineworkers [*in ministerium metallicorum*]) were made similar to slaves by virtue of their type of service, but that their status is different—they are *servi poenae*, or "slaves because of punishment" owned directly by the Roman state (D 48.19.8.8, L120; Hirt 2010, 97–98). Importantly, their status differs from enslaved people on three counts: they do not have a master as such, their enslavement is potentially limited in term, and it resulted from conviction for deviance.

As a slight aside, commentators have often read this passage to mean that "women serving mine workers almost certainly were expected to provide sexual services" (Hillner 2020, 20; citing Robinson 2007, 125). There is some evidence that jurists were at least concerned with the possibility that women condemned to the mines might give birth (D 40.5.24.5), but if the implication that women were sex slaves is present in any of the discussions of mineworkers, it is rather subtle. There is, additionally, evidence for paid prostitution within the garrison guarding the mines at Mons Claudianus in the first through third centuries, rather than condemned or enslaved sex workers (Bülow-Jacobsen 2022). Similarly,

Hélène Cuvigny (2010) has shown that soldiers from the Roman garrison at Berenice paid for the services of a prostitute by the month; it would be surprising if male inmates were provided with sexual services while soldiers paid out of pocket for the same. To further underscore the folly of reading legal prescriptions as if they were descriptions of universal practices, we note that even women working in mines overseen by the military did not *solely* work "in the service of mineworkers"—in the second century, for example, women worked in the emerald mines themselves, as documentary evidence proves (O. Did. 376 [early second century CE]).

The distinction between a "slave" and a "slave of punishment" was of continual interest to jurists and legislators. In his *On the Duty of the Proconsul*, Ulpian addresses a potential legal problem in which an enslaved person (*servus*) is condemned to work as a "punishment slave" (*servus poenae*) on account of deviance. If that person is subsequently released from his sentence, what is his new legal status? Does he revert to being a slave? The question is only intelligible if one understands that a *servus poenae* is not a subset of *servus*, but a different category altogether. Ulpian commends a rescript of Antoninus Pius as "most correct" (*rectissime*) in its judgment that, in the event of release of a "punishment slave," the person should not be returned to their former enslaver because they ceased to be their master's property when their legal status changed to *servus poenae*. To underscore the point further, Ulpian continues, "If, however, a slave is condemned to fetters [*in vincula*]—whether permanently or temporarily [*sive in perpetua . . . sive in temporalia*]—he remains the property of him who was his master before he was condemned" (D 48.19.8.12–13, L120 [early third century CE]). That is, a slave who is *not* sentenced to service as a *servus poenae* does not change legal status; as a result, he remains under the authority of his enslaver, to whom he is returned after his sentence is complete. Similarly, according to Ulpian, women who are condemned to forced labor in the mines become *servae poenae* only if they are condemned to permanent labor; if they are condemned only to a temporary sentence in the mines, their legal status remains intact and they remain citizens (D 48.19.8.8).

In some cases, jurists devise hypotheticals to test the limits and implications of a legal doctrine, with little real-world interest or application; the question of an incarcerated slave was not merely a hypothetical. Ulpian cites an imperial rescript that adjudicates this problem, presumably in response to at least one relevant case, and the distinction between enslaved people and imprisoned people appears in the papyrological record, as well. P. Oxy. 12.1423 is a letter from Flavius Ammonas, an attendant on the staff of the prefect of Egypt, charging another man to locate his runaway slave and "to bind him as a prisoner and return him" (*diadēsas* [amended *diadēsanti*] *desmion agagein*) (D132 [mid-third century CE]). The man was already liable to be chained simply by virtue of his enslaved status. This papyrus from an imperial official makes clear that it was his deviant behavior that changed the slave's status to "prisoner," leading him to be bound on account of his actions. Roman materials are not unique in referring to convict laborers as prisoners and in discussing convict labor among broader carceral practices. Documentary sources from the Ptolemaic period also refer to people laboring in mines as "prisoners" (*desmōtai*), and to mines as a "prison" (*desmōterion*) (PSI 4.423, D58 [263–29 BCE]; P. Cair. Zen. 2.59296; D33 [250 BCE]).

It is often assumed that Romans considered labor in the mines to be effectively a death sentence, but the breadth of evidence suggests that death was only one possible outcome, the likelihood of which depended on what form of condemnation the convict underwent—whether they were condemned *in metallum* or *ad opus metalli*. The jurist Callistratus points out that at least condemnation to mine service (*ad opus metalli*) was not a death sentence *de iure* by prescribing that, in certain circumstances, the penalty could be enhanced to become a death penalty (D 48.19.28.14, L122 [early third century CE]). Similarly, a rescript of the emperor Antoninus Pius stipulates that in some cases, people condemned to mine service (*in metallum damnati*) can be released owing to sickness or infirmity, provided that they "have served not less than ten years of their sentence" (D 48.19.22–23, L131 [138–61 CE]). Citing this rescript, the jurist Modestinus adds that sentences to mine labor should be understood as limited to ten years unless specifically indicated otherwise by the sentencing judge. He writes as follows: "If someone is sent to the mines without a predetermined time limit [*sine praefinito tempore in metallum dato*] on account of the inexperience of the person sentencing, it seems that his sentence is limited to ten years" (D 48.19.23, L131 [ca. 250 CE]). Perpetual condemnation to the mines existed as one option for judges, but the only sense in which a sentence of service in the mines (*ad opus metalli*) could *not* be time-bound, according to Modestinus, was when the judge made a mistake.

Documentary sources like SB 20.14631 provide corroborating evidence for limited-term sentences in the mines. This short and fragmentary letter from the prefect of Egypt to a mining official orders the release of a man sentenced by the previous prefect to labor in the mines for a period of five years. "I order that Petesuchos son of Petesuchos, condemned by the distinguished man Petronius Mamertinus to five years in the alabaster mines, be released because the time of his sentence is complete" (D106 [139 CE]; Bastianini 1988). Similarly, a papyrus written at the direction of the prefect of Egypt on December 27, 209 CE documents the release of a prisoner who had been sentenced to work in the mines and been incarcerated there for a period of five years. The document is similar to others of its type, recording conviction of a crime, length of incarceration, and completion of a sentence. It reads:

> From Subatianus Aquila to Theon the governor of the Arsinoite district. Greetings. Nigeras, son of Papirios, whom the most honorable Claudius Julianus condemned to the alabaster mine for a period of five years, and who has completed the time of his sentence, I released. (SB 1.4639, D109)

It is important to remember that mining camps that employed convict labor, like alabaster mines in the Nile Valley and marble mines in Egypt's eastern desert, are carceral facilities. *PSI* 4.423, discussed above, contains a report from a mine overseer in Ptolemaic Egypt, detailing the labor of ten prisoners (*desmōtai*) who worked the mine over the course of sixty-eight days. (p. 125–126; D58 [263–229 BCE]). The overseer specifically notes, moreover, that 130 further prisoners were being held in the camp, waiting for their turn to work. As we demonstrate in chapter 2 with investigation of the incarcerated miner's quarters at Simitthus (Chemtou, Tunisia), and the mines at Phaino (Wadi Feynan, Jordan), condemnation to labor was not an exemption from incarceration—it was a form of incarceration.

Limited-term sentencing and release was rather common, it seems. In fact, a similar papyrus from only a few months later mentions the same prefect of Egypt as employing a limited-term sentence.

> Anubion the governor [writes] . . . Since the most illustrious prefect Subatianus Aquila sent me a letter concerning Isidorus, who is also called Chaireos, who has completed the time of his sentence and has been released, this copy was sent to you all, so that you might know and act accordingly. (SB 14.11999, D105 [210 CE]; Schwartz 1971)

Again we find bureaucracy at the center of the Roman carceral system, with the colonial Roman administrator pronouncing the completion of a carceral sentence. Some commentators, like Arnaldo Marcone (1999), express reservations about the ubiquity of such releases for time served, but he nevertheless admits that "even if such releases didn't take place every day, they absolutely correspond to a regular practice which, on balance, speaks in favor of the smooth functioning of the administration of Roman Egypt"—an administration that had condemnation and release as part of its regular procedure (97). What this document fails to mention, however, is perhaps just as illuminating as the information it presents: first, it does not indicate how long the person had been incarcerated, only that he had completed the time of his sentence. Second, it does not clarify where he had been incarcerated. While the mines are a possible location, and perhaps the probable location, it is worth noting that the language of the document allows the possibility that he had been detained in a public prison.

In the late first century BCE, Diodorus Siculus noted that mine service is dangerous to health and to life, and that few are able to survive it indefinitely (*Library of History* 5.38, L168). Practically speaking, toxic air filled with heavy metals rendered it less likely that prisoners would survive their sentence of penal labor in the mines, and some late ancient laws prescribe perpetual condemnation to the mines as a criminal sanction, as in cases of fraudulent notices of ownership, or if an estate overseer allows heretics to congregate on his land (*CTh* 2.14.1 [400 CE]; *CTh* 16.5.40 [407 CE]). Just as penal incarceration was one option available to Roman judges, so too were limited-term or perpetual sentences of labor in the mines.

PRISON REFORMS

As we have argued, carceral ideology was hardly static through the period covered by our juristic sources; nor can a singular set of practices be distilled from a corpus punctuated by dissenting voices and intermittent efforts at reform. Nevertheless, the sources do reflect a couple periods of what might be described as prison reform, with a cluster of laws promulgated under Constantine, and again under Honorius and Theodosius II, that attempt to constrain some of the worst excesses of the carceral system. Since the period of the *Theodosian Code*, in which these laws are attested, spans almost precisely the space between the two periods of "reform," we cannot say that these emperors were unique in their concern over the plight of the incarcerated; other attempts at reform are almost certainly lost to history. Nevertheless, legal sources rarely discuss the material conditions of prisons, and we do well to pay attention to the few laws that place incarcerated individuals as subjects rather than objects.

Constantine's reforms were dispatched from Serdica (Sofia, Bulgaria) in 320/21 CE, and aimed to address some of the dangers of prison for people locked inside, first of all by limiting the time that accused people were jailed, as discussed above. The idea is that the accused "not perish from the punishments of prison" (*CTh* 9.3.1, L133). Accused persons in both private and public suits shall be kept in loose fitting chains rather than "iron fetters which fit close to the bone." The law addresses access to light, as well, stipulating that accused people should be allowed access to light during the day and moved to darker, inner areas of the prison only "when night doubles the need for detention." Even then, accused prisoners are intended only to be kept in the part of the prison closer to the entrance (*vestibulum*), rather than the dark inner prison reserved for convicts. At sunrise, "[the prisoner] ought to be immediately led back to the sunlight." Here we see Constantine speaking directly to the distinction between custodial and penal incarceration, and prescribing that both ought to happen in public prisons. It is not precisely a distinction between a prison and a jail in modern sense—another two hundred years passed before we have secure evidence of a separate pretrial jail facility specifically for the accused and not yet convicted—but it is certainly an explicit attestation of an operative legal distinction between custodial and punitive incarceration (p. 87).

The emperor was concerned, however, that prisons were fundamentally dangerous and unhealthy places, and that custodial incarceration could constitute an injustice for someone acquitted of charges for which they were jailed. He orders that "neither those who perform the duties of the prison-warden [*qui stratorum funguntur officio*] nor his assistants shall not be permitted to sell their cruelty to the accusers, nor to deliver innocent people to death in the confines of prisons or to allow them to waste away for chronic disease after they are denied a hearing." *This* is the context in which Constantine clarifies that death in prison "is regarded as pitiable for the innocent, though it is not sufficiently severe for the guilty." Constantine indicates that in many instances death in prison would not be enough for guilty people—they ought to be executed, as argued by Lovato (1994)—and also that conditions in public prisons were so dire that they constituted punishment in themselves (183–84). Squalid prison conditions could—and apparently did—kill people, and it was precisely this aspect that aborted justice for the innocent and guilty alike: a punishment that should not be visited on people awaiting trial, even though they are acceptable for those who have been convicted, and perhaps overly humane for convicts.

Nearly two centuries later the Ostrogothic king Theodoric restated Constantine's concern about the tortures of prison, adding a new facet of carceral ideology that doesn't appear in earlier Roman legal sources: reformatory incarceration. The king demanded that penal incarceration be dispensed selectively, "lest the innocent seem to endure harm to life on account of a zeal for punishment . . . let the guilty alone fall for the correction of many, since it is even a kind of piety to imprison the crime in its infancy, lest it should increase with maturity" (Cassiodorus, *Variae* 5.39.1–4, L7 [523–26 CE]). The prison was a social instrument in the hands of the Ostrogothic state, an integrated facet of the penal apparatus aimed at producing salubrious effects on its victims. Theodoric's ideal transparently reflects a much earlier precedent: Plato's suggestion that an ideal city would have three prisons, one called "the Reformatory" where penal control can instill moderation in offenders without ejecting them from society for good (*Laws* 908a–909c, L18 [mid-fourth century BCE], p. 94–95). In this instance we see Plato's ideal put into civic action—it is part of the long-term genesis of reformatory incarceration that Hillner details in her 2015 monograph, which traces the phenomenon from ideals of the Greek classical period into the practice of fifth- and sixth-century forced monastic confinement.

The widespread implementation of reformatory incarceration is one of the trends that Hillner advocates for in late Roman sources and society; we note four more trends here, each of which is discussed by Bernhard Raspels (1991) and expanded upon by Hillner. First, legal materials witness a desire to limit the number of prisons—as seen, for instance, in legislation addressing prison personnel. Citing three laws spanning the fourth century, Hillner (2015) writes "Secret agents [*agentes in rebus*] and soldiers acting as a police force in rural areas [*stationarii*] were urged not to put people in prison [*carcer*], but to refer their matter and the offenders themselves to a magistrate with judicial powers" (121). The point is correct in broad strokes, but its implications are muddled; the first two laws cited (*CTh* 8.4.2, 315 CE; 6.29.1, L87 [355 CE]) simply shift responsibility for imprisonment from the *agentes in rebus* to judges, prohibiting them from keeping their own prison facilities and sending people to them without proper trial. The laws attempt to limit who can oversee prison facilities, yes, but not to limit the use of prisons either pre- or posttrial; judges were still free to do so. The third law simply restates that these secret agents should not be casting anyone into prison, but instead should devote themselves to their other duties (*CTh* 6.29.8, 395 CE). As Hillner writes, these laws envision that "[secret agents'] official duties were purely supervisory and not judicial, but the laws show that these competences were sometimes exceeded" (121).

But abuses of the prison are still uses of the prison. The fact that laws spanning the fourth century reiterate the commonality of such abuses suggests that they were likely widespread and difficult to reign in. Such abuses are historical phenomena and instances of carceral practice—and, indeed, local carceral *policy* in some places. They deserve to be part of our analysis as much as the ideals of the legislators trying to limit them.

This late ancient attempt to place carceral control largely under the authority of judges leads Hillner to conclude that "prisons therefore were to be located only in the provincial capitals, although at this level there was no limit on the number of prisons, as different judges based in provincial capitals could maintain their own prisons" (122). Again, the point is technically true but muddled; as we demonstrate below, both archaeological and documentary data show that prison facilities appeared across the landscape, far beyond provincial capitals, even in the fourth-century horizon about which Hillner writes. If *true* prisons only occurred in provincial capitals, then the Mediterranean basin was littered with perhaps thousands of untrue prisons, which are still part of the story of incarceration in this period.

Three more broad-scale reforms are worth noting, as well: As Hillner notes, sources point to a desire that only people involved in criminal procedures are placed in prisons, that such people are brought to prompt trials, and that people in pretrial detention are protected from abuses by staff in the facilities where they waited (121–25). Although Hillner relies on Rivière's reading of Constantine's legislation that we have disputed above, late Roman legal sources certainly aim to limit the use of prisons in fiscal and civil matters, reserving incarceration for criminal cases. In attempting to secure prompt trials of the accused, legal sources are in harmony with literary and documentary sources that we discuss below, seeming to speak to a real problem: that the judges' dockets were perpetually backlogged, leaving countless hordes in prison awaiting trial, and often dying before their appearance (p. 99–101). The late fourth through mid-fifth century present another burst of legal reforms addressing a new reality in which Christians were both part of a religious community whose history was bound up in unjust incarceration and, in their position as governing officials, incarcerators themselves. In the late

360s CE, the emperors Valentinian II, Valens, and Gratian jointly pronounced a general amnesty on Easter, while another law of 385 CE exempted people guilty of certain crimes from any amnesty on account of their capacity to affect society negatively (*CTh* 9.38.3, L45 [367–69 CE]; *CTh* 9.38.8, L29 [385 CE]). Hillner (2015) is right to point to Easter amnesty laws as a salve to the issue of trial delays and prison guard abuses, noting especially the import of clerical visits to and oversight of carceral facilities (104–5, 123–24). The latter law presents perhaps the first Roman evidence of incarceration described explicitly as a communal good because of the prison's ability to incapacitate certain classes of offenders. In the early fifth century, the emperors Honorius and Theodosius II commanded stiff penalties for judges and their staffs who fail to follow certain "health-giving regulations" (*saluberrime statuta*) for people jailed as a result of an accusation against them. Custodial prisoners are ordered to receive a portion of food on Sunday, along with a guarded visit to the public bath (*CTh* 9.3.7, L44 [409 CE]). While these reforms are explicitly described as extending from a Christian concern for the poor, they appear to be intended solely for the benefit of accused persons and not for those suffering penal incarceration. The same emperors granted sanctuary to people who fled to churches to avoid incarceration and demanded that bishops be able to enter both churches and prisons to speak with people accused of crimes, in order that they might appeal to judges on behalf of the accused and on behalf of those "very many persons [who] are frequently thrust into prison in order that that may be deprived of the freedom to approach a judge" (*Sirmondian* 13, L100 [419 CE]). Late ancient Christians also occasionally promoted punitive incarceration for less serious crimes—a policy motivated by a squeamish desire to avoid bloodshed and executions, as Hillner (2015) points out (140–42; cf. esp. Cassiodorus, *Variae* 7.1.3; Ambrose, *Letter* 50).

BETWEEN LEGAL IDEALS AND CARCERAL PRACTICES

It was necessary to take a close, albeit brief, look at ideologies of incarceration prescribed by and reflected in juristic sources. Nevertheless, there are three fundamental flaws with a focus on legal sources when trying to understand incarceration in antiquity. First, juristic sources' claims about what the law is are often prescriptive. While we are on *somewhat* firmer ground in presuming that imperial pronouncements were carried out, we must conclude that the idealized world of the jurists has no obvious or necessary connection to facts on the ground—especially in the case of Ulpian's distaste for penal incarceration, which he couches in the admission that the practice was in fact widespread. Juristic opinions and even imperial pronouncements do not reflect practices in any one-to-one manner; in fact, we have seen that they are at times explicitly at odds. In other words, any scholar reading jurists and imperial pronouncements for clear insight into "everyday" carceral practices commits a category error.

There is some relationship between legal ideals and the practices that they undergird, but it is neither static nor predictable, and as we have shown, legal sources in particular attest to the impotence of jurists and emperors to reign in the prison's use. As Hubert Dreyfus and Paul Rabinow explain, in instances where we want to understand the diffuse connections between individual, empowered actors and broad systems that they influence, looking to practices is often the most obvious solution.

> This is the problem. How to talk about intentionality without a subject, a strategy without a strategist. The answer must lie in the practices themselves . . . There is a logic to the practices. There is a push towards a strategic objective, but no one is pushing. The objective emerged historically, taking particular forms and encountering specific obstacles, conditions and resistances. Will and calculation were involved. The overall effect, however, escaped the actors' intentions, as well as those of anybody else. As Foucault phrased it, "People know what they do; they frequently know why they do what they do; but what they don't know is what what they do does." (1982, 187)

What is surprising is that even scholars deeply knowledgeable about the range of documentary evidence and its dissimilarity with juristic prescriptions nevertheless let their own analysis of the normative materials speak before and in summation of countervailing evidence. For instance, a scholar no less than Jens-Uwe Krause (1996), who published a marvelous book detailing much of the documentary evidence for incarceration, nevertheless followed Mommsen in his conclusion that "incarceration in the Roman empire essentially comprised custodial and pre-execution detention . . . Nothing changed from this situation during the imperial period" (64). The Mommsenian and Foucauldian frames for the prison prove hard to escape.

Legal historians have recently sought to underline the disconnect between ideals preserved in ancient laws and practices preserved in documentary sources; there may be no larger gap than the one between the modern scholarly understanding of ancient incarceration based on legal sources and the reality of incarceration as seen through archaeological, documentary, and visual material. Still, as many have argued, Roman legal sources are replete with indications that limited-term penal incarceration was acceptable and operative from at least the period of the late republic and continuing through late antiquity (Eisenhut 1972; Lovato 1994, 85–89).

Nevertheless, legal sources are not univocal, and at times even jurists working under successive emperors fundamentally disagree with each other. For instance, Callistratus prescribed that prisoners should be stripped after their conviction, while his contemporary Ulpian advised that even convicted prisoners should be allowed to keep a modest amount of clothing and money so that they can purchase food while in prison (Callistratus, D 48.20.2, L33 [ca. 193–211 CE]; Ulpian, D 48.20.6, L124 [211–22 CE]). For his part, two centuries later, the orator, professor, and advocate for prisoners Libanius complained directly to the emperor that central legislation had little impact on civic practice, at least in his late fourth-century context; he knew it to be typical practice for wardens to allow prisoners their clothes only after extracting a bribe (*Oration* 33.30 [386 CE]). Nevertheless, legal sources also regularly prescribe practices that other evidence flatly contradicts, as we discuss at length in later chapters. Rather than being pictures of the final product, legal materials are selected snapshots from a constantly evolving recipe book.

To be fair, many contemporary scholars of Roman law are interested purely in the idealized world of the law—what the law *says* rather than how it was carried out. This is a fine and legitimate research agenda, though it is not ours. Even so, we have argued here that as a matter of legal theory—what the law says—penal incarceration is regularly attested as a legitimate, "legal" practice. Problems are compounded when social historians who do attend to practices take legal theories as if they reflect realities on the ground. Starting with Mommsen, historians who have written on the topic of Roman prisons constantly reduce the phenomenon to over-zealous and exploitative bureaucrats who abuse and dishonor the "real law." Even *if* limited-term and penal incarceration were illegal under the system of Roman law, we have to deal with the apparent fact, exclaimed by scores of documentary and literary sources, that it was practiced constantly across the ancient Mediterranean. Some of the men behind our legal sources would prefer if incarceration were little used and little discussed. Historians, by and large, have obliged.

The second issue with a purely legal frame for understanding incarceration is this: In the ancient Mediterranean basin, incarceration was not merely—or even primarily—a function of law. As we argue below at length, carceral systems were central to the economic and social life of many ancient cities; even emperors had a hard time reining in their use. In 355 CE, the emperor Constantius complained from Milan that imperial secret agents in Rome had a "wicked custom by which they have been sending any men to prison" (*CTh* 6.29.1, L87 [355 CE]). The emperor's order that such customs cease was apparently either disregarded, rescinded, or otherwise in need of reiteration, because forty years later another law prescribed the same thing on the basis of the same complaint about secret agents (*agentes in rebus*) abusing their power (*CTh* 6.29.8, L214 [395 CE]). Examples could be multiplied of bureaucrats complaining about the widespread use of prisons for unjust and illegal purposes, and of scholars dismissing the issue of penal incarceration as a problem of "a few bad apples"—forgetting, it seems, the rest of that famous bon mot: "A few bad apples spoil the barrel."

Literary sources, too, attest to the impotence of legal prohibitions. In a different oration before the emperor, this one exclusively taking up the plight of Antioch's civic prisoners, Libanius laments the ubiquity of prisoners dying even awaiting trial *despite* legal prohibitions that aim at holding governors liable in such cases (*Oration* 45.14, L52 [386 CE]). Eusebius of Vercelli even accused his Christian theological rivals of abusing the civic prison (*carcer publicus*) of Scythopolis in order to persecute coreligionists, shutting some of them up for long stints and arresting those visiting to bring them food, using the courts to exile others, and threatening the local destitute population with prison in order to keep them in line: "the Ariomaniacs terrify the rich, because they threaten them with proscription, and they terrify the poor, since they have the power to shut them up in prison" (*Letter* 2.5–8, L38 [355–59 CE]; cf. Hillner 2015: 223–224). Sources like these paint abuses as rampant. In what follows we will see a variety of prison spaces and a myriad of uses of those spaces, including custodial, penal, and coercive implementations, alongside a number of uses that are clearly abuses of prisons for personal, political, or religious aims. The point that we want to stress is that even abuses are *uses* of the prison. They are not "just" abuses, a locution that we have heard often, whose aim is to remove evidence from the discussion and whose effect is to marginalize experiences because they are deemed anomalous. If penal incarceration was an abuse, then it was a common one. And if abuse itself is common, as literary sources attest from the entire span of the period under discussion, then attending to abuses of the prison is to attend to the history of the prison itself.

There is one final issue with centering legal sources in our understanding of carceral practices: it is to forget the lives and bodies of people after their cage was secured. In the words of Keramet Reiter (2016), it is to allow the prison to become "the backdrop of a story whose center stage is occupied by bureaucrats and their politics" (7). And so, we turn to the core of our work: foregrounding archaeological and documentary evidence in the hope that we can glimpse the lives of people suffering incarceration and not merely the goals and scruples of their captors. Our aim in engaging these sources is almost never to enlighten *why* someone is in prison. What their captors intended is perhaps useful as a question of intellectual, institutional, or legal history, but it is not our primary aim here. We will ask, instead, "what was the prison to the person inside of it?"

2

Spaces of Incarceration

A Typology of Prisons in Antiquity

Since incarceration is a constellation of practices that take place in physical space, we are well served to pay close attention to such spaces, when possible—understanding the architecture of ancient carceral facilities sheds new light on old debates and raises previously unforeseen questions. As architectural historian Norman Johnston (2000) argues, "A realistic history of prisons—as opposed to a theoretical one that mistakes the rhetoric of the state and of educated elites for administrative practice—must document actual prisons, their goals, their methods, and their successes" (2). Yet, when it comes to ancient incarceration, the architectural aspects of prisons have been too easily dismissed. Take Mommsen's *Roman Criminal Law* (1899), for example: in the 1,078 pages of his tome, a physical prison is discussed only once—the famous Tullian Prison in Rome—and even then only in support of an etymological argument (301–2). Mommsen was surely aware of reports from Pompeii, and he even mentions carceral mining facilities in Sicily (the Lautumiae). Yet the archaeological material was of scant interest to Mommsen, who intended to understand legal ideals more than on-the-ground practices. A century later, Yann Rivière (1999) came to a similar position, though in his account archaeology—or the lack thereof—played a significantly expanded role. "The archaeological argument serves as my point of departure: the cramped conditions of the *carcer* and its internal organization leave no room for the correction of the individual and make the prison a space of abandonment where people die, sometimes strangled by the executioner" (57). In Rivière's estimation, punishment in prison was illegitimate as a matter of law and impractical as a matter of space; the Tullian Prison in Rome is simply too small for it to function as a true prison. Rivière's conception of Rome evokes an early second century stereotype of an imagined mythical past; "you'll consider lucky those generations who, once upon a time under kings and tribunes, saw Rome satisfied with a single prison," as Juvenal put it (*Satires* 3.299–314, L132 [early second century CE]). If the Tullian Prison were the only facility in Rome, the argument might hold; but it was not—not by a long shot. As we detail below, prisons of varying sizes dotted the landscape. At least three existed in Rome during the late republic, including a sprawling facility directly adjacent to the Tullian Prison. Exploring their spatial features will help us to understand their social functions.

Ancient carceral facilities took a variety of forms. From the Ptolemaic period to the Byzantine, and from the Levant to Hispania, we find remarkable architectural and technological diversity, and every prison is singular when considered in sufficient detail. Yet archaeological, documentary, and literary evidence allow us to group carceral spaces broadly into categories, which in turn illuminate family resemblances within categories and differences between prison types. We build on the pioneering work of Pilar Pavón Torrejón, who looked systematically at four sites of ancient incarceration—Athens, Rome, Cosa, and Paestum (2003, 33–39, 89–100, 118). Our list of archaeologically attested prisons began here, and over the past years it has grown to include several dozen sites—some securely identified, and some potential ones. We expect that more still will be added in coming years. With this chapter we add a number of new facilities to the conversation and sketch a typology of ancient carceral spaces in broad strokes.

Our typology distinguishes between two broad categories of carceral facilities in the ancient Mediterranean world: those that were purpose-built, and those that were not. Among purpose-built facilities, we discuss five further subcategories: civic prisons, military prisons, prisons attached to treasuries, prisons inside amphitheaters, and workers' prisons. The category of prisons that are not purpose-built can be further subdivided into two groupings: preexisting spaces that were permanently repurposed as prisons, and ad hoc prisons, or spaces used temporarily. Repurposed prisons in particular reveal general patterns that in turn provide unique insights into the logics of ancient carceral architecture because they allow us to pinpoint changes required to transform a space into a prison. We begin with purpose-built prisons.

PURPOSE-BUILT PRISONS

Civic Prisons

In cities, municipalities, colonies, and settlements, the Greek agora and the Roman forum and their associated public buildings served as a central crossroads organizing commerce, politics, law, and social endeavors. These centers were customarily equipped with civic prisons—that is, public carceral architecture purpose-built to serve local communal needs—with Roman archaeological sources providing the earliest secure material evidence. In his famous handbook of the first century

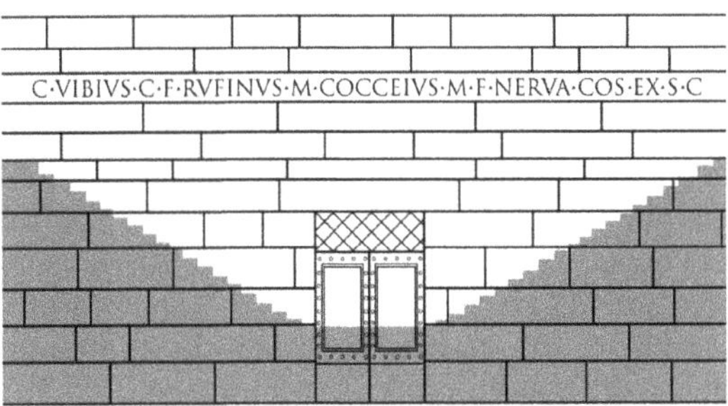

FIGURE 1. The Tullian Prison, before renovation in the early first century CE (A1; Rome, Italy). Inscription CIL 6.1539, 21–22 CE (Cerrone 2022). Drawing by Evan Levine, after Canina 1838, fig. 10.

BCE, the architect Vitruvius spoke at once descriptively about how the forum in Rome had been for centuries and prescriptively about how other forums around the Mediterranean should be built. Every forum should have three public facilities immediately in its vicinity, he writes: a treasury (*aerarium*), a meeting house (*curia*), and a prison (*carcer*), each in proportion to the size of the forum (*On Architecture* 5.2, L152 [ca. 30–20 BCE]).

For Vitruvius the ideal city center should imitate Rome, where the Tullian Prison stood directly next to the new meeting house of the Roman senate (*curia Julia*), on a narrow passageway between the older Roman Forum and the new Forum of Julius Caesar, directly across from the Temple of Saturn, which housed a particularly important treasury (*aerarium*) (Plutarch, *Life of Publicola* 12; Richardson 1980, 51–62) (fig. 1). Ancient historical (and in many ways mythical) accounts claim that Rome's fourth king, Ancus Marcius (r. 640–616 BCE), established "a prison at the center of the city, above the forum, in order to deter increasing lawlessness," and that a lower dungeon was added by the sixth king, Servius Tullius, after whom the entire facility was named (Livy, *From the Founding of the City* 1.33.8, L49 [31–17 BCE]; Varro, *Latin Language* 5.151, L187 [47–45 BCE]). Luckily, the Tullian Prison never needed to be rediscovered—its location and function has been known continuously since antiquity, and to this day it remains visible and accessible on the Roman forum, preserved underneath a sixteenth-century church built atop the prison where later Christians believed that the apostles Peter and Paul had been incarcerated.

We are lucky, too, that the space has been subjected to recent, detailed archaeological investigation under the direction of Patrizia Fortini, who argues that before it was converted into a prison in the fourth century BCE, the lower chamber was used for worship for underworld deities (Russo 2022). At least three significant phases of the prison are visible in the archaeological record, during all of which the facility was fully underground. In the fourth century BCE, a circular room serving a sacred well appears to have been covered over, transformed into a prison facility called the Tullianum that was built into defensive walls around Rome's Capitoline

Hill. In the third century BCE, the Tullianum was shortened, and another room added above it known as the Carcer (Susanna 2022a). Major renovations of the facility occurred in the mid-second century BCE and again in the early first century CE, including newly placed votive deposits to underworld deities, apparently intended to "keep intact its binding with the sphere of the sacred" (Susanna 2022b, 88). In its initial phase, the Tullianum stood on a major road through the nascent city, and in later phases the upper room of the Carcer-Tullianum opened toward the senate chambers in one direction and offered access to the lower chamber through a small manhole in the floor. The prison, as renovated in the early imperial period, is still visible today: it is a small, dark, wet, cold underground complex, with direct access to the forum but little light or air movement, a structure immediately recognizable even from historical descriptions like that of the Roman historian Sallust. "In the prison, when you have gone up a little way toward the left, there is a place called the Tullianum, about twelve feet below the surface of the ground. It is enclosed on all sides by walls, and overhead is a vaulted ceiling formed by stone arches; but neglect, darkness, and stench give it a hideous and terrifying appearance" (Sallust, *Catiline's War* 55, L48 [44–40 BCE]). The Carcer-Tullianum was hardly Rome's only prison; as we detail below, many other facilities dotted the cityscape that were used as prisons during the Republican period, including the much larger Lautumiae directly adjacent to the Tullian Prison, the Temple of Saturn, and the municipal archives (somewhat ironically) called the House of Freedom (*atrium libertatis*) (Pavón Torrejón 2003b, 109–12). Beginning in the late first century BCE under the reign of Augustus, a number of new carceral facilities under the command of prefects and the military were strewn across the city (Pavón Torrejón 2003a, 112–13; Zamora Manzano 2015, 40–50).

Outside the city of Rome, the earliest identifiable Roman civic prison imitates the form of the Tullian Prison. In the mid-third century BCE, the Roman Republic established a military veteran's colony at Cosa north of Rome, on the Etruscan coast. Among the first public buildings was a squat, stout structure just off the corner of the forum, a few steps from the meeting house (*curia*), with walls twice as thick as those of other public buildings constructed at the same time. The structure looks remarkably like a version of the Tullian Prison adapted to the local topography, and it is now widely accepted to have been the civic prison of Cosa (A20). Not only is this prison the earliest identifiable civic prison outside of Rome, it was also among the earliest to be identified by scholars: excavators in the 1950s initially considered the space to be a treasury, a cistern, or a cellar, and they later arrived at its carceral function, when in 1993 they wrote that "oddly enough, Cosa's Carcer, if that is what it was, seems to be the only one so far identified outside of Rome" (Brown et al. 1993, 41; cf. Brown 1951, 81). Of course, Albert Ballu had already identified the civic prison of Cuicul (Djemila, Algeria) seven decades earlier, but Cosa's facility has received more scholarly attention and the identification has been widely accepted as convincing (even by Rivière himself) such that

FIGURE 2. Civic prison of Cosa (A20; Ansedonia, Italy). Reconstruction by Niels Bargfeldt.

today the identification is made on public signage at the archaeological site (Pavón Torrejón 2003b, 118–19; Rivière 2004a, 56).

Cosa's civic prison stands just off the northeast corner of the forum, and comprises a large room above ground that opens to a public street (fig. 2). Two chambers communicate with the entry: an inner chamber at street level and secured through an internal door, and a second room underground, accessible only through a small manhole that was secured with a heavy lid (0.78 long x 0.70 wide), which would have been clamped down to prevent it from being dislodged from below. The lower chamber is partly cut into the bedrock and partly built in stone, and it was not plastered in a way that might suggest its design or use as a cistern. The double-thickness of the walls throughout suggest that security was a design priority, and the presence of two different chambers, one upper and one lower, suggests perhaps that separating people into different classes was an ideological aim with an architectural expression. We return to this theme below (p. 85–87).

A similar structure appears at the Roman colony of Ulpia Traiana Sarmizegetusa (Sarmizegetusa, Romania), established in the early second century CE. In figure 3 the *curia* stands imposing on the south edge of the forum, and two tribunals (*tribunalia*) flank it to the east and west—platforms from which two local administrators (*duoviri*) heard petitions and handed down decisions. Underneath the eastern tribunal excavators found a now-familiar structure: two underground rooms, with an antechamber and secure inner chamber. Archaeologists at the site offered a firm identification for the chambers underneath the western tribunal—"it is certain that underneath the eastern tribunal is the prison, based on the underground Roman Tullianum, and no area in Sarmizegetusa is more suited to this function" (Étienne et al. 1990, 279; fig. 3). In 1990, it was the fourth such Roman civic prison plausibly identified, and one that shows clear similarities with Cuicul, Cosa, and Rome. The prison at Sarmizegetusa was a later addition to the tribunal, constructed by doubling the width of the walls, blocking up an old, insecure door, and installing a new, thicker door secured by two bolts a meter in length that prevented it from being opened by someone locked inside. In the words of the site's most recent excavators, the architectural changes implemented "signify that a number of precautions were taken against a danger that was not found on the outside, but rather on the inside" of the prison (Étienne et al. 2002, 141).

Intriguingly, another space at Sarmizegetusa shares features with a number of prisons discussed here; it is possible that a second, significantly larger civic prison stood just steps away underneath the civic *curia* dedicated to the goddess Concord. These two, parallel chambers are four meters deep, with one access point—through a door communicating directly with the forum, and high, narrow windows that open directly to the public street behind the forum. Étienne and others (1990) identify this space as the civic treasury of Sarmizegetusa (285). We propose here that its features intriguingly evoke other prisons explored below, including direct forum access, windows opening to the public, separate cells that do not communicate with one another, and a cultic space appearing above a carceral facility, each of which are widely attested. It is possible that these two parallel cells likewise served a carceral function. Cities with multiple carceral facilities are well-attested, too: documentary evidence explored below demonstrates that even a midsize city like Oxyrhynchus had at least three active prisons during the Roman period, and by the time it served as an occasional imperial capital in the late fourth century, Antioch had at least two large public prisons, with prisoners regularly transferring back and forth between the facilities (Matter 2004, 64).

Placing civic prisons directly adjacent to the city's economic, social, and political center is not a uniquely Roman architectural choice—these locations at the center of the city have antecedents, and the trend endured well into the early modern period. Plato and Demosthenes, for example, both remark on the placement of the state prison of classical Athens in the agora (Plato, *Laws* 907d–910d, L18 [360–347 BCE]; Demosthenes, *Against Timocrates* 24.146, 151, L27 [353 BCE]; Athens Civic Prison A23; Vanderpool 1980; Hunter 1997). Likewise, during the same period when the prison at Cosa was in use, the Achaean general Philopoemen was imprisoned in the municipal prison of Messene, in the Greek Peloponnese (Messene Civic Prison, A16). In his account of the general's life, Plutarch described the civic prison of Messene, to which the locals had given a darkly ironic nickname: they called their prison "the Treasury." Plutarch narrates the course of Philopoemen's incarceration and ultimately his death within the dreadful space, which admitted neither air nor light and had no door, and "it is shut by a stone that is dragged over" (*Life of Philopoemen* 19–20, L148 [early second century CE]).

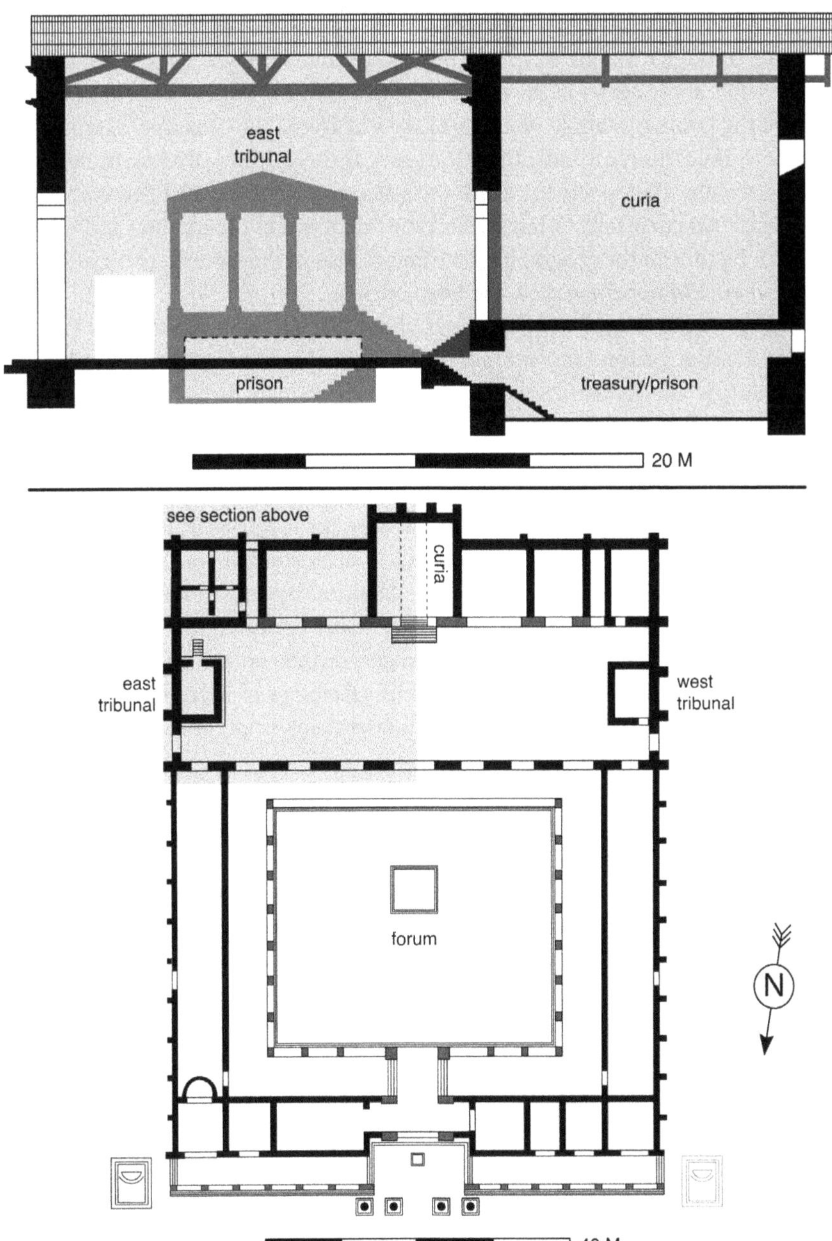

FIGURE 3. Reconstructed elevation of curia and east tribunal in the old forum at Ulpia Traiana Sarmizegetusa (A27; Sarmizegetusa, Romania). Plan and reconstruction by Evan Levine, based on Étienne et al. 2002, 99, 144.

Astonishingly, the space that Plutarch describes remains intact to this day. It comprises two underground chambers directly adjacent to the city's agora, accessible only through a manhole covered by a stone lid that weighs 1,500 kilograms. A hole is visible at the center of the stone, used to attach a hook and a hoisting device to move the cover and allow entrance to, or exit from "the Treasury." Archaeologist Petros Themelis (2010) identified the space as the treasury of Messene, arguing that shortly after Philopoemen's death the space was intentionally filled with earth and at least two curse tablets, having become "an object of superstition and magic" (122–24). By time of the geographer Pausanias's visit in the second century CE, the prison where Philopoemen died had been buried.

There are a number of striking things about this space: its description by Plutarch as the civic prison (*desmōtērion*) of Messene that locals had taken to calling "The Treasury" (*ton kaloumenon Thēsauron*), its placement directly on the agora—like a Roman forum, the economic, political, and social center of the city—and its material aspects as a small, underground space accessible only through a hole, covered by a stone that secured prisoners inside, and kept the public out. While Themelis identifies the site as Messene's treasury, the language of Plutarch implies that the site was not a treasury briefly used to imprison but was in fact the civic prison that was nicknamed the "Treasury." All these aspects overlap with what we have seen both in Rome and Cosa during the same period in the second century BCE. These correspondences suggest that such practices are not peculiarly Roman and that Romans took part in practices and ideologies of incarceration attested across the ancient Mediterranean. We will encounter ample further evidence of this point across the pages that follow.

The civic prison of the Roman city of Cuicul shares many similarities with the three prisons already discussed, and it presents a few interesting differences (Cuicul Prison, A5; Ballu 1921, 1926; Leschi 1953). The city's municipal forum was constructed as part of its founding, around 97 CE, while a number of adjacent buildings were constructed somewhat later. A man named Gaius Julius Crescens Didius Crescentianus sponsored the city's courthouse, dedicating a structure in 169 CE with judicial chambers above and a civic prison below (*ILAlg* 2.7793–94; Cagnat 1920). The prison comprises two large underground rooms, with gates which restrict movement between them. The entire complex has a single entrance, opening to an antechamber (a) that itself has gates on either side—one gate opens to the first chamber of the prison, and the other opens directly to the *cardo*, one of two main roads through the heart of the city (fig. 4).

Not only does this space directly adjoin the forum, as we might expect given Vitruvius's famous pronouncement, but the prison lies directly underneath the civic basilica. A rear stairwell (d) provided easy access between the courtroom above and the prison below, on the shortest possible route. Inside, two rooms held prisoners, each built in large blocks of local limestone with pillars at the center holding a vaulted concrete ceiling. Stone benches line two sides of the first room (b);

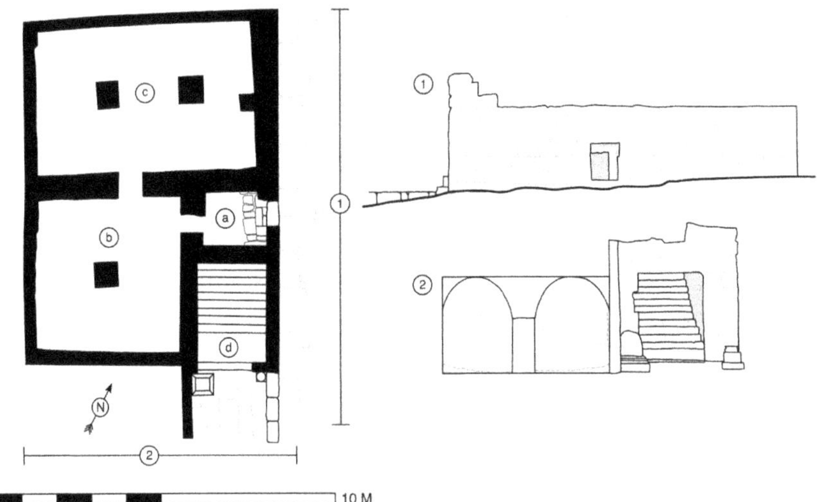

FIGURE 4. Cuicul civic prison complex, underneath the civic basilica (A5; Djemila, Algeria). Plan by Gina Tibbott and Evan Levine. A 3D model of the archaeological remains and a reconstruction of the space are available in the Ancient Mediterranean Incarceration Database.

if the doors were barred rather than solid, then a small amount of natural light would have passed through the entrance and antechamber to reach prisoners. An internal door controlled access between chambers—the innermost chamber (c) is the larger of the two, and received no natural light whatsoever.

The architect leading excavations at Cuicul was among the few scholars working in the wake of Mommsen who rejected the trend by which prisons were disappearing from the archaeological record. In 1926, Albert Ballu (1926) concluded definitively that the subterranean structure underneath the civic basilica "was none other than the prison necessary for any establishment of justice" (65). Perhaps Ballu was uniquely primed to see the connection between courts and prisons; some thirty years earlier he had collaborated with another architect to design the sprawling Palace of Justice in Bucharest, complete with magnificent courtrooms in French Renaissance style and, at its back, a prison.

Since the first excavation report in 1827, a two-room structure in Pompeii (18 square meters and 25 square meters), set slightly below ground level and next to the public latrines, has been identified as either the civic prison, or the city treasury. The rooms communicate with the forum: the first opened directly up to the forum through a small iron-barred door, while a small skylight allowed some minimal amount of light to enter and air to exchange from outside (Mau 1899, 91). Like at Cuicul, the inner chamber was yet more bleak: an internal door controlled movement between rooms, and the chamber farthest from the entrance was likely bathed in continual darkness. As we noted in the introduction, the first excavator recalled finding an underground facility whose narrow doors were fitted with iron bars and contained human remains, apparently locked inside during the eruption (Bonucci 1827, 151). In 1884, Johannes Overbeck repeated the conclusion and in 1900, Antonio Sogliano dismissed suggestions that the site could possibly have served as a treasury because the conclusion was based on the faulty assumption that the municipal offices above had anything to do with the vaulted chambers below; there is no stair or passage connecting them, and no reason to think their functions related (Overbeck and Mau 1884, 73; Sogliano 1900, 236–38; Rivière 2004a, 591). Scholars have returned to the question repeatedly in the intervening years, with recent opinion trending toward the identification of the rooms as the prison of Pompeii rather than a treasury (Pavón Torrejón 2003b, 146). Without clarifying inscriptions or literary accounts it is difficult to arrive at a firm conclusion; given the state of the evidence along with the parallels discussed here, it is probable that the space served as one of Pompeii's civic prisons. In fact, a number of other strong candidates appear in the archaeological record at Pompeii, including barrel-vaulted chambers directly under the tribunal in the civic basilica, accessible only through a set of stairs that lead directly to the tribunal platform; this was identified tentatively as a civic prison already in 1877 (Nissen 1877, 311–12). Likewise, a set of vaulted chambers underneath the Capitoline Temple on the forum are suited to a carceral function; similarly to the structure at Sufetula discussed below (p. 76–80), they stand directly underneath a tribunal intended for legal proceedings and are accessible by a single gated entrance on the podium's eastern face (Ulrich 1994, 236–38).

One further space bears mentioning here, not because it is extraordinary but because it is ordinary. A pair of small cells underneath a large building in Tiberias, on the Sea of Galilee in Syria Palaestina, has recently been identified as the late Roman civic prison underneath an administrative palace (*praetorium*) boasting some thirty above-ground rooms and intended to host an imperial governor's assize court. The identification coheres with other data presented here, and the parallels support the excavator's suspicion that the facility was built to serve as the civic prison of Tiberias. The compound was constructed shortly after 363 CE and "in the northernmost wing are the unique remains of two small underground cells, each with a plaster floor and a bench. Low, narrow slot-like windows open to the outside (two windows in the eastern cell, one in the western), excluding the possibility that these were storage spaces" (Patrich et al. 2022, 82).

The two underground rooms are two by three meters and appear directly underneath the place of judicial proceedings in Tiberias, with walls 1.23 meters thick—just wide enough for outstretched hands from either side to touch in the middle—and boasting two small windows allowing direct access to the public street outside of the structure. As one of the excavators points out, "The slits in the walls allow small items to be transferred to the cells by those outside the building as well as to and from them, but do not allow exit from them. The entrance to the cells is possible only from above, from inside the [*praetorium*]" (Meir 2012,

99). Similar to the civic prisons at Rome and at Cosa, a small manhole in the upper floor would have provided the only access point to the cells, and prisoners were left to wait for their trial, or perhaps serve their sentence of incarceration, on small benches built in stone and still intact on the site, reminiscent of the benches at Cuicul.

Doubtless, more prisons will be unearthed in the archaeological record—perhaps even in cities already treated here. Underground, vaulted chambers appear directly underneath the tribunal platform in both the basilica of Pompeii and the Curia of Cosa—is it possible that these are further carceral spaces, and not treasuries (*aeraria*) or record halls (*tabularia*), as is most commonly assumed? (David 1983, 223–25). Time, we hope, will tell.

We have argued that it is ill advised to read literary accounts of what ancient societies should look like as if they were descriptions of how ancient cities functioned. And yet, in the civic prisons of Cosa and Cuicul, we see that Vitruvius's prescription was also broadly descriptive of practices on the ground. Relying on Libanius's orations, Alberto De Simoni (2022) has recently proposed a carceral topography of fourth-century Antioch "with certain precision," arguing that the forum featured "on one side, the *bouleuterion* [political center of Antioch], the general's quarters, and a prison, and on the other side the *dikasterion* [courthouse]" (199). Byzantine Egypt presents another parallel: based on papyrological sources in Greek and Coptic, Sofía Torallas Tovar concluded that "there were public prisons in every city and even in towns. They were supported by a special tax, called *desmofulakia*, which had existed since the Ptolemaic period" (Torallas Tovar 1999, 48). The identification of the civic prison of Messene in early second-century BCE Achaia further suggests that Vitruvius's text reflects a wider Mediterranean cultural practice, in which purpose-built public prisons appeared at the center of the city, as well as underground. In other words, we need not understand the Tullian Prison as the architectural progenitor of civic prisons throughout the Roman empire, much less throughout the Mediterranean. In this and in many other aspects of ancient carceral practice, Romans were inheritors of a long-standing tradition.

Military Prisons

Civic prisons are one type of purpose-built carceral space among many. In the Roman period, an often blurry line separated what we might today consider "purely military" duties from general policing and civil service functions undertaken by legionaries. Nevertheless, we can distinguish between military and civic prisons: Roman military bases were outfitted with at least one proprietary carceral facility (*carcer castrensis*), employed by the legion for a number of functions, but primarily as part of local policing operations. In some cases, residences (particularly of magistrates) or other domestic spaces were also used for military incarceration (Hillner 2015, 129–30).

Roman soldiers performed a wide variety of duties, from hydraulic engineering and road construction to arresting people for petty theft (P. Oslo 2.21, D89 [71 CE]) and roughing up the local population (P. Wisc. 2.48, D97 [154–59 CE]; Bowman 1994, 42–49). They were sometimes detailed to oversee civic prisons in their jurisdiction, as Pliny the Younger's letters suggest, and literary sources regularly attest to dedicated carceral spaces and prison staff on military bases themselves (*Letters* 10.19–20, L24 [109–10 CE]). Soldiers, of course, often found themselves as prisoners, both in civic and military contexts (Diodorus Siculus, *Library of History* 1.79.1–2, L65 [mid-first century BCE], *D* 48.19.38.11, L123 [early third century CE]). Nevertheless, it should be emphasized that military prisons were not used solely to detain members of the military or even war captives—the prisons are "military" insofar as they are placed on army bases and staffed by soldiers, even while they often held civilian prisoners. For instance, the civilian Perpetua and her companions were depicted moving between a number of different types of carceral facility in the early third century CE: they were first held under house arrest, then transferred to a civic prison, and only thereafter transferred to a military prison before finally being placed in an amphitheater prison, where they awaited death (*Martyrdom of Perpetua and Felicity*, L15 [ca. third or fourth century CE]). Movement between carceral facilities reflected neither their alleged crime nor their identity but rather the identity of their incarcerators and the stage of their prosecution and sentencing process. One trend visible throughout the corpus of literary and documentary evidence is that in the ancient world, different prisons did not typically pertain to different types of prisoners but to different classes of imprisoner; even military prisons were used for public purposes, both in the city of Rome and on the imperial frontier (Pavón Torrejón 2003a).

We should expect that at least in the Roman period, nearly every military base had some carceral facility, although to date only one such dedicated military prison has been securely identified: at Lambaesis, in modern-day Tazoult, Algeria (fig. 5).

The prison at Lambaesis sits in the legionary *principia*—the central administrative complex where speeches and trainings were held, associations of soldiers met, and the legion's standards were kept safe alongside their pay. In the upper diagram of figure 5, the Temple of the Standards (*aedes signorum*, 1) appears at the center, a religious space where flags and symbols of the legion are kept, and meeting rooms flank the temple to the east (2, 3) and west (II, III). While the fifth-century CE military historian Vegetius suggests that the area underneath the Temple of the Standards was typically used as a treasury, at Lambaesis we find five parallel cells, each secured with a gate, opening to a common antechamber (*Epitome of Military Science* 2.20). The antechamber was itself connected, through another locking door, to the portico in front of the temple's entrance. Each cell contains a significant amount of graffiti; some are single letters or fragments of words, but most are small tables for games or for keeping track of days and weeks, scratched into the wall by people with ample time, poor light, and rudimentary tools. Each cell has a

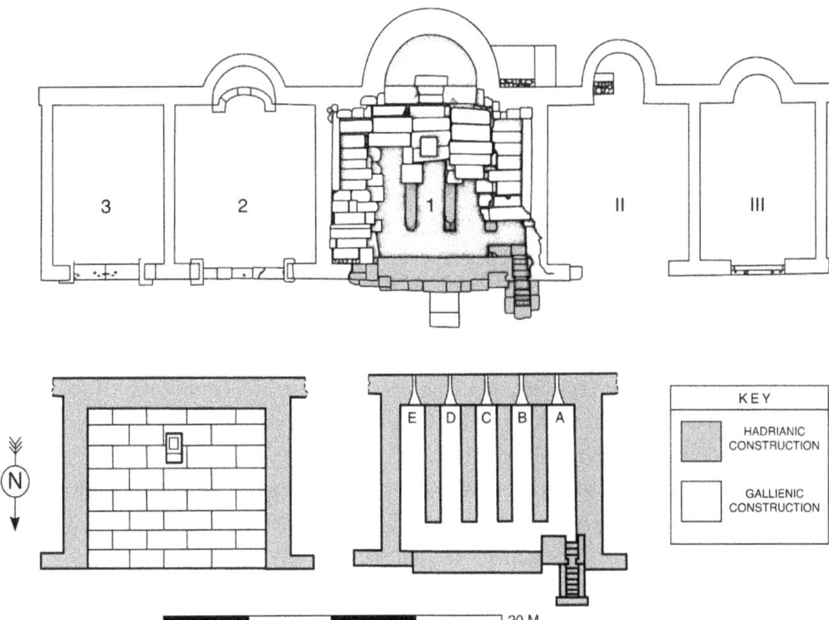

FIGURE 5. Military prison at Lambaesis, current status above, and initial Hadrianic phase below (A7; Tazoult, Algeria; Letteney and Larsen 2019). Drawings by Gina Tibbott and Evan Levine, after Besnier 1899, 230.

window, opening high above the floor of the prison onto the public street through the center of the military camp. This architecture, commended in a different context by the agricultural writer Columella for underground *ergastula* (slave prisons) for its healthsome effects, also allowed people outside to pass small objects like food, water, lamps, and clothing from the (semi)public street to the people incarcerated below (*On Agriculture* 1.6.3, L47 [mid-first century CE]). It is clear that the windows were used this way, as well: they are visibly worn down from many years of arms and objects passing through to those incarcerated within (Letteney and Larsen 2019, 76–77). Typologically similar spaces were recently discovered in the Roman military base at Vindobona (Vienna, Austria), which the excavators propose as a prison for use by legions stationed there, and Apulum (Alba Iulia, Romania), where an underground space with nearly identical windows has recently been identified on analogy with Lambaesis and aided by additional epigraphic evidence (Mosser 2024; Cupcea 2024).

While few military prisons have been identified archaeologically, documentary and literary sources make clear that during the Ptolemaic and Roman period, a primary function of military outposts was to coordinate police activity and facilitate incarceration for a wide variety of offenses and offenders, restraining both soldiers and civilians alike (Bauschatz 2013, 99–159; Fuhrmann 2012, 203–38).

In this respect, the ancient Mediterranean is not unique. In the contemporary world, the military industrial complex and the prison industrial complex are co-constituting, and both are implicated with the broader economy, as Ruth Wilson Gilmore taught us in *Golden Gulag* (2007). This interplay between the military, civic, and economic is a critical facet of our typology—the prison was bound up in all three. We see the connection between economic production and carcerality already in the Ptolemaic period, to which we now turn.

Treasury Prisons

In Ptolemaic Egypt, civic prisons were often attached to local municipal treasuries, and overseen by the office of the tax collector (*praktor*) or treasurer. In documentary papyri, people are regularly held in a treasury prison (*praktoreion*) for both public and private debts, often until they could secure bail money, a guarantor for their debt, or full payment (Muhs 2018).

Still, the treasury prison was not the only carceral facility available in the Ptolemaic period, as we see in a complaint from February of 221 BCE, in which a woman traveling in Oxyrhynchus complained directly to the king that she had been attacked by another woman in the bath house, robbed, and thrown in a local jail (*fulakē*) under the jurisdiction of the village leader (*kōmarchēs*), only to be released four days later on bail paid in the form of her own clothing (P. Enteux. 83, D71). A note appended to her complaint, apparently from the royal administration, commands the local administrator (*epistatēs*) to reconcile the women and, if he is unable, to send their case for adjudication before the local court for native appellants (*laokritēs*).

In other words, a variety of carceral facilities formed the infrastructure of society in Ptolemaic Egypt, and a notice from 228 CE about a prisoner who died in custody in the *praktoreion* of Oxyrhynchus shows that prisons attached to treasuries continued to be used for centuries after the Roman conquest, functioning as a type of civic prison (P. Oxy. 43.3104, D15). Nevertheless, an edict from 68 CE, discussed in a different context above, explicitly distinguishes the tax collector's prison (*praktoreion*) from civic prisons (*fulakas*), and urges that civic prisoners ought not to be held in prisons intended for debtors. To this day, the inscription appears on the north jamb of the outer gateway of the temple of Hibis in Kharga, Egypt, reading: "In accordance with the will of the divine Augustus, I command that no one under cover of the public treasury shall have debts transferred to himself which he did not contract originally, nor shall he in any way hold any free man in any prison whatsoever unless he is a criminal, nor shall anyone except a debtor of the public treasury be confined in a tax collector's prison [*praktoreion*]" (OGIS 669, D185 [68 CE]; second copy Temple of Hibis 2.4, D177). The edict assumes that imprisoning public debtors inside a treasury prison was both common and proper procedure in Roman Egypt—so much so that the term for public treasury, *dēmosios*, became another term for prison, such as we find in the Yakto Mosaic (V5) from late Roman Antioch, discussed below (Pavón Torrejón 2003b, 30–31; p. 141). Documentary sources like this suggest that in both the Ptolemaic and Roman period, Egyptian treasury prisons were conceptually distinct from civic prisons, and that both remained in use.

To date, no plausible identification of such a facility's archaeological remains has been made, and it is not currently clear how such a structure would differ architecturally from other known civic or military prisons. The remaining two types of purpose-built prisons, however, have more distinctive features.

Amphitheater Prisons

Ancient Mediterranean civic prisoners were exemplary, and confinement at the center of cities rendered their deviance visible. Amphitheater prisons present an even more spectacular form of carcerality, in which gladiators and prisoners condemned to die in the ring were confined within the space of their pending execution, and paraded out to live their final moments before a crowd of onlookers. In the middle of the second century the jurist Gaius remarked on long-term detention of condemned criminals, stipulating that they lose both their citizenship and their freedom, a fate that "anticipates their death, sometimes by a long period, as happens in the persons of those who are condemned to the beasts"—adding that it is customary that they be kept secure and alive for a significant period so that they could be interrogated under torture against others, and, as Kathleen Coleman points out, so that gladiators and beasts could be sourced and arrangements made for a properly spectacular public execution (D 48.19.29, L169 [mid-second century CE]; Coleman 1990, 57).

Surviving archaeological evidence suggests that some amphitheaters had dedicated carceral spaces for each actor in this drama: prisons for condemned people, prisons for gladiators, and even cages for animals who battled prisoners (which in Latin are also referred to as *carceres*). Some spaces, like a subterranean cross-vaulted chamber in the Carthage amphitheater identified by David Bomgardner (1989) as a *spoliarium* (used to strip bodies of the deceased), in fact appear more consistent with an identification as one of that facility's prisons (100). Roman amphitheaters are carceral spaces in the fullest sense, designed to hold people condemned to spectacular death for a significant length of time. The amphitheater at Carales (Cagliari, Italy) presents the clearest example of these three different spaces, all visible in one remarkably well preserved site—though only two of these types of *carceres* were purpose-built, and the third will be discussed further in a subsequent section (p. 68–71).

Figure 6 presents a schematic drawing of the site. The amphitheater center appears at the right, with its bedrock-cut features outlined. The square room on the right (A) is the gladiator prison (fig. 7). This space is cut directly into the bedrock,

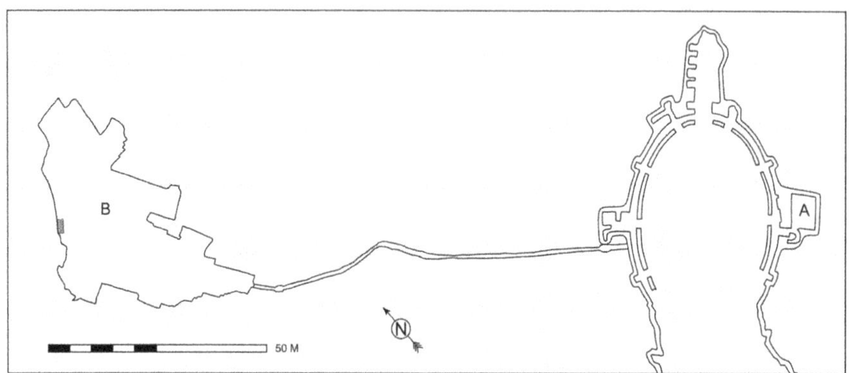

FIGURE 6. Amphitheater of Carales with Gladiator Prison (label A, A33) and Prison for the Condemned (label B, A24) (Cagliari, Italy). Drawing by Gina Tibbott.

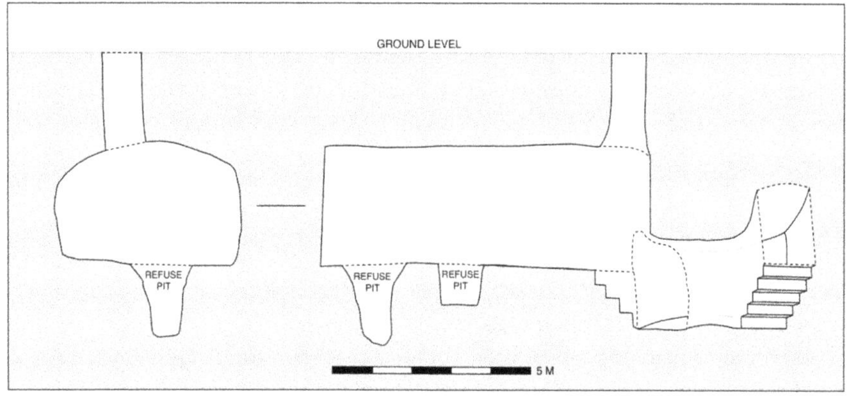

FIGURE 7. Gladiator Prison within the Carales amphitheater (A33). Drawing by Gina Tibbott.

including a vaulted ceiling and two pits in the floor serviced by small canals, apparently intended as toilets for the people locked inside (Pala 1994, 136). A skylight to the south rises some five meters from the floor of the prison to the surface, far above, allowing fresh air and light into the space without sacrificing security. Such features indicate a (rudimentary) concern for the health of the imprisoned gladiators. Eleven anchor points are cut into the walls approximately one meter above the floor with a regular distance between them of 0.7 meters, interspersed with niches for oil lamps, eight in all, cut into walls that were originally plastered and painted (Dadea 2006, 52–53; Spano 1868, 28). All the anchors show signs of wear from chains or ropes being passed through them to secure prisoners to the walls, and are identical to those in the Prison for the Condemned discussed below (fig. 6 label B, fig. 10 below). A gated door secured the space, opening to a small shrine dedicated to the god Nemesis and two stairwells: one leading into the arena and another to the seating area, through a second locking gate (Dadea 2006, 53–57).

Workers' Prisons

The final type of purpose-built carceral facility for which we have clear evidence is the workers' prison, designed to secure condemned prisoners, often alongside enslaved workers, in locations where their labor could be exploited. Some literary sources speak to smaller quarters in elite houses for enslaved workers, along with incarcerated individuals being sent to work in bakeries within the city of Rome, which Hillner (2015) discussed as places of confinement along with brothels, factories, and mills (201–10). Here we will focus on the workers' prison at the mines of Simitthus (Chemtou, Tunisia) as an example of an expansive carceral facility with architectural features apparently intended to keep incarcerated and enslaved workers securely within, separated into groups, and, with the help of a wall separating the quarries from the town, perhaps also apart from the local population (Röder 1993, 21).

Simitthus was the single source for *giallo antico*: a fine yellow marble prized throughout the Mediterranean world. During the Roman period, it was quarried under imperial monopoly and overseen by the army, which had a significant permanent outpost on the site. Both literary and documentary sources suggest that mines were typically staffed by a mix of local overseers and centrally dispatched specialists, but that manual labor was provided by incarcerated and enslaved workers who were housed in a purpose-built carceral facility (Hirt 2010, 332–36). Archaeologist Friedrich Rakob identified one such facility at Simitthus, arguing that it was built sometime after 154 CE, and in its first two phases it was designed and used to hold prisoners and enslaved workers some 250 meters northwest of the mine where they labored. At 80 meters by 37 meters, the workers' prison was more than twice the size of any other courtyard or building in the camp, and it stood under direct military supervision in three distinct zones sealed off from one another. Not only were the prison's external walls significantly wider and stronger than the internal walls separating the six cells, but the outer walls significantly "exceeded their static function," according to Rakob (1994)—that is, they were built to withstand internal horizontal forces related to escape (66).

Latrines were added to the north end of each cell in a second phase that was constructed around 190 CE, complementing a small bathing facility already inside the secure area to the east (fig. 8; Rakob 1994, 82; Mackensen 2000, 492–23). En suite lavatories were a rarity in carceral facilities, and as we discuss below, prisoners were commonly forced to relieve themselves in their cells and, at times, to sit in the filth (p. 106). Nevertheless, the Gladiator Prison at Cagliari included two pits and a trough for prisoners to relieve themselves, and a facility underneath the Julian Basilica at Corinth, which has been identified as either the civic prison or municipal treasury, also included a small bathroom facility in the gated

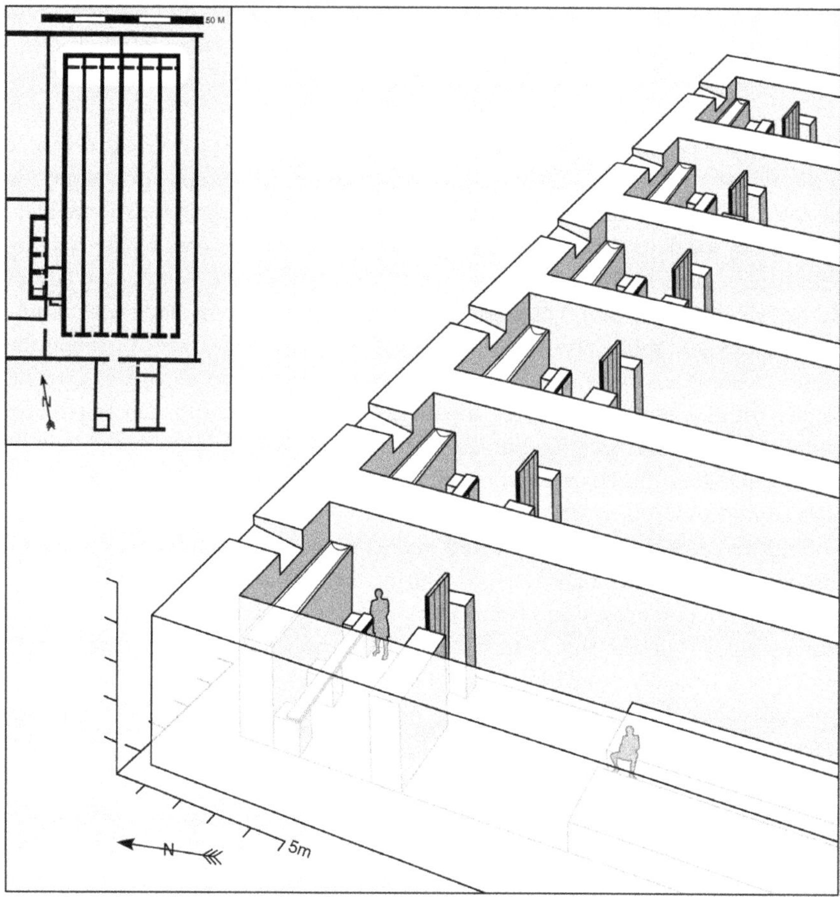

FIGURE 8. Second phase of the incarcerated and enslaved workers' quarters at Simitthus, showing separate cells with benches along the length, latrines at the north end of each cell, and a small bath facility to the east, inside the complex (A13; Chemtou, Tunisia). Illustration by Gina Tibbott after Rakob 1994, 93, fig. 94, and 72, fig. 67.

antechamber (Gladiator Prison, A33; Corinth Basilica, A14; Scotton 2020, 218; Larsen 2024, 370–71). At Simitthus, a lead pressure line supplied water through the wall of each latrine, allowing the facilities to be used both as a toilet and bath. Rather than constructing a single sewer for the toilet facility in each cell (which would have been a more straightforward and efficient solution), engineers at Simitthus designed and built six separate sewers—one for each toilet—which pass through two minuscule apertures before connecting with the common sewer to the north, increasing expense and compromising functionality but adding to the main aim of the facility: both security and separation between prisoners held in each cell. Some sixteen hundred years later, the architect of Eastern State Penitentiary in Philadelphia employed an identical tactic with the explicit aim of preventing prisoner communication through empty pipes (Johnston 2000, 71). The inclusion of a latrine within the facility at Simitthus points further toward a carceral function for the space, allowing for people to be held in moderately sanitary conditions for long periods of time. In the words of Rakob (1994), the peculiar techniques of construction and their stark difference from other toilets in the facility are "indications of the different quality of their users"—they are prison toilets, designed with security in mind rather than efficiency (101).

Each of the six cells each had a strong, locking door and communicated only with an outer corridor which was itself accessed through two gated entrances. Today the doorframe is visibly worn by repeated use over the hundred or so active years of the facility (Rakob 1994, 70). A guard tower oversaw the outer corridor, controlling access to the facility. As Rakob notes, the facility's watchtowers do not look out toward the valley but inward—these vantage points were intended to oversee people locked inside (53). Each cell measures nearly eighty meters in length and six meters in width, with benches installed along both sides. In its earliest phase, a wall separated the entrance to the three eastern cells from the entrance to the three western cells, but this subdivision was removed when latrines were installed in each cell, perhaps indicating that the facility was initially subdivided by sex, with common latrines serving the three eastern and three western cells.

Rakob estimated that each cell could house approximately 180 people, meaning that the facility had the capacity to hold over one thousand people in segregated, secure compartments. Many ancient civic prisons would have had a maximum capacity of roughly twenty-five to seventy-five people; given its size, separate cells, communal bathing facilities, and entrance guarded by towers, workers' prisons like Simitthus appear to be a facility of a different type—a type that resonates most clearly with the large, industrialized prisons in the modern US criminal justice system. For reference, Eastern State Penitentiary in Philadelphia was initially designed to incarcerate 250 prisoners, though in subsequent decades it would far exceed its design capacity (Rubin 2021, 23). Around 230 CE the prison camp at Simitthus was converted into workshops, and it remains the only such workers' prison identified in the archaeological record to date, though as Alfred Michael Hirt (2010) points out, Roman imperial mining facilities in Egypt's eastern desert include watchtowers that may have been used to guard convict labor (15, 225). Hirt also notes that it is unclear *who* was condemned to spaces like these—literary sources widely attest the use of prisoner labor in imperial mines and legal materials suggest that sentences were often intended to be limited term—but they do not appear in the epigraphic record (185).

As Wendy Warren remarks in this book's afterword, "the *mass* of our own era's 'mass incarceration' is certainly historically distinct"—the first well-attested instance of widespread carceral control at a scale similar to that in the contemporary United States only appeared in Germany in the fifteenth century (p. 198;

Weinreich 2023). Additionally, the term "mass incarceration" speaks not only to scale but to the insidious interimplication of state profit, labor, economics, and carcerality typified by the modern "prison industrial complex" (McLennan 2018, 151). The prisons of the ancient world were undoubtedly different from their modern counterparts. Nevertheless, the scale of the workers' prison at Simitthus, and its relationship with the market economy, suggests pausing to rethink claims that some of the core features of mass incarceration are wholly unprecedented.

Writing in the second century CE, the physician Galen recorded his impression of a visit to a mining camp in Cyprus that sounds strikingly similar to Simitthus—noting specifically that the space had both mine shafts where prisoners labored and a warehouse where they slept nearby (*Simple Remedies* 9.3.11–34, L160 [late second century CE]; Mattern 2013, 99–103). Such evidence raises another important question, sticky, but not intractable: what spaces count as a prison? No simple answer will be universally satisfying, but in this case documentary evidence offers some insight. A quarry overseer's report from the mid-third century BCE records that ten men worked in the mines over a sixty-eight-day period while during that same period, another 130 prisoners sat idle, waiting for their turn to work (PSI 4.423, D58; p. 126). At this Ptolemaic mine, the scenario in which an idle prisoner was activated as a forced laborer appears to have been rather circumscribed: either one of the ten current workers had died, or if limited-term sentences in the mines existed in the Ptolemaic period as they did during the Roman period, perhaps when the worker's sentence had been served. It is possible that some of the men waiting to work were sent there as slaves while others were transferred to the miner's prison as convicts, but the papyrus labels them all as prisoners (*desmōtai*). The report makes clear that over the course of two months, more than *ninety percent* of these prisoners sat idle, detained in a carceral facility. In so doing, it illustrates that a strong distinction between convict labor and other forms of penal incarceration can be a distinction without a difference, as we also saw in the legal record; facilities for holding condemned miners were prisons and, in at least some instances, they were likely filled with bodies waiting for their turn to work rather than simply acting as secure facilities for rest between shifts. Even though it dates centuries before the construction of the workers prison at Simitthus, documentary evidence like PSI 4.423 helps us to understand such sprawling carceral facilities and suggests the possibility that at any given time, only a select number of laborers worked in the mines, while the great majority lingered inside the prison for months or years, awaiting their turn underground.

Seen together, purpose-built prisons suggest a number of family resemblances, both in their design and in their archaeological remains. With the exception of the incarcerated workers' quarters at Simitthus, every purpose-built prison surveyed here is underground, and many were built directly underneath places of judicial or religious authority. What the Simitthus facility lacked in subterranean security, however, it more than made up for with a guarded entry corridor surveilled by a watchtower above. Every prison surveyed had the capacity to separate prisoners into cells either through stone-built walls, as at Lambaesis and Cuicul, or through upper and lower chambers, like at Rome and Cosa. Most often these spaces were constructed in the immediate vicinity of the city's civic, economic, and social center (forum/agora), and the great majority boasted small windows opening to the public street, rendering the space simultaneously secure and porous to visitors.

The other branch of our taxonomy concerns spaces designed for other purposes that nevertheless came to be used as sites of incarceration. Repurposing spaces for confinement often involved significant architectural interventions, though in some cases it did not. Paying attention to these non-purpose-built prisons allows us another glimpse at carceral logics: by tracking the architectural changes involved in outfitting a facility to serve a carceral function, we are able to trace what features incarcerators deemed necessary to the prison's function. We will argue that these repurposed spaces also shared several features with purpose-built prisons, and that together they suggest that ancient incarcerators applied models from public prison architecture to guide their selection of and intervention in repurposed carceral spaces.

OTHER PRISONS: REPURPOSED, AD HOC, AND PRIVATE

Our second category distinguishes between repurposed prisons and ad hoc prisons. Repurposed prisons are spaces that have been modified from their initial use in order to secure people for an indefinite period of time. Ad hoc prisons, on the other hand, often involve only minimal renovation and serve a carceral purpose only for a limited period, after which the space may conceivably revert to its initial function. Put differently, repurposed prisons were outfitted to become formal sites of incarceration; ad hoc prisons merely functioned as such for a limited period. Both categories reveal important aspects of carcerality.

By the imperial period, the city of Rome had multiple civic prisons. Pilar Pavón Torrejón (2003) counts at least seven: the Tullian Prison (A1), the nearby Lautumiae, a prison in the Forum Holitorium on the banks of the Tiber, and four others (89–110; cf. Juvenal, *Satires* 3.299–314, L132 [early second century CE]). It is striking to note that the two most commonly discussed civic prisons in Rome are, in fact, both repurposed spaces. As discussed above, archaeological evidence suggests that the Tullian Prison initially served as a site of cultic activity associated with underworld deities, and continued to be used for this function even during its tenure as the iconic civic prison of Rome.

Literary materials suggest that another civic prison of Rome was even more dramatically repurposed: the Lautumiae, quarries for local stone modeled on similar carceral facilities in Sicily (A12). As T. J. Cadoux (2008) argues, by the second century BCE, large underground caverns in Rome had been repurposed to serve as a site of long-term incarceration for common, "non-prestige" prisoners (203–8). Cadoux explains this as follows: "Why should the Romans require two places of detention, the *carcer* and the *lautumiae?* The answer is obvious: the *carcer* was a solid building in which criminals awaiting trial or execution could be securely held; the *lautumiae* provided hollows or caves, where a considerable number of people could be hindered from escaping by a few sentries, and if a few did escape it was no great disaster" (203). Remains of the Lautumiae have not yet been securely identified, but archaeologists agree on their general location: Cadoux argues that the facility was north of the Tullian Prison, while Filippo Coarelli (2014) suggests that it was an adjacent part of the same complex (68). These carceral facilities at the foot of the Capitoline Hill in Rome remained in use throughout the imperial period.

A repurposed prison in late ancient Corinth (Greece) allows us to track the renovations involved in transforming a space into a prison (fig. 9). In the late first or early second century CE, a row of shops were built on the northwest side of Corinth's forum, itself established as the center of a new Roman colony more than a hundred years prior. At some point between the late second and late fourth century CE, however, several of the shops were remodeled into a new prison space, opening directly onto the forum. Why remodel shops to serve as a prison? Some evidence suggests that the initial civic prison of Roman Corinth was located directly underneath the Julian Basilica, following a pattern known from other first- and second-century Roman cities like Cuicul, discussed above (Scotton et al. 2020, 217–18). The city's basilica collapsed in the late fourth century, however; if the civic prison was underneath, a new facility would be needed, and in a hurry (Larsen 2024, 369–76). Prison graffiti dated between the fifth and sixth centuries indicate the city repurposed an existing space—the Northwest Shops—into a prison shortly after the collapse of the basilica (Sironen 2016, 11–17).

The shops comprise a series of fifteen rooms, each approximately four by five meters, with a larger central chamber referred to as the Boudroumi (a Turkish loanword for dungeon) that had at least two floors: one at ground level and a second suspended above, supported by wood beams. We are sure that at least the Boudroumi and the adjacent chambers to the west were used for incarceration in the late ancient period because over two dozen prisoner graffiti remain scratched into the floors of the facility, excavated by a team of archaeologists in 1901 (*IG* 4.2.3.1270–94: D236–60 [fifth through sixth centuries CE]; Larsen 2024). Some graffiti speak to the conditions of confinement or call down divine curses on the prisoners' captors, while others are simple drawings and even tables for gaming or keeping track of time. A number of graffiti contain game boards, offering glimpses of how incarcerated people developed tactics to pass time. Some of these prisoner graffiti even appear on floor tiles immediately outside the facility, suggesting that prisoners were kept under guard in the forum's colonnade, likely in order that they could beg from passersby, a practice that attested in a

FIGURE 9. Late Roman prison at Corinth (A15; Corinth, Greece; Larsen 2024). Top: elevation of the Northwest shops as seen from the Forum. Middle: cutaway elevation of the prison entrances, with upper windows blocked up and a small window appearing in the center chamber (Boudroumi), opening to the forum. A passageway connects the room to the left and the center chamber. Bottom: cutaway elevation of prison interior. Reconstruction by Niels Bargfeldt. A 3D model of the archaeological remains and a reconstruction of the space are available in the Ancient Mediterranean Incarceration Database.

roughly contemporary source from Antioch (Antakya, Turkey; John Chrysostom, *Homilies on John* 60, L158 [ca. 390 CE]).

Renovations of the shops allow us to see what architects prioritized in repurposing the site as a prison, offering essential insight into what features render a space carceral. First, they installed a wall between the Boudroumi and the forum, making the largest chamber also the most secure, and they created a window in the new wall to allow communication between those inside the prison and those outside, mirroring civic prison architecture known across the Mediterranean. Second, a small passageway was built to connect the Boudroumi with the chamber immediately to its west, creating the now-familiar multi-celled structure well attested elsewhere. Graffiti appear on the floor of both chambers. Finally, the second story of the Boudroumi appears to have been left intact, rendering the ground floor a cramped 1.6 meters in from floor to ceiling, while graffiti on the walls suggests that the second floor was also used to detain prisoners high above the ground. Architects in late ancient Corinth took features common to purpose-built Roman prisons and implemented them in this repurposed space: location on the forum; multiple communicating chambers; ability to separate prisoners within the same facility; and windows connecting public space outside the prison with its largest chamber. The most striking divergence from the established pattern is that the Corinth prison is not underground. Nevertheless, the space retains the common feature of including an upper and lower prison, as is known from Cosa and Rome, the difference being that in this case, Corinth's upper prison was further from the entrance, unlike in subterranean examples.

We previously discussed the amphitheater in Carales and its two separate prison facilities: one purpose-built prison for gladiators included in the amphitheater's initial design (fig. 6, A), and a second prison for people condemned to die in spectacles, which was constructed subsequently in a repurposed quarry (Prison for the Condemned, A24; Dadea 2006, 79–87). The amphitheater sits at the center of an extensive complex where tunnels connect facilities above the ground with those underneath. It was built into the end of a deep limestone valley, with tunnels dug out of the bedrock on three sides and seating placed on top, while on the remaining end the oval shape was completed with seating built in large limestone blocks that were quarried in a small mine one hundred meters to the northwest. When the project was complete, an underground aqueduct was cut to channel rainwater from the newly built amphitheater into the cavity left by mining blocks for the facility (fig. 6, B). Walls of the disused quarry were covered in a thick layer of hydraulic plaster, preparing it for use as a cistern which stored winter rains and increased hydraulic capacity in a city with a ballooning population but no significant source of spring or groundwater. The space is as oppressive as it is astonishing; it is ten meters from floor to ceiling, and over fifty at its widest point. When in use as a cistern, it was capable of holding more than a million liters of water.

FIGURE 10. Inscribed wall in the Prison for the Condemned at Carales, with a worn anchor cut through hydraulic plaster visible in the upper left. Facing Northeast (A24; Cagliari, Italy). Author image.

At some point prior to the fourth century CE, the quarry-turned-cistern was repurposed yet again, this time into a prison for people condemned to die in the arena. It is unclear exactly when this cistern was transformed into a prison, but mineral buildup on the hydraulic plaster proves that the cavern held water for a significant period of time. The relative chronology is absolutely clear because of one more fact about the space: dozens of anchors were cut through the plaster into the bedrock, letting water escape but allowing prisoners to be affixed directly to the bedrock, so that they could not. The anchors are worn from use, having been threaded with ropes or chains, and numerous graffiti remain scratched into the walls throughout the space (fig. 10). Many graffiti appear directly beneath anchors, while post holes in the wall suggest some of the condemned received the barest of final comforts: a wooden platform on which to sit and wait.

An entrance gate at the northwest opened onto steep stairs cut into the bedrock, descending five meters from the surface outside to the floor of the prison. A wooden scaffold opposite the entrance was its only exit, allowing prisoners to climb eight meters into the aqueduct that led to the center of the amphitheater. Two skylights illuminated the aqueduct, allowing prisoner's eyes to adjust over the one-hundred-meter walk from darkness into the light of the arena. Not far from this exit is another curious feature: a series of nonsequential Roman numerals cut into the wall underneath anchors—these may relate to staging, perhaps allowing the order of prisoners to be set before the games began. At one point, water flowed from the sky to the arena to a long aqueduct before it splashed down into the cistern at Carales. Eventually, bodies flowed in the opposite direction, ascending a wooden scaffold and walking the same path backward, to meet their death in the arena.

Compared with the extensive renovations required at Corinth, the cistern in Carales began as a relatively secure space. Renovations were less extensive as a consequence: water was drained; anchors were cut through the hydraulic plaster into the walls for stocks; wooden platforms were constructed for sitting; and a scaffold rose to the aqueduct to ferry people out. It appears that people confined in the space, or perhaps their captors, outfitted the facility themselves, as well: cutting footholds into the wall that allowed access to high niches created during quarrying—niches that would have supplied access to less damp and rancid air than that below, along with a degree of privacy, albeit a paltry one. Prisoners scratched in their own touches, too, in the form of countless small crosses, lines, and at least one early Christian graffito carved with poor tools in limited light by someone sitting directly below an anchor point—likely attached to the wall, with little hope left for deliverance (fig. 11). The Christogram atop the ship's mast did not become a significant symbol before the reign of Constantine, suggesting that imperial pronouncements outlawing gladiator games in 325 and again in 357 may have been either specific to the city of Rome, or not widely heeded (*CTh* 15.12.1–2).

While worker's prisons like Simitthus were often purpose-built to warehouse convicted and enslaved laborers, literary sources regularly consider mine shafts themselves one species of the genus "prison," as they were used to detain those working underground—often for weeks or even months on end (Pliny the Elder, *Natural History* 33.70, L159 [ca. 77 CE]). The copper mines at Phaino (Wadi Feynan, Jordan) were among the most famous carceral facilities in the ancient world, regularly and graphically described as facilities teeming with overworked and brutally mutilated convict laborers, a place "where even a condemned murderer is hardly able to live a few days" (Athanasius, *History of the Arians* 60; Hillner 2015, 202–3). At Phaino, cavernous galleries were carved out of the bedrock in order to maximize surveillance capabilities, allowing a skeleton staff of guards to detain a large number of laborers extracting copper, and sleeping, inside (Friedman 2009).

The mining facility at Wadi Khalid, near the ruins of ancient Phaino, gives a sense of the experience to which miners were subjected and the architectural interventions necessary to keep these facilities productive. The mine comprises three shafts, with surface openings one meter across leading to tunnels that plunge a hundred meters into the earth. Two of the shafts were opened already in the Iron Age, with a third added during the Roman period, as evidenced by late

FIGURE 11. Drawing of early Christian graffito of ship with Christogram on top of the mast and alpha and omega hanging from the sail, twelve oars, and a small Greek inscription reading *ian*. Image by Evan Levine after Dadea 2006, 85, fig. 37.

first-century coins in the newer shaft and Roman masonry in the older shafts, apparently added to shore up the aging underground infrastructure (A37; Hauptmann 2007, 121). Footholds cut into the walls aided miners as they descended, where literary sources suggest that they would be left for weeks or even months on end, sustenance lowered down in baskets and hard-earned copper ore lifted up to the surface above. The air was toxic deep underground; minimal ventilation allowed heavy metals to lodge in laborers' lungs, as Strabo notes: "Air in the mines is both deadly and hard to endure on account of the grievous odor of the ore, so that the workmen are doomed to a quick death" (Strabo, *Geography* 12.3.40, L167 [early first century CE]). Enslaved and incarcerated miners crawled on hands and knees through underground galleries and, inevitably, felt their bodies deteriorate over time. As Pliny the Elder reports, "in every mine, the legs are injured" (Pliny the Elder, *Natural History* 36.28 [ca. 77 CE]).

Roman phases of a copper mine at nearby Wadi Amram (Israel) give a sense both of the scale and discomfort of daily life in and within these kinds of sites. Beno Rothenberg has mapped out an entire constellation of mine shafts, each with an average diameter of just seventy centimeters and occasionally opening into wide arcades, where shafts were cut to allow an exchange of air, ore, and bodies from above. Niches in the wall were made for accommodated small oil lamps, offering "the only source of light in these complex dark workings," though at the expense of the oxygen that they consumed as prisoners crawled through underground galleries, following veins of copper nodules. A basket made from reed and rope, roughly the size "of a modern shopping basket," used for hauling ore to the surface above, was found in one of the lowest areas of the mines (Rothenberg 1999, 164–65, see esp. fig. 22). The mining complex at Wadi Amram offers us a glimpse into a warren of carcerality, forced labor, and terror.

Eusebius, writing in the fourth century CE, speaks regularly of "the mines at Phaino," "the mines in Palestine," "the mines at Cilicia," or "the mines of Thebais" as landscapes of incarceration to which Christians were sent for punishment (*Martyrs of Palestine* 7, 8, 13, L54 [early fourth century CE]). Even so, while condemned prisoners were used as some of the labor force in places like Phaino, particularly for the more brutal and body-destroying aspects of work, we must remember that "the mines in Faynan were not normally run as a large-scale penal colony with a big military garrison"; rather, convict laborers were one cog in a much larger ecosystem of imperial power and extraction (Mattingly 2013, 190). To borrow a phrase from geographer Dominique Moran, Phaino itself was a "carceral geography," insofar as the whole region—the mining town, shafts, surveilled roads, and the surrounding landscape—was bound up in its carceral function, rather than incarceration being localized in a single prison structure (2015). Today, the region remains largely as it was in antiquity: harsh and remote, with exceedingly rugged and barren terrain that rendered escape without notice nearly impossible. Narrow exits from mines were distant enough from any population center that an escaped convict would perhaps find a harsher reality outside the mine than inside, even if they could evade guards above and checkpoints securing the landscape. The typical miner's appearance—mostly naked, with half-shaved heads, shackles, and often tattoos—would make them easy to spot and hard to mistake, incorporating the landscape itself into the carceral infrastructure rather than simply serving as its host (Millar 1984, 128; Larsen 2019, 561; Cyprian, *Letters* 77.3, L141 [250–58 CE]; Petronius, *Satyricon* 103, L185 [late first century CE]).

For the most part, ancient prisoners were kept underground, but a few sources speak to the use of towers as sites of incarceration. In the late sixth century CE, Gregory of Tours told a story about a hermit named Hospicius living in chains in an old tower, whom the invading Lombard army had mistaken for a prisoner (*Histories* 6.6, L162 [late sixth century CE]; Hillner 2015, 271). The story's logic relies on a durable association across the Mediterranean between towers and long-term incarceration, an association backed up by archaeological evidence. Sarah Morris and John Papadopoulos (2005) have argued that dozens of towers from both urban and rural Greece in the classical and Hellenistic periods exhibit features associated with incarceration: designed apparently to keep people in rather than out, "as places for temporary incarceration of unfree labor" and, unsubtly, the spatial inverse of a mineshaft, exploited for similar ends (193).

Incarceration often occurred outside formal prisons, in existing structures, with little or no renovation, that were used to detain people for a period of time. We refer to such sites as ad hoc prisons. Here we discuss an exemplary, but not exhaustive, series of examples: cisterns, temples, baths, markets, and rooms in private homes. As we have seen, Roman prisons especially share structural similarities with cisterns—they are mostly underground spaces, often at the center of settlements and connected to other municipal infrastructure—and a number of Roman- and Byzantine-era prisons were structurally repurposed from their initial use as a cistern (Herodian Palace Prison, A8; Dara Prison, A11; Prison for the Condemned, A24; cf. Philippi Prison, A19; Mentzos 2005, 152). Around 238 CE, a large Roman estate outside the ancient capital of Tarraco (Tarragona, Spain) was sacked and many of the buildings were destroyed. A large kitchen facility servicing the main house was lost in the attack, including a cistern that had been repurposed by doubling the wall width on three sides, and tripling the wall that opened into the villa. When excavators unearthed the facility in the late 1960s, there were a few "notable surprises, since in the lower stratum, destroyed and burned, we found *in situ* some iron shackles, one of them containing within the rusty metal the heel bones of a person and, next to it, fragments of a burned skull; without a doubt it was the prison or cell for punishment, perhaps intended for the villa's rebellious slaves" (Berges 1969–70, 142; Els Munts, A28).

The space was renovated to double the width of the walls, apparently in relation to its use as a prison. As such, it could be categorized as a private prison, repurposed from cistern, rather than an ad hoc prison in a strict sense. Even so, the cistern at Els Munts differs in important ways from other repurposed prisons like the Prison for the Condemned at Carales; apart from reinforcing the walls and adding shackles, there do not appear to have been any significant architectural changes implemented to turn the space into a private prison. Such ad hoc use of cisterns for temporary incarceration follows a wider pattern across the Mediterranean which stretches beyond the parameters of this book. Sources as distant as the biblical book of Jeremiah, set in Jerusalem in the seventh and sixth centuries BCE, envisions disused cisterns used to hold prisoners (37:11–38:13, L43 [sixth/fifth centuries BCE]), and in the medieval period a cistern on the acropolis at Cosa was apparently converted into a prison, as evidenced by the dense attestation of graffiti in the space. One composition at Cosa from 1210 CE is eerily similar to the fourth-century prisoner graffito at Carales, comprising "two boats painted with dark brown pigment, one larger than the other, both sailing toward the north . . . To the south of the ships is a series of six simple crosses" (Hobart 2003, 126; cf. fig. 11).

Documentary and literary sources often attest the use of temples as ad hoc sites for temporary incarceration. For instance, in the fourth century CE, a man from Oxyrhynchus wrote a letter to his brother Heras, asking him to bring a significant amount of money that he apparently owed. Unable to repay his debt, he complains: "by heaven I am locked up in the temple of Hadrian!" (*P. Oxy.* 17.2154, D18 [fourth century CE]). As discussed below, the prisoner may indicate that he was incarcerated in a formal prison structure like the one underneath the central temple at Sufetula, but more likely we have here evidence of the temple treasury being used to detain a prisoner temporarily; Cassius Dio apparently reported that the treasury inside the Temple of Saturn on the Roman forum was used to detain inhabitants of Praeneste during a war against Pirro (A39; Cassius Dio, *Roman History* [Zonaras Annales 8, 3 (D)], L60 [ca. 230 CE]; Pavón Torrejón 2003b, 30, 109). Prisons connected to temples are attested across the ancient world, including Neo-Babylonian legal sources, to which we can add the Lambaesis military prison complex, discussed above (Joannès 2023, 533–39).

Any secure room could conceivably function as a temporary carceral space, and in addition to their common central location in cities, temples were uniquely equipped with such rooms. They were an obvious choice for temporary incarceration, and a choice taken from time to time, it seems. With the civic prison at Messene nicknamed "The Treasury" and treasuries used as prisons, our data point to an intertwined relationship between these two civic structures: two of the three structures the Vitruvius prescribes for every Roman forum. Both respond to criminality within society, the only fundamental difference being that prisons are intended to keep people in, while treasuries keep people out.

Some sources suggest that in times when cities had an unexpected influx of prisoners, baths could be used as ad hoc prisons. In a fifth- or sixth-century hagiography about Demetrios, the patron saint of Thessaloniki (Greece), the emperor Maximian is depicted temporarily requisitioning baths near the city's forum to incarcerate large numbers of Christians (*Martyrdom of Demetrios of Thessalonike* 4–7, L164). The holy man was eventually killed in his cell at the baths, the narrative reports: a detail which his martyrdom account deploys to explain why, already in late antiquity, the city's Roman baths doubled as a cultic site associated with Demetrios. Today, the martyr is celebrated in the Church of Holy Demetrios at Thessaloniki, and excavations in the 1930s and 1940s underneath the church established that there is, in fact, a Roman bathhouse underneath the church (Bakirtzis 1988, 11).

Macella, or food markets, are also attested as ad hoc sites of incarceration. In a letter from 335 CE, a man named Callistos complains that Athanasius, the bishop of Alexandria, colluded with a group of drunken local soldiers to incarcerate Christians in a variety of places, including "in the store chambers [*en tais kellais*]" and "among the standards [*en tois signois*]" of the military camp, "in the shops [*en tōi malekkōi*]," "in the military camp prison," and even "in the biggest prison [*en tēi megistēi foilakēi*]" (*P. Lond.* 6.1914, D118). While most of these appear to refer to purpose-built or repurposed prisons, the *cella* and the *macella*—both of which have their Latin name preserved in this Greek letter—are ad hoc sites, and both fit the criteria of secure, easily guardable rooms which could be used to detain prisoners in a pinch. This source reports that Athanasius and his Roman military henchmen were in precisely such a pinch.

Private prisons had capacious uses. Essentially, they could be used for all kinds of nonpublic bodily immobilization: domestic confinement of family members to correct or chastise; punitive incarceration of slaves in domestic or rural contexts; even debt management and monastic confinement (Hillner 2015, 151–93). Although regularly outlawed, private prisons are attested and used in every period covered by this book, eventually being coopted into the Byzantine Egyptian carceral system as semipublic prisons (Torallas Tovar 1999, 50–53; 2003, 221–23; Berkes 2015; Hillner 2015, 177–85).

Many larger villas had a place that could function to incarcerate, and documentary evidence indicates that individuals used underground strongrooms or basements to detain people through both lawful and extrajudicial means. As Torallas Tovar has argued, "A city with meager finances preferred to keep prisoners in the estate owners' prison, because it was expensive to maintain [public prisons]." Doing so required close coordination between municipal magistrates and estate staff, for instance in the case of *Stud. Pal.* 10.252, where public and private officials teamed up to arrest and imprison men for a robbery in the sixth century CE (D296 [6th c CE]; Torallas Tovar 1999, 53). As an example of the extrajudicial use of such private prisons, a fourth-century woman's affidavit against her husband reports that among his many outrages, he "shut up his own slaves and mine with my foster-daughters and his agent and son for seven whole days in his basement" (P. Oxy. 6.903, D85; Hillner 2015, 162–69).

Archaeological evidence perhaps offers further insight into such private prisons even in an earlier period. When Mount Vesuvius erupted and destroyed the cities of Pompeii and Herculaneum in 79 CE, a significant portion of the city fled, though an unlucky segment remained in the city and were buried under ash and pyroclastic flow. One victim of the eruption was not given the option to evacuate: they were fettered and attached to the wall in an underground room at the Villa of the Mosaic Columns. On October 17, 1905, excavators found two human tibia in that underground room, a cellar attached to the elite villa's kitchen, still detained in the shackles that affixed them to the wall (*Notizie degli scavi* 1910, 259–60). As in the case of the cistern at Els Munts discussed above, it is possible to classify the space at the Villa of the Mosaic Columns as a repurposed rather than ad hoc prison, given that the shackles were affixed to the wall. We include it here because affixing shackles represents a comparatively minimal update to the cellar's architecture. The villa's initial excavators did not complete their removal of ash from the room, stopping just inside the threshold where the prisoner's legs were found. The space is still visible today, and still today the majority of it remains filled to the brim with ancient ash. Only future archaeological work will reveal what remains below the surface; it is possible that the remains of more victims remain buried.

This cellar in the Villa of the Mosaic Columns, as well as the Els Munts cistern discussed above, are typically understood as *ergastula*: holding cells where enslaved workers rested after performing chained work during the day (Étienne 1974; Joshel and Petersen 2014, 96). What precisely counts as an *ergastulum* is debated. The term applies to spaces for confining exploited involuntary laborers, often with a punitive purpose (Hillner 2015, 169–70). The fact is, we do not know if these individuals were enslaved; it is impossible to make the distinction based on their remains alone. All we know is that they were shackled. Archaeologically attested cases of private incarceration are slippery, because enslaved and non-enslaved people were bound using identical technologies, but for divergent reasons. The material is illuminating nevertheless, suggesting that when Romans considered where and how to bind bodies in their private homes, they did so in spaces that mirrored the public facilities designed for the same: they are deep underground, with a single entrance and anchors on the wall for affixing shackles, and yet the spaces remain accessible, such that slaves or prisoners could be cared for and retrieved.

The preceding typology is a rough sketch—a series of broad categories pieced together from fragmentary evidence that can help us to think spatially and materially about the literary, documentary, and visual evidence engaged in subsequent chapters. More work is required. Nevertheless, even a tentative typology can help to identify other spaces that have broadly carceral features. We conclude by applying our typology to one such site.

Little can be said for certain about the foundation of Sufetula (Sbeitla, Tunisia), though Roman inhabitation is evidenced from the middle of the first century CE forward, and the city's forum was heavily renovated in the middle of the second century (Duval 1990, 501–12). At the northwest side of Sufetula's forum lies a spectacular cultic complex: three temples stand side by side, perhaps dedicated to each of the three gods worshiped in the Capitoline Temple at Rome, or to the Roman emperor Antoninus Pius and his two adoptive sons, Marcus Aurelius and Lucius Verus (fig. 12; Naddari 2018). The forum complex was built in 156/57 CE, and each temple at its western end stands high on an imposing pediment. The two outer structures sit on top of narrow architectural arcades, with doors on the north and south leading from inside the adjacent buildings into the long windowless corridors underneath the outer temples.

Above, the central temple looks similar to those on its south and north—marginally larger and lacking stairs connecting the porch to the forum but otherwise similar in style and grandeur (fig. 13). Underneath, however, the central temple could hardly be more different. Wide alleyways run along either side, connecting the forum to the public street running behind the temples and past narrow windows, allowing light and small objects to pass into two parallel chambers that run underneath the temple's central cultic area (*cella*) (B and C, fig. 14). An antechamber (A) stands underneath the temple's porch and directly behind a platform that likely served as the city's tribunal. This underground complex had a single access point: an antechamber accessible through a large door, with its own narrow windows opening to the north alley. Thresholds for further doors stand between

FIGURE 12. Temple complex at Sufetula (Sbeitla, Tunisia). Author photo.

the antechamber and chambers B and C, and a wall divides chamber B into two. Another threshold for a door divides chambers C and D.

The function of the secure complex underneath Sufetula's central temple is unclear, but its design betrays a purpose distinct from the areas underneath the outer temples, which were not publicly accessible and have neither windows nor secure antechambers. It is possible that at Sufetula, similar to the military prison at Lambaesis, we have an instance of a temple built for cultic devotion above and storage of prisoners below. In analogy with the site of Timgad, 240 kilometers west, the excavators of Sufetula suggest that the municipal *curia*, where criminal court cases were heard, must have stood on the southwest corner of the forum, directly adjacent to the southern temple, and a number of architectural elements suggest this identification is likely correct (Duval and Baratte 1973, 23).

There are only two temple complexes of this type extant from the ancient world, and the differences between them are illuminating. At the site of Baelo Claudia just north of the Strait of Gibraltar, three temples dating from the first century CE adjoin the forum, parallel to each other. They are similarly interpreted as a Triple Capitolium, though the identification is debated. The temples at Baelo Claudia have one major difference with their sibling at Sufetula—they have no windowed, underground complex, but rather a small crypt underneath one of the outer

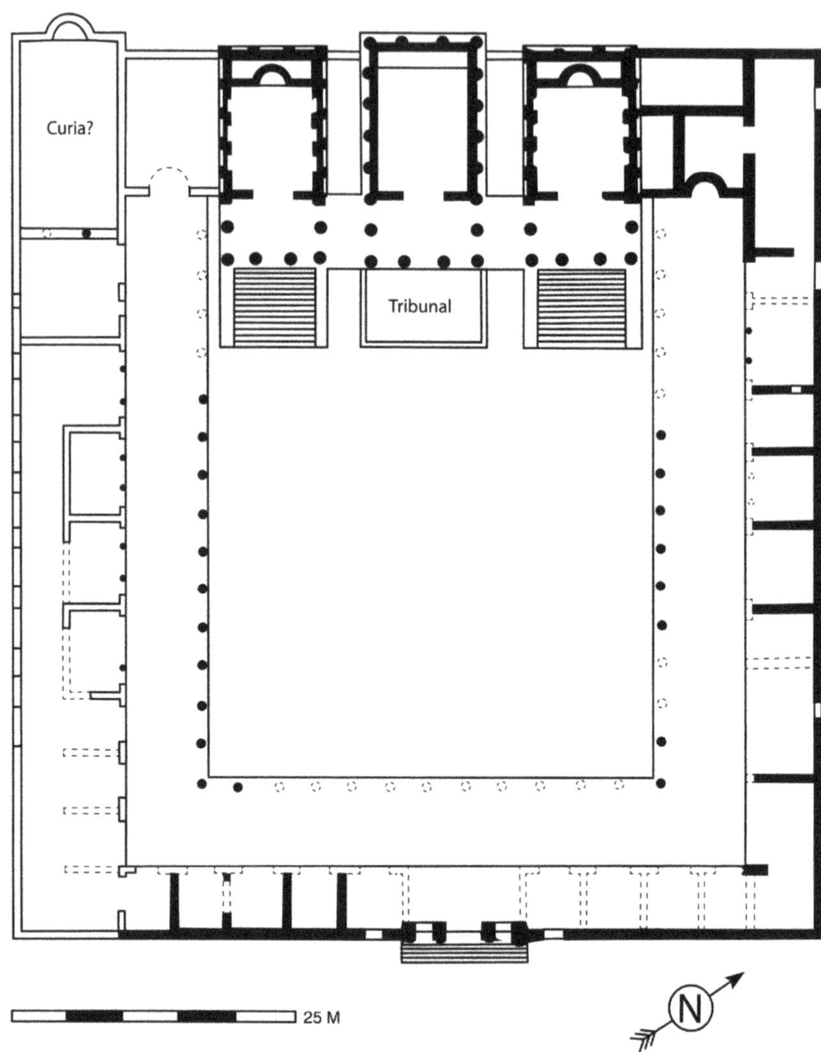

FIGURE 13. Sufetula, forum baseplan. Plan by Gina Tibbott after Duval and Baratte 1973, 18, fig. 8. Duval and Baratte propose an apsidal building on the northwest corner of the forum as the Curia.

temples, with no public access, antechamber, or other signs of carceral design or use (Bonneville et al. 2000, 103; 189–90).

Slit windows underneath temple podia are not uncommon, and no single feature of this space points to a carceral intention or use in itself. Nevertheless, the space underneath the central temple at Sufetula is stunning because it presents a collocation of features that suggest it was perhaps designed to be the municipal

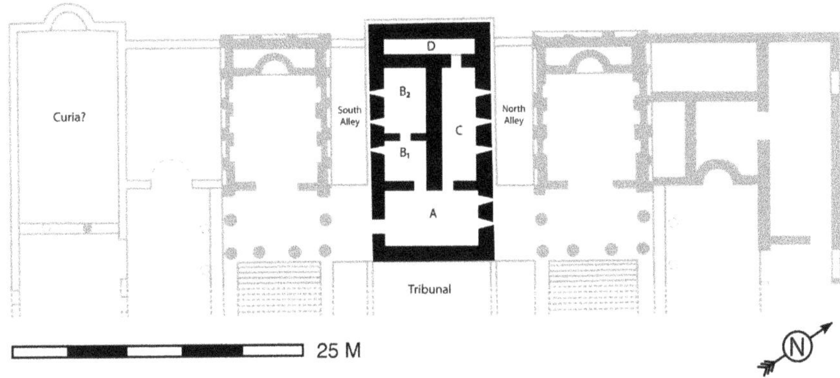

FIGURE 14. Sufetula, proposed civic prison underneath the central temple (A24; Sbeitla, Tunisia). Plan by Gina Tibbott.

carcer: the space sits directly on the forum, as Vitruvius prescribes, and with close, direct access to the municipal *curia*, like we see in Cuicul, which was established at around the same time 325 kilometers to the northwest. Unlike Cuicul, where the prison lies directly underneath the *curia*, at Sufetula the proposed prison sits directly underneath a temple dedicated to the gods—and political domination—of Rome, like we see two hundred kilometers west at Lambaesis. The placement of a carceral space underneath the tribunal resembles the identical setup at Sarmize-getusa, and echoes the civic basilica at Tipasa six hundred kilometers northwest on the Mediterranean coast, where the bodies of captives decorate the basilica's apse and illustrate materially the power of Roman political officials *over* the bodies of prisoners (p. 83–84, 136–138). Similar tribunals with chambers underneath are preserved nearby at Timgad and a particularly striking example at Leptis Magna, apparently built in imitation of the Temple of the Divine Julius in Rome and including two stairwells that lead directly from the chambers underneath the temple to the tribunal platform above (Ulrich 1994, 253–66, 283–301).

In the absence of inscriptions, graffiti, anchors, shackles, or literary sources indicating the precise use of the space, we cannot make a secure identification of the facility at Sufetula. Nevertheless, no other explanation has been forwarded—in fact, Noël Duval and François Baratte's 1973 plan of the forum remains the standard depiction of the temple complex, omitting the underground facility altogether (fig. 13). Our typology helps us to see the striking parallels to this space among broader North African and Roman civic architecture of the second century CE, and suggests reappraisal of other parallel and contemporary sites like the tribunals at Leptis Magna, Sabratha, and Timgad. In fact, Albert Ballu, the excavator of the prison in Cuicul, made a similar suggestion about Timgad already in 1910, suggesting that a pair of stout, two-chambered subterranean rooms may have served as the city's prison. Like at parallel sites, the facility is accessible only from above, and is directly adjacent to the *curia* (Ballu 1910, 46–47, 54).

Each of the spaces detailed above had diverse functions: some were used to hold defendants in custody before trial or execution while some undoubtedly held debt prisoners or political detainees with a coercive aim. Other prisoners sat in these prisons as punishment. These spaces were multipurpose and, as we have shown, multifaceted. Still, carceral architecture encodes ideologies of imprisonment, and we must see spaces of incarceration before we can understand the practices undertaken inside them. The history of prison architecture matters, in other words: it presents a key to understanding carceral ideologies, practices, and experiences. Having investigated places of confinement, we turn now to the relationship between ancient ideologies of incarceration and their material expressions.

IDEOLOGY READ FROM SPACES OF INCARCERATION

Archaeological remains do not speak for themselves, and ideologies mobilized in architecture are hardly self-evident. Nevertheless, as Caroline Humphrey (2005) has argued, "ideology is found not only in texts and speeches; it is a political practice that is also manifest in constructing material objects" (39). By paying close attention to the material aspects of a space, historians may speculate about its use—speculations that are rendered more plausible when corroborated by other forms of evidence trending in the same direction. Architecture offers us one more avenue for understanding ideologies of incarceration as they morph and grow, as Norman Johnston (2000) showed regarding early modern and modern prisons: "Throughout the evolution of prison architecture, competing philosophies of punishment and theories of prison design resulted in a preferred type of layout that was thought capable of accomplishing the goals of imprisonment, only to change in the next" (1). A panoptic prison, for instance, encodes an ideology of surveillance and order as a corrective to criminality. What might ancient infrastructure have communicated about conceptions of law, order, and social deviance? Broad correspondences between ancient carceral sites are suggestive of an underlying set of practices, lived experiences, and perhaps even intentions expressed by engineers or builders in the spaces that they created. In this section we situate spaces of incarceration alongside a broader archive, attempting to understand the ideologies that the spaces encoded. We attend to five ideals that recur across the built environment of the ancient Mediterranean: centrality, surveillance, separation, depth, and punitive variability.

As a starting point, venues of incarceration indicate one aspect of the prison's role in society. Contemporary US mega-prisons like the famous Pelican Bay Prison in California or the New York State correctional facility at Attica are located far from metropolitan centers, in areas of low-population density; while local jails hold the accused close to courthouses, most convicts are "locked *away*" (Reiter

2016, 99–102). Quite the opposite was the case in antiquity; archaeological, documentary, and literary evidence uniformly reveal that civic prisons were situated at the center of cities. Vitruvius's proposal that Roman civic prisons should be built immediately adjacent to the municipal forum appears to reflect common practice; more often than not, they were built directly on the forum. The proximity of civic prisons to other central public architecture, and their apparent construction as part and parcel of outfitting new cities with civic infrastructure, suggests that city planners understood the prison to be a key part of the cityscape, one integral to the social functioning of a city. In the words of Christopher J. Fuhrmann, "the state's punishment of crime and disorder was a public highlight of Rome's most central topography," and as Guy Geltner has demonstrated, the centrality of Italian prisons within cities continued through the Middle Ages down to modernity (Fuhrmann 2016, 299; Geltner 2008, 29). Far from being a normal or obvious outcome, the thoroughgoing ruralization of penal and correctional facilities is a contemporary anomaly.

Without exception these spaces were built to be simultaneously physically secure and socially permeable, accessible directly from the forum through small windows or doors, sometimes with purpose-built antechambers overseen by a guard. Their regular placement at the city center is not haphazard but intentional, and it appears that part of that intention was for prisons to be readily accessible to the public at large—especially to family and friends who often bore the burden of care for prisoners, but perhaps also to advertise their deviance. Finally, civic prisons were uniformly proximate to courtrooms, and at times directly underneath them: civic basilicas, *curiae*, and *tribunalia*, often with direct passage between, perhaps indicating a security concern in moving prisoners to their place of judgment, or a practical one, keeping them close by for ease of access.

Even the placement of prisons near temples may be understood within the matrix of Roman judicial ideology. As Richard Neudecker (2010) argues, both in the Roman republic and in the empire, "divine presence—be it by way of statues or by altars—was necessary to give validity to legal acts," and while we argue below that incarceration was never solely a judicial act, the prominent colocation of sacred, judicial, and carceral infrastructure across the Roman world was unsurprising, but meaningful (161). The prominence of prisons within the urban landscape communicates architecturally what documentary and literary evidence reveals to have been the case: prisons were a fully integrated feature of the political and social structure of the ancient world. Libanius reports on a conversation with a municipal prison warden, who claimed that even the atmosphere of New Year celebrations penetrated the prison and brought a modicum of joy to prisoners, "sometimes even causing a smile" (*Oration* 9.12 [ca. 390 CE]). The relationship between a carceral society and its prisoners was, in other words, multidirectional; in the words of Jens-Uwe Krause, "Every inhabitant of a city was more or less directly confronted with the prison, and with the condition of the prisoners.

Prisons did not have the function of hiding prisoners away. Instead, their presence in the center of the city served as a deterrent" (1996, 272).

The facility in Cuicul is paradigmatic: it is underground, directly adjacent to the forum, and part of the initial design of the forum complex itself, opening to an adjacent public street. The prison is built into the foundation of the civic basilica, and the courtroom has two points of access: one monumental entrance allowed access from Cuicul's forum, while a second set of doors allowed access from the prison below. Judges and lawyers, it seems, entered through the front door while prisoners were ferried in from the back, five meters along the *cardo* and up the stairs, under guard. Most of the civic prisons identified to date have a single point of entrance and exit, and communicate not the forum itself but rather with an adjacent public street. The prison in the praetorian palace in Caesarea Maritima (Israel) adds complexity to this pattern, but the same themes recur: it has a narrow, winding entrance leading down from the prison guard offices to the eastern chamber of the prison, below. A second chamber allows prisoners to move from the prison, up a set of stairs, to the trial chambers above. (Herodian Palace Prison, A8; CIIP 2.1273, D206 [second century CE]). Prisons were often centrally located, but in comparison to other public buildings their presence was veiled; the prison lies just down an alley, through a gate, or underneath a temple—accessible, but requiring mediation of a guard or a gate or a window wide enough only for a hand and a voice.

Second, nearly all carceral sites were underground. This pattern holds across the entirety of the Mediterranean and the time period under discussion in this book, for both purpose-built and repurposed facilities. It is not surprising, then, that visual, documentary, and literary sources overwhelmingly depict prisons as dark, wet, cold places (p. 106–110). Subterranean spaces may be more secure than those built above ground by making escape more difficult, but literary and visual sources allow us to understand other ideological resonances implicated in the uniform decision to bury prisoners underground. In what follows, we discuss two further aspects of ideology encoded in prison architecture: first, ancient prisons are frequently described as liminal spaces, connecting the world of the living to that of the dead; second, sources from the Roman imperial period almost uniformly depict prisoners as low and diminutive, cowering beneath symbols of governmental power.

Before it was a carceral facility, the Tullian Prison in Rome was a space devoted to the worship of underworld deities, and recent excavations show that even after its transformation into a prison that cultic connection remained—during renovations in the early first century CE, a fresh dedication to underworld deities was placed underneath floor pavers in the lower prison (Susanna 2022b). This material practice reflects a common theme: from the earliest surviving material and into the Byzantine period, literary sources regularly portray prisons as shallow parts of the underworld (Reid 2022, 28; Hesiod, *Theogony* 720–820 [late eighth to early seventh century BCE]; John Climacus, *Ladder of Divine Ascent* 4 [early seventh century CE]). Pliny the Elder explicitly understands mines as a type of carceral space, and in the first century CE he described mining practices as a form of stealing from the earth, a sacred parent. "We penetrate her inner parts and seek for riches in the abode of the spirits of the underworld [*manes*]," he laments, "as though the part where we tread upon her were not sufficiently bountiful and fertile" (*Natural History* 33.1, L165 [ca. 77 CE]; trans. LCL 294). The connection is not solely literary; three laws of Constantine speak to condemned prisoners being "thrown into the mines [*in metallum detrudetur*]"—in the words of Hervé Huntzinger, "these three constitutions evoke the image of the condemned thrown from the surface of the earth (the world of the living), into underground mines (the world of the dead)" (2005, 28; *CTh* 12.1.6 [318/9 CE]; 1.5.3 [331 CE]; 4.8.8 [332 CE]). Early Christian sources in particular stress both the subterranean aspect of prisons and the relationship between depth and the underworld and, as Meghan Henning (2021) has shown, a stunning variety of early Christian materials describe hell using peculiarly carceral language and imagery (38–43, 99–100).

Constructing prisons underground also extends a political ideology of domination, at least in Roman sources. North African evidence is particularly illuminating. The civic prison in Cuicul and the military prison in Lambaesis are both underground, though the former is under the civic basilica while the latter was built under a sanctuary that housed the standards of the Roman army's Third Legion (Cuicul A5, Lambaesis A7). Nevertheless, both are situated under symbols of Roman imperial rule and military domination: in the case of Cuicul, the civic basilica where trials were held, and in the case of Lambaesis, under the symbols of the Roman army's military might. Prisoners were quite literally detained beneath the feet of Roman administrators and beneath the objects that they chose to symbolize military domination. Placing prisons underground further reinforced the visual cliché of incarceration as a form of state dominance and social disappearance—a combined function that continues in modern carceral practices and that deserves further comparative consideration (Zarrugh 2020). A similar ideological impetus may have been present in Greek spaces and sources as well, but we simply have much less evidence and are unwilling to make a strong claim regarding this possibility; the one plausibly identified prison from the Hellenistic period discussed here—the civic prison of Messene—is certainly underground, though perhaps simply to enhance security. Likewise, a site that has been identified as the state prison of classical Athens stands at ground level, though that identification is contested (Messene A16, Athens A23; Vanderpool 1980; Hunter 1997).

Political dominion over captive bodies is one of the most common themes across Roman-period sources, though as we see at Cuicul and Lambaesis, the theme is often played in subtly different keys. A third site in Roman North Africa clarifies this commonality: the civic basilica in the colony of Tipasa on the Mediterranean coast, used as a courthouse in the same period when the Cuicul and

Lambaesis prisons were in use inland. No civic prison lies underneath the basilica at Tipasa. Instead, the floor of the civic basilica was decorated with a mosaic depicting the bodies of prisoners, again placing Roman imperial power, in the form of judges, above incarcerated bodies. The Mosaic of the Captives at Tipasa depicts portraits of thirteen individuals surrounding a central scene of an incarcerated family, including a man, woman, and child—apparently native Berbers (fig. 15; V8 [late second century CE]). In the absence of a prison underneath the civic basilica, however, artisans and image makers in service of the city of Tipasa chose to decorate the courthouse floor with the bodies of captives, depicted not only as subdued but as indigenous, further assimilating a Roman ideology of carcerality with its identity as a colonizing state.

Taken together, these first two points—the centrality of carceral spaces and their placement underneath the society responsible for their captivity—gesture toward a tension in carceral ideology. Incarceration was proximate to the public life of cities, yet it was also a form of disappearance. Prisoners were not physically removed from civic life but carefully hidden from the eye. Prisons were built in such a way that the spaces were accessible, while prisoners themselves were harder to see than to hear, to touch, or to smell. They were, to use Michael T. Taussig's (1999) phrase, avatars of a public secret (49–55).

The third aspect of carceral ideology that can be read from these spaces is perhaps unsurprising, at least to modern audiences, but it nevertheless bears pause: archaeological remains of prisons point to an ideology of surveillance. In addition to letting food and other necessities to be passed to people inside, prison windows allowed for oversight of prisoners without the need to open doors and jeopardize the security of the facility. Some visual sources corroborate this surveillance function. For instance, a fresco found in a house on Via Stabiae in Pompeii depicts the myth of Pero and Micon—an ancient story about the virtue of filial piety that appears in a variety of literary sources, in addition to frescoes and statues (fig. 16, Naples Archaeological Museum 115398, V12 [first century CE]). Details shift from telling to telling, but at its core the story is about a young mother visiting her parent who was condemned to death by starvation in prison. On regular visits she nurses the parent at her breast until a guard discovers the scheme and, instead of punishing the daughter, allows both to go free on account of the daughter's *pietas*—faithfulness. This fresco makes explicit a matter left ambiguous in the literary accounts: how did the guard know about the arrangement? The answer is that the prison had a window, through which the guard is depicted outside the prison peering down into the cell at the moment of discovery. Windows opening to public spaces remained part of prison architecture long after the Pompeii fresco was buried in the late first century CE: the late antique prison at Corinth had a similar window opening to the forum, presumably with a dual function of access and surveillance; a similar arrangement appears in the remains of the prison underneath a late Roman administrative building at Tiberias in the province of Palestine (Corinth, A15; Tiberias, A40).

We can glimpse an aspect of surveillance in the architectural features of mining camps, as well. By the Roman period, the arched galleries of Umm al-Amad mine at Phaino had lain fallow for many centuries. When Romans reopened the mines, they widened galleries inside but not the entrances, which remained accessible through minuscule entrances passable only on hands and knees. As archaeologist Hannah Friedman (2009) argues, "Entrances were purposefully kept small. The difficulty in exiting the mine is so great that it suggests that individuals rarely if ever left" (6). Adding to the restrictive entrances, which are common features of mines across the empire, Friedman notes that towers on the landscape fulfill the conditions of panoptic surveillance in a squarely Foucauldian sense, in which "individuals are under surveillance and know that they are being watched" (8). In many important aspects, these mining facilities look and function differently than civic prisons discussed above. Nevertheless, we see striking ideological correspondences between the two types of facility, especially regarding the importance of surveillance.

Fourth, archaeological evidence suggests a prevalent ideology of separation that literary sources corroborate. Significant expense and effort were deployed at Lambaesis and Simitthus to construct facilities where people could be segregated from one another within the prison complex, and if the space identified at Sufetula is indeed a civic prison of the city, we have yet another example of parallel cells opening to a common antechamber. Cuicul, Cosa, and Pompeii likewise have multiple chambers conceivably used to separate prisoners of different sorts, though the architecture alone does not betray the operative lines of difference. Some materials distinguish between prisoners kept in fetters and those in looser custody, like Diodorus Siculus's first-century BCE account of the civic prison at Alba Fucens in which King Perseus of Macedon was kept "in free custody [*eis eleutheran . . . fulakēn*]" as a favor, or an official letter on papyrus from the second or third century CE reporting on the names of prisoners under transport, some of whom were "in chains [*en desmois*]" while others were "under free guard [*eleutherai tērēsei*]" (*Library of History* 31.8.2, L57 [ca. 60 BCE]; P. Bagnall 29, D101 [175–225 CE]). In fact, Diodorus speaks of at least three different types of custody, including one prison at Alba Fucens reserved for people awaiting execution. He clarifies that "this prison is a pit deep underground [*esti de ho karkaros orugma katageion bathu*]"—a practice of separation that Diodorus notes was common "in that period," perhaps implying that categories or practices had changed between the time of the events, in the mid-second century BCE, and his recounting of them one hundred years later (31.9.2).

The phenomenon of prisoner separation is corroborated in the city of Rome by the second-century CE historian Suetonius, who records an attempt to control prisoners through punitive isolation. In what is perhaps the earliest extant evidence for punitive solitary confinement, Suetonius notes that certain prisoners in Rome were detained in such a way that guards could prevent them from reading or even interacting with other prisoners (*Life of Tiberius* 61, L19 [ca. 120 CE]). It is unclear how such solitary confinement was accomplished; there are no obvious architectural elements in the Tullian Prison that would readily allow for installation of barriers (and we do not know what the other prisons of Rome looked like), though this does not preclude the possibility that wooden dividers were installed in the lower chamber. In fact, in his epitome of Verrius Flaccus's first-century BCE work, Festus indicates that the Tullian Prison had a secure housing unit referred to as the *robus*, where prisoners were segregated, named after the hard oak boxes (*arcis robusteis*) to which criminals were once condemned, though Calpurnius Flaccus uses the term *robus* to refer simply to the Tullianum's lower, darker room (*On the Meanings of Words* 17 s.v. Robum [second century CE]; Calpurnius Flaccus, *Declamation* 4, L46 [second century CE]). Cicero, too, wrote of prisoners being separated "incommunicado" into cells—literally boxes (*arcae*); interestingly, hanging wooden boxes or cages continued in European use through the late medieval and early modern period, for instance at the prison in Mont St. Michel, Normandy (*On Behalf of Milo* 60 [52 BCE]; Cadoux 2008, 219; Johnston 2000, 8–9). Perhaps this is what Suetonius had in mind when speaking of punitive isolation within the civic prison at Rome. It is worth noting that the Latin word at issue here—*arca*—is also used to denote a coffin. Even if not intended, the double entendre would be hard for a native speaker to miss.

A further, gendered aspect of prisoner separation appears in a law of the emperor Constantius from 340 CE. The law provides that both males and females should be confined as punishment for the crimes for which they had been convicted but that they should be detained in separate facilities (*CTh* 9.3.3, L72). This evidence is admittedly late, more likely coinciding with use of the prisons at Corinth, Rome, and Tiberias than some of the other facilities that underlie our analysis; moreover, it is of course possible that in different periods and locations, the operative lines of separation differed. We note, however, that the evidence for one particular type of separation is later still: our first evidence for a *jail*—a purpose-built facility explicitly intended solely for pretrial detention—is from 539 or 540 CE, when a bishop named Paul consecrated a "holy detention center" in Gerasa (Jerash, Jordan). According to its dedicatory inscription, the gleaming new facility was built precisely to keep different types of prisoners separate, "and in the name of the lord he blessed this [detention center] to be for all the accused [*hupaitiōn*] apart from the condemned, so that no person found guilty [*katadikon*] could be put there with impunity, nor anyone could be transferred from the detention center to the prison of the condemned [*eis tēn tōn katakritōn fulakēn*]" (*SEG* 35.1571, D168 [539–40 CE]; Hillner 2015, 287). One facility, in other words, was a jail, while the other was a prison—in the modern sense of both terms. It has been repeated over and again that the jail has always existed since time immemorial, while the prison only came along much later. So far as the evidence suggests, the opposite is true.

Finally, prisons were architecturally designed as spaces of punishment. On the one hand, it was, and still is, rather obvious—both to ancients and moderns alike—that these spaces were unpleasant; they were, at base, a dark, dank, cold, feces-filled pit. The punitive aspect of this displeasure influenced even the language that people use to describe carceral spaces—numerous sites carry a name which highlights their punitive nature—names like "Dark Hole" and "Prison of Oblivion" (*Acts of Shmona and Gurya* 30, L1 [310 CE]; Procopius, *History of the Wars* 1.5, L157 [event 496, account 533 CE]). In this, they follow a long tradition. Already in 400/399 BCE, we hear of limited-term incarceration used as a formal punishment (Lysias, *Against Andocides* 20–25, L219). Later in the same century, Plato imagined an ideal city having three prisons: "one that is public, in the area of the agora, for general offenders," a second similarly within the city's administrative district called "The Reformatory," and a third outside the city, "having as its name some word for punishment [*timōrias echōn epōnumian fēmēn tina*]" (*Laws* 908, L18 [360–347 BCE]). Centuries later, a man named Zebatus wrote a petition from a prison in Seleucid Maresha, claiming that he was writing "from The Punishments" (*ek tōn timō[riōn]*)—apparently a name for the facility where he had been incarcerated for three years already (*CIIP* 4.3.3689, D170 [second century BCE]). We return to Zebatus below; for now, it is sufficient to note that the idea of prisons as punitive spaces endures across much of Mediterranean antiquity.

Woven together, these strands suggest an ideology of punitive variability: prisons were designed so that incarcerators could increase or decrease punitive aspects through material changes in the time, location, and nature of detention. Put another way, the ability to dial up the degree of punishment through variable forms and spaces of incarceration, often taken as an innovative hallmark of the modern prison, is in fact quite ancient. Archaeological evidence from civic, military, worker, and amphitheater prisons show separation into more and less harsh venues, and literary sources speak to their effects. For instance, in the third- or fourth-century CE *Passion of Perpetua and Felicity*, Christians bribe prison guards to move the martyr and her companions to a less taxing part of the civic prison, with cleaner air and readier access to light (1, L15 [third to fourth centuries CE]). Variable conditions are not simply a fantasy of martyrdom accounts, either—around the turn of the third century CE, the jurist Paul prescribed that wardens should be punished if they accepted a bribe to allow prisoners to be held in better conditions (D. 48.3.8, L108 [late second to early third century CE]). A Syriac text from Edessa speaks to some of the built features of prisons in 310 CE, along with the tactics that prison staff used to coerce those within. Guards "stopped up the doors and windows before them, so that they could not see the light at all; and they were three days in the month of August in the summer, and no one brought them bread and they drank no water," remaining in such conditions from August to November (*Acts of Shmona and Gurya* 27–36, L1). When the literary and archaeological material are placed in conversation with each other, we see that windows and doors did more than mediate access to prisoners inside—they also allowed administrators to control the modality and degree of punishment within a carceral space.

Worker prisons show similar features related to punitive variability. In his treatise *On Agriculture*, Columella expresses a concern similar to Constantine's about the need for additional security measures after sunset in secure rooms used to contain enslaved workers. Columella distinguishes between two different types of spaces: small rooms (*cellae*), which were appropriate to lock enslaved people who were not typically held in chains during the day, and slaves who typically wore chains during the day should ideally be kept "in an underground workers prison (*subterraneum ergastulum*), as wholesome as possible, receiving light through a number of narrow windows built so high from the ground that they cannot be reached with the hand" (1.6.3, L47 [first century CE]). The idealized space, in other words, looked like a real one: it sounds like a rather precise description of the military prison at Lambaesis. Columella's business was teaching enslavers how to ply their despotic task with efficiency, and along the way to put a positive spin on dire and inhuman practices of mastery (Howley 2025). From the position of the enslaved worker, on the other hand, it is hard to imagine much comfort in the notion that, after each day of body-destroying labor, the subterranean facility where they spent the night was "as wholesome as possible." Enslaved and imprisoned people were bound for divergent ideological reasons, but they were often bound using identical technologies. In Columella's despotic prescriptions we see the cross-fertilization of enslaver tactics and carceral technologies.

The architecture of carceral spaces can be interpreted fruitfully in light of literary, documentary, and visual materials, allowing glimpses at broader ideologies of incarceration across Mediterranean antiquity. The five features outlined here are distinct but mutually reinforcing: centrality, surveillance, separation, depth, and punitive variability. Together, they corroborate evidence indicating that the prison was a state-sponsored good—a fundamental, ubiquitous, yet carefully hidden aspect of civic life—and that incarceration was often conceived of in punitive terms.

While there is not yet relevant archaeological evidence from Ptolemaic Egypt, as we shall see, each of these themes are articulated similarly in documentary sources, the other broad archive that forms a basis for this project. Having investigated spaces of incarceration and the ideologies that they appear to encode, we now turn to sources that document what they might have felt like to inhabit, often in the words of prisoners themselves.

PART TWO

Experiences and Perceptions

3

Experiences of Incarceration

Kalief Browder spent three years in pretrial detention at New York City's Rikers Island jail. He spent seven hundred of those days in solitary confinement, at a facility famous enough for its horrors that the Department of Justice took action against what it called a "culture of violence and overuse of punitive segregation" against a population of detainees, 85 percent of whom have received no sentence (Department of Justice 2021). Even as of 2021, 30 percent of those detainees will wait more than a year before receiving a judgment, in conditions designed to isolate men, and to break them. Rikers broke Kalief Browder. He committed suicide on June 6, 2015. He was twenty-two years old, accused of stealing a backpack. His pretrial detention proved, in effect, to be a death sentence.

Was Kalief Browder being "punished"? No, not in a strict legal sense—he was in jail, having only been accused of a crime. But at some point, the question itself becomes meaningless, a distinction without a difference. We hide behind impotent technicalities when we insist that prolonged pretrial incarceration is not a form of punishment, denying the lived experience of prisoners and diverting blame to a "broken system." In broad strokes, this system has been in place for over two thousand years at least. Perhaps a system that has been "broken" since antiquity is, in fact, functioning as designed, even if that design is veiled, misnamed, or unintentional. It is cold comfort to the Browder family to know that Kalief "wasn't technically being punished." If it is not already clear to readers why we choose to weigh lived experience and theoretical ideals separately, perhaps this example clarifies the issue. Whether incarceration is punitive is a matter of whose perspective we choose to privilege, and in the case of this peculiar and abiding institution, intentions and effects have only rarely aligned.

Punitive aspects of incarceration can be viewed from several angles, each with attendant questions and offering different vantage points. The intentions of lawmakers, jurists, and judges differ not only from the experiences of prisoners, but also from societal discourses about what incarceration is and how it ought to be used. In chapter 1 we argued that at least in contexts where Roman law dominated, incarceration was regularly intended as a form of punishment by legal experts and political leaders. We now turn directly to an issue that we've tried to hold firmly in mind all along: the cage as viewed by those inside of it. While this chapter could cover almost endless topics, we pick three because they offer sometimes overlooked angles of analysis. In order to understand individual prisoner experiences, we attend to bodily concerns — especially death, hunger, sexual violence, and the cold, damp, and foul environment of ancient prisons. To understand how individual experiences relate to broader societal questions, we consider the role of food, both food insecurity and consumption. But first, we begin with a section that picks up and counterbalances chapter 1: the experience of incarceration as punishment.

EXPERIENCE OF INCARCERATION AS PUNITIVE

Here we argue that prisoners often experienced their incarceration as punishment, and that broader society often understood it as such. Moreover, we detail aspects of time and space that incarcerators in antiquity calibrated to have specific punitive effects. We are not the first to forward such an argument. In her magisterial book, Pilar Pavón Torrejón (2003) argues for the punitive use of incarceration as a normal part of the ancient Mediterranean world, alongside other uses such as repression, prevention, as well as pretrial segregation and custodial functions (186–208). More recently, Alberto De Simoni (2022) has argued that "For prison to be a punishment it needed not to be recognized as such by a statute, rather it needed to be *perceived* as punishment," offering a broad selection of literary sources in support of the widespread perception of penal incarceration from classical Athenian and imperial Roman contexts (32). Here we introduce a number of documentary sources to the conversation, framed in a new way to show that they point in the same direction as literary materials, suggesting that incarceration was widely understood as punishment by carceral victims and societies alike. Nearly half the documentary evidence directly relating to ancient Mediterranean incarceration are letters from captives themselves, on their behalf, or about them. In most of these cases it is no longer possible to determine the intention of the prisoner's captors; more often, the prisoner's own description of their plight is readily accessible, which we submit is at least as important—and qualitatively more important if the aim is to understand incarceration as experienced by its victims. Across the archive we hear repeatedly hear prisoners describe their captivity as a form of punishment. Consider, for instance, a letter from the Zeno archive in which two prisoners admit they committed a crime and express their understanding of their time in prison as punishment for that crime.

To Zeno, from the swineherds Petenouris, Samoys, greetings. We beg you, have mercy on us—sure, we are being punished for our sins [*hēmartomen tetimōrēmetha*], but no one is sinless—so that the pigs don't die, on which we depend! So you must understand that you are making trial of us. You know that we have been here already for three days. Will you not let us free to work, or to depart for the pigs, so that they won't die with us stuck in prison? For we have nothing that we need, and we will die in this way. So you must consider if it seems to you right to release us. (P. Cair. Zen. 3.59495, D141 [263–229 BCE])

These swineherds wrote to Zeno to request mercy and release from prison, which they referred to explicitly as a punishment for their actions. They admit having committed wrongdoing, but they seek release through a desperate plea—if their punishment is not brought to an end, pigs who they depend on will die needlessly. The nature of these men's transgression is not clear, nor is the capacity in which they were incarcerated. We know only that they thought Zeno had the ability to affect their release.

Another document from the same archive betrays a similar situation: a letter from an Egyptian man who failed to fulfill contractual obligations to finish work on time and was imprisoned as a result. Zeno's agency is somewhat clearer in this instance—it is likely that the other party to the contract was Zeno himself.

I have repeatedly asked you to be released and to be discharged, so that I can be released and that I can see. For it won't be the case that forty days pass without the work being finished. So that you don't distrust, in the presence of people should you prefer, I will write an oath to you in Crocodilopolis or in Memphis to finish the current work and whatever else you should require. For I have been punished enough [*hikanōs gar tetimōrēmai*]. I ask you not to overlook me [*deomai sou mē me periidēis*] ... (P. Cair. Zen. 4.59639, D213 [263–229 BCE])

This letter brings together a number of themes we see elsewhere: request for release, the intersection of economic debt and incarceration, language of "overlooking," (p. 165–168) and the experience of incarceration as punitive. Regardless of the specific legal rationale, the letter writer considered the prison itself to be punishment for his deviance and wrote "I have been punished enough." There is an entire vernacular theory of justice implied in this astonishing statement, one whose contours we can only begin to glimpse, juxtaposing an admitted guilt with a subjective sense of penal proportionality. These are Ptolemaic documents, but the notion that prisons are fundamentally penal facilities persists in letters from subsequent periods as well. Perhaps a century later, a man with an Aramaic name in the Idumean city of Maresha scratched a letter into a limestone slab. The Greek is poorly rendered and fragmentary, the letter opening mid-sentence with,

... who is also called Zebatus, sent this from The Punishments [*apestalkan ek tōn timō[riōn]*]. Health and life. I believe to know that I am innocently near death, since it was three years ago that I was arrested, and because Theon came to have my possessions ... (CIIP 4.3.3689, D170 [second century BCE])

The startling letter continues, and merits further sustained attention elsewhere. For our purposes it is worth noting that, while the addressee of this plea is lost, we know the place from which Zebatus writes and how he characterizes the space: he is in prison, a place he calls "The Punishments," where he has been held for three years as a result of his failure to pay a fine. Was this man being *punished* for his failure to pay up? While later Roman lawyers (and modern historians) might have disagreed or equivocated, for Zebatus the answer was clear: he viewed his time in prison as punitive, an ideal blended even into the name of the place from which he begged for release.

This idea of prison as a place of punishment, and one named accordingly, appears across the Mediterranean during the period under discussion. As discussed, already in the mid-fourth century BCE, Plato imagined an ideal society with three different types of prison. The first, at the civic center, accords rather well with the prison as it seems to have functioned in classical Athens: serving to hold both people in pretrial detention along with people serving a punishment of incarceration. Plato's characters envision two other facilities as well, serving further purposes.

> For anyone found guilty (of impiety), the court must impose [*timatō to dikastērion*] one penalty [*timēma*] for each act of impiety. Imprisonment is to be imposed in all cases [*desmos men oun huparchetō pasi*]. There should be three prisons [*desmōtēriōn*] in the state: one that is public, in the area of the agora, for general offenders [*henos men koinou tois pleistois peri agoran*], for the safe custody of a large number of bodies [*somatōn*]; another near the meeting place of the Nocturnal Council, given the name "The Reformatory [*sōfronistērion*]"; and another in the middle of the countryside, in the barest and most desolate place possible, and having as its name some word for punishment [*timōrias echōn epōnumian fēmēn tina*]. (Plato, *Laws* 907e–908a, L18 [360–347 BCE])

Plato imagines "The Reformatory" prison situated in the city, near the seat of government, and his prescription belongs within a broader set of ideals about how to cure, improve, or educate people out of their ignorance through a minimum term of five years of incarceration in that facility (Allen 2000, 71, 247–51, 280; Hillner 2015, 28–38; Abolafia 2021, 68). Importantly, the third proposed prison, which Plato envisions "in the middle of the countryside, in the barest and most desolate place possible" is explicitly connected with punishment and intended to "have as its name some word for punishment [*timōria*]."

Plato's ideas about punitive and reformatory incarceration predate the period covered by this book, but thinkers exploited his ideas throughout antiquity. In the first century CE, Philo of Alexandria wrote a commentary on the biblical figure of Joseph, paying close attention to the character's time incarcerated in Egypt and his subsequent career as a prison warden. Philo makes no distinction between Roman and Pharaonic carceral systems, seeing the prison as a transhistorical and transregional phenomenon in most of its particulars, with little change except for one implemented by the biblical patriarch himself. He writes that when Joseph was placed in charge of the prison, he changed it from a place of punishment to a place of correction—noting specifically that, as a result, the space could no longer be called just a "prison" (*heirktē*) but that it had become instead a "reformatory" (*sōfronistērion*), using precisely Plato's name for the institution (*On Joseph* 15–16, L12 [mid-first century CE]). Elsewhere, Philo explicitly imagined prisons and millhouses as places of carceral punishment, again understanding practices known from his own Roman provincial context to be universal and transhistorical (*On Dreams* 4, L186 [mid-first century CE]).

A Platonist of the following generation, Plutarch, reports that Cicero also raised the idea of penal life sentences of incarceration in late republican Rome, as a response to the Catilinarian conspiracy (*Life of Cicero* 20–21, L85 [early second century CE]). Plutarch picks up on Plato's distinction, as well, relating the purpose of incarceration to both the nature of the crime and the status of the convict—his Cicero proposes that, for Roman senators, a life sentence in prison was the most "extreme penalty" feasible—likely because people of high social status (*honestiores*) were typically not punished in a way that violated their bodies, rendering terminal incarceration a logical alternative to maiming or executing the elite (Garnsey 1970, 140–52; Robinson 1995, 39; 2007, 106; Harries 2007, 36). Since the conspirators could not be reformed, Plutarch's Cicero suggests, life sentences of retribution were among the "best practices" of the late republican period, again following the Platonic trichotomy (Eisenhut 1972, 270–72). This was neither an aberration, an oddity, or a one-off: almost 150 years earlier the playwright Plautus had already invoked the idea of life in prison, and a century and a half hence, the historian Josephus would report that the emperor Vespasian granted mercy to one revolting Judaean general, who was condemned to lifetime imprisonment (*desmois aiōniois*) instead of execution in an imperial triumph (Plautus, *The Rope* 713–16, L178 [205–184 BCE]; Josephus, *Judaean War* 7.434, L292 [ca. 75 CE]).

While the prison offered a unique mechanism for punishing high-status individuals without violating their bodily integrity, literary sources reiterate what we learn from documents: low-status individuals were also subject to its torments. In his telling of the myth of Pero and Micon, Pliny the Elder goes so far as to stress the low status of the daughter, even though the point of the story, for him, was not to bemoan the use of the prison as class-based punishment but to record an example of filial piety in the extreme. "A plebeian woman of low position and therefore unknown, who had just given birth to a child, had permission to visit her mother who had been shut up in prison as a punishment" (*Natural History* 7.36, L150 [ca. 77 CE]). Read alongside the documentary of evidence analyzed here, literary sources support the idea that Romans envisioned the prison as a flexible institution capable of punishing the bodies of different classes of people in divergent ways. In an idealized penal order, these methods were calibrated not only to the crime but to the identity of the convicted.

A similar idea endured into Late Antiquity. Procopius, a late Roman historian, offers a glimpse into (at least his understanding of) Sasanian carceral practices, which were themselves legible within the Platonic and Roman penal tradition. An account set in 496/98 CE tells of a cross-dressing escape from the "Prison of Oblivion" in Persia, where a king was said to have been incarcerated as a form of punishment. Like the Catilinarian conspirators, the king's eligibility for a life sentence, rather than for capital punishment, is explicitly predicated on his status—in Procopius's words, his "kingly blood" (*History of the Wars* 1.5–6, L157 [ca. 565 CE]). These sources give a sense of the available parameters, and the attempt to ensure that retribution was carefully calibrated not only to the crime being punished but to the status of the individual concerned. Interestingly, Plato's word for a "reformatory" prison (*sōfronistērion*) appears abbreviated in a tax account from the sixth century CE, suggesting the possibility that a prison following the Platonic pattern was actually implemented almost nine centuries after the Athenian philosopher wrote about it, and—according to the standard Foucauldian account—more than a millennium before such reformatory prisons were allegedly "born" (P. Cair. Masp. 1.67057, D182 [551–52 CE]; Hillner 2015, 147).

The Platonic notion of prison as reformatory has an important reception in imperial Roman contexts (Hillner 2015, 45–63). Writing *On Anger*, first-century Stoic philosopher and statesman Seneca the Younger argues that "different considerations should in different cases restrain us." In certain cases, he argues, "we resort to the sword and to capital punishment," whereas "an act that deserves the censure of a very light flogging we punish by chains, the prison, and starvation" (3.32.2–3, L93 [ca. 41–50 CE]). In Seneca's estimation, the three punishments—chains, prison, and starvation—are virtually synonymous, available for implementation, and harsher than a physical beating. In fact, Seneca envisions an entire spectrum of punishment, each of which are reformatory in intention. "I will resort to every form of punishment [*genus poenae*], but only as a remedy." Occasional but regular errors can be rehabilitated with private rebuke followed by public disgrace. More serious offenses can be reformed through exile, and "if your wickedness has become deep rooted, demanding harsher remedies to meet your case, we shall have to resort to public chains and the prison [*vincula publica et carcer*]." Only in the case of inveterate criminality does Seneca think that reform is not possible, at which point capital punishment is justified as a form of pity over the incurable mind (*On Anger* 3.32, L93 [ca. 41–50 CE]; cf. Hillner 2015, 52–55). A century later, Calpurnius Flaccus suggested prisoners convicted of parricide ought to linger in prison for a precisely calibrated amount of time (one year, in this case), and only thereafter be properly executed (*Declamations* 4, L46 [second century CE]). Here, it seems, both time served and execution were intended as punitive measures. These literary sources offer further context to the prisoner letters discussed above: the notion that the prison could be used to punish crime was widespread, including finely calibrated modalities of describing its punitive aims.

Such close calibration of time, space, and culpability is not solely a literary ideal but even shows up in sources like a dedicatory inscription from northwest Lydia (western Turkey) in the third century CE, given on behalf of a prisoner named Theodorus who had served his time, and thanked the gods for his salvation from prison. It reads: "in the month of Panemos, according to the enlightenment given by the gods by Zeus and Men the Great Artemidoros: 'I have punished Theodorus in respect to his eyes in consequence of the sins, which he committed.'" Theodorus goes on to explain the nature of his crimes and the sacrifices that he has made to expiate the guilt. The inscription ends with Theodorus claiming, "I have Zeus as my legal advocate." The god (or more likely, a priest who serves the god) responds:

> "Behold, I had blinded him in consequence for his actions, but now he has made good his mistakes by propitiating the gods and by erecting an inscribed stele."
>
> Asked by the council: "I am merciful because my stele was erected on the day that I appointed. You may open the prison, I release the condemned [*anuxais tēn fulakēn, exafiō ton katadikon*] after one year and ten months have passed." (SEG 38.1237, D167 [235–36 CE]; trans. Malay 1988, 151–52)

Here, in the middle of the third century CE, we see a rather clear example of incarceration that is understood to be both reformatory and limited-term. While the inscription reflects a bit of ritual performance, it also implies the fixed place of the limited-term carceral sentencing in the social imagination of Roman East, as argued by Angelos Chaniotis (2009). Two facets in particular are worth noting. First, the inscription situates the sentence not in a convict labor camp but rather in a civic prison. Second, the inscription calibrates specifically between the number of crimes (three), the severity of each, and the amount of time in which Theodorus was held in the prison as part of his punishment. A curiously specific sentence is pronounced: twenty-two months. While the inscription describes a scene within a religious literary frame, it clearly reflects some judicial context; it seems unlikely that Theodorus invented from whole cloth the crimes and times detailed in his stele. It is yet another example of time in prison as calibrated according to crimes committed.

Beyond calibrating time, we have evidence for Romans particularly implementing spatial sanctions in order to heighten the punitive aspect of incarceration. For example, two of Tiberius's biographers record that the emperor used the prison to neutralize enemies and otherwise segregate unwanted members of society for long periods of time—up to seven years, in some instances (Cassius Dio, *Roman History* 59.6.1–3, L126 [ca. 230 CE]). Suetonius adds that the emperor also prescribed spatial sanctions within the prison, such that "some of those in custody in prison were denied not only the comfort of studying, but even the privilege of conversing and talking together" (*Life of Tiberius* 61, L19 [121 CE]). While some carceral facilities have small cells or subdividers that would allow for segregation within the prison, Suetonius does not tell us enough about how separation was implemented to compare it directly to modern instantiations of the same. Nevertheless, it is difficult to find a modern English phrase to describe these spatial aspects of penal incarceration in the early first century CE beyond what it appears to be: the earliest attestation of punitive solitary confinement.

Sources describe punitive isolation of prisoners from the first century CE through the sixth; we offer just one more example, which draws together punitive time and punitive space. It comes from a context of monastic confinement, where punitive uses of space and spatial segregation were often applied (Hillner 2015, 188–89). In the early fourth century CE, an influential Christian monk named Pachomius established a community north of Thebes, Egypt, and a set of rules for the men focused on holiness, asceticism, and labor, producing goods that could be used by the community, or sold to support it. Biographies of Pachomius quickly spread, relating stories of his sanctity and the rigor that he imposed on monks under his charge. One recounts the story of a monk who, having been charged with weaving one mat per day, instead produced two and displayed them in front of his cell in hopes of attracting the eye, and the praise, of the monastery superior. On seeing the mats, however, and realizing that the monk labored in search of earthly praise rather than "the praise of God," Pachomius grows angry and prescribes the monk's punishment: he was to stand behind the other brothers at prayer time and in their midst during mealtime, begging for forgiveness. Thereafter Pachomius "ordered him to be locked up in his cell for five months, make two mats every day, eat only bread with salt, and none of the brothers to visit him" (*Paralipomena* 34, L201 [ca. fourth century CE]; Hillner 2015, 189–91). The brother's crime related to commodity production and his punishment was calibrated to fit that crime— he was sentenced to a limited-term punitive sentence of five months of solitary confinement, including enhanced labor obligations and punitive food rations. The story weaves together punitive intention and experience, along with punitive uses of space, along with a goal of reforming the offender.

We have argued that treatments of ancient incarceration to date have tended to privilege legal and literary sources, and have been prone to mistaking normative discussions for descriptions of how prisons functioned in reality. Literary materials have a lot to teach us and, as we argued above, in some cases they corroborate other types of evidence, like the punitive variability and ideology of separation embedded in ancient prison architecture, and even the common perception of prisons as punitive facilities. John Bauschatz and Brian Muhs have added significantly to our understanding of carceral practices as seen in documentary sources from the Ptolemaic period, and Sofía Torallas Tovar has analyzed late ancient Egyptian sources in a number of brief, important studies (Bauschatz 2007, 2013; Muhs 2018; Torallas Tovar 1999, 2003, 2006). Documentary sources have rarely been allowed to control the discussion, however, and in the few instances where documents from the Roman imperial era have been explored extensively, Mommsen's conclusion that incarceration was a marginal aspect of ancient society has been uncritically appropriated as an interpretive lens and, in the end, a Procrustean bed. Documentary sources do not simply offer different information; they offer a different kind of knowledge about experiences and ideologies of incarceration.

In what follows, we mine the collection of documentary sources related to incarceration in the Mediterranean from 300 BCE to 600 CE, pausing on only the most relevant pieces useful for the task at hand. Having written at some length about types of prisons and the ideology that these spaces encode, we turn in the remaining chapters to the most proximate data available, aiming to elucidate some aspects of the experience of incarceration in the ancient world as seen in prisoner letters and petitions, warrants, bail bonds, orders of appearance and release, and the like. We outline the personal experience of incarceration with respect to bodily concerns and the complex relationship between food and incarceration—material also covered by Jens-Uwe Krause (1996), though from a different angle and with reference predominantly to literary rather than documentary evidence (271–301).

BODILY CONCERNS

The intention of an incarcerator often has little effect on the experience of the incarcerated. Behind Stephen Duguid's question "Can prisons work?" and Angela Davis's "Are prisons obsolete?" lies a fundamental problem that appears in antiquity as much as modernity: more often than not, even a humanistic plan to rehabilitate someone through incarceration has the effect of restraining them in a facility that they experience as torture (Duguid 2000; Davis 2003). The problem is particularly acute in the ancient Mediterranean, and startlingly well-attested in our sources: carceral facilities exposed prisoners to tortuous environments with immensely heightened risks of hunger, sexual violence, and death.

Death

Prisons were treacherous places to be, no matter whether a person was under carceral control for custodial, coercive, or punitive, or even reformatory reasons. The documentary and literary record is replete with reports of prisoner deaths, and also with documents in which people express fear of prison on the grounds that incarceration itself presented an imminent mortal risk. For instance, P. Oxy. 43.3104 is a large, professionally produced notice of a prisoner's death: a tax farmer named Aurelius Epinicus who was incarcerated in 228 CE (D15). The report introduces the deceased by both his Latin and Egyptian names, and records that he had purchased the right to collect a 2.5 percent tax on woolen objects. Aurelius was incarcerated in late April of 228 CE, likely because he failed to fulfill his tax farming obligation. The report states that he survived only fifty-six days in prison, dying on June 24. His incarceration for a relatively minor financial infraction ultimately proved to be a death sentence. A roughly contemporary source offers another glimpse at the practice of registering the death of prisoners, this time in the North African city of Carthage whose bishop Cyprian wrote to fellow clergy about incarcerated Christians, clarifying that they should be considered martyrs even if they weren't executed publicly. Cyprian specifies that even those who die in prison are to be honored as martyrs for the faith, and that a record should be kept of the exact dates when their incarceration caused their death (*Letter* 12, L23 [ca. 250 CE]). The practice, begun somewhat earlier by a man named Tertullus, resulted in a new calendrical system for Christians—a system modeled directly on the form of recordkeeping produced upon the death of prisoners like Aurelius Epinicus.

Another document from the mid-third century CE speaks to the danger of a swift death in prison. SB 16.12949 is a fragmentary record of court proceedings before the Roman governor (*prefect*) of Egypt, who adjourned the case before him while relevant documents could be located (D62 [207–68 CE]). The governor ordered that the defendant be incarcerated while the archival search took place, eliciting a request from his lawyer that the defendant be released on bail instead, "so that he may be able to remain alive." Embedded in each of these sources is the assumption that prisons are potentially lethal places—even a short custodial stay ran the very real risk of death.

Even so, a swift death was not the only possibility; some individuals lingered quite a while before succumbing. In P. Petr. 3.36, a prisoner writes to a Ptolemaic city manager (*epimelētēs*), complaining that he has been left to suffer in prison for ten months already, and is on the verge of death. With a palpable sense of anguish and terror, he begs, "I pray for you not to let me perish of hunger in prison, but write to the governor about these things or send me to him . . . in order that I may be saved" (D3 [218–217 BCE]). Similarly, in 177 BCE, a man incarcerated in "Big Prison" at Oxyrhynchus wrote that he was imprisoned unjustly, having already been acquitted of the accused crime. "I have up to now been confined already for three years," he writes, "lacking the necessities." The letter breaks off in the middle of his request, ending with "therefore, so that I may not waste away in [prison], neglected, contrary to all decency, I beg you with every plea to order . . ." (P. Coll. Youtie 1.12, D4). Perhaps six hundred years later, another Egyptian prisoner—this one in Thebes and writing in Coptic—expressed a familiar plea: "I am dying in prison, and I still do not know why" (BKU 1.144, D210 [sixth–seventh centuries CE]; Torallas Tovar 2003, 218–19).

The earliest known papyri attest a concern over death in prison, and the theme is common among late Roman literary sources. Both legislators like Constantine and orators like Libanius, for instance, speak to the reality of innocent people suffering at length and ultimately expiring in their cell without ever having been convicted of a crime (*CI* 9.4.1, L133 [320 CE], Libanius, *Oration* 45, L52 [386 CE]). Ammianus Marcellinus even tells the story of a wealthy woman who preferred to commit suicide rather than encounter the dangers of prison (*History* 28.1.47; Pavón

Torrejón 2004, 119). Late literary attention to the issue should not be confused with its early absence—the papyri show clearly that the issue remained across the time covered by our book, and John Bauschatz (2013) detailed the prevalence of long-term detention without trial or bail under the Ptolemaic regime, writing that "the Ptolemies do not seem to have made allowances for prisoners for whom no bail was posted or for whom no trial arrangements were made. They doubtless realized that such detentions occasionally took place but did little to prevent them" (222). Despite Bauschatz's assertion to the contrary, the Ptolemies were manifestly not unique in this practice. Rather, among the various regions, cultures, and periods covered by this book, perhaps the most common bodily concern expressed by prisoners and imprisoners alike is the heightened risk of death for people suffering incarceration, and the extraordinary common fact that prisoners died after long periods inside—even those "only" in pretrial detention.

Hunger

Next to worries about death, the most common complaint of prisoners in the papyri is that they were hungry. While food insecurity was doubtless of concern to nearly all prisoners, the issue was rendered more acute for people far from home who lacked a local network of support to bring them supplies. The connection between hunger and incarceration was so clear throughout our time period that Hesychios, a lexicographer in late antique Alexandria, offers "the prison" (*to desmōtērion*) as a gloss for a word meaning "the place with no food at all" (Hesychius, α 5831 *apasiton* [ca. 400–600 CE]; Curbera 2018, 14–15). At the other end of our timeframe, three men who had been summoned to Philadelphia in the mid-third century BCE wrote to Zeno, an influential retainer for an aristocrat who later became an aristocrat himself, with this very concern. "Rhodon, Menippos, and Pausanias send greetings to Zeno. We beg you to ask Philoskos [chief treasurer/*oikonomos* of Arsinoites] that when we arrive, we might receive judgment from Dionysios concerning the accusations against us, lest we be destroyed by hunger in prison, given that we are foreigners, but rather, having received judgment through your intercession, we might obtain justice" (PSI 4.419, D57 [263–229 BCE]). These men's worry was clear: they might accede to their summons only to be thrown into a local prison to await trial. Given that they were foreigners with no local network of support, they worried that they would die from lack of supplies while they waited. These men's plight was hardly unique—in fact, it seems that foreigners were especially vulnerable to the dangers of imprisonment. A woman visiting Oxyrhynchus in the early Ptolemaic period ended up in jail after being attacked by a local; in her complaint to the king, she specifically notes that, in her view, the entire incident was motivated by the fact that she was a stranger in the city (P. Enteux. 83, D71 [221 BCE]). Similarly, a professional grain measurer from outside Alexandria wrote to Zeno with a similar request as the men above, asking that he send "a cloak or some money, as much as you please," because he "has no one in this city [whom he knows]," and that it would take time for his family to sail down the Nile to care for him while he was in prison (P. Cair. Zen. 3.59519, D134 [263–229 BCE]). It is worth noting that even the centrality of Mediterranean prisons within cities does not mean that incarceration did not entail geographic displacement; confinement in a city far from home would be no less jarring or arduous for someone familiar with rural farm life than confinement in a contemporary, ruralized prison is for city dwellers. Incarceration means displacement and isolation, in body and from society.

Even prisoners with local networks of support often express an acute concern over hunger. A Byzantine potsherd containing a letter written in Coptic speaks to the bind that two women found themselves in while incarcerated. They write, "we were at pains and wrote to you, and you have forgotten us in the captivity where we are . . . For as the Lord lives, if you don't reach us today with the money, there will be no life left in us. Send the rations for us to the jailer and give loaves and . . ." (O. Mon. Epiph. 177, D139 [sixth–seventh centuries CE]). It seems the women were left in prison as collateral for the debts of their husbands, who were released to work and pay off what they owed. As part of the deal the men were tasked with sending food to their wives in prison, but they had failed to do so. As such, the women threatened to end their collateral incarceration, sending the guards directly to the husbands, who would presumably be arrested and incarcerated while the women went free. In a similar way, centuries earlier, a woman named Tryphas wrote to her son and daughter, reminding them to feed the slaves (lit., "the bodies") that she had left in prison as debt collateral. Tryphas was waiting for grain prices to rise so that she could make a bigger profit on her crop before she recovered the people whom she enslaved and then imprisoned on account of her own personal debt. She reminds her children, "I have often written to you to care for the slaves. They will die in the prison" (BGU 16.2618, D146 [7 BCE]).

In the documentary record, across the time period covered by our book, we find that the most dangerous way to be incarcerated was far from family and, even worse, in poverty. "I am in great need," complained a man named Poseidonios in the late third century BCE, "and I am very poor, and I perceive that I am close to death in the prison because of my lack [of basic necessities]" (P. Petr. 3.36r, D147 [218–217 BCE]). A roughly contemporary document echoes the same themes: P. Petr. 2.19(2) is a fragmentary papyrus containing two petitions from prisoners who complain that they will die if they are not supplied with necessities. One man appears to have been condemned to a work camp (*ergastērion*) and complains that that he won't last much longer there before he dies—he claims that he "is being destroyed in the prison [*en tēi fulakēi kataftharēnai*]"; apparently the conditions of the work exacerbated his caloric needs, which were not being met (D108 [260–200 BCE]).

Documents also commonly attest cases in which a single incarcerated person plunged an entire family into hunger. P. Cair. Masp. 1.67020 is a sixth-century CE petition for release of a group of friends held in a public prison. The petitioners offer a number of reasons for the request, including a pathetic plea for the welfare of the prisoners' children. "You must be appealed to through your innate love for God to act on their behalf, and to order their release, first because of the profiting of your soul and then because of the great poverty that they have, and the lack of food for their children" (D112 [566–73 CE]). Besides, the petitioner argues, the "season demands the family members for the cultivation," arguing that prolonged incarceration at public expense was deleterious to the family and community alike; it was time for the harvest and, as a result, their labor would benefit the public. On November 20, 464 CE, a prisoner named Aurelis Macarius petitioned the public defender of his section of the city, claiming to be unjustly incarcerated and promising to pay any properly documented debt (which his accuser had failed to produce). The brother of his (by then deceased) employer charged Macarius with a debt and confiscated eight of his cattle as collateral, placing him in prison for three months, during which time the man was unable to receive a hearing in his case. In the absence of a hearing or judgment, the remainder of Macarius's herd died (P. Oxy. 6.902, D16 [464 CE]). While both these sources come from the later end of our timeframe, complaints about the economic hardship caused by even temporary incarceration span the period from 300 BCE to 600 CE, demonstrating in the starkest of terms that incarceration affected not only the accused and condemned, but also that their loss of economic production caused ripple effects, which endangered the dependents of those in prison. The problem persists even today, where modern studies linking food security and incarceration push us to think about such impacts not only on incarcerated individuals but also their household, especially children (Cox and Wallace 2016). Sources speak regularly of the imprisonment of a male primary wage earner causing a cascade of precarity leading even to family reorientations in which, Libanius reports, "wives, sisters, and daughters who were supported *by* them before their imprisonment have to become their nourishers now." Prisoners are "doubly afflicted, by the actual imprisonment and by the manner of it," in which rationed food is "much below their needs," and families step in to fill the gap. Libanius reports that "ugly and aged women" are reduced to begging to feed themselves and their incarcerated family members, while physically desirable women sell their bodies to buy sustenance. "For the prisoners this is even more bitter than their imprisonment, for they are bound to ask about the source of the support, and to be told the answer" (*Oration* 45.9, L52 [386 CE]).

Sexual Violence

We have seen the effects on families of incarceration, which Libanius reported in the fourth century resulted in countless wives and children selling their bodies to provide for those inside. Christian sources from the second and fifth centuries both suggest that women faced an increased threat of rape in prison, and the *Mishnah*, a second-century collection of rabbinic Jewish materials, indicates that women ought to be normally rescued from prison (*beit hashevi*, "house of confinement") before a man because she is more vulnerable to sexual violence (cf. *Acts of Paul and Thecla* 27, L277 [second century CE]; Augustine, *City of God* 1.16, L258 [413–26 CE]; *Mishnah Horayot* 3.7 [late second century CE]; cf. Schellenberg 2021, 93n11). Interestingly, the passage in the *Mishnah* specifies that in cases in which both a man and woman are incarcerated and both are vulnerable to sexual violence, the man ought to be released first. In the sixth-century the historian Procopius spoke precisely to the risk of sexual violation at the hands of wardens controlling access to the prison in the Sasanian east (*History of the Wars* 1.5–6, L157). King Kavad I faced a revolt in 496 CE: his opponents "rose against him, removed him from the throne, and kept him in prison in chains," but they were "unwilling to put to death a man of the royal blood, and decided to confine him in a prison which it is their habit to call the Prison of Oblivion." The prison guard made advances on the king's wife, Procopius tells us, and Kavad "told her to give herself over to the man, to treat as he wished. In this way the keeper of the prison slept with the wife, and he conceived for her an extraordinary love, and as a result permitted her to go in to her husband just as she wished and to depart from there again without interference from anyone." Eventually, Kavad escaped the prison dressed in his wife's clothes, returning to the throne shortly thereafter. The logic of Procopius's mythical narrative assumes the normalcy of such sexual bribery to gain entrance and care for incarcerated loved ones, and it betrays a common assumption that women were not safe from sexual exploitation and violation even when delivering food to the prison.

Sexual violence lies quietly in the background of many sources engaged here, but the theme is rarely discussed directly. Although it was undoubtedly the case that the bodies of incarcerated men and women were themselves exploited for sex by guards and other prisoners, the issue appears only rarely in our dataset. Even so, sources occasionally address a heightened concern over sexual violence against incarcerated women directly. A law of the emperor Justinian dated to May 1, 556 CE, prohibits the incarceration of women in a civic prison and instead demands confinement in a monastic setting, especially for charges "of an exceedingly serious nature," reading as follows: "We do not permit a woman to be placed in prison, or guarded by men on account of a fiscal obligation, in any private proceeding, or for any criminal offense, lest she be violated on such premises" (Nov. Just. 134.9.1, L3 [556 CE]; Hillner 2015, 337). The emperor presents himself in the noble role of a protector of women's chastity, and in so doing he presents an explicit rationale for prohibiting the incarceration of women: prisoners were at heightened risk of sexual violence. Such violence is explicitly named in a few instances, as in a fourth- or fifth-century petition from a woman named Aurelia Attiaina, who accused her ex-husband Paul of abducting her, locking her up in his house, and raping her until she bore a child. Attiaina requests that the Roman tribune summon Paul to court, extract money owed to her, and finally "that he be punished for the things he dared to do to me" (P. Oxy. 50.3581, D279 [ca. 4–5 CE]; Bryen 2013, 181–82; Hillner 2015, 162).

Sources from the Roman imperial period discuss convicted women performing forced, penal prostitution. As Hillner (2015) discusses at length, the earliest source for such forced sexual labor appears in Tertullian's *Apology*, written in 197 CE, and the practice continued through the fourth century at least—the fifth-century church historian Socrates records that on a visit to Rome in 391, the emperor Theodosius I abolished the practice (204–7; McGinn 1998, 166). Yet, as Hillner also notes, "None of these institutions [of forced labor], however, were state-run prison camps," and she argues that they are also importantly distinct from civic prisons and the Roman prison system, and the "primary purpose was not to prevent convicts' escape, but to operate a business" (207). Even so, they form one piece of the broader Roman carceral landscape, and in this regard—like other aspects of the carceral system—economics were tightly bound up with practices and places of incarceration. In the case of forced prostitution, the issue of sexual violence is front and center.

More often, however, sexual violence is implied rather than addressed outright, as is the case in a fourth-century CE affidavit from Oxyrhynchus in which a Christian wife accuses her husband of numerous offenses against her and members of her household (P. Oxy. 6.903, D85; Rowlandson 1998, 207–8). "Concerning all the outrages uttered by him against me. He shut up his own slaves and mine with my foster-daughters and his agent and son for seven whole days in his basement, having physically maltreated his slaves and my slave Zoe and killed them with blows, and he applied fire to my foster-daughters, having stripped them quite naked, which is contrary to the laws." Why were the enslaved and now imprisoned women and men stripped naked? What is implied in the word "outraged [*hubrisas*]"—an ambiguous term that can carry a sexual meaning, but need not? The document speaks clearly to the freedom of incarcerators to abuse their victims, here in a private rather than in a public prison, and it indicates that the use of such private prisons was not considered illegal even though some of their specific conditions may be "contrary to the laws" (presumably invoking third century CE legal norms like we find in *D* 48.20.2, L33). Nevertheless, sexual violence often must be looked for in the interstices. In a law from 384 CE, the emperors Gratian, Valentinian II, and Theodosius I prescribe that in celebration of a religious holiday, prisoners who have been accused or convicted of minor crimes should be released—in the source's words, exempt from the "danger of prison"—while those imprisoned for certain serious crimes should remain (*CTh* 9.38.7, L17). The list includes people in prison for homicide, seduction, adultery, sorcery and magic, and for *raptus*. But what does *raptus* mean? Should it be translated as "rape," or rather "kidnapping?" Does the word imply both? Similarly, when Philo of Alexandria noted in the first century CE that guards become more villainous because they absorb evil from prisoners, including evil from the "corrupter" (*fthoreus*), does he indicate someone incarcerated for perpetrating sexual violence? (*On Joseph* 15, L12 [30–50 CE])

Does he imply that prison guards themselves become more prone to perpetrate sexual violence because of their proximity to rapists? It is a possible reading, and perhaps it is the only reasonable reading of the text, but the source is typically and frustratingly vague. Sexual violation is hard to locate in the archive directly, but its stain is latent throughout.

Cold, Dark, Damp, and Foul-Smelling

A few ancient literary sources suggest that prisons were overfilled with bodies, and insufferably hot as a result: Lucian's *Toxaris* and the *Passion of Perpetua* (*Toxaris* 29, L143 [ca. 163 CE]; *Passion of Perpetua* 3, L15 [third–fourth centuries CE]). Both accounts offer insight into popular perceptions of North African prison conditions, while Ammianus Marcellinus speaks of stifling heat in an overcrowded civic prison at Constantinople in the early 370s CE (*History* 29.1.13 [late fourth century CE]). It is curious, then, that firsthand accounts and archaeological evidence more consistently attest to the opposite: prisons were dark, damp, underground spaces that left their inhabitants suffering from cold.

An ostracon from the monastery of Epiphanius in Thebes contains a prisoner letter that speaks to the tragic sensory realities of incarceration; a man who was apparently imprisoned as collateral for someone else's debt complains that he has "no kinsman . . . neither mother, nor father, nor brother, nor sister" able to care for him while incarcerated, while the conditions of his detention threaten his life. The guards were particularly harsh, first injuring his hands and then abandoning him shackled and left to his own devices. "They even forsook me, and I made water underneath me [i.e., urinated on myself], and I was not able to cover myself, because they had maimed my hands" (O. Mon. Epiph. 176, D195 [sixth to seventh centuries CE]). Further explanation is hardly needed for how such sickening conditions would have left the victim uncomfortable, cold, and unable to cover himself for warmth, beyond the other obvious indignities. An approximately contemporaneous source speaks to similar indignities even in a prison located in a hospital at Constantinople, where John of Ephesus complains of rats and mice, fleas, gnats, and bugs that were attracted by the hospital's fetid smell, only to find their way to attack the prisoners held inside (*Ecclesiastical History* 3.2.5, L92 [ca. 588 CE]).

Literary and archaeological evidence supports the documentary picture of prisons as dark, damp, and cold. Plutarch tells the story of Jugurtha, the Numidian king, who, having been defeated and brought to Rome as a captive in 104 BCE, was thrown down naked in the Tullian Prison: "in utter bewilderment and with a grin on his lips [Jugurtha] said: 'Hercules! How cold this Roman bath is!'" (*Life of Marius* 12.3–4; L228 [100–20 CE]). The punchline in Plutarch's anecdote only lands if the audience understands prisons as cold and wet places. A compilation of sayings from the third and fourth centuries CE records a monk speaking of his life in the Egyptian city of Oxyrhynchus, where he complained that "there are many rich people who are in prison, with their hands immobilized in shackles, or having their feet so firmly bound to wood that they can't even urinate freely" (*De vitis patrum* 5.46, L6 [early modern collection, saying third–fourth centuries CE]). As subterranean spaces, prisons tended to be damp and humid already; being continually soiled with urine would only exacerbate the experience of feeling chilled. On the other end of our temporal frame, in the third century BCE, Phaneisis the grain measurer's petition to Zeno (discussed above) similarly requests a cloak, perhaps for the same reason: he was cold (P. Cair. Zen. 3.59519, D134 [263–229 BCE]). Likewise, a letter forged in the name of the apostle Paul depicts him imprisoned in Rome, awaiting a potential death sentence and asking his associate Timothy to send a thick outer garment because winter was fast approaching (2 *Timothy* 4:13–21, L21 [early second century CE]). Both the real and imagined prisoner letters point to the same material reality, in which prisoners were often stripped naked, or nearly so, and suffered the chill of the prison as a result, especially during the colder months of the year. As discussed below, visual sources reflect this general picture, as well.

Even in the heat of the summer, underground spaces like the military prison at Lambaesis, the civic prison at Sufetula, and the prison for the condemned at Carales remain noticeably cool (Lambaesis, A7; Sufetula, A34; Carales, A24). In addition to the chill, sources comment regularly on persistent, overwhelming darkness. Calpurnius Flaccus envisioned a civic prison in an idealized set of legal disputes from the second century CE.

> I can see the civic prison (*carcerem publicam*), constructed of huge stone blocks, receiving through the narrow chinks just a faint semblance of light. Those thrown into it gaze into the lower prison (*robur tullianum*), and whenever the creaking of the iron-bound door stirs those people, lying ill, they are terrified, and by viewing someone else's punishment, they learn of their own soon to come. Whiplashes crack, food is delivered in the foul hands of the executioner even to those who refuse it. (*Declamations* 4, L46 [second century CE])

Similarly, a mid-fourth century CE funerary epigram for a martyr imagines prison as a dark, dirty, underground space. "A new punishment for every limb is added to the prison's filth: They lay out fragments of pottery to keep sleep at bay; twice six days passed, food is denied; he is thrown into a deep dungeon" (CLE 307, D165 [368–84 CE]; trans. Trout 2015, 18–19). Pliny the Elder reports of prisoners condemned to the mines who had it worse still, working ten-hour days underground, lit only by an oil lamp (*Natural History* 33.3; Huntzinger 2005, 26).

The sparse light that did reach the floor of public prisons came in through purpose-built apertures, as Columella suggested for enslaved workers quarters and as attested at a number of archeological sites, again pointing to the material overlap in structures for binding bodies whose legal status nevertheless differ (*On Agriculture* 1.6.3, L47 [mid-first century CE]). As discussed above, several prisons have such windows (Cosa, A20; Sufetula, A34; Tiberias, A40), with the Lambae-sis prison (A7) and the late antique prison in Corinth (A15) even facing south as Columella recommends, while the Carthage amphitheater prison (A25), and the gladiator prison in the amphitheater at Carales (A33) both have high sky-lights, inaccessible from the floor of the space, which allow light to pass without compromising security.

Ancient medical texts both corroborate documentary sources and illuminate the experience of darkness in prison. Galen, a prolific doctor of the second century CE, discusses the use of light to torture and blind prisoners who had been kept in the dark for extended periods.

> And I dare say have you never heard that Dionysius, tyrant of Sicily, built a chamber above his prison: a chamber that was completely covered with shining chalk and very bright in other respects too; that he brought his prisoners up into this chamber after a protracted stay below; and that they, coming into bright light from deep, long-continued gloom would of course gladly look up to the light and as they did so, would be blinded, unable to endure the sudden, instantaneous onslaught of brilliance. (*On the Usefulness of the Parts* 10.3, L61 [second century CE])

Galen's story not only assumes that prisons were typically dark underground spaces, but that this material reality was common knowledge—common enough to serve as a cornerstone of his theory of sight. The doctor deploys his story to highlight the Sicilian tyrant's cruelty, but one securely identified prison appears to have architectural elements designed precisely to allow prisoner eyes to adjust slowly as they moved from the dark underground of the prison to the light of day. As prisoners walked the one hundred meters from Prison for the Condemned to the amphitheater at Carales, they passed under two skylights which still today allow light to stream in from the surface some ten meters above the rock-cut passageway (A24). These skylights likely remain from the initial phase, originally intended to allow cleaning access to the aqueduct. Nevertheless, they are significantly larger than typical access points; it is certain that this slow reentry into the light allowed prisoner and guard's eyes to adjust, and it is possible that this feature is an intentional design element of the reuse of the space, ensuring that prisoners condemned to die by gladiator or beast were not blinded before the fight even began. The cruelty of prolonged time in darkness even animates the law of Constantine from 320 CE discussed above, who legislated that those under custodial control should be allowed to enjoy at least some light during the day, and brought into the prison's outer room (*vestibulum*) only "when night doubles the necessity for his guard" (*CTh* 9.3.1, L133 [320/21 CE]). In these sources, light deprivation was at once prescribed for its benefits in heightening security and also debated as a form of torture.

The Syriac *Acts of Shmona and Gurya* recounts the incarceration and execution of martyrs in 310 CE and speaks to the torture involved in the conditions of incarceration, including sustenance being withheld and windows stopped up, preventing both light and fresh air, as additional punishments by the guards (27–36, L1). In a perversely reminiscent manner, the South Carolina Department of Corrections has drawn criticism for using steel coverings of the windows to block sunlight from prison cells, which is part of a larger conversation about weaponizing sunlight deprivation as a form of torture (Kilpatrick et al. 2023; Alexander and Starosielski 2023, 133–36). The *Acts* speak also to the debilitation caused by fetters, in this case dislocating Shmona's knee. The concern was not an idle one: some ten years after the martyrs' deaths, Constantine instituted a law requiring prisoners to be kept in restraints that "do not fit too close to the bone," lest they be maimed (*CTh* 9.3.1 L133 [320/21 CE]). As discussed previously, evidence of shackling prisoners is prevalent: both the Prison for the Condemned and the Gladiator Prison in the amphitheater of Carales have anchors on the walls worn down from use to hold ropes or chains, and when the Villa of the Mosaic Columns in Pompeii was excavated in the early twentieth century, tibia were found still encased in iron fetters and attached to the wall.

Seen together, the relevant evidence presents a coherent and gruesome picture of the bodily experience of incarceration that holds remarkably stable across the period under discussion. Prisoners were often placed underground with little light and access only to meager food rations, or such food and drink as were delivered to them by friends, family, or patrons, and they were peculiarly vulnerable to death. Death by starvation is most commonly attested in the sources, but one must imagine that disease was a distinct threat in cold, damp, feculent conditions where multiple prisoners were kept in close quarters, especially in late summer and midwinter when pathogens became most lethal (Shaw 1996; Harper 2017, 81–86). Prisons were so well-known as disease vectors that instead of enumerating illnesses, John Chrysostom suggests that an ideal reader can visit a prison, hostel, and poorhouse, to encounter "every category of disease." "From [the hostel] he enters into the prison [*desmōterion*], inspecting every cell in the facility, there he finds people using shit for clothes and straw for houses, lying naked, constantly besieged by frost and disease and hunger, calling to passersby with only a gaze and trembling body and the noise of chattering teeth; able neither to utter a word nor extend a hand, to such an extent that they now are wasting away in suffering" (*To Stagirius* 3.13, L289 [ca. 380 CE]). Chrysostom's vision of a public prison is fictive, but it also coheres with real facilities and concerns. Some facilities, like the workers' prison at Simitthus, had rudimentary bathrooms for prisoners. Most facilities seem to have had no such luxuries, rendering contact between human waste and prisoners' wounds and food all but inevitable. Such conditions, a veritable petri dish of diseases, made risk of infection virtually unavoidable.

Documentary sources do not speak of prisons as particularly malodorous. Literary sources, however, often dwell on the stench. Writing of the civic prison at Alba Fucens, Diodorus Siculus envisioned "a stench so terrible assail[ing] anyone who drew near that it could scarcely be endured" (*Library of History* 31.9.2, L57 [61–30 BCE]). The complaint, offered from the perspective of a mere passerby, is not surprising, and must reflect a common material reality in and around places where feces, urine, sweat, and body odor commingled, rising from the prison below and escaping through narrow apertures. Lucian's depiction of a public prison in Egypt dwells on the unbearable smell inside, and a popular martyr account from the late fifth century depicts the Tullian Prison at Rome as interfacing directly with the sewer system: "[There was] a lowly holding cell in the Tullian Prison from which a horrible stench rose up, because excrement produced by the nearby houses collected in the underground passageways of the sewers which flowed together there; and at this collection point, as we said, there was a filthy and low holding cell, so dark that the internal environment gave no indication that it was daytime, nor any trace of light. Into this cell Chrysanthus, bound up in iron, is thrust" (*Passion of Saints Chrysanthus and Daria* 22, L50 [late fifth century CE]; Lucian, *Toxaris* 29 L143 [ca. 163 CE]). Like many other depictions of Rome's most famous prison, the account imagines darkness, moisture, chill, and odor combining to form an insufferable space of sensory torture (Pavón Torrejón 1999, 106–10).

We must assume, too, that in places like the public prisons at Cosa and Cuicul, or the Gladiator Prison at Carales with its open latrines in the center of the room, festering feces turning to ammonia similarly confronted the nostrils. These material aspects of spaces, and their penal effect, even jumped from literal to metaphorical depictions of prisons. In the third-century CE *Acts of Thomas*, the eponymous apostle tours through hell with a murdered woman, where she looks through a small opening to an underground prison. "Leading me away again he showed me a chamber," the woman recounts, "very dark and breathing out a great stench, and many souls looked out from there, wishing to get something of the air, but their guards did not allow them to look out. And he who was with me said: 'This is the prison of those souls which you saw. For when they have fulfilled their punishments for what each one did, others later succeed them'" (57, L149 [third century CE]). The account makes metaphorical what must have been true for the majority of real prisons in the ancient world: the spaces "breathed out" putrid air from the depth of the prison to the public arena just outside.

FOOD INSECURITY AND CONSUMPTION

Above we wrote briefly about prisoners' hunger, as well as their often feeble attempts to mobilize local networks of support for provisions. The relationship between incarceration and alimentation is multifaceted, however, and deserves its own sustained analysis. Here we analyze three aspects of this nexus: (1) how food insecurity helps us understand incarceration as a particular threat to people of low social status, (2) how prisoners acquired food, and (3) the relationship between incarceration and food production. Each complements a larger picture of the manner in which incarceration was interwoven with social priorities, needs, and inequities.

Toward the beginning of his oration *On Prisons*, Libanius decried contemporary practices of incarceration in fourth-century Antioch, and the yawning chasm separating haughty juristic intentions for incarceration and the material realities of its practice in his city. Incarceration, he proclaimed, "is the normal treatment of the weaker at the hands of the influential, of the penniless at the hands of the wealthy, of the masses at the hands of the elite who expect any charge they make to count for more than proof . . . this is the treatment accorded to the manufacturing class by organizers of loyal addresses to you, and by the lackeys of the governors to those who do not please them in all respects" (*Oration* 45.4, L52 [386 CE]). Libanius's complaint—that incarceration was primarily a tool of the elites used to control the destitute—is undeniably rhetorical: he was, above all, a rhetorician, and these are the words of an elite scholar writing on behalf of an underclass of which he was never part. Nevertheless, Libanius addresses prisoners and their plight regularly in his letters, and he did have direct, first-person experience as a prisoner, which he narrates in his autobiography, having been accused of magic by a rival sophist (*Autobiography* 44–45 [374 CE]; *Letters* 391, 804, 1025, 1414, 1428, 1526; Matter 2004; Pavón Torrejón 2004, 113–14). His charge is not unwarranted—documentary sources largely corroborate his suggestion that the threat of incarceration to an individual was directly proportional to that person's social and economic status.

To begin, a number of documents indicate petty food theft as the reason for people's arrest and imprisonment. On the September 29, 71 CE, for instance, an Egyptian estate owner's scribe wrote to the local Roman centurion, asking the soldier to arrest two individuals who had stolen olives from the property (P. Oslo 2.21, D89). On the one hand, this papyrus shows the banality of the process of arrest and incarceration, and the ease with which landowners could cause laborers to be arrested over trivial offenses based solely on their personal testimony. On the other hand, the papyrus offers a glimpse at the relationship between status, food scarcity, and incarceration. The simplest explanation for why the two men named in the request stole olives (if, indeed, they did) is because they needed food. P. Mich. 6.421, written perhaps just a few years earlier, tells a similar story, in which two men are accused of stealing two donkeys (D201 [41–68 CE]). The papyrus notes specifically that upon arrest the men were stripped of their possessions, including their bread. Together, these documents show how, for the destitute, food scarcity could be both a cause of incarceration and its effect.

In his survey of Ptolemaic papyri related to imprisonment John Bauschatz showed that debt was the most common reason for incarceration, and the pattern holds in Roman and Byzantine documents (Bauschatz 2007; e.g. P. Fam. Tebt. 19, D232 [118 CE]; P. Oxy. 17.2154, D18 [fourth century CE]; PSI 7.824, D13 [late sixth/ early seventh centuries CE]). Bauschatz's comparative approach to the data allows us to begin to see how food scarcity, starvation, and poverty were linked to incarceration in documentary sources from the full stretch of time examined in our book, and archaeological evidence may gesture in a similar direction.

Although they were discovered far beyond the Mediterranean basin, the remains of a man who was crucified in Roman Britain between 130 and 360 CE may further underscore the relation between food scarcity and incarceration. Deformations in his skeletal remains suggest that the man was held in chains for a significant period—long enough to leave indentions in his ankle bones (Fenstanton, A38). Why was he held in chains? Of course, he may have been enslaved, but the fact of his crucifixion suggests strongly that this man was perceived as criminally deviant and possessing of low social status, whether or not he was enslaved. Osteological analysis offers a glimpse at a man who was malnourished for his entire life, struggling to acquire or absorb sufficient amounts of iron in his diet from childhood to his age at death, around thirty years old (Ingham and Duhig 2022, 24–29). It is doubtful that this unlucky man was executed simply for stealing food. Nevertheless, his remains suggest a person left shackled for long periods of time, who had lived a difficult life in which it was not always clear how, or when, his next meal might arrive. Placed alongside literary and documentary sources, we can see his case as one more instance of the stark relationship between people who dealt with food scarcity and those who were most likely to experience incarceration—people like Thamus and his sons, who wrote to Zeno in the middle of the third century BCE,

> I have done all the things so that you might not accuse us. I have a loan of twelve *artabas* of wheat and sixteen *artabas* of wheat mixed with barley from which I have measured out at the granary fourteen *artabas* of wheat mixed with barley. You would do well to arrange for the release of my sons from prison, and we will fulfill the work which you command. For, since we are in the prison, there will be nothing more for you, should we be destroyed in the prison. Farewell. (PSI 5.532, D59 [263–229 BCE])

Here a father pleads on behalf of his sons, who were incarcerated owing to a (not insignificant) debt of grain. Thamus does not claim to be solvent but rather uses a form of plea that we know from many other Ptolemaic debt prisoners: he requests release so that he and his sons can work off their debt, rather than them languishing, and perhaps dying, in prison.

Viewed together, these sources support the idea that the highest rates of incarceration in the ancient world were likely similar to those in the present day: the prison was disproportionately inflicted on the poor, manual laborers, and socially vulnerable (Wacquant 2009). This is hardly a surprising result of the Roman status system, in which criminal penalties were explicitly keyed to the status of the defendant, but it is nevertheless worth dwelling on for a moment. It was not a crime to be poor, but it was certainly the poor, and people who felt the need to steal food, who most often found themselves sitting in an ancient prison.

While food insecurity funneled some people into ancient prisons, even for those who enjoyed easy access to nutrition on the outside, incarceration presented new social and logistical problems that could leave them at death's door once detained inside a cell. Even if prisoners could get in touch with friends willing to bring them supplies, the road to nourishment was sometimes impeded. For instance, P. Petr. Kleon 54 relates a story of a certain Demetrios bringing food to a mining facility in 255 BCE; he "wanted to distribute five loaves of bread to everyone, since there is no bread in the camp," but upon arrival he was assaulted and hauled off to prison himself (D17). In a follow up letter to his employer, Demetrios pleads for aid, complaining that he is being "utterly afflicted," and that he "is in need of a lot of things in the prison" (P. Petr. Kleon 58, D55 [255 BCE]; p. 163–164).

In the second half of the third century BCE, another man ran into a similar issue. He loaded a donkey with food in Karanis and began the twenty-five kilometers journey to Crocodilopolis to deliver provisions to a prisoner there, only to have the animal confiscated en route by a police officer who subsequently demanded a bribe to return his property. The traveler fled the scene in order to avoid being incarcerated himself: "I made myself scarce for fear of being marched to prison for four *choinixes* [about a gallon] of barley," and even though he dispatched a complaint, he received no reply (SB 16.12468, D1).

Reports of family or friends bringing food to prisoners are relatively rare in the documentary record, and while it is methodologically dubious to read an absence of evidence as evidence of anything, it seems likely that people incarcerated in or near their hometown simply relied on word of mouth to alert local networks that they needed material support, rather than sending a letter of the sort that might survive to this day. Quite often, the evidence that survives comprises requests for food sent directly to local elites—although this fact may well result from overrepresentation of the administrator Zeno's personal archive in the documentary record. It is hard to estimate the extent to which the documentary record is representative of the normal order when it comes to individual prisoners requesting help. Implied in each of their pleas, however, is a broader pattern that holds in the Ptolemaic, Roman, and Byzantine period: prisoners were supplied with meager rations, if they were supplied by the prison warden at all, and they relied on the kindness of individuals outside the prison to provide what they lacked.

We even have evidence that prisoner supplies made it into the line items of some elite domestic budgets. P. Cair. Zen. 4.59707 is an account of wheat apportioned, consumed, and left over in a household in the third century BCE, including provision of supplies for a feast in honor of the Ptolemaic king and a small amount of wheat earmarked "for the body of Demetrios, who lies as a prisoner . . ." (D43 [263–229 BCE]). Demetrios was allotted one *choinix* of wheat per day. The measure is a traditional daily grain ration for slaves roughly equivalent to one US dry quart of wheat, which, if delivered in the form of a small loaf of bread, would supply somewhere around 1,700 calories to its recipient. We are cautious not to make too much of this single datum, but again the information is intriguing; the ration is sufficient to sustain life, but only barely so for a prisoner battling cold and disease in his place of confinement. It is a ration likely to leave the prisoner expressing one of the documentary archive's most common complaints: hunger.

A few sources attest supplies sent to prison guards in particular. A late ancient papyrus even orders wine to be sent to a prison along with a monastery, though it is interesting that the monks received ten times the volume of wine that the prison guards were allotted (*P. Oxy.* 16.1945, D12 [517 CE]). It is not clear whether the monks are more numerous, better paid, or less consequential when drunk. Other sources attest delivery of wine to prisons as a part of the bureaucracy of prison management, suggesting again that prison management comprised significantly more than sitting at the door to keep guard (to prison guards: PSI 13.1315, D83 [127 BCE]; to prisons: PSI 8.953, D23 [567/68 CE]).

Delivering food to prisoners involved its own risks. Not infrequently, we find reports of the people making a delivery of food for prisoners who were themselves arrested—perhaps a kind of "guilt by association" in the eyes of prison personnel (P. Petr. Kleon 54, D17 [255 BCE]; P. Petr. Kleon 58, D55 [255 BCE]). There was also the risk of extortion, as we saw in the case of the man bribed by a police officer above, and the occasional necessity of bribing one's way into a prison, or paying a guard in order that imprisoned associates could receive better treatment—an ancient version of practices institutionalized in the medieval Florentine *agevolatura* fee, which had the curious effect of reproducing external economic hierarchies within the prison (cf. *Acts of Paul and Thecla* 18, L28 [second century CE]; *Martyrdom of Perpetua and Felicity* 1, L15 [third–fourth centuries CE]; Geltner 2008, 20). While there is evidence that the position of prison guard was typically state-funded, as we discuss below, some personnel were perhaps at least equally motivated by the extrajudicial benefits of the position. Such practices are well-attested in the medieval period, and we have reason to think that they were common in antiquity, as well (Geltner 2008, 19–20).

The permeability of prison spaces is one of the more surprising aspects of ancient Mediterranean carceral practices, especially given contemporary regimes' attempts to restrict visitation and control the flow of goods in and out of prisons. We have already seen evidence of families and associates bringing food, clothing, and other items to prisoners, and prisoners asking for money with which to purchase food, lamps, or other necessities—implying that captives had some access to the broader system of economic exchange in the cities where they were held, however mediated. Legal sources corroborate this state of affairs: the Roman jurist Ulpian cited a rescript of Hadrian permitting prisoners to maintain a small sum of money with the express purpose of purchasing sustenance (D 48.20.6, L124 [117–38 CE]). In so far as the amount does not exceed five gold coins (*aurei*)—no small sum—prisoners were legally entitled to keep such funds with them while in prison, though the sheer mass of prisoner complaints against wardens militates against any suggestion that this legal ideal was ever meticulously observed.

Perhaps closer to practices on the ground, we have a sermon from the bishop of Constantinople in the late fourth century, speaking on Jesus's words of commendation for those who care for prisoners, as told in the *Gospel according to Matthew* (25:35–36, L213 [late first century CE]). Commenting on the passage, the bishop asks, "Tell me—what is easier than to walk and enter into the prison?" His argument relies on the notion that his late antique audience had the ability to visit a prison if they wished, yet few actually did so. Rather, prisoners beg pitifully and fruitlessly in the market of Constantinople, capital of the empire, at the end of the day "returning from the *agora* still in chains, and although begging all day, still not collecting even the barest of nourishment" (John Chrysostom, *Homilies on John* 60.4, L158 [ca. 390 CE]). It is interesting to note that these sources reinforce an ancient penal ideology that distinguishes between the necessity of keeping inmates from escaping prison, and the permissibility of members of the public to enter. Careful control of prisoners' movement is integral to the idea of a prison; segregating them from the public, however, is not.

Permeability extended to both people and objects. In letters between the bishop of Carthage and prisoners condemned to North African mines, we find reports of deliveries of both food and coin to the imprisoned (Cyprian, *Letters* 76–79, L141 [ca. September 257–September 258 CE]; Larsen 2019). From this instance, we can see that prisoners condemned to convict labor within mining camps had use for money and access to some kind of market in which to spend it. These letters continue, in the mid-third century CE, a trend of provisioning imprisoned miners visible already in the earliest Ptolemaic papyri, where food deliveries to mines aimed both at the comfort of prisoners there and provisioning them so that they could continue their extractive labor (PSI 4.423, D58 [263–229 BCE]). Mining complexes were not isolated prison labor warehouses, in other words. Rather, they were connected to a broader society and often embedded in small cities like Simitthus or regions like Phaino, whose economy revolved around extractive processes powered by enslaved and incarcerated labor. Other imperially controlled mining towns of Mons Claudianus and Mons Porphyrites in the eastern Egyptian desert are well understood through troves of documentary sources excavated among their ruins, and they offer a portrait of a bustling town complete with all the amenities (and vices) available in any city of an even moderate size (van der Veen 1998). Similarly, tablets from the mines at Vipasca (Aljustrel, Portugal) show the presence of shoemakers, fullers, schoolteachers, and barbers in and around the workers quarters whose business depended on the presence of miners, and we learn about baths with assigned hours for men, women, children, and slaves (Friedman 2009; Cummings et al. 1956). Incarcerated miners in late 257 or early 258 CE asked the bishop of Carthage to send money from his estate in Curubis, and they thanked him for doing so (Cyprian, *Letters* 77, L141). We should expect that their treatment was like those in civic prisons, in which a meager dole was supplemented by food and other items purchased on the open market, either through apertures in their living quarters or while released under guard.

Even so, while prisoners depended greatly on their social networks, they did not rely solely on friends, family, and associations to provide for their needs, as is often asserted (Krause 1996, 279–83). Like other orthodoxies engaged in this book, this flawed notion is based on unstated assumptions about the nature of legal sources. Specifically, a law from the early fifth century mandating that prison wardens supply prisoners with food has been read as an innovation in the ancient carceral system, indicating that prior to the reign of Honorius and Theodosius II, no such requirement or practice existed (*CTh* 9.3.7, L44 [409 CE]). It is possible that in the Ptolemaic period prisoners were exclusively reliant on support outside the prison, though, as we saw, those incarcerated as forced laborers in the mines had bread provided to sustain their bodies for labor. Yet, from the late classical Greek period and in both republican and imperial Rome, sources indicate overwhelmingly that the state delivered food rations to prisoners on a daily basis, however meager. For instance, in a play called *Men of Tarentum* (unfortunately extant only in fragments), the late classical Greek poet Alexis evoked the idea of a typical prison ration. About philosophers cast into prison he wrote: "Pythagorisms, subtle discourses, and finely chiseled meditations are what nourish those men, but their daily diet is this: one plain loaf of bread for each one and a cup of water—and that is all." To this another character responds: "That's prison fare [*desmōtēriou diaitan*] you're talking about!" (222 (219K), L183 [ca. 275 BCE]). The notion of a prison diet was common enough in the third century BCE that the poet Alexis deployed it without comment in his play, and when Athanaeus repeated the line at the end of the second century CE in his compendium of quotations from Greek literature, he similarly saw no reason to gloss the notion (*The Learned Banqueters* 4.161, L196). Simply put, these sources suggest a shared cultural assumption in which that prisoners were assumed to be given regular rations of food, and that those rations were meager and undesirable.

In the middle of the first century BCE, Diodorus Siculus wrote of the prison at Alba Fucens, in the Apennine Mountains one hundred kilometers east of Rome. Alba Fucens was a city where men of all ranks were imprisoned, but notably for our author, it was a place for incarceration of high-ranking men awaiting trial on capital and political charges. Diodorus writes of one such man, King Philip of Macedon, held in the civic prison (*carcer*) of Alba Fucens, "a deep underground dungeon, no larger than a nine-couch room, dark, and noisy because of the large numbers committed to the place." The crowded conditions caused prisoners' food to mix with the feces prevalent in the small, cramped space. Worst of all, Diodorus reports, during his seven days in the prison the king was "in such a sorry plight that he begged for aid even from men of the lowest status, whose food was the prison ration" (*Library of History* 31.9.2–3, L57 [first century BCE]). The assumption of the text is that loathsome food was supplied to all, but that high-status prisoners relied on superior food delivered from companions outside who could travel to a (relatively) remote city with aid. Several centuries later, Libanius complained that prisoners were supplied with only a small amount of alimentation but this time of a different character than we heard about above: soup and a few greens, and in an amount that was hardly enough to sustain life, which forced them to rely on the generosity of individuals simply to remain alive (*Oration* 45.9, L52 [386 CE]). Libanius considered this situation, in which prisoners were reliant on outside help, a corruption of the regular and acceptable order, and one of the many failures of the prison system in Antioch. At first glance the speech reflects the need for an outsider to provide food to prisoners to survive; yet it also attests this necessity as an aberration from the ideal.

State supply of prison rations suffuses Latin sources, as well. Around the same time that Diodorus Siculus wrote, the author Sallust composed a speech in the voice of the Roman tribune of the plebs about a recently passed law allowing certain citizens to purchase five pecks of grain per month at a subsidized rate. The amount was a pittance, "which cannot really be much greater than the rations in a prison," sustaining life by the barest of margins (*Histories* 3, fr. 15.19, L192 [first century BCE]). A third-century CE Syrian source, the *Didascalia Apostolorum*, records the story of the biblical king Manasseh taken away to Babylon, where his captors "shut him up in prison all bound and fettered with iron. And there was given him bran-bread by weight, and water mingled with gall in small measure, that he might be alive and be sore, afflicted and vexed" (7, L16). When prison rations appear in sources, they are most often depicted as a meticulously calibrated cruelty: enough food to keep someone alive while subduing their body and spirit.

Prison rations are a staple of the rhetorical tradition too. In his fifth Verrine Oration, Cicero tells a story about Apollonius of Palermo, who spent eighteen months sentenced to prison without the ability to receive visitors—a detail that Pavón Torrejón rightly understands as proof that he was provided with some sort of daily food rations from his incarcerators (*Against Verres* 5.21–24, L227 [70 BCE], Pavón Torrejón 2003b, 223). Likewise, in one of his rhetorical exercises, Seneca the Elder mentions a high-status prisoner on trial in the Roman senate who asked during his trial to be provided with something he expected but had not received: a *diarium*—daily ration (*Controversiae* 9.4.20, L198 [early first century CE]). Seneca's son wrote in his *Letters* of the philosopher Epicurus's intermittent fasting, noting that "even prison food is more generous [*liberaliora alimenta sunt carceris*]" than what the philosopher would eat, noting further that even those unlucky few who are in prison awaiting capital punishment did not receive such meager rations from the man who was soon to be their executioner (Seneca the Younger, *Letters* 18.10–11, L184 [mid-first century CE]). Likewise, in the second century CE, Calpurnius Flaccus's *Declamations* simply assumed that prison guards supplied food to inmates as a matter of course (4, L46 [second century CE]). Rations are not solely a literary or rhetorical affectation, however: a fragmentary inscription from the civic *curia* at Thamugadi (Timgad, Algeria) indicates that the citizenry of the town was responsible for feeding prisoners and guards alike (CIL 8.17897, D171 [361 or 363 CE]).

While the notion of a state-funded prison ration is hardly novel to the fifth century CE, as is often asserted, the practice received a new justification in 409 CE, when Emperors Honorius and Theodosius II decreed that judges were to inspect prisons on Sunday, that they were to ensure that guards were not blocking delivery of supplies to prisoners, and that those without food should be allotted whatever ration the prison registrar (*commentariensis*) estimated was necessary (*CTh* 9.3.7, L44). This law is interesting, insofar as it makes explicit something that remains implicit in the documentary and other literary materials discussed above. Namely, the emperors justify apportioning food to prisoners on the theory that prisoners will go hungry otherwise, and they further claim that it is a Christian's duty to care for the poor. The law also explicates another practice: a state-appointed agent entering the prison on a regular basis to gauge amounts of food necessary to keep prisoners alive—a bureaucratic act that is equal parts caring and sinister. Just under a century later, the Breviary of Alaric added a gloss to this law specifying that prisoner rations should be provided *a christianis*—"by Christians" (9.3.7 [506 CE]). The imperial justification for feeding prisoners—care for the poor—is surely inflected by their Christian profession, and by the long tradition of Christian care for those in prison that the satirist Lucian mocked two centuries before (McGowan 2003; Nicklas 2016). But the law also assumes that people in prison are the type of people who do not have access to food—they are poor, far from home, or otherwise without means to activate a social network to care for them during their incarceration. The destitute are more likely to be incarcerated in the first place, and in more danger as a result than those of means. The law, it seems, took all of it into account.

As our survey of the evidence demonstrates, the law of Honorius and Theodosius II mandating prison rations simply appended a new justification to an age-old practice of feeding prisoners some token amount of food, chiefly with the aim of keeping them alive. We should not confuse this modest aim with good-natured charity, however, and Christians were not of one mind about feeding prisoners. An early fourth-century account of the incarceration, torture, trial, and execution of the holy men Shmona and Gurya in Edessa depicts prison guards preventing delivery of food from fellow Christians precisely as a means of coercion and heightened punishment (*Acts of Shmona and Gurya* 31, L1 [ca. 310 CE]). Later in the fourth century, another martyr's funerary inscription lists denial of food as one of many tortures inflicted by wardens (CLE 307, D165 [368–84 CE]). Other Christian sources likewise complain that food had been denied to prisoners, though at times sources lay blame at the feet of coreligionists: for instance the *Acts of the Abitinian Martyrs*, discussed above, records an incident earlier in the fourth century of a soon-to-be bishop of Carthage accused of standing in front of the civic prison, armed and attacking people attempting to deliver provisions for prisoners inside. Furthermore, "the cups for the thirsty inside in chains were broken. At the entrance to the prison, food was scattered only to be torn apart by the dogs" (20, L32 [304–12 CE]). This source is antagonistic toward the bishop and worthy of the historian's skepticism, but the overwhelming violence perpetrated by both sides in the so-called "Donatist controversy" suggests that such prohibitions are well within the realm of possibility; moreover, this story needed to be believable to be effective, at least in the heat of sectarian violence at the dawn of the fifth century (Shaw 2011, 18–38). It is apparently the case that food could be provided or denied prisoners throughout antiquity, and at scale.

Close attention to the long history of feeding prisoners, and the common thread of keeping prisoners alive but weak, shows that rations formed part of the punishment of incarceration rather than a salve for it. Contemporary carceral practices are perhaps instructive here. Prison administrators in the United States sometimes provide bland, repulsive, but technically nutritious food to prisoners (under the names "Nutraloaf" and "Special Management Meal"), not in order to recognize their fundamental dignity and need for nutrition but as an exhibition of the incarcerator's "discretionary power" and as a means of heightened punishment (Locchi 2021). Today, some prisoners are punished through food aimed solely at keeping them alive. The complaints and descriptions above suggest that such practices are in fact quite ancient. Being kept alive was part of the punishment, and bland, unpalatable food was part of that process.

As discussed above, wine deliveries to prison guards are commonly attested, and in his oration *On Prisons* Libanius claims that at least some prisoners received wine, too. He commends the example of a "well-known Phoenician" who was in charge of prison policy in Palestine. Rather than incarcerating large numbers of people, Libanius reports, this administrator was accustomed to releasing some prisoners and treating the rest with wine and song while incarcerated (*Oration* 45.30, L52 [386 CE]). Libanius envisions the prison transformed into a tavern, and claims that drunken crooning was so effective a reformatory activity that the administrator "found such a speedy ending to every problem that beset him that he had no more need of prisons." It is worth pausing to note that in this instance we have a late antique writer attempting to imagine something difficult and utopian: a world without prisons, one of the very few instances even approaching abolitionism in our sources. It is unlikely that this sort of late ancient art therapy was common, but it is nevertheless notable that Libanius cited a festive sing-along as a positive example of prison management in an oration delivered to the emperor directly. The story also reminds us that carceral policies varied across the Mediterranean—sometimes dramatically—and were often directed and implemented by local officials and wardens themselves rather than resulting from top-down legal prescriptions.

The physical space of ancient prisons presented particular challenges at mealtime. Sources do not mention when rations were delivered, or by what means; the best we can say is that it is likely that visitors were limited to delivering food during daylight hours, and that meals were probably delivered in some sort of organic or ceramic packaging. In the few archaeologically attested prisons that have been excavated in the modern period (that is, when courseware pottery was collected and studied rather than discarded) significant numbers of simple table-wares, lamps, and jugs appear in the deposits. (For instance, in the prison for the condemned at Cagliari and the Gladiator Prison in the same facility [A24, A33], or lamps and jugs found in the eastern aisle of the cryptoporticus underneath the Julian Basilica in Corinth [A14; Scotton 2020, 218].) The presence of such coarse-wares may in fact prove to be another kind of diagnostic feature in disambiguating underground strongrooms as carceral spaces rather than treasuries, though less so than other features like stocks, anchors, or shackles; more research is needed here.

While scholars debate whether it represents a real or a fictionalized account, in Late Antiquity the *Passion of Perpetua and Felicity* was widely believed to be a true prison diary or at least a "beneficial representation" of an imprisoned martyr in third-century Carthage (Muehlberger 2022, 334; Rebillard 2020, 15–20). The account reflects the (imagined) experience of elite Roman prisoners receiving intermittently "good" treatment from guards who have accepted bribes from the prisoners' companions (*Passion of Perpetua and Felicity* 3, L15 [third–fourth century CE]). Perpetua and her companions receive visitors regularly in the account, and we hear of two meals explicitly. Perpetua recounts that, when she was rushed off to a judicial hearing, "we were lunching [*pranderemus*]"—eating a light meal in the earlier part of the day, with another more substantial meal implied (6.1). Later we hear of another practice that sounds strikingly modern: a final meal before execution, calling it a "free supper [*cena libera*]," perhaps implying that the prisoners were allowed to eat in the open and without chains, a practice attested also in Petronius's *Satyricon* (17.1; *Satryicon* 26, L229 [mid-first century CE]; Kyle 1998, 108n38). It is important to remember that prisoner meals were only rarely final: we should expect that most were taken in cramped quarters with minimal light and poor hygiene.

As briefly mentioned above, in the early second century CE, a Roman provincial governor wrote to the emperor with a question about how to handle the feeding of people sentenced to labor for the state. Pliny the Younger writes,

> In most cities—and notably at Nicomedia and Nicaea—certain men who had been condemned to forced labor or to the arena, and to punishments similar to these, are performing the duties and functions of public slaves—even to the point of drawing the yearly salary of the public slave! On hearing of this I thought long and hard about what I should do; I thought it extremely harsh after such a long interval to return them to their punishment, when several of them were now old, and by all accounts were living frugal and moderate lives. Yet I thought it insufficiently fitting to keep

condemned men engaged on public projects. On the other hand, I considered it un-profitable to feed them at public expense for doing nothing, while not to feed them was also dangerous. (*Letters* 10.31–2, L40 [109–10 CE])

Here we see a Roman official of the highest station struggling with a problem of food supply, cost, labor, and expedience, and seeking a solution that balances all factors for the benefit of the empire. His letter attests a state-funded system for feeding prisoners, writing that it would be "unprofitable to feed them at public expense for doing nothing" and concluding that they should be put to work on some public project or another. Nevertheless, the men were condemned to some more strict form of punishment than the lighter duties to which they had been assigned—duties typical of a publicly owned slave and not a prisoner condemned to work—and if the governor failed to feed them, or pay them such that they could buy food, they might die. Two important facets of state rations appear in this anecdote: first, quantity and cost were carefully calculated by administrators who were at least supposed to be concerned about the state's bottom line. Second, prisoners were fed so that they had the energy to work; the cost of their food ought to be significantly less than the benefit that their labor produced.

Writing in the mid first century BCE, Cicero noted that a runaway slave had been arrested and imprisoned, though he wasn't sure if he was sent to the public prison (*publicus*) or, alternatively, to a mill (*pistrina*) to perform forced labor. The equivalence is telling—both were available, legitimate punishments, and apparently interchangeable (*Letters to Quintus* 2.14, L210 [late 59 BCE]). Explicit laws condemning people convicted of "nonserious crimes" to work in the state-owned bakeries in the city of Rome appear in the early fourth century CE, when Constantine ordered that even people convicted of crimes on the island of Sardinia be shipped to the mainland for the purpose (*CTh* 9.40.3, L199 [319 CE]). These laws are the continuation of an earlier practice visible in sources from the first through third centuries CE, when people were sentenced to work in municipal bakeries, though in this earlier period it is not clear whether the punishment was reserved for enslaved people who were convicted of a crime. In the fifth century, the church historian Socrates described the emperor Theodosius I's visit to the city of Rome in 391 CE, noting that at that time the old municipal bakeries of Rome were still in use but short on labor. The bakers in charge, Socrates complains, built brothels nearby and abducted men (mostly travelers, he clarifies), who visited the prostitutes, forcing them to work in the bakeries until they were old and their friends assumed they had died (*Ecclesiastical History* 5.18). As Hillner (2015) points out, it is not clear whether Socrates "described an incident that actually occurred in late-fourth-century Rome, or was inspired by circumstances in mid-fifth-century Constantinople . . ." In any event, the story "suggests that *pistores* [bakers] at times had difficulties enlisting their workforce and may have welcomed a supply of convicts" (206).

A recent discovery at Pompeii perhaps brings archaeological texture to one such space: a series of cramped rooms in a private home, constructed in the middle of the first century CE, with a single point of entry and exit, iron grates on windows that only opened to the inside of the house, and a single barred skylight that allowed in the little light aside from that thrown off by the oven. The facility was in a state of transition: smaller atrium homes were in the process of agglomeration, being consumed and redeveloped into a mega-villa apparently owned by a local politician named Aulus Rustius Verus, whose initials appear on grinding stones inside the locked facility. As the archaeologists note, it was "a facility in which we must imagine the presence of people of servile status, whose freedom of movement the owner felt a need to restrict. It is the most shocking aspect of ancient slavery, which is devoid of relationships of trust and assurances of manumission, where we are reduced to brute violence: quarries, mines, prisons, and bake houses" (Iovino et al. 2023, 10). It is not clear whether the laborers in this locked bakery were enslaved or incarcerated—as Jared Benton (2024) has observed, the distinction appears to be, at most, one of scale, with larger bakeries more likely representing incarcerated labor and smaller bakeries mostly relying on enslaved labor. He remarks, "bakeries did serve as prisons occasionally in large cities where provisioning a populace with bread was a major concern. In these cases, it seems the state sometimes participated in a convict lease system as a way to meet labor needs in lieu of chattel slavery, primarily in cities where large populations and thick markets set the economic conditions for such deliberate exploitation" (20). The Pompeiian evidence is not sufficient to determine the status of the people working in this facility, but perhaps the very fact of the ambiguity is as enlightening as a clear distinction; either way, we find here a haunting thematic return to where we began in this discussion on food. Laws like Constantine's committing low-level offenders to baking facilities, along with this newly unearthed facility at Pompeii invite us to imagine the plight of the destitute in the ancient world, struggling with food scarcity and always on the precipice of disaster. They are the kind of people who might have committed an offense like food theft to quiet their hunger, only to be sentenced to convict labor and find themselves caught up as fuel for the machine of state food production.

As we have noted many times already, carceral intentions rarely align with prisoner experiences. We have argued that even custodial incarceration likely amounted to a death sentence for a startling proportion of ancient prisoners, and the common intention to build a secure facility often resulted in the construction of a gleaming new torture chamber. Yet another group of actors triangulated amid lawmakers' intentions and prisoners' experiences: the broader society from which these prisoners were drawn, and into which these prisons were integrated. A key aim of our book is to demonstrate the centrality of prison facilities and carceral systems more broadly in several ancient Mediterranean societies. We turn now to these social aspects of incarceration.

4

Ancient Mediterranean Prison Societies

The previous chapter considered prisoner experiences inside carceral facilities, both real and imagined. This chapter turns to those "outside," asking about the impact of incarceration on the wider society, and how members of those societies recognized, imagined, or described life in chains. We focus on four topics that illustrate interactions between the prison and the communities that hosted them: (1) economic impacts of the prison, (2) social support for inmates, (3) public pressure on prison proprietors, and (4) the public transcript of incarceration.

ECONOMIC REALITIES

Ancient prison policies and practices responded to economic demands, as the circulation of goods fueled the carceral engine. As shown by Brian Muhs (2018, 99), already in the Ptolemaic period civic prisons played an important role in the collection of public and private debts, and John Bauschatz (2007) argues that debt was the single most common reason for incarceration at the time (47). The trend did not end with Ptolemaic rule: scores of papyri from the Roman and Byzantine periods show that incarceration continued to be a central facet of the debt economy.

Debt incarceration and bail release, however, only form the tip of the iceberg; other economic factors play a role at least as significant in driving practices of incarceration. Frequently, we find evidence of prisoners requesting release not because they were innocent or solvent, but because it was a critical season and the local economy required their labor. A beekeeper petitioned Zeno in the third century BCE, asking for release because he had been in prison already twenty-two days and it was time to transport hives to their pastures (P. Cair. Zen. 3.59520,

123

D38 [263–229 BCE]). Another letter from the same archive shows two men complaining that they will die in prison if they aren't released, and that their pigs will die, too, for lack of being tended to (P. Cair. Zen. 3.59495, D141 [263–229 BCE]). A third letter dispenses with all pretenses toward magnanimity, demanding that Zeno consider his own self-interest: "Have you fallen asleep, overlooking me in prison? Think of your flocks and herds! Know that if the goats of Demetrios remain here, they will perish; for the road down which he drives them to the pastures is enough to kill them" (P. Mich. 1.87, D50 [263–229 BCE]). The debtor even offers a form of bail: "If it seems good to you I will leave my wife in prison to be answerable for me, until you inquire into the matters about which they accuse me." In the few instances in which petitions like this address a prisoner's guilt or innocence, the issue is secondary—they request release on the basis of economic expediency, and on the idea that their solvency is directly related to their capacity to ply a trade. A Coptic ostracon from late antique Karnak (Egypt) likewise speaks to the import of prisoners for the seasonal labor force. A man named Komes begs a local official to have mercy on a prisoner, and to release him "because it is the season of work and I need him, as I have no one else" (Oxford, Ashmolean Museum 1168.B, D297; Crum 1902, 79). Interestingly, in this example we see that an earlier Greek word typically reserved for war captives (*aichmalōtos*) has shifted to be a general term for prisoners in Coptic.

In the late Roman period, even debt collection was bound up in seasonal economic forces. In the fourth century CE, a son wrote to his father, threatening to send soldiers to incarcerate him for a debt of vegetable seed that he had owed his son for a year and that now should be available, given that the harvest season had arrived (P. Fay. 135, D119). Prisoners regularly complain of economic hardship incurred through incarceration, too, like a farmer at the turn of the Common Era who complains of being imprisoned for failure to pay taxes (even though he has a receipt of payment), causing him to miss the sowing season for his fields and the opportunity to labor on public lands that he had lawfully leased (P. Col. 8.209, D69 [3 CE]). In these cases we see the peculiar double vulnerability of the destitute, in which incarceration for debt compromised their ability to tend to their only source of revenue by which they might, eventually, pay and be released. The rural poor and migrant laborers, already vulnerable to incarceration, are also those most attuned to the waxing and waning of seasons and the ongoing life of their crops, a flux rendered in acute relief by the artificial stasis of the prison and by the whims of urban officials, whose lack of attention to the round of seasons reflect a different lived reality. The distinct relationship between stasis and seasonality shows up even in the visual record, with the largest proportion of depictions of the natural cycle of seasons occurring in the houses of African landowners whose seasonal laborers, in a very real sense, fed the Roman Empire (Shaw 2013, 176). These examples illustrate how prisons were a mechanism within a larger economic system. Seasonal needs drove both incarceration and the release of laborers. Yet even this is only one side of the coin.

The interimplication of the prison and economy is perhaps clearest on the other side of the coin: in the case of forced convict labor, especially mining operations. Ancient Mediterranean regimes required vast mining operations to meet demands for stone and metals—such a demand that in the Roman period, extractive industries left a significant geographical and environmental mark that is still detectable across the Mediterranean basin and even as far as the polar ice caps (Rosman et al. 1997; Hirt 2010; A. Hillman et al. 2017). Romans extracted hundreds of tons of copper per year from the island of Cyprus alone, which was just one among many centrally operated mines turning incarcerated and enslaved labor into revenue for the state (Raber 1987).

Polybius wrote that in the second century BCE, forty thousand laborers worked the mines near New Carthage, Spain, producing twenty-five thousand drachmae each day "for the benefit of the Roman people" (Quoted in Strabo, *Geography* 3.2.10, L142 [early first century CE]). Such numbers represent little more than a guess, but even if inflated they give a sense of the scale, and they indicate social understandings about the scale of Roman mining practices along with their economic importance. Writing in the first century BCE, Diodorus Siculus lamented that those mining under the earth give their bodies in search of revenue for their captors. "Those working for the mine overseers produce revenues in sums defying belief, while they themselves wear out their bodies in the diggings under the earth day and night, dying in large numbers because of the exceptional hardships they endure" (*Library of History* 5.38, L168). Likewise, Strabo tells us that when mining operations were unprofitable, they were temporarily shuttered. "What is more, the mine [at Mount Sandaracurgium] is often left idle because of the unprofitableness of it, since the workmen are not only more than two hundred in number, but are continually spent by disease and death" (*Geography* 12.3.40, L167 [early first century CE]). In these instances, the bodies of forced laborers were the fuel of the industry, and if mining concerns weren't profitable, these authors urged that the operation should cease. While Fergus Millar (1984) questioned whether mining operations were in fact profitable, sources like Polybius, Diodorus Siculus, and Strabo insist that they were intended to turn the bodies of incarcerated and enslaved miners into profit for the state. Nevertheless, to reduce carceral practices solely to questions of economic rationality is to dispense with the fact that prisons have almost never been profitable—even modern private prisons produce a profit only through redirecting public money to private hands, not purely through the labor of their captives. Ultimately, the prison's utility (if that is the right word) derives from the input of captive bodies, and not from the output of labor.

As Alfred Michael Hirt (2010) has argued, extractive mining efforts were of utmost importance to the central Roman state, but quarries like Simitthus, Mons Claudianus, and others "were thus run primarily for non-economic reasons connected with the display of imperial power and its projection through the means of art and architecture" (366–67). A letter from the middle of the third century BCE illustrates the economic exploitation of prisoners by private contractors overseeing mines owned by the Ptolemaic king. The address, on the back, reads: "Notice from Horos the stonecutter concerning the prisoners [*desmōtai*] working the *aōilia* [unit of measure, two cubic cubits] and concerning the mine-shafts." It is worth quoting in full.

> To Zeno. Greetings from Horos the stonecutter. Herieus reports concerning the prisoners, from the second of (the month of) Phaophi until the tenth of (the month of) Choiak, that each man has worked two *aōilia* every day, there being ten men in all, so that within each month 600 *aōilia* have been worked, and within the two month period 1,200 have been worked, and over the course of eight days 160 have been worked. The total of *aōilia* worked is 1,360. If it seems best to you, send someone who will make a measurement, for there are 130 (prisoners) who have not yet worked. And know that we have received the contract for the excavation of the mineshafts, so that we may work. But Herieus, after receiving grain from you for the work, has not worked, but . . . the workers (?) . . . . And the channels for which we received the contract, (at a cost of) 2.5 obols per five *aōilia* of rock and 1.5 obols for those transporting ten *aōilia* of rock, these I have completed at a cost of two obols and one obol, respectively. For I have workers here with me, so that the work was completed very quickly. And we have worked the royal stone from the rock toward the south at a cost of one obol, and we have received nothing for it. Therefore you would do well, if it seems best to you, to please give us some grain, so that we may be able to keep working until you make an examination about these matters. Farewell. (PSI 4.423, D58 [263–229 BCE]; trans. Bauschatz 2013, 256)

This fascinating report offers a window into nearly every aspect of the economic exploitation of prisoners in Ptolemaic Egypt. Laborers called prisoners were detailed to mines under the authority of Hereius and Horos, contractors who were awarded (or who likely purchased) the right to quarry royal mines and were paid a set fee for each unit quarried and delivered. The overseer indicates that he has 140 men at his disposal, and yet that over a period of sixty-eight days, only ten of them worked in the mines while the remaining prisoners sat idle, awaiting their turn to work in what must have been a sizable detention facility. We don't have archaeological evidence for this particular incarcerated miner's quarters, but the facility at Simitthus is a relevant comparandum, capable of holding more than one thousand workers. Also relevant is the report discussed above in which prisoners were ordered by the Ptolemaic king to be moved out of a local prison and transported up the Nile in order to labor in the mines (SB 28.16854, D5 [225 BCE]). Horos, the mine overseer, notes precisely the payment schedule and the costs incurred, and requests that administrator Zeno send grain "so that we may be able to keep working." The logic motivating the transaction can be rendered clearly enough: food was allotted to captive workers as fuel to power extraction.

Similarly, a fragmentary papyrus from the early second century CE, apparently a daily report on the troop movements and whereabouts of a Roman auxiliary cohort in Lower Moesia (modern-day Romania and Bulgaria), notes personnel missing from the ranks for various duties. Some soldiers were across the Danube on expedition; some had been sent to Gaul to bring back wheat for the troops. Some were sick and some, it notes, had been sent on official duty to oversee the mines in Dardania (C. Pap. Lat 112 [mid-September, 100–105 CE]; Fink 1971, 224–25). Taken together, these sources allow us to imagine how mining camps could function as a (quite literal) prison-industrial complex built on a convict leasing model. Even so, it seems that most days the typical laborer sat inside a carceral complex, waiting their turn in the mines and being kept alive for that purpose by the contractors who purchased the right to their bodies. Prisoners supplied gold, silver, copper, alabaster, marble, and other precious natural resources for public buildings and private homes, for coins and weapons, for jewelry and housewares. The deployment of unpaid convict labor was one of the cornerstones of the economy.

As we have noted a number of times already, Ulpian was a legal reformer, with dissenting opinions, most famous in carceral studies for his pronouncement that prisons should not be used for punishment (D 48.19.8.9, L120 [early third century CE]). His regular refrain, that lower-class deviants ought be condemned to labor of various sorts rather than simply imprisoned, perhaps indicates something about the nature of his objection to penal incarceration: prisons should not be used for punishment because doing so involves a wasted opportunity for labor extraction benefiting the public good, instead holding prisoners and feeding them at public expense (D 48.19.9). If this was the rationale underlying Ulpian's infamous objection, he was not alone. In the early second century CE, the Roman governor of Pontus and Bithynia (two provinces in the eastern Mediterranean on the coast of the Black Sea) wrote to the emperor Trajan about the matter of prisoners condemned to forced labor instead of serving lighter sentences as public slaves. In his letter, Pliny the Younger worries about the prudence of returning sometimes elderly men to their initial punishment and about the cost of feeding them a prison ration without forcing them to work. The emperor takes a hard line in his response: anyone sentenced within the last ten years was to return to serve their sentence, while those who were sentenced more than ten years prior (and were thereby advanced in age) should be sent to do similar, though lighter, work than that to which they were originally sentenced. Such men, the emperor suggests, "are usually assigned to the baths, or to clearing the sewers, or again, to laying roads and streets" (*Letters* 10.32, L40 [109–10 CE]). Trajan's response illustrates how, while idle incarceration was an available punishment for crimes, it was not lost on the powers that be that captive bodies could and should be put to labor within the broader economy. A fragmentary inscription of a law from the mid-sixth century (likely from Justinian) appears to take a different tack, opposing this exact practice by forbidding the use of prisoners as labor on public projects, except when the schedule is tight and prisoners are necessary to complete the work on time (SEG 8.355, D166 [542 CE?]).

In all, the evidence paints a telling picture. In the hands of the powerful, incarceration was a multipurpose tool, capable of suppressing undesirable behavior and reorienting free people to perform unpaid labor for the benefit of state priorities. Economic and social factors inflected carceral vulnerability, as well: the destitute were more likely to end up in prison in the first instance, and when convicted of a crime, they were more likely than those of means to be sentenced to punishment by prison or forced labor. It is simultaneously optimistic and naïve to view carceral systems exclusively under the rubric of crime and punishment. In the prison's position as a cornerstone of the ancient economy, we witness instead the disarticulation of crime from punishment, and find instead a clear vista onto incarceration's other, less noble uses (Davis 2006). Prisoners did more than pay a debt, whether private or societal. They were a useful resource for society itself, cogs in a machine that fit tongue and groove with economic priorities of successive empires that quite simply could not function in the absence of a carceral system that consumed their labor and, often, their lives.

SOCIAL SUPPORT AND ASSOCIATIONS

As we have argued, ancient judicial sources on incarceration, and the contemporary historiographical analysis of them, leads to the false impression that incarceration in antiquity was primarily a matter of justice delayed and that "prison" is the wrong term altogether to describe these spaces; instead, they were merely jails or "lockups"—temporary holding cells used sparingly with little social impact, and even less impact on the historical record. From their placement at the center of cities, however, to their use as one form of punishment, to the exploitation of prisoners in extractive and labor-intensive industries, and even incarcerated people's reliance on external aid, we see that prisons were fully integrated into the life of ancient cities across the Mediterranean. The prison was a social institution, involving the family members and community of the incarcerated, as well as local politics, public relations, and the local and transregional economy.

First, prisoners relied heavily on community support—above all, for food, as discussed at length in the previous chapter. Prison windows that opened to public spaces, common in the archaeological record, apparently served as sites of social networking. A number of early Christian accounts of incarceration and martyrdom speak to regular visiting hours for family and community members, along with the apparently common tactic of bribing prison officials to gain access to those inside (*Acts of Paul and Thecla* 18, L28 [mid-second century, CE]; *Passion of Perpetua and Felicity* 3, L15 [third–fourth centuries CE]). In the first century CE, the apostle Paul claims to have both received visitors while in prison and dispatched them to others with letters in tow, and in the third-century *Acts of Thomas*, a visitor is depicted bribing a guard with 363 staters of silver in order to gain access to the apostle Thomas locked inside (Paul, *Philemon* 12, L80 [mid-first century CE]; *Acts of Thomas* 151, L36 [early third century CE]).

Associations, or social groups, often played a key role in caring for imprisoned members. A letter from an Egyptian gravediggers' association shows the group petitioning the Ptolemaic king for release of one of their members, requesting that he not be harassed by the head prison guard while he awaits trial (P. Tarich. 5, D138 [ca. 189 BCE]). The letter, from the early second century BCE, includes what might be construed as a threat of collective action, with the gravediggers reminding the king that they are useful to him as justification for local authorities to leave them in peace. The association was quite active in this space, it seems: their archive records two more similar petitions on behalf of incarcerated gravediggers within the span of about a year (P. Tarich. 3, D156 [189 BCE]; P. Tarich. 4 (a & b), D157 [188 BCE]; Armoni 2013, 40–59). While food itself is not explicated in these documents, given the thoroughgoing financial and legal effort to support their associates, it is reasonable to imagine that they also sought to ensure the nourishment of incarcerated gravediggers within their association that were wrongly being "destroyed in the prison . . . [not] having the necessities," and that "spending [their] own" in these cases referred also to supplying food to prisoners for sustenance (P. Tarich. 3 ll. 35–37, D156 [189 BCE]). By Late Antiquity, even associations of sports fans were banding together to influence politics in major cities like Antioch, Alexandria, and Constantinople, including petitioning for the release of prisoners during the famous Nika riots of 532 CE (Bond 2025, 179).

Religious associations were particularly prominent as caretakers for incarcerated members. In the middle of the second century BCE, members of an association of Jews in Herakleopolis wrote a petition on behalf of members incarcerated in Tebtunis, requesting that they be released from prison (P. Polit. Jud. 17, D202 [143 BCE]). Another member of the same Jewish community wrote about a decade later to the leader of the group, claiming "since I happen to be duly admonished, and grasp the experience of prison and have wasted away for enough days, being away from home and not having the basic necessities, I beg and pray with supplication not to overlook [*huperidein*] me but, should it seem right, to assist me and dispose that I may be called from the [prison] . . ." (P. Polit. Jud. 2, D272 [ca. 135 BCE]). In the first century CE, another religious community—this time followers of a Jewish messiah—made visits and wrote petitions in an attempt to secure release for one of their leaders (Paul, *Letter to the Philippians* 1:18; 2:25–30; 4:10–20, L66 [mid-first century CE]). Roughly contemporaneous Christian sources speak to the care for incarcerated associates as incumbent on the community, including, importantly, provisioning Christian prisoners with food (*Gospel according to Matthew* 25, L213 [late first century CE]; *Letter to the Hebrews* 13:3, L220 [late first century CE]). By the second century, Christians were known to a broader public not only for providing for their own incarcerated coreligionists, but as an association of people particularly invested in caring for all prisoners in need of help. Lucian of Samosata openly mocked Christians for their gullibility and ostentation in caring for prisoners who called on them for aid, including the religious freelancer and (in Lucian's estimation) scam artist Peregrinus.

> When [Peregrinus] had been shackled, the Christians, regarding the incident as a calamity, left nothing undone in the effort to release him. Then, because this was not feasible, every other form of amenity was furnished to him, not casually but eagerly. From the break of day old widows and orphan children could be seen waiting near the prison, while their higher-ups even slept inside with him, having bribed the prison guards. Then elaborate meals were brought in, and sacred texts of theirs were read aloud, and most blessed Peregrinus (for he was still called this) was called "new Socrates" by them. (*Passing of Peregrinus* 12, L197 [late second century CE])

It has long been noted that civic associations—professional, religious, or social—were particularly attractive to people who lacked other networks of social security and were also in need of protection against such risks of litigation and assurance of proper burial. However, association support in prison has also been recently discussed at length (Last and Harland 2020, 151–86). To these benefits we should add another important benefit: insurance against incarceration and assurance of aid should people of little means find themselves on the wrong side of the prison gate.

Incarceration had impact beyond the individual, as social risk radiated from the condemned to those in their orbit. Diodorus Siculus wrote about the relatives of convicts also sent to the mines, and Seneca the Younger complained of people deserting incarcerated friends "at the first rattle of the chain" (*Library of History* 3.12–13, L71 [60–30 BCE]; *Letter* 9.9, L215 [63–65 CE]). Eusebius recorded among other outrages of the emperor Licinius that during his short reign over the eastern Roman empire he legislated "that those suffering hardship in prisons should receive no human kindness in the form of food distributions," and further that people caught delivering food to prisoners should be imprisoned themselves, "that those offering any humane service be bound in chains in prison and endure the same punishment as those who had been so sentenced" (*Ecclesiastical History* 10.8.11 [ca. 324 CE]). He also spoke of the physical risks of certain Christians being stopped by guards at the gate while visiting other Christians imprisoned in the mines, thereby putting their own lives at risk (*Martyrs of Palestine* 11.6, L77 [325 CE]). Visitation was not limited to exchange of supplies and words of support: the luckiest captives awaiting trial were able to procure legal assistance, as in the case of SB 16.12949, an account of legal proceedings in the third century CE where an advocate speaks in defense of an accused prisoner (D62). The detailed nature of the litigation strongly implies that the advocate did not take the case sight unseen, but rather that he had met with his incarcerated client and prepared a defense on their behalf. The papyrus does not indicate whether this meeting occurred through a window or during a supervised visitation, but, taken together, sources like these speak to prisons as socially porous spaces where visitors came and went on a daily basis with provisions, support, and services. In the fourth century CE, Libanius even spoke of the blessings that visitors bestow on prisoners "through a little window" (*Letter* 1428.1 [363 CE]; De Simoni 2022, 170).

Windows, gates, and even supervised visitation inside kept prisoners in touch with their social networks. The narrative of Lucian's *Toxaris* draws on a cultural assumption of set hours and specific procedures for prisoner visitation, with prison guards locking up and slaves overseeing the facility at night (30, L143 [163 CE]). While separation was a priority in some prison facilities, we have argued that prisoner access was also an intentional design feature of carceral spaces, and while some sources speak to the subversive nature of prisoner contact with the public, others demonstrate that prisoner contact with the broader public was a feature of the carceral system, and not a bug. In his *Autobiography*, Libanius speaks of personally persuading the governor to release a student's father from prison so that he could return home—apparently, a regular task for the professor (232 [385 CE]; Schouler 2006, 284). In late ancient Egypt, monks commonly replaced politicians and businessmen in the position of carceral go-between, as we see in P. Lond. 6.1914 and O. Mon. Epiph. 163 (D118 [335 CE]; D194 [sixth–seventh centuries CE]). While the offices and identities of the elite changed, the social logic remained static: having friends in high places just might save a prisoner's life, and in order to receive a hearing, bail, or work release, prisoners often relied on influential members of society to manipulate the judicial system.

Scores of letters in the Zeno archive illustrate this fact from the earliest period of our study. Zeno was a complex social actor: on paper, he was first a business associate and secretary of a man named Apollonius, a local Ptolemaic finance minister (*dioiketes*), then he was the manager of Apollonius's estate in Philadelphia, and eventually he became a private businessman in Philadelphia. His private archive is substantial, comprising over 1,800 individual papyri spanning the period between 263 and 229 BCE, and including over two dozen letters from or about prisoners, each of which demonstrate his abiding ability to influence the actions and decisions of judges and wardens, both as an associate of a powerful man and as a power broker in his own right (Vandorpe 2013). Zeno is one such well-attested power broker, but he is hardly unique. Letters from or about prisoners were often to local elites—retainers or representatives of the political establishment and local businessmen—requesting release from prison or aid for those inside. The evidence suggests that across Mediterranean antiquity, if you hoped to get released from prison, knowing the right people and how to get a communication to them was at least equally important to knowing how to navigate the judicial system.

Documents rarely offer full insight into networks of movement that carried these letters from the prison to the public, but the archive offers glimpses. For instance, another prisoner letter in the Zeno archive indicates that "the bearer of the letter is a brother of the detained person" (P. Mich. 1.85, D120 [263–229 BCE]), while a Coptic ostracon from the opposite end of our time period suggests that letters could be sent through carriers to be paid upon arrival, by its recipient. Two women, held in prison as collateral for their husband's debts, write, "Pay the wage of . . . who shall bring this potsherd to you" (O. Mon. Epiph. 177, D139 [500–799 CE]). Evidence for modes of dispatch is scant, preventing us from saying, for instance, that family letter carriers were more common in the Ptolemaic period and postpaid on arrival was common in the Byzantine period. Rather, we ought to view each as one option among many for a prisoner wanting to communicate with those outside.

Physically speaking, prisoners were separated from the general population through infrastructure that segregated their bodies while allowing limited interaction with the public. And yet, incarcerated individuals were connected to the broader society through a number of key nodes. While it is often noted that prisoners relied on the support of friends and family to stay alive, in chapter 5 we suggest two further modes of connection: regular prison visitation by trained writers, passing by to take and dispatch petitions; and communication networks based on letters whose postage was paid by the recipient upon delivery, again implying that private couriers visited prisons with some regularity, hoping to contract business with a prisoner inside (p. 165–168).

There is, in fact, a letter from the late sixth or early seventh century CE that speaks to one such private courier who was himself in danger of incarceration. In PSI 7.824, the administrator of a private estate wrote to the estate supervisor Iulianus, reporting "the letter-carrier came saying that you are holding his wife in the prison and that you seized his other possessions [or: his horses]. Please release his horses and keep his wife under guard" (D13 [575–625 CE]; emendation Berkes 2015). The letter carrier needed to keep working to pay off his debt; he needed his horses to work, carrying letters like this one, as well as those discussed above. While he worked, his wife sat in prison as collateral. Such were the impossible choices faced by the economically vulnerable captured by a carceral system intent on making them pay.

Connections between social networks and carceral facilities happened in a variety of ways, most of which never took material form and thus never left a trace in the documentary record. Nevertheless, the sheer quantity of preserved petitions, often written in a trained hand and sent to local administrators, indicates that prisoners had ongoing access to people who could understand, record, dispatch, and ultimately communicate their needs to the relevant parties. Prisoners were in regular contact with the "outside world." But what did the public think about the plight of the prisoner?

PUBLIC PRESSURE AND CONSENT

In the preface of his book *On Medicine*, the Roman physician Celsus remarks on the practice of advancing science by vivisecting "criminal people received from the prison" (*nocentes homines . . . ex carcere acceptos*). It is an awful and gruesome story, at the end of which the doctor contemplates whether the ends justify the means. He reports that most people in his day contended that the execution of criminals through medical vivisection was cruel and unjustified, while others, himself included, thought that such violence against convicts was justified because it allowed doctors to "seek remedies for innocent people of all future ages" (*On Medicine* pref. 23–25, L195 [47 CE]). Celsus's brief anecdote reveals a live issue in the middle of the first century CE: a public debate over the treatment of public prisoners. Some saw vivisection as fundamentally cruel and hoped for its end, while others saw the practice as necessary for scientific progress and found it worthwhile to destroy the bodies of the convicted with hopes of saving the innocent. Celsus's anecdote shows that broader publics were aware of practices of incarceration, and that many had opinions about them, all of which inflected prisoners' experience. The issue was debated in antiquity, and experimentation on incarcerated populations is not a relic of a bygone era—debate over the validity of such practices continues today (Knight and Flynn 2012).

Incarceration is a social phenomenon implicating more than just a prisoner and that prisoner's captor; the public has always played a role in legitimizing the carceral apparatus. Across Mediterranean antiquity rulers were often criticized for excessive use of the prison, and they regularly opened the prison's doors in hopes of gaining the favor of a public that variously protested, or consented to, its abuses. To our knowledge, no source from the ancient world questions the validity of the institution of the prison itself—there were no ancient prison abolitionists, in other words, though the notion that tyrants abuse the prison system, while good leaders reform it, is common enough to constitute something of a late antique literary trope (Hillner 2013, 389–90).

In his *Roman History*, Cassius Dio reports that toward the end of his reign the emperor Tiberius came under increasing public pressure for abusive practices of incarceration (59.6.1–3, L126 [ca. 230 CE]; Chauvot 1999b). As a political remedy, his young successor Gaius (Caligula) released people who had been held in prison, including political prisoners who had reportedly been incarcerated already for seven years. Dio reports that Gaius burned legal evidence from the prisoner's cases in order to form a contrast with his predecessor; without the relevant documents, the new emperor would be "unable to punish" these alleged enemies of the state with indefinite incarceration, as Tiberius had done repeatedly. A century earlier, the historian Suetonius similarly accused Tiberius of tyrannical abuse of the prison to punish his rivals, and in some instances to avenge mistreatment of imperial officials by local populations (*Life of Tiberius* 61, L19 [ca. 120 CE]). In one instance, Suetonius reports that the emperor dispatched two cohorts of soldiers to a small city east of the Apennine Mountains, where locals were holding a centurion's body ransom. Soldiers entered the city quietly through two different gates and "sent the majority of the plebeians and the city councilors [*decuriones*] to prison for life [*in perpetua vincula*]" (*Life of Tiberius* 37 [ca. 120 CE]).

Written during the late first century CE, the *Gospel according to Mark* tells a story of another instance of politically expedient prisoner release by one of Tiberius's provincial governors, Pontius Pilate. In this account, the governor was said to be in the habit of releasing one prisoner each year on the occasion of a Jewish Passover holiday, and the public had some say over which prisoner was released (15:6–15, L62 [late first century CE]). The historical details of this story are unlikely to be true. Nevertheless, the circumstances described by the gospel account were legible within its ancient context, in which the identities of current prisoners were known to the populace, the public could effect incarceration or release of prisoners through popular pressure, and that rulers used the prison as a tool not solely to coerce and punish individuals but also to intimidate and placate the broader population.

Local populations and administrators alike used prisoners as a bargaining chip to pressure or appease the other, while elites could use their sway to effect the release even of people who had been convicted and condemned to prison as part of their punishment. In the late fourth century, Libanius's speech before emperor Theodosius I noted precisely that at Antioch, the whole swath of punishments available to a governor were intended as a public institution through which the state telegraphs ideas about deviance to the broader society, with salubrious deterrent effects. It is the governor's task, he argues, to execute people who deserve death so as to "restrain the others through fear of a similar fate" (*Oration* 45.28, L52 [386 CE]). Punishments are part of a well-ordered society, Libanius argues, including the punishment of being cast into a public prison. But to let people die in prison before they have been tried and convicted is a moral catastrophe of a high order (45.29). Over a century later, a letter from the Ostrogothic king Athalaric to the urban prefect of Rome reports a familiar story of judicial abuse: two residents of the city suspected of sedition during the reign of King Theodoric sat in prison—either having been convicted with minimal deliberation, or perhaps simply awaiting trial—and as a result were "wasting away under the punishment of lengthy incarceration [*longae custodiae poena maceratos*]" (Cassiodorus, *Variae* 9.17, L8 [533–34 CE]). Theodoric had died at least seven years prior, which strongly suggests that the men in question were not still awaiting trial—perhaps the allegations never went to trial or, alternatively, the conspirators were convicted and left to rot in the civic prison of Rome as punishment. Either way, it was described as a punishment (9.17.2: *longae custodiae poena*; cf. Hillner 2015, 134n78). The king's letter makes clear that the bishop of Rome was aware of the plight of these prisoners because he checked on them, an interesting correlation with the law of Honorius suggesting precisely that local bishops were responsible to check on the prison population in their jurisdiction once a week, on Sunday (*CTh* 9.3.7, L44 [409 CE]). As in earlier cases, these men were granted pardons and released on a royal order—this time at the behest of John, the bishop of Rome; Shane Bjornlie (2019) points out that these letters comprise the first evidence within Cassiodorus's collection of royal assent to a papal petition (375). In assenting to such a request of a well-heeled local, King Athalaric followed a precedent in evidence already for a thousand years, by which prisoners petition elites for release, appealing to the incarcerator's sense of justice along with their desire to appear merciful in the eyes of a public who knew the identity of those incarcerated in their cities (cf. P. Cair. Zen. 3.59482, D35 [263–229 BCE]; O. Mon. Epiph. 163, D194 [sixth–seventh centuries CE]). An influential figure petitioning for a specific prisoner's release was not novel—what's new was that a Christian cleric had risen to the role of the influential figure doing so. King Athalaric's letter specifically notes that there was a public outcry about these prisoners, suggesting again that the deviance of prisoners was purposefully on public display.

Then as now, the public had a role in an individual's experience of incarceration. Those who opposed the imprisonment of specific people could do something about it: they could write to local leadership, issue their complaint, and plead their case. Likewise, if prisoners or their immediate social circle felt their incarceration was unjust or unwarranted, they could appeal to a public, who had opinions about the case and could supply and bottom-up political influence. And it appears that these actions sometimes worked to put someone in prison, or to have them released. It is perhaps worth pausing to consider what it might mean that, at either end of our timeframe, we regularly meet local power brokers who stood outside of the formal legal apparatus but nevertheless possessed the power to loose and bind. The broader public was at times well aware of who was incarcerated in their midst, even though their bodies were carefully hidden from view and direct access.

Representations of prisoners, on the other hand, were everywhere: sometimes in stories about their plight, and sometimes in artistic renderings that broadcasted to society messages about their experience, culpability, and social status. Prisoners were not the only members of ancient society to experience the prison, in other words—depictions of prisoners invited society as a whole to reflect on the place of incarceration within it. We turn now to public and private depictions of prisoners, asking about the experience of the prison for those outside of it, and for those involved in its day-to-day operation. Or, put differently, we ask: How did nonincarcerated members of society recognize the prison and its captives?

PUBLIC TRANSCRIPT

Prisoners were depicted in a staggering array of places and media across the ancient world: on monumental civic architecture, in private domestic spaces, on tombstones and dedications, figurines, and even on clothes. These representations offer insight into the public transcript of incarceration: the visual lexicon available to residents of the ancient Mediterranean when imagining prisoners and places of their incarceration. This public transcript results from images commissioned by individuals, communities, and the state, and manufactured by artisans. James C. Scott (1990) describes the public transcript as "the *self*-portrait of dominant elites as they would have themselves seen . . . It is designed to be impressive, to affirm and naturalize the power of dominant elites, and to conceal or euphemize the dirty linen of their rule" (18). We extend Scott's usage to consider how elites represented themselves publicly in relation to carceral facilities and imprisoned subjects. Together, these representations of prisons, prisoners, and the idealized judicial order by elites and for an elite gaze created and reified a series of visual typecasts of incarceration to the public. Put differently, they announced to pass-ersby how to "know a prisoner when you see one."

In what follows we offer readings of visual sources, attempting to understand typical features common among representations of prisoners and prisons. One goal is to understand what a typical person in antiquity might have conceived when faced with stories and reports of incarcerated people—what the broader public's experience of incarceration looked like, even outside of carceral facili-ties. Another goal is to understand the visual lexicon produced by those com-missioning and crafting images of deviant bodies that had come into contact with state power. How do representations of prisons stereotype the bodies of prisoners and sites of their incarceration, and how do both relate to the visual discourse of gender, racial or ethnic stereotypes, and other depictions of state power?

Thus far our analysis has focused primarily on civic prisoners, bracketing for a moment both prisoners of war and slaves. From a purely material perspective this distinction is artificial and academic, as the methods of binding were often identical for all three categories; shackles used for civic prisoners are visually and materially indistinguishable from those used to bind slaves or prisoners of war. Nevertheless, literary and documentary sources tend to use different words for each type of bound body, and they distinguish between the three based on the rationale for their unfreedom: civic prisoners were bound on account of perceived criminality or deviance, prisoners of war as a result of military campaigns, and slaves owing to formal, legal enslavement. When it comes to visual sources, however, the distinction between bound bodies is both less clear and less useful. Relatively few surviving sources explicitly depict civic prisoners in clear distinc-tion from prisoners of war or enslaved people; in most cases, it is not possible to determine what kind of bound bodies are represented. But slippage between these categories is not a purely modern issue: Romans themselves exploited the ambigu-ity. In many cases we find a studied lack of distinction that is itself both telling and analytically useful.

Consider for instance the Mosaic of the Captives, which decorated the central apse of Tipasa's civic basilica on the coast of Mauritania in Roman North Africa (fig. 15). This late second-century CE mosaic depicts a captive native (Berber) man joined by a woman and a young boy, who are presumably intended to depict a family unit. The male captive appears muscled and nude, looking into the dis-tance with hands bound behind their back and casting long shadows from their feet, while the woman peers directly at the viewer over her shackled hands, in a

FIGURE 15. Mosaic of the Captives (V8; Tipasa, Tunisia) Late second century CE. Image courtesy Carole Raddato. See Dunbabin 1978, 26; Ferris 2000, 102–3; Bradley 2004, 300.

more sympathetic depiction. These are military captives—the man sits on a shield, unmistakably identifying him and the others as prisoners of war. But this scene was not chosen for a martial context. Designers in Tipasa chose to depict *military* captives as the central decorative motif on the floor of the *civic* basilica. A variety of events take place in civic basilicas, including human trafficking in a variety of guises; local decisions to loose and to bind captives in the civic prison were undertaken here, along with decisions about slaves sold and manumitted. It was a choice to depict military prisoners in a place where civic prisoners were presented and tried. We argue that such a decision suggests that, in relevant visual lexica, bound bodies of different types were functionally interchangeable. Further, there was utility in intentionally blurring the line between civic prisoners and prisoners of war in provincial settings like Tipasa, where such ambiguity and interchangeability served a colonizing purpose: intimidating the native local population, who were all dominated subjects of Roman military presence to one degree or another. It could hardly have been lost to indigenous populations called to the curia, basilica, or tribunal to receive judgment that Romans represented local populations as already and perpetually dominated through incarceration and trampled underneath the feet of judges.

The Mosaic of the Captives is not unique, either: a similar choice was made in Corinth in the design of the Lechaion Road basilica, variously dated from the late first to the early third century CE (V16). The southern facade of the basilica faced the forum and featured several larger-than-life captives in an Orientalized guise, two of which survive almost in their entirety (Stillwell 1941, 55–88; Richardson 1902). The exact date of their installation at the entrance to the basilica is debated (and the details need not concern us here) but a second-century CE time frame is a reasonable hypothesis (Ajootian 2014, 364). Visually, the captives follow a common pattern in imperial Roman sculpture that Rolf Michael Schneider (2012) has called the handsome Asian: "a clean-shaven face framed by long coiffured hair and crowned by the Phrygian cap . . . a visual stereotype [that] made it possible to represent all the people of the Asian East as uniform and thus essentially the same" (85–86). At Sarmizegetusa, too, Dacian prisoners of war decorated the facade of the basilica complex, directly adjacent to the civic prison that stood underneath the eastern tribunal (Étienne et al. 2002, 135). At these sites, war captives decorate the entrance to a space where civic judicial matters were decided, even though it was civil prisoners, and not war captives, who would have seen and passed these objects to receive judgment. We do not know what any particular person in antiquity thought about the visualization of military prisoners to decorate a civic basilica. Nevertheless, it is reasonable to think that an ancient observer standing in the forum in Corinth or Sarmizegetusa would have seen a correspondence between the chained prisoners of war depicted at the basilica entrance and the chained civil prisoners moving beneath them. The same holds for the floor of the basilica in Tipasa. That this motif appears regularly in civic basilicas suggests further that military captives could be employed as visual representations of prisoners writ large.

Visual sources, then, often deployed stock imagery depicting captives of various types with a sort of determined obfuscation. Since visual cultures as geographically disparate as Mauritania, Dacia, and Greece conflate civic and martial prisoners, we cautiously proceed in our consideration of how ambiguous imagery offers insight into the ways image makers and governmental officials employed incarceration within the visual lexicon of state power. In this way, visual sources are a particularly interesting point of contrast to prison graffiti: while the former offer an elite-funded view of bound bodies and their relationship with civil society, the latter give insight into tactics of resistance that incarcerated people deployed in response to such depictions, for instance in the prisoner graffiti from late ancient Corinth (Larsen 2024).

Images of incarceration were ubiquitous, appearing in a wide variety of media on different objects and visual contexts. Our dataset is intended to be broadly representative rather than comprehensive, but even selecting judiciously, sources include images of prisoners on statues, decorative columns and reliefs, wall frescoes, floor mosaics, coins, gems, pendants, plates, vases, tunics, dolls, figurines, keys, manuscripts, mummy wrapping, and sarcophagi. Such a broad range of depictions and media suggests that prisoners were represented to a wide variety of viewers. Prisoners appear on public structures, home decor, elite private objects, magical handbooks, funerary art, and on mass-produced objects available to people across the social spectrum. These images were displayed in judicial and non-judicial spaces, in public and in private, on monuments and personal trinkets, and in formats large and small. We find prisoners depicted in Ptolemaic Egypt, early and late in the Roman Empire, and in Byzantine sources, from every corner of the Mediterranean basin and beyond. Just about anywhere an image was to be regularly found, prisoners appeared.

Incarcerated bodies populate the public transcript more than carceral spaces; representations of prisons themselves are comparatively rare. Even so, a number are extant, all from Roman and Byzantine contexts. These sources depict prisons as dark, underground chambers with small windows opening to the outdoors. For instance, at Pompeii we find the myth of Pero and Micon depicted in four different places—three frescoes in private residences along with a small terracotta statue found at the entrance to a public bath complex. The story is extant in three different literary versions, each involving a parent convicted of an unspecified crime and sentenced to die in prison by starvation, and a daughter keeping the parent alive by feeding them with her breast milk on repeated visits (Valerius Maximus, *Memorable Doings and Sayings* 5.4.7, L14 [14–37 CE]; Hyginus, *Fables* 254.3 [early first century CE]; Pliny, *Natural History* 7.36, L150 [ca. 77 CE]). While the names of the characters change between tellings, and even the gender of the parent is in flux, the tale is recognizably stable and undoubtedly what is depicted in the Pompeiian frescoes.

All three frescoes appear to be based on a portrayal of the mythical prison scene in Rome, and each depicts a dark space with a window high on one wall (Rohden 1880, 57–60). Bars cover the window in depictions at the house on the Via Stabiae (9.2.5, V12 [mid-first century CE]; fig. 16) and the House of Marcus Lucretius Fronto (5.4.a, V13 [mid-first century CE], while the opening appears to be unbarred in the depiction at the House of Bacchus (7.4.10, V15 [mid-first century CE])—though this last depiction seems to have significantly decayed shortly after excavation in 1826, and we are reliant on early drawings. In all three frescoes, light beams diagonally through the window, emphasizing that the prison is a dark and underground space, with a window opening to the public, as seen in the person peering down from above in figure 16. Critically, in these frescoes the prison is not the focus of the story but merely its setting: it is a stage built from stock features and is meant to be immediately recognizable to viewers as a civic prison. The proliferation of this particular image, from Rome to at least three houses in Pompeii and undoubtedly to countless others, as well as its representation across the late Roman period, makes these scenes important indicators of how the material aspects of a Roman prison were popularly imagined.

Just within Pompeii, the myth appears in a variety of spaces: the fresco preserved at the House of Bacchus (7.4.10, V15) is from a public space—the atrium at the entrance to the home—while the version preserved on the Via Stabiae (9.2.5, V12) decorated the triclinium of a combination storefront/home, in a semipublic

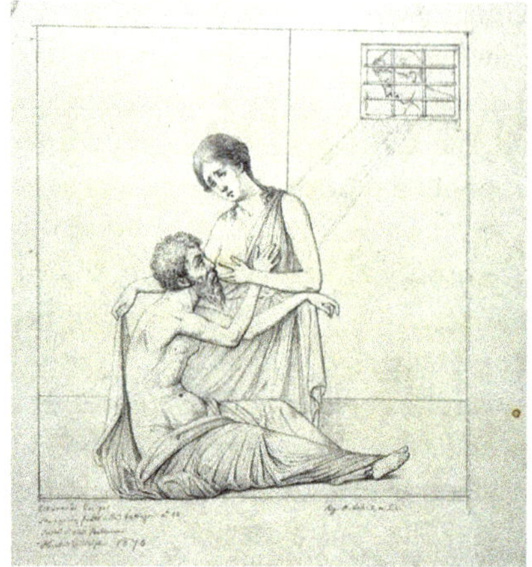

FIGURE 16. Left: Fresco of Pero and Micon, Via Stabiae, Pompeii (9.2.5, V12 [mid-first century CE]); MANN inv. 115398. Photo by Giorgio Albano. Right: Drawing of fresco by Nicola Vople, 1870. MANN inv. ADS 970. Both copyright, courtesy of the Ministry of Culture, National Archaeological Museum of Naples.

room intended for entertaining and display. A statue depicting the myth was found at the entrance to a public bath complex (2.4.6, V14), while the version of the myth in the House of Marcus Lucretius Fronto graced the wall of a *cubiculum*: a bedroom opening to the house's atrium. This version, decorating a private bedroom, offers further insight into why the homeowner elected to have this scene represented in their home, because it includes a Latin elegiac poem written within its frame. The poem reads,

> The food which the mother was preparing for her little children
> hostile Fortune has turned into food for her father.
> The deed is worthy of eternity. [See how] the old veins in the thin neck [shine as]
>   the milk [passes through.]
> At the same time, she herself, Pero, strokes Micon with her face pressed to him:
> along with piety there is in her a sad modesty. (CLE 2048, D199 [first century CE];
>   trans. Milnor)

The homeowner chose a fresco evoking this story because it presents the virtue of filial piety, not because it depicted a prison. Nevertheless, for the story to be effective, viewers must already have a stereotyped idea of what a prison looks like, and of the people inside of them. Literary accounts of the myth depict lower status people as peculiarly vulnerable to incarceration, and these frescoes participate in a larger visual pattern of viewing prisoners as particularly worthy of charity (Harley-McGowan 2015). Because a civic prison is merely the setting of this story, it provides us insight into what these homeowners were led to believe the inside of a public prison looked like. As we have seen, these facilities look surprisingly similar to the civic prisons that are attested archaeologically, even though the images were intended to present a moralizing tale and in at least some cases to remind viewers of a social debt owed to their families.

Carceral facilities appear in a few other depictions, as well. For instance, a large mosaic uncovered outside Antioch depicts a succession of public buildings and monuments as they appeared in the fifth century CE, including two identical large buildings on a central urban artery, "imposing and austere in appearance." A high-ranking official stands in front of one of these buildings while a figure rushes towards it carrying a loaf of bread and a small white bag. The building features a legend reading *to dēmosin*—"the public facility," or, as Michel Matter (2004, 65–67) argues, the public prison—a usage of the term that goes all the way back to Thucydides (Yakto Mosaic, Hatay Archaeology Museum, V5 [late fifth century CE]; Thucydides, *Peloponnesian War* 5.18.7 [late fifth century BCE]). As we discuss below, another story taking place in a prison—the Christian apostle Peter drawing water from a rock in the Tullian Prison—appears in a few depictions, though both dwell on the characters in the story more than the space of the prison itself. A sixth-century manuscript illustration represents the Roman client king Herod's prison at Machaerus as a dark space with a barred door as its entrance, inhabited by prisoners with long, haggard hair and beards wrapped in heavy brown cloaks, while a roughly contemporaneous depiction of the biblical patriarch Joseph from Antioch presents his prison as small and cramped, with vaulted ceilings (BnF Sup. grec 1286(10v), V61 [sixth century CE]; Weitzmann 1979, 491–92, no. 442; Princeton Art Museum, Antioch C515-S630, V7 [490–550 CE]).

Soldiers serve as guards more often than not in extant representations of prisoners and prisons, which has led some interpreters to understand the scenes as depicting prisoners of war. Across the Roman world, however, soldiers were regularly detailed to public prisons; conversely, civilians were regularly incarcerated in military prisons and guarded by military personnel (Pliny the Younger, *Letters* 10.19–20, L24 [109–10 CE], *Passion of Perpetua and Felicity* 7–9, L15 [third–fourth centuries CE]). In other words, the depiction of a soldier serving as a guard is not an indication of the status of their prisoners. A first-century CE limestone relief from Nickenich (Germany) represents an imposing Roman soldier in the upper register transporting two prisoners, hunched and small in the lower register (Landesmuseum Bonn inv. 31.86, V21 [first century CE]). In one hand the soldier holds a club; with the other hand he controls a chain connected to collars around prisoners' necks. As noted above, the methods of binding civil prisoners, prisoners of war, and slaves were often formally identical, and the presence of a soldier as guard does not shed any interpretive light on the intended status of the bound individuals. What we can say, however, is this: the image depicts prisoner transport with startling fidelity to the material aspects known from archaeological sources, including extant remains of shackles, and it echoes what someone might have seen as any sort of prisoner was marched through their town (Thompson 1993, 233–40).

Prisoner transports were common in various parts of the ancient world, so far as literary and documentary sources attest—and especially so in Asia Minor, as described in the edict of Hadrian concerning the treatment of soldiers transporting prisoners discussed in chapter 5, for instance, along with the letters of the early second-century CE bishop Ignatius depicting the movement of prisoners over land in the provinces (p. 184; SEG 59.1365, D175 [129 CE]; Ignatius of Antioch, *Romans* 5.1, L216 [early second century CE]). A second- or third-century CE relief from Miletus (Balat, Turkey) represents a similar scene: a soldier controls a chain connected to the hand of one prisoner, who is in turn attached through chains and collars to two others (Istanbul, Archaeological Museum inv. 2042, V43 [second–third centuries CE]). The motif is repeated in roughly contemporaneous reliefs from Smyrna and Ephesus, both of which depict *damnati*: prisoners en route to die in the arena, often holding placards apparently intended to indicate their crime to the public as they pass by (Oxford, Ashmolean inv. ANMichaelis.137, V44 [ca. 200 CE]; Selçuk, Ephesos Museum inv. 244, V45 [second/third century CE]; Vismara 2001, 42–43). It is often impossible to say whether the prisoners depicted are civic or martial, but the ambiguity persists from antiquity, along with the visual effect of the images, which stress the dominance of Roman order over deviant bodies. We argue this ambiguity is itself analytically useful because it reflects well a common and sustained metonymy in the public transcripts of the ancient Mediterranean world.

Nevertheless, there are some unambiguous depictions of Roman soldiers guarding civic prisoners. For instance, a pair of fourth-century CE sarcophagi from Rome, along with a fifth-century ivory box from Rome, depict the arrest of the apostle Peter and his miracle of causing a rock to flow with water so that he could baptize the guards overseeing him in the Tullian Prison (MET 1991.366, V6 [early fourth century CE]; MV 31551.0.0, V26 [early fourth century CE]; BM 1856,0623.10, V40 [ca. 430 CE]). In all the depictions the guards are soldiers: they wear a short tunic, military boots, and Pannonian caps, and in one literary source they are even given names and described as "senior agents of the Master of the Offices [*melloprincipes magistrani*]"—an usual phrase that seems to refer in this instance to agents of the emperor Nero's personal military cadre (*Acts of Martinian and Processus* 1, L171 [500–550 CE]; Lapidge 2018, 385n14–15). These objects show the use of common visual identifiers for prisoners being adapted creatively in a new mythical context, and they show that soldiers could be depicted as guards in an unequivocally civic facility. And importantly, viewers were expected to recognize relatively stable visual codes of incarceration, rendering it possible to deploy the same motifs in service of a new, Christian narrative.

As represented in visual sources, the job of a prison guard consisted primarily in transport and surveillance, and the common presence of both small antechambers and windows into individual cells suggest that direct oversight was a design ideal implemented in many carceral facilities. The Pero and Micon fresco in the house on the Via Stabia in Pompeii gives further insight into the function of these windows (9.2.5 V12 [first century CE]; fig. 16). While literary accounts of the myth simply record that the guard was able to look into the prison, this fresco depicts the moment of discovery itself: the guard, standing outside the prison, peers in from the window above and, representing the story's audience, catches the daughter in the midst of her act of filial piety. The detail, faded on the fresco but clear in the drawing that Nicola La Volpe made some twenty years after its excavation, offers insight into the public transcript of how a prison guard might surveil inmates without needing to enter the prison.

When sources have more than one register, prisoners are almost uniformly depicted in the lower part of the composition. Put differently, in the public transcript, power is consistently mapped upward, and captivity downward. The representation of prisoners as physically lower in visual sources connects to a coherent ideology of state power literally *over* bodies, as we see, for instance, in the placement of the Mosaic of the Captives physically underneath the seat of judgment, and in the common trope of prisons placed directly underneath courts and temples (Mosaic of the Captives, V8 [late second century CE]); Cuicul Prison, A5 [169 CE], Lambaesis Prison, A7 [early second century CE]). Likewise, it was important to the designer of the Sousse relief (fig. 20) to place the triumphant emperor physically over the body of his captive, and in the first century CE relief from Nickenich, a single soldier stands alone in the upper register, controlling with a chain two captives who appear underneath his feet, at three quarters his height (Sousse Archaeological Museum, V29 [third century CE]; fig. 20; Landesmuseum Bonn inv. 31.86, V21 [first century CE]). The theme continues even in depictions far removed from elite imperial display; a terracotta statue of Pero and Micon from a Pompeiian bath presents the prisoner noticeably smaller than his daughter and seated at her feet (V14 [mid-first century CE]). Visual sources consistently employ size and position to reiterate that prisoners are subdued and weakened in relation to free people; they are both socially and physically inferior. The famous Gemma Augustea and the Grand camée de France are large, carved stone depictions of the Roman emperor in triumph—among the most elite, refined, and rare works of imperial art produced in or surviving from antiquity. Both depict the effortless dominance of the emperor, and by extension Roman imperial power, over captive bodies (KMW Antikensammlung IXa 79, V24 [9–12 CE]; BnF camée 264, V63 [early first century CE]). They are what Keith Bradley (2004) designates "abstract symbols of Roman power," and each gem depicts an emperor in heroic nudity in the upper register, crowned by the goddess Victory, while the lower register displays vanquished prisoners alongside their captured military equipment (300). These prisoners are unambiguously martial, but nevertheless they appear remarkably similar to representations of other types of bound bodies: they are wrought low, hands bound behind their back, haggard and dejected, men and women alike. Both objects depict captives being prepared for display as a battlefield trophy, a typical scene extending from classical Greek to late Roman contexts in which captives were stripped naked, with their bodies and armor set for display (Havener 2018; Nielson 1983). This same visual language of power persists into early Christian art, as we see for instance in an early fourth century CE sarcophagus from the catacomb of Domitilla in Rome that directly inverts common symbols of Roman dominance, porting them into a triumphalist Christian register (MV 31525.0.0, V73 [ca. 350 CE]). Thus, rather than the crowning of an emperor by the goddess Victory, Christ is crowned in laurel by a Roman soldier, while in the central panel a cross dominates, topped by a Christogram. Under the cross's arms sit two Roman soldiers, their heads hung, dejected under the symbol of Christ's resurrection. In place of legionary standards, this object, from roughly 350 CE, depicts the Christian cross topped and below it, instead of prisoners, Roman soldiers. Likewise, in another sarcophagus that depicts Peter baptizing a soldier-guard in the Tullian Prison, the apostle stands tall, towering over the soldier, who is rendered small and subordinate (MV 31551.0.0, V26 [300–330 CE]). In the late Roman period, then, we find Christian imagery that inverts the registers of the traditional Roman program of displaying guards and criminals, even as broader visual codes remain intact.

Such scenes of prison guards are not depicted solely on prestige items like a sarcophagus fit for display, or items connected to the imperial family—we find them also on media with much wider circulation. For instance, a bronze coin minted in Rome in 176 and 177 CE depicts a familiar scene on its reverse: a battlefield trophy towering over a seated, captive Sarmatian woman and man (RIC 3.1188, V62). An early first-century terracotta plaque also from the city of Rome represents a similar scene: a Gaulish prisoner guarded by a Roman soldier, arms chained, looking at his armor hung for display on a tree to his left (fig. 17).

No matter their status as prisoners, slaves, or spoils of war, captives are most often depicted with hands chained behind their back. We find this particular motif across vast stretches of time and space: in Rome in the Augustan era (V24, V41), Palestine in the first quarter of the first century BCE (V56), in Italy in the first century BCE/CE (V27), in Germany in the late first century or second century CE (V10, V11), North Africa of the second (V8), third (V29), and fourth centuries (V57), Cilicia in 251–53 CE (V60), and fourth-century Egypt (V58). As a motif it is not universal, however: occasionally, hands are tied in the front, clasped in what Cassius Dio calls "the manner of captives" (*Roman History* 68.10.1 [ca. 230 CE]). Extant examples include scenes from the Arch of Septimius Severus in Rome and a small but growing collection of bronze figurines from sites on the edges of the Roman Empire (V17 [203 CE]; Jackson 2005). Likewise, prisoners' arms are bound both behind the back and in front in a series of sixteen figurines of captives from the Idumean city of Maresha (Beit Guvrin, Israel), dated roughly to the second century BCE, all deposited together in a single room of what the excavators understood as a Seleucid military barracks (fig. 18, V55). Hands bound by ropes or chains are the most common visual indication of a prisoner, simplifying for

FIGURE 17. British Museum 1805,0703.314 (V32 [ca. 1–20 CE]). The inscription reads M(arcus) Anton(ius) Epaphra.

ease of identification a rather wider panoply of restraint modes and styles known archaeologically (Thompson 2003, 217–44).

Like visual sources, literary materials typically depict prisoners as naked, dirty, and miserable, with males often sporting a beard and long, unkempt hair. An anecdote of Quintilian offers a good example of the public typecasting of a stripped prisoner. In his *Orator's Education*, he mentions a certain Quintus Curius, whose accuser had painted a picture on a canvas as a visual aid to argument. While he mobilizes the depiction in service of a different point, Quintilian notes specifically that the prisoner was portrayed as stripped naked, conforming

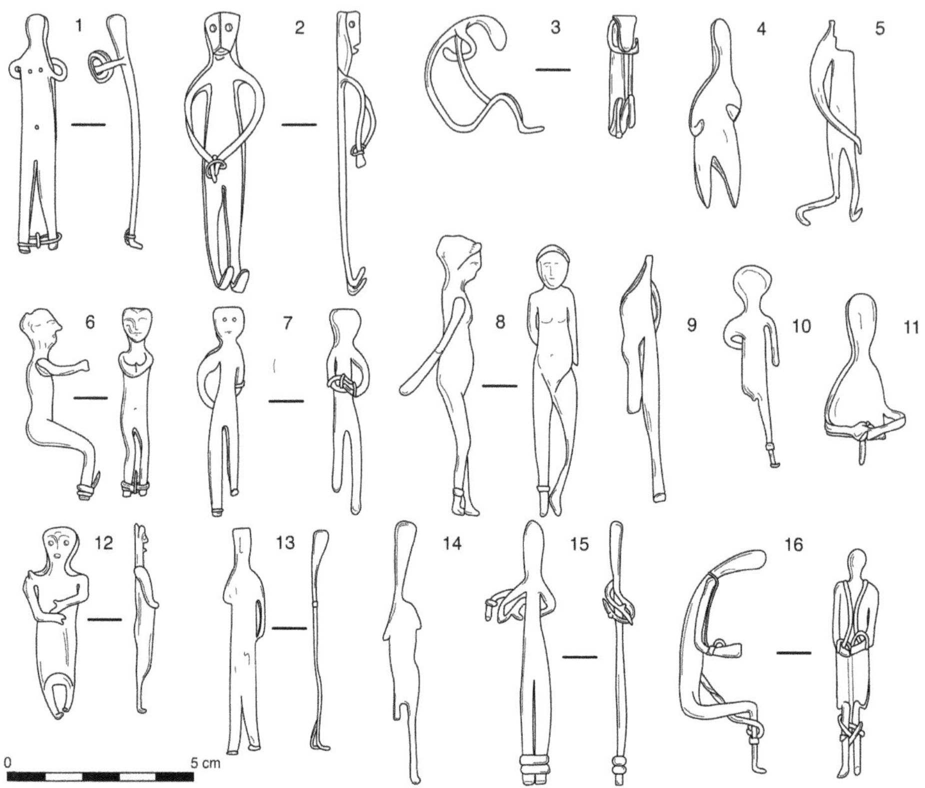

FIGURE 18. Sixteen lead figurines depicting prisoners in a variety of styles and positions. Excavated at floor level of a Seleucid military outpost, understood as either "votive offerings after a battle, in the form of bound captives," or "they represent the intended victims of incantation" (Bliss and Macalister 1902, 154). Image by Evan Levine after Bliss and Macalister 1902, plate 85.

to stereotypes of prisoner representation and pointing again to a durable connection in the visual lexicon between the act of incarceration and the physical exposure of prisoner bodies (6.3.72–73, L194 [late first century CE]). A century later, the satirist Lucian imagined a civic prisoner in an iron collar and manacles, shackled to stocks alongside other prisoners and "having become unrecognizable through his miseries . . . [with] long hair, all unkempt and matted" (*Toxaris* 29–30, L143 [ca. 163 CE]). The early fourth-century astrologer Firmicus Maternus likewise warns that the moon ought to be observed as part of any person's full birth chart, and that in certain configurations it "places some in custody, some it throws into the prison, some are subjected to public trials; some are condemned, others are crushed by the filth of the prison and of public incarceration [*squalore carceris et publicarum custodiarum*] and die covered in filth and repulsive" (*Mathesis* 4.14.2, L20). Third-century Christians condemned to work in imperial mines wrote back to the bishop Cyprian with a vision of their own plight: a vignette at once representative of their experience, and also, one suspects, intended by them (or the ancient editor of the collection) to be legible as a portrait of people toiling deep underground:

> Those condemned with us give the greatest thanks to you before God, dearly be-loved Cyprian, because you have refreshed struggling hearts by your letters; you have cured members wounded by cudgels; you have released feet bound with chains; you have smoothed the hair of half-shaved heads; you have illuminated the darkness of the prison; you have brought the mountains of the mine down to the plains; you have even brought fragrant flowers to noses and have dissipated the foul odor of smoke. (Cyprian, *Letter* 77.3, L141 [ca. September 257–September 258 CE])

Asked to draw a generic prisoner, a contemporary American might depict a figure in an orange or black and white striped jumpsuit; an ancient Roman would more likely have drawn a haggard man stripped naked, hands bound behind his back.

Some sources depict clothing that has been removed from prisoners, and even the stripped prisoners themselves—for instance, in the Gemma Augustea and the Mosaic of the Captives, both discussed above (KMW Antikensammlung IXa 79, V24 [9–12 CE]; Mosaic of the Captives, V8 [late second century CE]; fig. 15). One telling example is the Mosaic of the Damnati, which decorated the floor of a private home near ancient Thysdrus (El Djem, Tunisia) in the second century CE (fig. 19). Two men appear with long, unkempt hair, matted beards, and hands tied behind their backs as trained animal handlers (*bestiarii*) hold them upright and guide them to the teeth of an advancing leopard. Military standards decorate a stage at the center of the arena where these men were sent to die. Their mortifying state reinforces not only their violent fate but implies also that their suffering as prisoners has lingered for a substantial period already: they awaited their execution with no access to facilities for such hygienic activities as bathing or trimming hair. The dark, damp filth of the Prison for the Condemned in Cagliari brings affective texture to the scene, and helps to illuminate some of the carceral realities embedded in a depiction like the Mosaic of the Damnati. The viewer is supposed to grasp intuitively why the prisoners' hair was matted and their beards were unruly: these men languished in dire circumstances for a long time prior to their final moments in the light of the arena.

A contemporaneous literary source from across the Mediterranean deploys a similar stock image, with the same readerly expectation. The *Mishnah* tractate *Moed Qatan* enumerates acceptable actions during festivals, including exceptions to a general prohibition on cutting one's hair and washing one's clothes. Those allowed to groom themselves include people who have traveled from overseas, men and women who have become ritually impure through menstruation or genital emissions, and prisoners who have been released from a "place of [martial] captivity [*beit hashivyah*]" or a "prison [*beit haʾasurin*]" (3.1, L144 [compiled late second century CE]). This Roman provincial text assumes that prisons were places

FIGURE 19 Mosaic of the Damnati (V28 [second century CE]), El Djem Archaeological Museum, Patio de l'Amphithéatre (west, Room 3). El Djem, Tunisia. Author photo.

from which someone could be released, and that when they were, they would need two things in particular: a haircut and a change of clothes. Whatever the historicity of the source, such an idea accords with the visual public transcript of how prisoners were imagined to look as they left a stay in a carceral facility. The common impression that prisoners typically sport long, disheveled hair appears even in later legal materials, including in a fourth-century law from emperors Valentinian II, Theodosius I, and Arcadius concerning the release of low-level offenders from prison on the occasion of Easter. They decree that "accused persons, with their disheveled hair in deathly disorder should [not] be dragged [out of the prison] as objects of the common pity," as their appearance was out of place in "in the midst of festive ceremonies and the venerable rites of a sacred season" (*Sirmondian* 8, L99 [386 CE]). The phrase, "disheveled hair in deathly disorder [*horrentibus passis feraliter crinibus*]," while clearly rhetorical, does in fact capture something of the essence of the public transcript of what a prisoner was imagined to look like—a sorry state evoking public pity.

As in the documentary record, male prisoners are overrepresented in visual sources. Even so, female prisoners appear in representations across the period covered here, from Ptolemaic Egypt (V2) and Seleucid Palestine (V55) to Rome near the turn of the Common Era (V24), to Greece in the first or second century CE (V16), to North Africa of the second (V8) and third centuries (V9), and to Rome (V53) and Asia Minor of the fourth century CE (V50, V54). Two sources in particular demonstrate typical differences in the depiction of female captives in particular, both discussed above: the Gemma Augustea, from Rome of the early first century CE, and the Mosaic of the Captives, from the second century CE in Tipasa on the North African coast. In both, male captives are stripped naked with hands bound behind their back while female captives remain clothed, hands tied in front of their bodies. These depictions are likely idealized, and certainly prudish; they do not indicate that female prisoners were not stripped in reality, nor that depicting as much was discouraged. For instance, while the left side of the lower register on the Gemma Augustea depicts a clothed female bound next to a stripped male, a stripped female captive sits to the far right, holding her hand to her exposed breast as her body is pulled by her hair (KMW, Antikensammlung IXa 79, V24 [9–12 CE]). Late Roman literary sources also describe the stripping of female prisoners, a practice echoed in roughly contemporary visual sources (*Passion of Perpetua and Felicity* 3.2, 6.3, L15 [third–fourth centuries CE]; V52–53). For their part, juristic sources commend both options: some prescribe that all prisoners should be stripped after conviction without distinction of gender, while others suggest that prisoners should be allowed to keep some modest amount of clothing, regardless of their conviction status (D 48.20.2, L33 [198–211 CE, though with reference to a rescript of Hadrian of 117–38 CE]; D 48.20.6, L124 [early third century CE]). Again, legal sources attest to their own secondary status: they prescribe a variety of ideal worlds that are neither internally consistent nor coherent with contemporary practices.

Similarly, child incarceration is rare in the visual record, but it nevertheless appears at times, like in the Mosaic of the Captives above, and is mirrored in both documentary and literary materials (Mosaic of the Captives, V8 [second century CE]; P. Cair. Masp.1.67005, D86 [568 CE]; *Passion of Perpetua and Felicity* 2.2, 5.2, L15 [third–fourth centuries CE]). Like literary and juristic materials, visual sources suggest that practices varied from place to place, even as certain practices appear as regular tropes. Together, common depictions offer insight into what ancient people might have considered as typical, like stripping men while allowing women to remain clothed, or generally avoiding the incarceration of children. While the documentary record shows that this last point is certainly wrong—children were at times incarcerated with their mothers, especially in the later Roman

FIGURE 20. Relief of a triumphing emperor, with a prisoner of war in tow (V29 [third century CE]), Sousse Archaeological Museum (Sousse, Tunisia). Author Photo. A 3D model of the relief is available in the Ancient Mediterranean Incarceration Database with the ID V29.

world—the visual record allows us to see incarceration through the eyes of the public, who would not be privy to the letters, receipts, and legal proceedings explored here.

While it is often impossible to tell what type of captive is represented, some differences stand out, especially between prisoners of war and civic prisoners. Prisoners of war are generally muscular and imposing; a third-century CE relief from Sousse offers a typical depiction (fig. 20). A triumphant emperor is depicted dominating a muscular prisoner, himself stripped down to a short cloak. The physical prowess of the captive appears exaggerated, with bulging shoulders and pectoral musculature. In this and similar cases the rationale for representing captured warriors as physically intimidating is reasonably clear: enemies of the state are presented as strong and visually impressive in their own right in a manner that stresses the comparative strength of the empire that subdued them. Presenting formidable captive enemies facilitated the notion that a great public service had been done in maintaining peace against such worthy foes, and it justified a continued widespread military presence. We see particularly muscular prisoners of war on the Gemma Augustea, (V24 [9–12 CE]), a marble column base from Mainz depicting a prisoner in the guise of the Farnese Hercules (V10 [late first century CE?]), a grave relief from Neumagen, (V11 [second century CE]), the Mosaic of Captives (V8 [late second century CE]), a Phrygian relief depicting men condemned to death, (V42 [second century CE]) and the Mosaic of Triumph of Dionysius from Setif (V9 [third century CE]).

On the other hand, civic prisoners are often represented as slight and emaciated, as we saw above in the Mosaic of the Damnati (V28 [second century CE]). The various visualizations of Pero, the father condemned to die and nursed at his daughter's breast, uniformly present the body of a man weakened by his incarceration. The accompanying poem in the House of Marcus Lucretius Fronto stresses the old man's frailty, echoing and focalizing the emaciated body depicted visually: "See how the old veins in the thin neck shine as the milk passes through . . ." (CLE 2048, D199 [first century CE]). The attenuated bodies of condemned prisoners serve a similar, albeit inverted, principle from the substantial bodies of prisoners of war: such representations stress the state's ability and prerogative to use incarceration to eviscerate subjects deemed problematic.

We have argued that the theme of triumphant incarcerators above and emaciated prisoners below is prevalent in the public transcript, and though many of our data come from the period of the Roman Empire, earlier Ptolemaic sources present similar themes. For example, a bronze prisoner in the Metropolitan Museum of Art (New York) is a Ptolemaic example of a type known widely in the Hellenistic world: statuettes depicting dwarves held in a pillory (MET 23.6.27, V1 [332–30 BCE]). Their Ptolemaic mummy wrapping is another example of a widely attested type—depicting bound captives underneath the feet of the deceased, along with an inscription indicating the power of the gods to vanquish chaos and political enemies of the state, represented by the prisoners (MET 90.6.87, V2 [fourth–first centuries BCE]). Only the legs of this mummy cartonnage survives, so it is hard to say what the rest of the decorating entailed. Nevertheless, it is telling that the artist tasked with memorializing the person wrapped inside chose the soles of the mummy's feet to depict subjugated bodies: haggard, emaciated, and bound— altogether prepared to be trampled upon for eternity in a not so subtle repetition of the conceptual imbrication of imprisonment and death. The "bound prisoner motif" is attested in Egyptian funerary art from the predynastic period (ending ca. 3,000 BCE) through the Roman period, beginning in royal burials and jumping to nonroyal uses by the early Ptolemaic period, symbolizing state domination of foreign enemies, divine conquering of forces of chaos, and the establishment of peace through governmental subjugation (Corcoran 1995, 53–55). The Ptolemaic example at the Metropolitan Museum of Art presents eighteen figures, both male and female, while an early Roman example of the type depicts only two highly stylized men: one Libyan and one Asian, restrained at their hands and feet and attached to one another with a chain (Fitzwilliam Museum E.103b.1911, V22

[30 BCE–100 CE]). In both instances, captives are stripped to loincloths with their hands and feet bound behind their back, with some attached to a post or beam and affixed to the ground, such as we also find in Roman archaeological sources (A10, A49). In Egypt this common trope lasted more than three thousand years, and it resonates with trends visible in art from Roman North Africa of the first centuries CE: captive bodies existed under the foot of the incarcerator, both visually and architecturally.

One peculiarity of Roman visual depictions is a commitment to marking prisoners as "other" through common motifs of foreignness (Schneider 2012). A third-century CE mosaic from Sitifis (Setif, Algeria) is typical: the god Dionysus is depicted in triumph, returning from India with black prisoners in tow, hands shackled behind their back, or held in chains attached to a satyr who leads the prisoners, and captive tigers, ahead of the god's chariot (Setif Archaeological Museum cat. 21, V9 [third century CE]). The god and his attendants have a range of complexions between fair and olive, while the prisoners, by contrast, all have the same dark skin and meticulously detailed "corkscrew" hair (Ako-Adounvo 1999, 192–97). Similarly, the three central figures of the Mosaic of the Captives are clearly depicted as Berbers, with each prisoner boasting the typical features of the indigenous population surrounding Roman Tipasa (fig. 15). A second-century CE mosaic from Zliten, some thirty-five kilometers east of the Roman city of Leptis Magna (Khoms, Libya) depicts another scene of prisoners in the act of execution by animals (*damnatio ad bestias*) (Tripoli Archaeological Museum, V46 [175–225 CE]). One of the most striking features of this gruesome home decor is the yellow skin tone of the condemned prisoners, which contrasts with the pink tones chosen for their executioners (*bestiarii*)—a distinction that led Kathleen Coleman (1990) to conclude that the prisoners are purposefully depicted as indigenous tribesmen (54). Visual tropes of foreignness mark prisoners' bodies across our archive: in a cameo vase in Berlin, (V35 [37–27 BCE]) in the Captives' Facade from Corinth, (V16 [first–second centuries CE]) the Tropaeum of Trajan in Moesia Inferior, (V37 [98–117 CE]), in Rome on the Column of Trajan (V36 [98–117 CE]), the Trajanic Statues of Dacian Prisoners included in the Arch of Constantine (V38 [98–117 CE]), on the Column of Marcus Aurelius, (V39 [ca.193 CE]), and the Arch of Septimius Severus, (V17 [203 CE]) and in the Sousse relief (fig. 20 [third century CE]). Again, the lesson is reasonably clear: prisoner bodies were often represented as foreign and other, both physically and by virtue of their deviance, attributes that are meticulously contrasted with Roman ideals of peace, law, and order (Carroll 2020).

As is the case with legal sources, in visual sources one finds a brazen disconnect and sustained distraction from the lived realities of prisoners. Nevertheless, we find unmistakable resonances between visual depictions and the documentary, literary, and archaeological sources discussed above. Visual sources reflect back to a culture its own practices and ideals but they are not a mirror. Even when they seem to be veristic representations, they refract and focus, vignette and occlude. And yet, these representations were the closest that many ancient people came to seeing the inside of a prison. Inhabitants of Ptolemaic Philadelphia, or Roman Corinth, or just about any other city in the Mediterranean basin likely saw depictions of prisoners more frequently than they saw incarcerated people, perhaps by many orders of magnitude. This is not because prisoners were absent from ancient society—as we argued above, they were often accessible at the center of cities—but rather because depictions of prisoners were ever-present. When interpreting the prevalence and coherence of the corpus of visual sources, we must remember that we are not gazing at an uninterested archive; prisoners were represented for a reason.

The public monuments and imperial images offer access to an official message, carefully curated to the masses: this is what prisoners look like, these are society's deviants, and this is how state power crushed them. What we learn from these materials is that, above all, across Mediterranean antiquity prisoners were represented in service of an ideology of domination, or what Giorgio Agamben (1998) has called sovereign power over bare life; the ability to decide when life is "politically relevant," and for what political purpose it is relevant to display (142). Ultimately, the key issue here is that those in power felt the need to project their dominance over dangerous forces. Defeating and capturing, however, were only the first steps; the next step was controlling, which required careful systems of management, planning, and personnel.

5

Prison Management

We have suggested that ancient Mediterranean states employed punitive carceral practices which touched nearly every aspect of society. Yet such a deleterious state power to incarcerate also had a banality to it, emerging in the emotionless, tedious routines of bureaucracy—carceral regimes etched in administrative triplicate. (Arendt 1994, 287). As Traianos Gagos and Peter Sijpesteijn (1996) have observed, in the Roman period "several hundreds of petitions of all sorts, some complaining about injustice committed against certain individuals or reports on smaller and larger scale crimes, as well as reports and declarations on every imaginable aspect of the administration swamped the office of these administrators every day. The documents that have survived represent but a small portion of the amount of daily paperwork reaching these headquarters" (83). The sheer quantity of surviving documents illuminating the prison, its captives, and its oversight speaks to one of the central features of incarceration in antiquity: the system was fundamentally bureaucratic, involving not only judges and laws but private individuals and interpersonal conflict, all of which resulted in documents being produced, copied, reproduced, disseminated, collected, filed, consulted, and ultimately discarded, only to be excavated as part of the great scramble for ancient papyri in the nineteenth and twentieth centuries. In this section we survey documents produced in the process of incarcerating individuals and maintaining carceral spaces.

It is important to keep in mind that our archive skews our vision most profoundly when discussing the topic of bureaucracy in particular. There is no doubt that the overwhelming majority of ancient prisoners left no discernible mark on the archive. It is impossible to quantify the extent of what we have lost, though we can be certain of a few facts: papyrological sources survive overwhelmingly from the urban centers of Egypt, and they survive in significantly greater numbers from the early centuries of Ptolemaic and Roman rule than from later periods. Inconsistent patterns of preservation require us to take care in extrapolation from Egypt to other settlements in the Mediterranean basin, and the archive leaves rural contexts poorly understood and the late Ptolemaic period difficult to characterize. What's more, channels of documentary production differ between the Ptolemaic and Roman periods, while the turn of the third century CE witnessed another revolution in documentary production in what has been called the "municipalization of writing" in Roman Egypt (Claytor 2018). All this together might lead one to be reasonably skeptical that useful conclusions could be drawn from such an archive.

It is striking, however, that the papyrological archive includes prison documents from the entire breadth of our time period and represents prisoners from all segments of society. That is to say, the documentary record offers a window into the institution that does not seem irreparably skewed by class, location, or time period; it is a cross-section of society, though one cut with a dull and imprecise knife. While documentary production changed between the Ptolemaic, Roman, and Byzantine periods—especially when it came to contracts and legal proceedings—the underlying carceral *practices*, it seems, remained remarkably intact.

Even individual documents attest to the extent of the bureaucracy inherent in carceral systems. In November of 22 CE, an agent working at the estate of a woman named Antonia wrote to the governor of Arsinoites, complaining that fifteen days earlier a group of herdsmen had led their flocks into his employer's fields and that the animals had consumed a modest quantity of wheat (P. Oslo 3.123, D90). The agent's letter ends: "I request that you write to the head administrator of Philadelphia so that the accused can be brought before you quickly for the necessary punishment, lest I be disadvantaged, given what I sent in the other petitions. Farewell." A second person supplemented the document in different handwriting, recording the day that the request was processed along with the governor's response: "On the sixteenth [November 11]. Send them up [from the prison to be tried?]." P. Oslo 3.123 is only one document, but it speaks to the grand paper trail following along behind accusations of even minor crimes.

Based on similar cases in our archive, we should expect some variation of the following chain of events occurring in connection with this single extant document: first (1) a letter had been written to the local authorities requesting the arrest of the accused and that, as a result of the accusation, (2) an arrest warrant was drawn up. Upon arrest their names would have been added to (3) a roll of prisoners when they arrived in jail. (4) A letter from an agent of the victim (P. Oslo

3.123, above) often elicited (5) a response from the governor back to the sender and (6) a further letter from the governor to the head administrator in Philadelphia (perhaps this same letter was simply forwarded, given that an order was appended to end with the decision of the governor). When the head administrator acted on the governor's order to transfer prisoners, they may be sent with (7) a written notice of transfer, and when the prisoners arrived, the governor would have likely written back to the victim's agent, with (8) a notice to appear for the trial. For their part, the prisoners may have done what countless others did in their position: (9) written a letter (perhaps several) to the governor to request that they be released on bail and also, perhaps (10) another letter to a family member, friend, or acquaintance in order to secure funds or assurances resulting in their release on bail. If granted, bail would be attested in a receipt, often in two copies: (11) one to be retained by the prison registrar, and (12) one kept by the imprisoned person.

Before the prisoner ever arrived before a judge, twelve distinct documents, involving no fewer than six people, are likely to have been produced by this one case—some in multiple copies—and the trial itself involved a flurry of additional documentary production. Further, many of these documents pertain to just one of the arrested men, but P. Oslo 3.123 points to three prisoners accused of the same crime, each of whom were at liberty to write their own letters seeking supplies or release. Even if administrative corners were cut and the men sat quietly with their accused crimes, sending no requests for aid, documents already start to pile up—*even if* these men were only in prison for the fourteen days between their accused crime and the processing of this letter, as opposed to the more than three years that other prisoners waited for release in evidence from the second century BCE (P. Coll. Youtie 1.12, D4 [177 BCE]; *CIIP* 4.3.3689, D170 [second century BCE]). The corpus includes examples of every type of document listed above. In a handful of instances, we have more than one document from a single prisoner, though in the vast majority of cases only one piece survives. Every puzzle piece implies an entire lost dossier. We are fortunate, however, that enough bureaucratic papyri survive that it is possible to understand the typical flow of documents resulting from even brief incarceration. This production and flow of bureaucratic documents is itself meaningful and worth careful consideration.

The preponderance of bureaucratic sources for the carceral system relate to the movement, status, and provisioning of captives: arrest warrants, lists of prisoners, and individual requests and records of prison deliveries, along with reports on labor, release, escape, and death. Of this group, the largest collection is arrest reports, which survive from every period covered by this book. As noted above, the fastest track to incarceration across the ancient world was to owe somebody money, especially someone of high social status who had well-established connections to social and political power, and a willingness to grease the wheels of the carceral apparatus to turn in their favor. The decision to arrest someone could be taken by any number of people, and, as Gagos and Sijpesteijn (1996) have noted, at least in the Roman period such orders were only drawn up if the accused were already assumed to be guilty (78). Papyri like P. Hib. 1.34 and 1.73 are typical of early Ptolemaic sources, according to which a prison guard himself was tasked by a local administrator with locating and arresting a debtor and extracting from him either the loaned item (a donkey), or its monetary equivalent. In a complaint to the king, the guard claims that another man (apparently the head prison guard of the region) released the debtor without exacting payment (P. Hib. 1.34, D48 [244–243 BCE]; P. Hib. 1.73 D49 [244–243 BCE]; Bauschatz 2013, 107–9). Interestingly, P. Hib. 1.73 is only a draft of the guard's complaint to the local administrator (*epistatēs*)—before the document was dispatched a clean copy was likely composed, adding yet another layer to the proliferating paperwork that was part of the carceral apparatus.

One letter to Zeno speaks expressly about the "regular procedure" of documentary production on behalf of people in prison. A man named Philo writes to Zeno, thanking him for attempting to secure the release of a man named Hermokrates who had been arrested. He claims that in addition to Zeno, "several other people put themselves to trouble on his behalf, but the most effective was Kaphisophon son of Philippos, the physician. The written report of the inquiry, which acquits him of all the charges, is already in the hands of Dositheos the recordkeeper [*hupomnēmatographos*] in order that the king may read it before letting him be released, as this is the regular procedure [*para to ethos einai houtos ginesthai*]" (P. Mich. 1.55, D87 [240 BCE]). Here we see explicitly stated what other papyri simply imply—prisoners would write to multiple people with the hope that at least one recipient would be able to secure their release.

Documentary production was a regular part of the social institution of incarceration in Ptolemaic Egypt and, as we have seen, a sense of "regular procedure" continued in the Roman and Byzantine period. It is this environment, in which documents ensure a prisoner's bondage as much as the fetters affixing them to their prison, that makes sense of the report about the emperor Gaius (Caligula) burning records so that he would be "unable to punish" political prisoners (Cassius Dio, *Roman History* 59.6.1–3, L126 [ca. 230 CE]). Two papyri from the late antique Apion archive are nearly identical—using the same format and language to request release on bail for different defendants, showing that the formulaic and bureaucratic nature of paperwork for requesting release on bail for Egyptian debt prisoners continued largely intact throughout the period covered by this book (P. Oxy. 83.5373, D217 [552 CE]; P. Oxy. 83.5375, D216 [557 CE]).

P. Hib. 2.249, from the mid-250s BCE, highlights another standard procedure: an Oxyrhynchite official wrote a letter ordering the arrest of a number of local grain gatherers. While it is not precisely clear to whom the letter was written, in the Ptolemaic period these letters were often written to either the treasurer (*oikonomos*) or head administrator (*epistatēs*) of the city, or to one of the chiefs of police, either the *archephodos* or the *archiphulakitēs*, while in the Roman period, such orders were typically addressed to a prison guard or local official like a governor (*stratēgos*) (D53 [258–254 BCE]). P. Oslo 2.21 is a typical example: a request that a man named Apollonios from the city of Karanis be arrested, having been accused of the crime of picking olives earlier than the appointed harvest season. This letter, dated September 29, 71 CE, is addressed not to the governor, however, or to the local prison guard, but to the local Roman centurion (D89). Documentary sources like these confirm what we see in literary materials: Roman soldiers were not reserved for strictly "military operations." Rather, they regularly appear in papyri and literary accounts alike as police officers. In the late fourth century, the orator Libanius reiterated the use of soldiers to carry out arrests, complaining to the emperor that rich landlords regularly lodge false accusations against their impoverished tenants; "just a word or two is needed, and a soldier goes down to the farm, complete with fetters, they are arrested, and the prison takes them in" (*Oration* 45.5, L52 [386 CE]). It may be the case that the centurion of P. Oslo 2.21 arrested the accused and delivered him to a civic prison, but it is perhaps at least as likely that this civil prisoner was incarcerated in a military prison, as we see in the *Passion of Perpetua and Felicity* 7. In either case, it is clear that the military played a hands-on role in arrests, even for petty crimes. The modern world mirrors the ancient in this respect: the boundary between the carceral and the military state is porous and often wholly indeterminate (Moran, Turner, and Arnold 2019).

The surviving summons are quite cursory, many resembling P. Mich. Mchl. 5, a small slip of papyrus from the second century CE roughly the size of a playing card that reads in its entirety as follows: "To the chief of police [*archifodōi*] of Taampemou. Send Markos surnamed Mallos and Eutyches with a guard, being accused by Sarapion" (fig. 21). Even our English translation inflates the text—in Greek it comprises a mere twelve words, and yet it contains all the necessary information for the local police chief. The order is written in a quick but trained hand, unsurprising given the ubiquity of such summons, many of which were apparently mass produced (Gagos and Sijpesteijn 1996, 83–85). Here we have an explicit order to move imprisoned individuals under guard, though it is not clear whether they have already been apprehended and are waiting in a jail or whether they are to be arrested and delivered. Following the text, the scribe wrote two lines of small strokes that are either decorative or, more likely, intended to hedge against a subsequent writer adding further text to the order—similar to a quickly disappearing relic of the modern era, in which entries on personal checks are completed with a horizontal line to guard against appended text that changes the meaning of the document. This scribe's concern was not unwarranted: the documentary archive includes accusations from the Ptolemaic and Roman periods of carceral records being altered or fabricated, leading to further conflict and accusations of unjust imprisonment (P. Mich. 1.36, D214 [254 BCE]; BGU 16.2639, D212 [10–9 BCE]).

Even simple summons could sometimes elicit replies from the officers charged with carrying out the task, as in the case of P. Oxy. 7.1033. On October 19, 392 CE, a

FIGURE 21. P. Mich. Mchl. 5, D64 (second century CE). Image courtesy University of Michigan Libraries.

pair of night guards wrote to the police magistrates of Oxyrhynchus complaining about the danger inherent in their jobs (D20). They ask either to receive backup when performing arrests or, alternatively, to be relieved of the duty—it was apparently too much to ask two men to perform both guard duties and arrests. This curious complaint underlines the ubiquity of arrest warrants; it is striking that two night guards were apparently insufficient to service a mid-sized city like Oxyrhynchus owing to the danger of the task ordered, and perhaps the workload itself, which, in addition to controlling the movement of inmates, involved managing complex bureaucratic files.

Once prisoners were taken into custody, they had to be both locked and logged in by the imprisoning authorities. Only a few of these lists remain intact, and mostly from the early Byzantine period, but they are nevertheless illustrative. For instance, Stud. Pal. 10.252 is a sixth-century prisoner roll noting the names of people incarcerated in the month of Mesoré, along with the crimes of which they are accused: the shepherds Neilammon and Georgios are accused of having stolen sheep, a city council member named Kosmos allegedly stole a postal worker's cloak, and a butcher named Ana was incarcerated because her brother stole money from a police officer (D296 [sixth century CE]; Torallas Tovar 2003, 213–14).

A number of sources speak to the position of registrars who were responsible for keeping records relating to prisoners. For instance, a trial record from the third century CE records a case brought before Quintus Maecius Laetus, prefect of Egypt, regarding a group of 650 rioters who were arrested and held in custody (SB 16.12949, D62 [207–68 CE]). A question arose during the legal proceedings about whether the defendant was in fact one of the rioters, and in order to adjudicate, the prefect asked that the *colletio* be brought in for inspection: apparently a list of people arrested, or perhaps simply the person who took down the testimony about the riot, which was extracted through torture. Because the request could not be fulfilled, the prefect ordered the prison registrar (*commentariensis*) to hold a man in custody until the proper documentation was produced. According to John R. Rea, editor of the papyrus, *commentarienses* "were in all probability not employed in recording the trial but rather were in charge of prison records"; they were the registrars of the prison, collecting records that could be produced during legal proceedings, such as in the trial against Verres in which Cicero demanded "let us have the prison record [*rationem carceris*], which is carefully kept so as to show the dates on which prisoners are received, and on which they die, or are put to death" (Rea 1983, 100; Cicero, *Against Verres* 2.5.147, L203 [70 BCE]). Given that such records were intended to be provisional, it is likely that many were kept on wax tablets rather than more permanent media like papyrus or parchment. If so, this would account for their relative absence in the documentary record.

A law of 380 CE specifies what information such prisoner lists were intended to include, assessing a fine of twenty pounds of gold if a prison *commentariensis* failed to record and report "the number of persons, the types of offenses, the form of incarceration, and the ages of the imprisoned" at least every thirty days (CI 9.4.5, L63 [380 CE]). In their capacity as filing clerks, *commentarienses* would have been peculiarly situated to receive bribes in exchange for inserting or deleting names from records, accusations that we saw above in P. Mich. 1.36 and BGU 16.2639, and perhaps the type of chicanery that the scribe of P. Mich. Mchl. 5 attempted to head off with his line of X's at the end of his cursory arrest warrant (fig. 21; P. Mich. 1.36, D214 [254 BCE]; BGU 16.2639, D212 [10–9 BCE]). Likewise, the Jewish philosopher Philo recounted precisely this type of administrative duplicity in Alexandria during the third decade of the first century CE, painting a vivid picture of record tampering by a certain man named Lampo.

> For [Lampo] stood alongside the governors as they issued judgments and he took down notes [*hypemnēmatizeto*] on the cases and introduced an organization [to the notes; *eisagōn hōs echōn taxin*]. Then, in some cases, he erased certain parts or purposefully omitted other things. Sometimes he interpolated some things that were not said. And other times he changed by remodeling, inverting, and turning the notes upside down, making money by the syllable, or rather by every letter stroke, the paper-porer. (*Against Flaccus* 131, L64)

Philo reports that this court registrar was so ruthlessly effective in documentary subterfuge that the populace regularly condemned him as a "pen-murderer" (*kalamosfaktēs*), but that the "perpetual flood of new cases private and public" prevented governors from properly scrutinizing the work of their staffs (132–33). He vehemently disapproved of the registrar's performance and aimed with his treatise to expose these abuses of the prison and the bureaucracy that (sometimes) underlies carceral practices. Nevertheless, his attempt to expose abuse betrays a broader cultural assumption that court documents were fluid and contested, and that record keepers were hardly immune from temptation to capitalize on their unique position within the bureaucracy.

Together, these sources situate the record keeper as a figure wielding surprising amounts of power in Ptolemaic, Roman, and Byzantine Egyptian carceral systems, and they speak further to the prison cell as an extension of the registrar's chambers. The prefect's order in the case before Quintus Maecius Laetus about the 650 rioters, discussed above, further underscores the power of the *commentariensis*. In a sense, it was prison registrars who were tasked with holding people in custody: "[Laetus] said to the *commentarienses*, 'Let the *duplicarius* be held in custody . . .'" (SB 16.12949, D62 [207–68 CE]). Unless we are to assume that *commentarienses* performed double duty as registrar and bailiff, then in the logic of this Roman court proceeding, the physical sequestering of a prisoner is a secondary operation, with the primary force of incarceration accomplished through the bonds of bureaucracy. This vast sea of legal protocols, checks and balances, and paperwork took time to work. In this case, it was bureaucracy's slow clockwork that held these rioters lingering in prison.

Sometimes notices about captives moved between prisons, as we see in P. Sorb. 3.135, from 224 BCE, in which a prison guard from the village of Mouchis wrote to the local governor (*stratēgos*) about a man arrested in Crocodilopolis for a debt owed to a man from Cyrene (D60). The short notice explicitly references three further documents that do not survive, letters of various sorts, along with a registration of a triflingly minor debt—on the order of a few obols—and a report moving between the prison in the regional center of Crocodilopolis and its the outlying village of Mouchis, roughly thirty kilometers away (Winkler 2018). The fragmentary nature of the papyrus precludes a full picture of the situation, but it nevertheless speaks to the intricately bureaucratized nature of the Ptolemaic carceral apparatus.

Prisoners, too, moved between carceral spaces, often with an escort carrying documentation, as we show below in the section on prisoner transport. More numerous than orders to move large numbers of prisoners between carceral facilities are orders for single prisoners or small groups to appear before government officials. P. Tebt. 2.290 is a paradigmatic record in an exemplary state of preservation (fig. 22). In it we find a short note, written in the late first or early second century CE from the governor (*stratēgos*) to the head administrator (*epistatēs*) of Tebtunis, summoning a man named Galates and his wife to appear before the governor. It also records the name of their accuser, Semele, the daughter of Akousilaos. It is possible that Galates and his wife were free, but it is just as likely that they had already been arrested, and the administrator was simply being asked to send prisoners for trial. The possibility is stronger still in cases where authorities

FIGURE 22. P. Tebt. 2.290, D78 (75–125 CE). "[To the chi]ef [*epistatei*] of Tebtunis. Send up Galates and his wife, [bo]th children of Kronion, who are accused by Semele daughter of Akousilaos [Seal]. The governor summons you." Order for arrest with attached clay seal showing the bust of an emperor. Note that the papyrus is mounted between thick glass, with a hole cut to accommodate the seal. Photo courtesy of the Center for the Tebtunis Papyri, University of California, Berkeley.

order that people be sent "with a guard," as is the case in SB 24.16005 and P. Mich. Mchl. 5, above, indicating that they are to arrive under carceral control (D67 [second century CE]). As we saw above in a Ptolemaic example, P. Tebt. 2.290 from the Roman period uses a seal to authenticate the document: a small clay disk remains on the surface of this papyrus to this day, bearing the bust of an emperor, a partial fingerprint of the official who attached it, and an inscription reading "the governor summons you."

Complaints are the most common type of document found among the surviving records of carceral bureaucracy, and they often double as petitions for release. In 177 BCE a man wrote a letter complaining of his false imprisonment at "Big Prison" in Crocodilopolis, to which he had been transferred three years earlier and where he feared that he would die if not released soon (P. Coll. Youtie. 1.12, D4). It seems that the man was initially arrested on account of a tax debt, along with his guarantors. The man claims that he was arrested without proper legal proceedings and should have not been subject to arrest in the first place given that he had a pardon from the governor, as well as from King Ptolemy and Queen Cleopatra, extending down to 177 BCE. Interestingly, the surviving document doesn't appear to be the official version dispatched from the prison, but rather a draft: numerous phrases are crossed out and rewritten above the line, implying that the text, once established, was transferred to a fair copy, with this version discarded to be excavated some two millennia later.

Changes in local prison oversight could also spell trouble for prisoners and necessitate further bureaucratic wrangling. Between the years 7 and 4 BCE a man named Satabous and his son were accused of murder by two men, both named Opis. The father and son had been thrown into prison after their trial before

Cordus, the chief of police in the town of Arsinoites. The prisoners dispatched a petition to the prefect of Egypt, written in beautiful handwriting more common in ancient books than petitions (P. Lond. 2.354, D80). CPR 15.15, on the other hand, appears to be a draft of this same petition, written in cursive script more common among documentary sources and recording extra details that were later edited out of the formal petition (D131 [7–4 BCE]; Jördens 2017, 272). Together, these papyri suggest that a scribe may have visited the men in prison to take notes and work up a draft, and sometime later produced another copy for dispatch. In their complaint, the two incarcerated men allege that they had been cleared for release by Cordus, "but before we were released from the prison, Cordus was transferred and Brison took his place." The men request that the prefect write to the governor of Arsinoites and demand their release so that they can get back to their work as tenant farmers, along with an investigation into the situation. In this petition and its draft we see a common theme again, present across the sources and time period under discussion: incarceration often began and ended according to the whims of local officials, with prisoners' only recourse being somehow to attract the attention of a yet more senior official, sometimes through petitions written by trained, professional writers resulting from multiple successive drafts. Quite opposed to the traditional notion of bureaucracy as the depersonalization of state power, these documents show just how personal the bureaucracy of incarceration could be. The changing political configuration, the transfer of a prison guard overseeing a carceral facility, the failure to deliver a prisoner's petition to the relevant administrator: each was tied to a bureaucratic process that was entirely out of the hands of a prisoner yet could seal their fate.

Occasionally the same petitions were drafted and dispatched to different recipients, as is the case in PSI 4.419 from the mid-third century BCE, in which three men write to Zeno asking for release, "lest we be destroyed by hunger in prison, given that we are foreigners" and, one suspects, as a result not receiving visitors to help tend to their basic material needs (D57 [262–229 BCE]). They ask Zeno to approach Philiskon, the chief treasurer of Arsinoites, to effect their release, and they end their letter informing him that they have written another letter presenting their request to Philiskon directly.

Follow-up letters are common, as well. P. Petr. Kleon 58 is a relatively unremarkable request for release in which a man named Demetrios writes to Kleon, an engineer responsible for water infrastructure in Arsiniotes during the mid-third century BCE: "To Kleon, greetings from Demetrios. I have already written to you before about the arrest for which I have been arrested now . . . Think of me as your own son and get me out of prison. You will not suffer any harm. For I am in need of a lot of things in the prison. Respectfully" (D55 [255 BCE]). Demetrios's letter does not speak to the reason for his imprisonment, but Demetrios claims to have already written to Kleon and sends this follow-up letter because he had already informed Kleon of the events leading to his arrest.

In this case, remarkably, the first letter that Demetrios sent to Kleon also sur-vives, and it at least partially hints at why this prisoner writes to a water engineer for aid. Demetrios tells a complex story in his initial complaint: he was a regu-lar at the mining camp he calls "the Works," and on a recent visit, he had picked up a chisel and was accused of attempting to steal it (P. Petr. Kleon 54, D17 [255 BCE]). Five days later, while bringing bread to the prisoners in the camp, one of the foremen's brothers came to Arsinoites and attacked Demetrios; the ensuing brawl was broken up by the city elders. Demetrios was responsible for provision-ing the prison camp, and in his letter to Kleon he complains that the rift between him and the camp's overseers was so serious that the mining itself may not be able to proceed for lack of food deliveries. In these two letters we glimpse a bit of the bureaucratic infrastructure supporting the prison labor system, the precarity of even the people tasked with provisioning the laborers, and their direct relationship with the industries benefiting from the extractive labor that runs on the input of incarcerated bodies. Demetrios was a mid-level staffer, shuffling between the office of a water engineer and a mining complex; it would not be surprising to learn that the mines, as well as its prison labor, were running to supply Kleon with raw mate-rial for his hydraulic projects. Demetrios exploits his position as middleman in his request for supplies in prison, claiming that "you know that we have been hard pressed during the works [ie. the mining activities], and now I am being utterly afflicted since I have been carried off to prison . . ." (P. Petr. Kleon 58, D55 [255 BCE]). Having served as a cog in the carceral system, Demetrios wrote as one who now had first-hand knowledge of its oppressive character.

Death notices of all types are common in the papyri, produced primarily to amend the tax record, including notices about people who died in prison. P. Oxy. 43.3104 is one such record, from Oxyrhynchus in 228 CE, recording the death of a tax farmer who contracted an illness in prison and died some eight weeks into his incarceration (D15). This notice comes from the Roman imperial period, but it speaks to the durability of carceral structures from the Ptolemaic period onward: this man was imprisoned for a fiscal debt and the notice explicitly states that he was incarcerated in the tax office prison (*logistērion*), as we see in numerous Ptolemaic era sources. One of the prison guards was illiterate, and signed the notice through another man named Aurelius Theon, while the other guard signed his own name.

How were all these documents created? In the case of official orders, prisoner lists, and the like, we should expect that the prison registrar, either as part of the tax office or as dedicated to the prison itself, produced and maintained bureau-cratic papers. As we just saw in P. Oxy. 43.3104, sometimes even the prison staff members possessed enough functional literacy to sign documents, and it is pos-sible that they were involved in production at times, as well. Prisoner petitions and letters present more of a puzzle, but the question is not intractable. Ancient prisons were porous spaces, allowing for the delivery of supplies to prisoners and communication between the inside and the outside, often through embrasures or barred windows of the sort we explored in chapter 2. Perhaps prisoners were released to consult with legal agents and scribes at times, but archaeological evidence suggests that this was hardly necessary in many cases. In the case of civic prisons especially, where one could stand on a public street and communicate through a window, it was often possible to interact with prisoners without ever having to enter the prison.

How is it that so many letters emerged from the dark, feculent carceral facilities, seemingly packed with lower-social status offenders within a largely illiterate society? Here the evidence allows us only an educated guess. In at least a few instances it is possible that multiple prisoner letters were written by the same person on behalf of prisoners. It is notoriously difficult to identify writers based solely on the appearance of the handwriting, though as Trevor Evans (2005) notes, "documents written in informal hands, which have a greater tendency toward 'individualistic' features, are especially promising." Four prisoner letters from Zeno's archive display precisely such features, including remarkably similar handwriting, phrasing, and layout—enough to suggest that they were either written by the same person or that they were produced by writers with remarkably similar training (P. Cair. Zen. 3.59492, D37; P. Mich. 1.87, D50; PSI 4.419, D57; P. Lond. 7.2045, D81 [all 263–229 BCE]). Together, these papyri offer insight into the production of prisoner letters, an aspect of incarceration that remains invisible in the vast majority of cases, where we have access only to a single document, disconnected from any further context.

All four letters begin with "To Zeno, Greetings," with a space between the words, followed by another space and the name of the sender (fig. 23). The letters have identical final greetings, as well, ending with "Good wishes" (*eutuchei*), written alone on a separate line, detached from the body. Both of these generic formatting features are common in letters from the Zeno archive, though they are by no means universally attested in the collection. Nevertheless, the cluster of coincidences is striking. If we add to this writing with the fibers in P. Cair. Zen. 3.59492 (D37), suggesting a new piece of papyrus used for a clean copy, compared with P. Mich. 1.87 (D50), which is written against the fibers, suggesting a reused scrap of papyrus, then we start to get a picture, perhaps, of a single writer who wrote a quick draft of a requested prisoner letter represented in P. Mich. 1.87, while P. Cair. Zen. 3.59492 is another prisoner's request which has already gone through the drafting stage and been transferred to a clean copy on a fresh piece of papyrus. Different levels of refinement add to this impression: P. Mich. 1.87 is written across the fibers and riddled with small spelling mistakes and missing words, some of which are corrected above the line, suggesting that it was written more quickly, while P. Cair. Zen. 3.59492 is written along the fibers, perhaps a final product after editing; it even includes the name of its addressee written on the back.

To similarity of handwriting, greetings, and format, we can add similarity of phrasing: P. Cair. Zen. 3.59492, P. Mich. 1.87, and PSI 4.419 use a phrase in common,

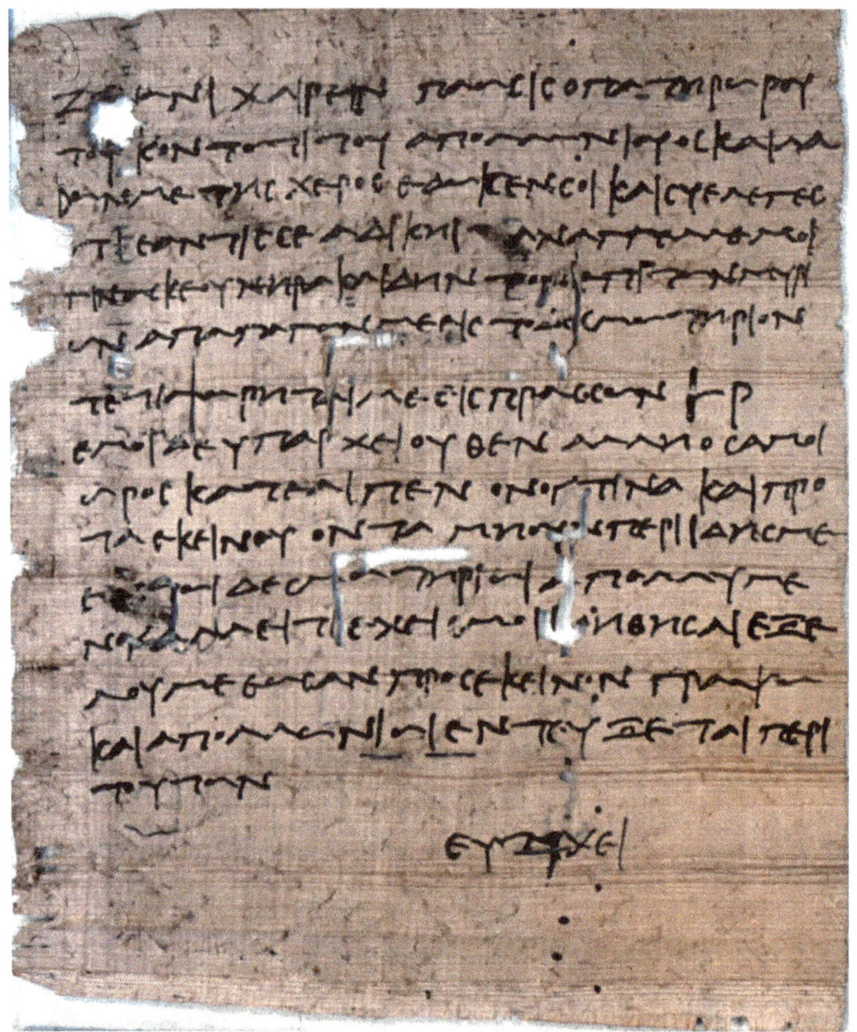

FIGURE 23. P. Cair. Zen. 3.59492, D37 (263–229 BCE).

"in the prison [*en tōi desmōtēriōi*]," with only slight orthographic changes, and both
P. Cair. Zen. 3.59492 and P. Mich. 1.87 use a peculiar construction with the verb "to
overlook" (*perioran*), inflected in the aorist subjunctive, to render their plea. This
phrasing is peculiar, found only in the third and second centuries BCE, and even
then in an exiguously small number of examples—six, by our count, of which half
are prisoner letters in the Zeno archive (D37, D50, D213). In P. Cair. Zen. 3.59492
we find "So, do not overlook me perishing in the prison [*mē oun periidēis me en
tōi desmōtēriōi apollumenon*]"; and in P. Mich. 1.87 we have "I pray and beseech

Ζήνωνι χαίρειν Κάλλιππος

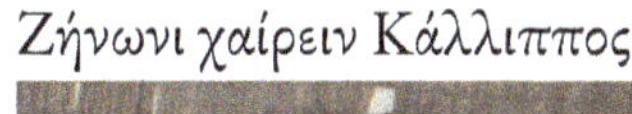

P. Mich. 1.87
D50, l. 1

P. Cair. Zen.
3.59492
D37, l. 1

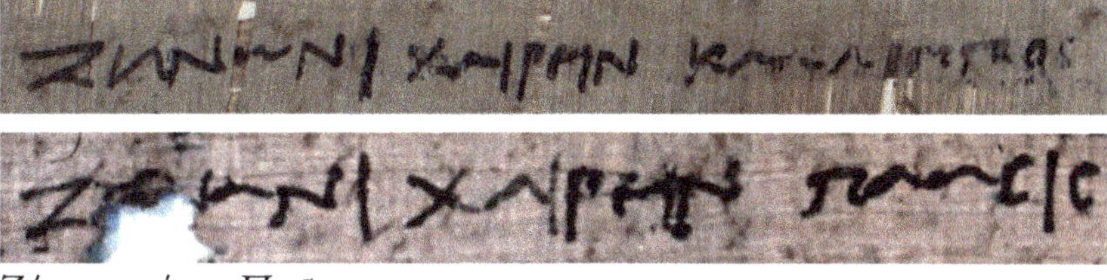

Ζήνωνι χαίρειν Παῶσις

μὴ περιίδῃς μη ἐν τῶι δεζμωτηρίωι

P. Mich. 1.87
D50, l. 5

P. Cair. Zen.
3.59492
D37, l. 10–11

μὴ οὖν περιίδῃς με / ἐν τῶι δεσμωτηρίωι

ἐν / τῶι δεζμωτηρίωι

P. Mich. 1.87
D50, l. 8–9

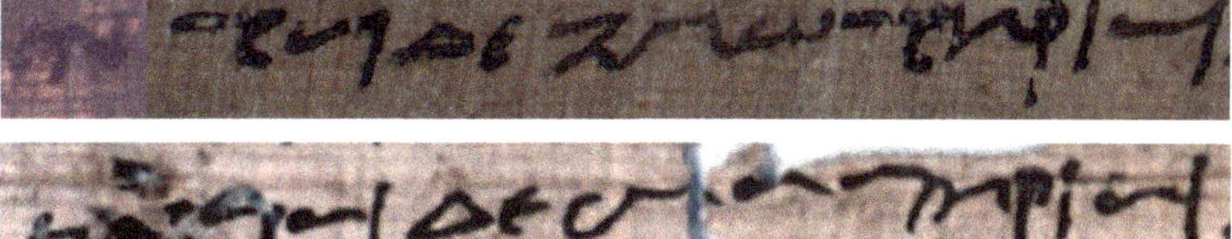

P. Cair. Zen.
3.59492
D37, l. 11

ἐν τῶι δεσμωτηρίωι

FIGURE 24. Script comparison of P. Mich. 1.87 (D50) and P. Cair. Zen. 3.59492 (D37 [both 263–229 BCE]). Images courtesy of the Cairo Museum, University of Michigan Libraries, and Adam Bülow-Jacobsen.

you, do not overlook me in the prison [*deomai sou kai iketeō, mē periidēs mē en tōi dezmōtēriōi*]" (fig. 24). A number of other points of comparison are possible that needn't detain us here, including the striking similarity of ligatures in these two letters. It is possible that these requests from prisoners to Zeno were all written by the same person. More certain is that they were produced by writers with remarkably similar training, analogous formats for such letters, and who even use identical stock phrases to render a prisoner's pleas.

In either case, similarities among the corpus of prisoner letters in the Zeno archive suggest strongly that these letters are not written by prisoners themselves. (The only real contender for a letter written "from the inside" is P. Cair. Zen. 3.59519, where the thick strokes may indicate writing in low-light conditions [D134, 263–229 BCE].) Rather, this cluster of letters gives the impression that trained writers periodically visited the local prison to record petitions. Given the often-discussed bureaucratic "thinness," especially in rural Egypt, the list of candidates for *who* produced these documents is rather short, pointing to professional writers as the primary producers of petitions in both the Ptolemaic and Roman periods (Hengstl 1997, 286–87; Kelly 2011, 41–45). Maybe these petitions were taken by a scribe on Zeno's staff or perhaps a staffer in the local writing office (*grapheion*), which was a regular institution in even small cities during the Ptolemaic, Roman, and Byzantine periods. What is clear is that the writer or writers had a durable notion of what a prisoner letter should look like and sound like. It would be easy to read too much into this small grouping of papyri. Whether written by the same writer or a small group of writers, they demonstrate materially what we know, a priori, must have occurred: professional writers found a way to take letters from prisoners and dispatch them to local power brokers. The many surviving petitions, sometimes in multiple drafts, suggest that drafting prisoner petitions was a routine task of a local scribe in the Ptolemaic and Roman periods, either officially or as a side job.

Prisoners were sometimes released outright, as we saw above. Often, however, they were released on bail, like we see in P. Oxy. 2.259 from 23 CE, creating yet another stream of paperwork (D72). This papyrus begins by noting that it is a "copy of a bond" written to the "overseer of the Zeus prison," in which a Persian man named Theon swears by the name of the emperor Tiberius that he is responsible for a prisoner that he has bailed out, and that he will return him within thirty days of a formal request to do so. If Theon fails to return the prisoner, he will pay two minae of gold; further, he will be arrested himself. He agrees that "I have no authority to obtain a further period of time nor to transfer myself to another prison." We have dozens of such receipts for cash bail from across the period under discussion, all of which together point to the ubiquity of bail as part of the institution of incarceration in antiquity, as well as to the attendant documentary burden: receipts were often produced in duplicate, with one held by the guarantor and another by the prison registrar. There are a handful of summons addressed to the accused or to another family member or close associate. (e.g., P. Oxy. 74.5004, D281 [third century CE]). These, again, seem not to be orders for arrest but summons to trial of the accused, who had been bailed out of prison in connection with their guarantor, who had given security.

A number of tax receipts record money paid for the maintenance of prisons and the payment of guards. P. Princ. 2.44, from 141 CE, is one of many such receipts from the second century CE that detail taxes levied specifically in support of both the local police and the guards of public prisons. It reads:

> In the fifth year of the emperor Caesar Titus Aelius Hadrianus Antoninus Augustus Pius, the fifth of Choiak, Heron son of Phaseis . . . whose mother is Tha[. . .] paid through Didymos and the assistants of the tax collectors on account of the poll-tax for the same year twelve drachmas and a half-obol[?] in silver and two chalki, totals

twelve drachmae, 1/2 obol two chalki; on account of the pig tax, one drachma one obol, on account of the tax concerning manning the watch-tower and guarding tax [*fulakias*], one drachma three obols, on account of the prison tax [*desmofulakias*] and the river guard tax [*potamofulakias*], 2 1/2 obols. (D123)

This papyrus records three taxes that are relevant for our analysis, and it is important to distinguish carefully between them. The "guarding" tax and the "river guard tax" seem to be levied in support of local police and, as the excavators and editors Grenfell and Hunt note, they are likely the Roman equivalent of the generalized *fulaktikon* tax known from the Ptolemaic period (P. Fayyum 178). The earliest Roman era evidence that we have for this type of tax is from 68 CE, in a receipt that raises funds specifically "for guard/police provisions" (O. Wilcken 2.422, D149 [68 CE]). Tax registers from the second century abbreviated the "prison guard tax" (*desmofulakia*) in a variety of ways, and this tax appears to have been levied specifically in support of the public prison (P. Mich. 6.383, D128 [106 CE]; P. Ryl. 2.191, D124 [117 CE]; P. Ryl. 2.193, D126 [135 CE]; P. Ryl. 2.194, D125 [136CE]; P. Princ. 2.44, D123 [141 CE]). The earliest securely dated attestation of this tax is from 110 CE, with the majority of receipts clustering in the middle decades of the second century and the latest attestation dating to the early 190s CE (O. Petr. Mus. 260, D151). It is hard to say whether taxes specifically earmarked for support of public prisons are new to Roman Egypt of the second century or if they are simply newly specified in documents from this period. An answer to this question is important for understanding changes in prison administration over time, but the fact of the tax, its apparent durability over the course of the Nerva-Antonine dynasty, and its prevalence in the documentary record all point to the notion that incarceration was a central public service in Roman-era Egypt and that the imperial bureaucracy had active structures in place to ensure that prisons were regularly staffed and maintained as a public good. Similar taxes apparently aimed at provisioning prison guards, phrased in slightly different ways, are found in receipts from a longer period of time, beginning with O. Wilcken 2.422, from 68 CE (D149), and continuing through P. Tebt. 2.354, from 186–90 CE (D66). They span that period, with regular attestation, for instance in: P. Fay. 53, D144 [111 CE]; P. Strasb. 5.415, D102 [128 CE]; and SB 24.16185, D68 [151 CE]. Such evidence raises the question of prison personnel, to which we turn momentarily.

A discussion of bureaucracy, by nature, may not promise the book's most gripping moments. Even so, it is a key thread in understanding how incarceration was stitched into the fabric of broader societies. To attend to the documentary aspects of incarceration in Mediterranean antiquity is to see an intricate and banal system of bureaucratic control, in which physical restraints on captive humans are reflections of an institution whose operative materials were not primarily chains and cells but warrants and lists, orders and receipts, contracts and petitions, affidavits and expense sheets. In this sense it is not an overreach to refer to the ancient carceral *system*—at times centralized and unified, and at other times a constellation of overlapping micro-institutions. The image reflects chiefly Egyptian documents, but the verisimilitude with literary and archaeological finds across the Mediterranean, as well as the durability of these structures across a period of nearly a thousand years, suggests that documentary productions, and the social systems that they record, were appreciably similar even in areas where such carceral ephemera do not remain naturally.

PERSONNEL

Bureaucracy requires bureaucrats, and carceral facilities do not run themselves. Prisons require a network of human resources that, when understood, shed light on the various ideologies of incarceration in the ancient Mediterranean and the people who enabled them daily. We find a variety of hierarchies among prison personnel across the immense stretch of time and space covered by this book, and we should not expect to see uniformity between different periods and locations. The current state of the evidence precludes us from providing a complete historical picture. Nevertheless, here we offer a general sketch.

At its most basic level, prison administration was a hierarchy presided over by a government official, who exercised a degree of ultimate responsibility and who delegated tasks to supervisors and lower-ranking assistants who attended to day-to-day operations. This varied across time and regions. As John Bauschatz (2013) showed, in Ptolemaic Egypt, the hierarchy descended from the regional governor (*stratēgos*) to the local police administrator (*epistatēs ton fylakitōn*), who, in turn, oversaw prison guards (*desmofulakes*) that worked as jailors and bailiffs, in conjunction with other police officials (138, 247). As discussed above, the Ptolemaic prison system, and municipal prisons themselves, were connected to the public treasury office in both formal and informal ways (p. 58–59).

Roman sources attest a broadly comparable model, though bureaucrats and staffers bore different titles and worked under a somewhat clearer hierarchy. In the city of Rome, prison supervision ultimately fell to the office of the prefect of the city, while in the provinces, governors deputized a head of the prison (*optio carceris*), or, in military contexts, a head of carceral facilities (*optio custodiarum*). The distinction in title appears to reflect different types of prison, with the head of the prison mostly serving in civic contexts while the head of carceral facilities served as part of a military legion, though soldiers could serve in either role, and some variation is visible, especially in documentary sources. For instance, a cinerary urn likely from Rome in the third century CE attests to a Pannonian man named Vitalis who served as both a centurion and as the *optio carceris*—presumably, the head of the civic prison of Rome (AE 1983, 48, D164 [third century CE, possibly 222–35]). Nevertheless, a soldier named Caesius Verus, who died at the rank of legionary centurion in the middle of the second century CE, served both as the military band director (*ordinatus tubicem*) and as head of the prison (*optio carcarem*) in an explicitly military context (Mitford 1988, 176–78, D186 [161–69 CE]). As elsewhere, we must let these documentary sources disturb the neat categories that literary material offers. Soldiers serving as prison managers bear titles ranging from *optio custodiarum* (CIL 13.6739, D203 [70–86 CE]) to *praepositus carceris* (IGLSyr 13.1.9088, D178 [238–44 CE]; Augustine, *Commentary on John* 49.9, L2 [419 CE]) to *agens curam carceris* (CIL 3.433, D263 [ca. mid-second century CE]). As Pilar Pavón Torrejón (2003) has argued, by the fourth century CE, across the Roman world the prison registrar (*commentariensis*) seems to have taken on primary responsibility as the prison supervisor (127–29, 229–34).

Under the direct supervision of the prison head, we meet a host of attendants holding various titles; often, the exact hierarchy of their relationship is difficult to untangle. In Latin sources we hear of low-level "prison staff" (*carcerarii*, AE 1978, 730, D163 [late second century CE]), somewhat higher-ranking "registrars" (*commentariis custodiarum*, CIL 9.6343, D265 [48–51 CE]), "keyholders" (*clavicularii*, CIL 13.1780, D169 [first century CE]), "gatekeepers" (*cataractarii*, *Passion of Montanus and Lucius* 9.2, L263 [late third century CE]) or "assistants to the gatekeepers" (*cataractariorum ministri*, *Passion of Perpetua and Felicity* 15.4, L15 [third–fourth centuries CE]), and even simply "attendants" (*officialii*, IGLSyr 13.1.9088, D178 [238–44 CE]). The last three—keyholders, assistants, and attendants—seem to have been lower-ranking, and their duties were often assigned to military personnel holding other titles, such as *frumentarii, beneficiarii, applicitarii, agentes in rebus*, and *chartularii*. For his part, Pliny the Elder, in his account of the Pero and Micon myth, calls the person guarding the gate a "doorkeeper" (*ianitor*) (*Natural History* 7.36, L150 [77 CE]). A prison staff position might have been one avenue for a nonelite member of society to work and secure a livelihood. It provided a possible yet still humble advancement opportunity for people of a certain status to rise above their station—for instance, from *carcerarius* to *optio carceris* (an advancement in name more than rank, as the *optio carceris* remained a junior staffer, while the *optio* was among the legion's senior staff; Bruun 1988).

To this general and imprecise organizational chart we can add auxiliary officials detailed to the prison who had received specific training in torture tactics, as mentioned by a variety of sources across our time period (*Gospel according to Matthew* 18:34, L151 [late first–early second century CE]; Firmicus Maternus, *Mathesis* 3.4.26, L20 [334 CE]; O. Mon. Epiph. 177, D139 [sixth–seventh centuries CE]). A prisoner in Maresha during the Seleucid period appears to use a slang term, "dogs," perhaps to refer to professional torturers detailed to his prison (*CIIP* 4.3.3689, D170). Other sources, such as P. Oxy. 2.259 from 23 CE, deploy only vague terms like "overseer [*tetagmenōs*] of the Zeus prison," leaving us to wonder about the goings on inside (D72).

A handful of sources from the late Roman period offer insight into the quantity of personnel assigned to carceral facilities, though hardly enough survive to speak in any more than anecdotal terms. Nevertheless, numbers appear from time to time—for instance, in two inscriptions from Ostia (outside Rome) dedicated to the emperor Caracalla by soldiers of the night guard (*vigiles*) (CIL 6.1057 and 1058, D65 [198–217 CE]). Pavón Torrejón (2003) writes, "they had three *optiones carceris* [heads of the prison] in each cohort, assisted by three *carcerarii* [prison guards]. That is, there were 21 officers in charge of the prisons along with 21 other soldiers. This data indicates that there were 6 members in care of the prisons in each of the *vigiles* [night guard] cohorts" (128). In this instance, we see a relatively robust prison staff operating in rotating shifts. Other documentary and literary evidence cohere with this general scale of approximately five to ten guards per facility. For example, Modestinus, a jurist and a student of Ulpian, indicates in book four of his work on *Punishments* that prisoners should never be handed over to the care of a single guard, but instead to a minimum of two, and a late Roman imperial decree found in Ptolemais (Tolmeita, Libya) assigns "seven soldiers for the guards at the public prison" (*eis parafulakēn tou dēmosiou desmōtēriou*) (D 48.3.14, L113 [ca. 250 CE]; SEG 9.356, D176 [501 CE]). A fragmentary Egyptian papyrus of the first century CE may indicate a similar situation—it appears to be a daily legionary report legion in which a presiding officer calls roll and then assigns guards to various posts, including to the gate, ramparts, granaries, market, and possibly one soldier to aid in guard duties at the prison (PSI 13.1307; Fink 1971, 200n13). This implies supplementary help from military personnel to aid otherwise nonmilitary guards. In sum, across our period, it appears rare that prison facilities had only a single guard, while a staff numbering more than ten is also unusual. So far, as we can tell from fragmentary evidence, a half-dozen guards is typical for the average facility, and soldiers were regularly detailed to public prisons as part of their policing duties.

A papyrus from the second century CE contains the names of people assigned to various offices, including the declaration "I give the office of guardian of the prisoners in the prisons [*tōn kata fulakēn desmiōn*] to the one written below," followed by a rather telling clause, "who is rich and suitable . . ." (P. Oxy. 3.580, D84 [second century CE]). The papyrus does not clarify why wealth would be advantageous in prison administrators, but one suspects such people were harder to bribe, or at least more expensive. Less noble reasons are also possible, of course. In any case, the grant of guard duties further underlines the social stratification of carceral spaces; the overseer was appointed on account of his wealth while the inmates often came from more socially vulnerable segments of society, with a bevy of guards likely representing a lower social status than the overseer. By the mid-second century in Asia Minor it was common that police personnel in leadership positions were centrally appointed, judging precisely on the basis of the candidates' wealth, integrity, and reputation (Brélaz 2020, 162). Here we see similar procedures in Egypt.

While some prison guards worked only for a time as specialized laborers on contract or assignment, some evidence suggests that other guards retained longer-term associations with particular carceral facilities. P. Hib. 1.73 is a draft complaint to a Ptolemaic governor from a man named Antigonus against a man named Patron. One piece of information, added subsequently by the scribe above the line, records that Patron works as head prison guard for a portion of the name of Oxyrhynchus and that he lives some eight kilometers away in the town of Takona, from where the complaint was issued (D49 [244–243 BCE]). The pattern holds in the late Roman period, as well. P. Wash. Univ. 1.57 is a sixth-century CE inventory of individuals, listed by name and including two who are noted as "prison guard" (*desmofulax*)—Pamouthis, a guard at "Big Prison," and Kalamon, a guard at another facility (D61).

Often we hear the names of individual guards in complaints, but not all prison managers were uniformly disliked. IGLSyr 13.1.9088 is a dedicatory inscription from the low-level attendants to a centurion named Ulpius Philippus, who served as supervisor of the prison in the third legion. The inscription does not speak to exact numbers but gives the sense of a single man overseeing a staff of attendants, retaining Latin titles even in the Greek inscription. "To Ulpius Philippus, centurion of the third Cyrenic legion of Gordian, supervisor of the carceral facilities [*praipositon koustōdiōn*], an incomparable supervisor [*praipositon*]. The attendants of the prisoners [*officialii hoi tōn desmōtōn*], in memory" (D178 [238–44 CE]). This honorary inscription offers a glimpse at a sort of camaraderie developing within a cohort of guards working at a single facility over a long period, and their desire (or perhaps requirement) to honor their supervisor in one way or another.

Epigraphic and archaeological data suggest that guards sometimes worked in bespoke spaces—whether rooms attached to the prison, independent offices, or other quarters. One such space appears within Herod's promontory palace in Caesarea Maritima (Caesarea, Israel), where we find a basilica for judicial hearings above a T-shaped cistern that was converted into a prison during the Herodian period (A8). About thirty meters from the facility we find a small room with a mosaic floor holding a Latin inscription that reads: "Good hope to the assistants of the office in charge of prison" (CIIP 2.1273, D206 [second century CE]). The mosaic offers well wishes to the attendants of the prison from their overseers and suggests strongly that this was their space: an office, breakroom, or something of the sort. In the civic prison of Cuicul, the archaeologist Louis Leschi proposed that the antechamber had a similar purpose, serving as a combination guard room and reserved space for prison officials (A5; Leschi 1953, 23). Such a room between the city's main thoroughfare and the main carceral chamber, with a locking door between each, would have the dual effect of increasing security and providing dedicated space for the guards proximate and separate from the imprisoned population. The subterranean complex in the Julian Basilica of Corinth, recently discussed by Paul Scotton, may have had a similar function: an inner cell has been interpreted as a possible civic prison, while the antechamber had both closer access to light and, unique among our archive, its own toilet (A14; Scotton 2022, 218). Finally, four intriguing stone altars were excavated in a small room inside the legionary base at Carnuntum (Petronell-Carnuntum, Austria; CIL 3.15190, D114; CIL 3.15191, D273; CIL 3.15192, D277 [all second century CE]). All four altars show signs of use—to this day white and black ash remain visible on their surfaces from sacrifices offered in them. Today one altar is blank, likely because its decoration was painted on, but three others were inscribed by *clavicularii* (key holders) with dedications to the goddess Nemesis—something of the patron deity of legionary jailers, to judge by the ubiquity of dedications to her (RIU 3.671, D275 [216 CE]; CIL 3.3484, D276 [219 CE]; CIL 3.15192, D277 [third century CE]). It is not possible to identify the precise function of this room in the legionary base with certainty, but the presence of three altars from key holders, one painted altar, and no other ritual material, suggests that it may have been the meeting room or office of Carnuntum's prison guards (Kremer 2012, 361–62).

Our evidence is spotty, but it appears that prison staff often held salaried positions funded by public tax dollars, and those running the prison system received both monetary remuneration as well as unofficial, fringe benefits. A Ptolemaic account of payments mentions a number of different types of guards and prison personnel, distinguishing them by place of origin—ten local guards from Philadelphia along with ten Arabs for general police activities, along with six watchmen to look after canal embankments during the yearly Nile inundation and six guards posted to the prison (*desmōterion*) (P. Cair. Zen. 2.59296, D33 [250 BCE]). Again, we find a single carceral facility with six guards, and we learn that guards posted to the prison and general police earn an identical salary of six drachmas per month, while people posted to watch over the embankment make only 2.5 drachmas over the same period. As the initial editor of this papyrus notes, it is possible that the estate from which the papyrus comes paid for the guards, but it is significantly more likely that the money came from the local municipality, as we see in parallel cases (Edgar 1926, 162; cf. PSI 4.344). As noted above, a similar conclusion is certain in the Roman period, as evidenced by a slew of second century CE receipts for taxes paid specifically in support of prison guards. John Bauschatz (2013) argues that during the Ptolemaic period, prison guards were the only members of the police force working "full-time" in the public prisons (247). In the Roman period visual and literary sources suggest that day-to-day operation of prisons was largely taken over by soldiers, though it is hard to say whether these are simply visual and literary tropes or evidence of a real change in staffing.

Prison staff received other work benefits like food and drink. Two Ptolemaic papyri, one from Memphis and another from Tebtunis, indicate customary delivery of wine to prison guards—a trend that continues into the late Roman period (UPZ 1.149, D54 [208–206 BCE]; PSI 13.1315, D83 [127 BCE]). As the party responsible for allowing visitors access to prisoners, guards were in a position of having regular and often absolute power over their charges. In addition to official payments of money, food, and wine, guards were often suspected of abusing their position by accepting bribes. The issue is so common as to be something of a stock trope in early Christian and other late antique sources (*Acts of Paul and Thecla* 17–20, L28 [mid-second century CE]; *Passion of Perpetua and Felicity*, L15 [third–fourth centuries CE]; Libanius, *Oration* 45.10, L52 [386 CE]; Procopius, *History of the Wars* 1.5–6, L157 [ca. 550 CE]). In the early third century CE, the jurist Paul prescribed that "if the officer in charge of a prison [*carceri praepositus*] is bribed to keep someone in custody without chains or has allowed a weapon or poison to be brought into the prison, he must be punished by the court" (D 48.3.8, L108 [early third century CE]). In the early second century CE, Pliny the Younger addressed a question to the emperor Trajan about the proper makeup of a public prison staff in his province.

> I am in doubt whether I should maintain guard over prisoners by employing the public slaves of the cities, which has hitherto been the practice, or whether I should employ soldiers; for my fear is that the use of public slaves may result in less reliable supervision, but on the other hand this duty may divert a not inconsiderable number of soldiers from military tasks. Meanwhile I have reinforced the public slaves with a few soldiers, but I see that there is a danger that this practice may lead to neglect of duty by both, as each side feels sure that they can pin the guilt they share on the other. (*Letters* 10.19–20, L24 [109–10 CE])

The emperor answered that Pliny was right to be concerned about the mixing of public slaves and soldiers, because they were likely to blame each other when something went wrong, concluding that public slaves should continue to be used as prison guards in the province. Trajan's ultimate concern is clear: "We must rather abide by the practice that as few soldiers as possible should be called away from the Standards [of the legion, i.e. from active duty]." The emperor's reply is complicated by another letter that he received from Pliny, perhaps later in the same year, expressing concern that people who had been condemned to various punishments were instead serving as public slaves in the city of Nicomedia (10.31, L40 [110 CE]). If prisoners served as public slaves and slaves sometimes watched over the prison and the prison was a publicly funded institution, then together these two letters, along with second-century documentary sources, leave open the real possibility that people condemned to prison, labor, or death, were instead serving as incarcerators themselves as menial prison labor. To put it delicately, such a situation would present a potential conflict of interest. As Noel Lenski points out, the use of public slaves to guard municipal prisons continued long into Late Antiquity, at least in the east: the mid-fifth century *Life of the Sleepless Alexander* notes that its eponymous monk was imprisoned in the public prison of Chalkis, and "guarded by the city's municipal slaves, since the magistrates feared him" (41; Lenski 2006, 344–45).

Anxiety about the identity and commitments of prison guards was a particular concern in late ancient sources. In 438 CE, the emperor Theodosius II promulgated a law stipulating that Jews, Samaritans, pagans, and other heretics "shall not have command over custody in prisons, so that Christians, as it often happens, may not, at times, be locked up and suffer a second imprisonment because of the hatred of the guards . . ." (*NTh* 3.7, L101 [438 CE]). The opposite concern—that (Nicene) Christians might serve as guards for Jews, Samaritans, or "heretical" Christians—was apparently not pressing. The legislation addresses an inherent bias embedded in carceral practices, and especially in the policing and surveillance of minoritized prisoners by guards of the majority class. Today, such practices continue, though often through negligence; in the fifth century, majority supremacy in carceral implementation was a matter of explicit legislation.

What did prison staff do? First and foremost, of course, they kept prisoners inside and oversaw visitor interactions. As mentioned above, one of the frescoes of Pero and Micon from a house and shop complex on the Via Stabiae in Pompeii provides a rare example of the representation of a prison guard stationed outside, peering through a prison window to surveil inmates inside (fig. 16). It seems that lower-ranking prison guards often sat near the doors or windows to the prison and were responsible for distribution of rations. Calpurnius Flaccus's fourth *Declamation*, discussed above, addressed prison guards' delivery of food to prisoners: "Whip lashes crack, food is delivered in the foul hands of the executioner even to those who refuse it. The hard-hearted doorkeeper sits by, a man whose eyes would remain dry even when his mother weeps" (L46 [second century CE]). The rhetor imagines two types of prison staff: the callous doorkeeper and the executioner, both of whom are tasked with delivery of prison rations.

As Ryan Schellenberg has recently discussed, prison staff also occasionally had the responsibility of preventing prisoner suicide—a phenomenon in evidence at least from the early Roman republic, and painstakingly catalogued by Jens-Uwe Krause (Schellenberg 2021, 72–73; Krause 1996, 302–3). In keeping with Pavón Torrejón's observation about the shift to prison registrars as ultimate authorities in the fourth century CE, legal sources suggest that thereafter, registrars were also responsible for distributing food. Honorius and Theodosius II issued a law in 409 CE demanding that prison registrars were to "make sure that food is supplied to those prisoners who do not have it" (*CTh* 9.3.7, L44).

Finally, as we showed in the preceding section, guards and registrars produced a flurry of documents for each case of incarceration. In the Ptolemaic period we have evidence of prison guards involved in writing petitions to higher-ranking government officials, and in the Roman period we see from documentary and legal sources that production of ongoing reports was also a part of daily duties of prison staff (P.Sorb. 3.135, D60 [225–224 BCE]; P. Oxy. 43.3104, D15 [228 CE]; *CTh* 9.3.6, L174 [380 CE]).

Considered together, literary, documentary, and visual sources speak to prison personnel as thoroughly integrated in the social and economic life of cities from the Ptolemaic period forward, even as aspects of hierarchy, identity, documentation, and duties evolved over time. They were important enough to the state that across our time period, we see facilities receiving around half a dozen dedicated staff, often paid with public funds. They help us consider how carceral facilities were viewed as a civic good, integrally related to numerous other societal systems. These staff were chiefly invested in keeping prisoners secure. Their charges, however, as well as their titles and hierarchical structures, were hardly static.

TRANSPORT

Incarceration is fundamentally a system of controlling movement, often taking the form of relative immobilization within a facility. Nevertheless, sources frequently dwell on prisoner movement, both within carceral facilities and across broader landscapes. Perhaps counterintuitively, transport of prisoners was an integral, everyday aspect of incarceration across the Mediterranean. Only in the most extreme cases of punitive incarceration do we hear of total immobilization. More often, prisoners moved within carceral spaces on a daily basis, and were regularly transported to and from legal proceedings, between carceral facilities like civic prisons and labor camps, and within such facilities—for instance, from the surface of mining camps down into the earth. Prisoners condemned to death were transported from prison facilities to places of execution; after death, their bodies were transported for disposal. When prisons are seen as temporary holding tanks, the movement of prisoners is not a critical or obvious area of analysis, beyond transport between jails and places of judgment and condemnation. And yet, prisoner transport is a central concern of a variety of ancient sources, both within the prison and outside of it. We turn now to each of these aspects of prisoner movement.

Within the Prison

The multichambered prison is a staple of literary and archaeological evidence. So far as archaeological evidence survives, celled prisons typically included an antechamber (presumably for guards) along with at least two further spaces meant for holding prisoners—one closer to the entrance, with limited access to natural light, and another chamber further from the entrance, often oppressively dark and sometimes subdivided further. The darkness of the inner prison was one of the "torments of prison" deemed in a law of Constantine as "pitiable for the innocent but not severe enough for the guilty"; as a result, one common and ongoing task of prison guards was the transport of prisoners between facilities and perhaps even between chambers within the facility, depending on the time of day (*CTh* 9.3.1, L133 [320/21 CE]).

Like many laws extant in late ancient codifications, this law appears to restate common practices in which prisoners moved daily between different parts of the prison. If there is an innovation here, it is perhaps Constantine's reserving the temporary, daily reprieve from darkness as a kindness offered only to those still awaiting trial, while convicted prisoners remained in the secure inner chamber. Discussion of the increased security of the "inner prison" predates Constantine's legislation by at least centuries, as we see for instance in the *Acts of the Apostles*, where Roman magistrates are depicted punishing itinerant preachers with flogging before "they threw them into prison and ordered the prison guard to keep them securely. Following these instructions, [the prison guard] put them in the inner prison [*eis tēn esōteran fulakēn*] and secured their feet in the stocks" (16:23–24, L67 [early second century CE]).

Archaeological evidence allows us to think spatially about movement between prison chambers and suggests that a number of different models were available. First, many prisons had a simple dual chamber architecture. The civic prison at Cuicul is a good example, with its three rooms built directly underneath the civic basilica (fig. 4). The first room is the smallest, comprising little more than an antechamber communicating directly with the public street through a small, locking door. The antechamber appears to be a space for guards to sit, between one gate opening from the street and another opening into the prison's first cell (A5, Chamber A; Leschi 1953, 23). Yet another secure door separates the outer cell from the larger inner cell, to the south (chamber B). In the case of Roman Cuicul, movement between the outer and inner part of the civic prison involved prison guards simply shuffling prisoners from chamber A to chamber B and securing the doors between. We find similar architecture in the prisons at Caesarea Maritima, Pompeii, and Corinth (Caesarea Maritima, A8; Pompeii, A9; Corinth, A15).

Other prisons comprised multiple cells connected by a single corridor, itself secured by a locking door leading outside, as exemplified by the military prison at Lambaesis (fig. 5; A7). This prison is situated underneath the legionary Sanctuary of the Standards, with a "stout locking device" securing a door to a narrow corridor that communicated with five small, gated cells (Rakob and Storz 1974, 276). In this case, movement of prisoners between cells was similarly simple, though in the facility's first phase no cell appears to have had more access to light than any other, suggesting that if prisoners were to be moved to lighter spaces during the day, they must have exited through the prison's only door into the open space at the center of the legionary headquarters. A later phase blocked windows to all of the cells. If the prison remained in use, the renovation rendered an even starker difference between the completely dark underground and the light available above. The workers' prison at Simitthus has a strikingly similar structure to that at Lambaesis, though at a significantly larger scale (Simitthus, A13; fig. 8).

Finally, some prisons had upper and lower chambers rather than parallel cells or inner and outer chambers. This is the structure of the most famous prison from the ancient world—the Tullian Prison at Rome—but the architecture is repeated across the Mediterranean, most clearly in the civic prison of Cosa and in the late Roman prison at Tiberias. In these cases, movement between cells was restricted not by a door but rather through a covered manhole, allowing access from above to the lower cells below. Such manholes have been discovered at Cosa, Messene, and Rome and are implied by the architectural structure remaining in Tiberias, and they are discussed in the late antique *Acts of Matthew*, which speaks of "sealing up the floor" of a prison to secure those within (Brown 1993, 40; *Acts and Martyrdom of Matthew* 14, L205 [late fourth century CE]). The *Revelation of John* also imagines the act of throwing a prisoner down into a prison called "the Abyss" and sealing it from above. (20:1–7, L13 [late first/early second century CE]). In these facilities, prisoners would enter and exit the darkest part of the prison with the aid of a ladder, rope, or in the case of the Prison for the Condemned in Carales, a wooden scaffold rising from the prison floor to the exit. The variety of archaeologically attested carceral spaces helps bring texture to sources like Constantine's law calling for the movement of accused prisoners between the "darkness of the inner prison" (*sedis intimae tenebras*) the "entrances of the prison and healthful locales" (*vestibulis carcerum et salubribus locis*) still inside the facility, and the "common light" (*publicum lumen*) (*CTh* 9.3.1, L133 [320/21 CE]). Yann Rivière (2004b) suggests that the law is unclear as to whether the "common light" indicates another section of the prison, an adjacent, open-air but enclosed space, or the public square of the city (215). Attending to the archaeology suggests that all three of these possibilities were likely employed.

Across our period, prison guards directed the movement of prisoners within carceral spaces and mediated access to visitors from the outside, policing interactions by surveillance through secure prison windows or allowing bodily access to those inside, both of which are attested in various visual representations of the Pero and Micon myth from Pompeii and in numerous narrative accounts (V12–15). In the *Acts of Thomas*, a text reflecting Roman Syria of the early third century, visitors are imagined bribing guards with silver coins to gain access to the apostle locked inside. Later, when the apostle tells a young acolyte to leave and gather necessities for the group of imprisoned Christians, he complains that there is no one to open the doors for him "because the prison guards have locked them and gone to sleep" (151, 154, L149 [ca. 200–250 CE]). Together, our sources depict prison guards providing scheduled, ongoing, daily surveillance of prisoners and their movements and, occasionally, admittance of visitors during what we might anachronistically call "visitor's hours."

Finally, unsanctioned movements—prison breaks—were not uncommon, appearing in sources across the timespan of the book. The prison break is a common theme in ancient literature, with Dionysius's escape in *The Bacchae* serving as a sort of paradigm for subsequent literary portrayals (Weaver 2004, 29–63). We find a similar prison break scene poetically inscribed in stone at Mylasa (Turkey), where a stele was found with a Hellenistic poem of Hyssaldomos telling the dramatic prison escape, aided by a deity, of a certain Pytheas (Marek and Zingg 2018, 1–139, esp. 13–31; L139 [250 BCE–150 BCE]). But escape was not purely the realm of literary fantasy; SB 22.15767 is a letter informing the governor (*strategos*) of Memphis and a number of other officials that two tax collectors had escaped from the prison—one of a handful of notices of escape to survive in the documentary record (D6 [199–100 BCE]). From a few decades earlier, on January 9, 255 BCE, we have a document giving notice to a commissioner named Kleon from a certain Nikeratos about a need to repair a wall of a carceral faculty in Arsinoites, lest prisoners escape:

> Nikeratos to Kleon, greetings. The southern wall of the stronghold—a part of it has collapsed, and the rest is in such a state that if it falls there is a danger that some of the people [lit. bodies, *sōmata*] will be lost. So please draw up a contract for this and give it to Dionysios the building contractor so he can get to work. For we shall bring them straight out and shall have to use even more space for the prisoners [*desmōtai*] which the finance minister Apollonios has now handed over to us. Be well. (P. Petr. Kleon 52, D93 [255 BCE]; trans. Bauschatz 2013, 245–46)

In addition to the issue of bureaucratic record keeping discussed above, this notice uses the Greek word *diafōnēsai* to refer to "escape," but this word could literally mean here to fail to answer roll call (LSJ, s.v. *diafōneō* 3). Especially when read alongside other documents that contain or refer to lists of prisoners' names (including many female prisoners), we can imagine that this may refer to a literal roll call process in which names of prisoners are read out and they are required to present themselves in some way to a prison guard (SB 28.16854, D5 [255 CE]; SB 24.16117, D99 [601–50 CE]). If such a roll call is in fact implied here, the source would add another layer to our understanding of controlled and unsanctioned movements within the prison. A recently published papyrus from Roman Judaea or Arabia details the trial of a number of individuals accused of having forged documents in an elaborate tax fraud scheme during the reign of Hadrian. In the memorandum we hear of a man named Gadalias, including "his committing violence and sedition and banditry, and the money that he counterfeited, and how he escaped from prison [*hōs apo heirktēs efugen*]," though the editors note that "it is unclear if Gadalias literally fled from incarceration or whether this is a figure of speech for one who managed to evade sentencing or punishment" (P. Cotton, D298 [129–32 CE]; Dolganov et al. 2023, 105).

The phenomenon of prison breaks shows up in more than a few literary sources, as well, including a letter from Pliny the Younger asking the emperor Trajan about the case of a philosopher who had been condemned to the mines for forgery only to break out and return to polite society—even exchanging letters with the emperor Domitian and receiving an acclamation from the people of Prusa (*Letters* 10.58, L193 [109–10 CE]). Livy tells a story of Phileas of Tarentum bribing guards to break hostages from Tarentum and Thurii out of the Atrium Libertatis in Rome, where they were being detained; although initially successful, they were all were caught shortly thereafter and executed (*From the Founding of the City* 25.7.12, L200 [27 BCE–17 CE]). Perhaps the most enticing, however, is Procopius's Orientalizing description of a Sasanian king serving a life sentence of incarceration in 496/498 CE at a facility called the "Prison of Oblivion," who manages a daring, cross-dressing escape (*History of the Wars* 1.5–6, L157 [ca. 550 CE]).

Outside the Prison

Legal Proceedings.   Outside the prison, a guard's most visible duty was transportation between carceral facilities and judicial chambers, a task aided by architecture in many contexts. As discussed above, the architect Vitruvius prescribed that every Roman municipality had a forum with a prison and *curia* directly adjacent, and as we have seen a number of times already it was typical for civic prisons to be built near or underneath spaces of judicial proceedings. Even in later Syriac sources, the same typical collocation of facilities is common: the fourth-century CE *Acts of Shmona and Gurya* describe a trial on November 15, 310 CE in Edessa, in which "the governor rose and went down to the court of justice . . . and when he had sat down on his tribunal in the basilica by the winter baths, at the same time he had sent eight soldiers with the jailor for Gurya and Shmona. And he brought them both up from that hole" (41, L1). The shared assumption here is that, as Vitruvius might have us expect, the tribunal in the basilica and the public prison were proximate to each other.

This pattern repeats across the Mediterranean. In a city like Sarmizegetusa, guards would have simply marched prisoners out from the space underneath the tribunal for their hearings in front of it. Conveniently, the facility was already inside the civic basilica complex (fig. 3, A27). At Rome and Cosa, we should similarly imagine guards escorting prisoners from the facility just a few steps to the forum and into the courthouse, while at Cuicul prisoners exited through the antechamber and walked some five meters down the main city street to the civic basilica's back entrance (fig. 4). The prison in Herod's promontory palace at Caesarea Maritima shows a similar logic, with cells underneath the trial platform (*bema*) and the office of the prison guards located some thirty meters away from the entrance to the underground space, on the corner of the promontory palace (Eck 2007, 87–89, CIIP 2.1273, D206 [second century CE]). Common to each of these examples is a built environment designed to create a brief yet highly visible public route for prisoners brought to trial. Beyond making trips to the court, guards were occasionally responsible for chaining prisoners and escorting them to the city center so that they could beg for food, though in a letter to the governor of Syria in 363 CE, Libanius hinted that even these occasional outings could constitute a form of torture. He begs for the end of his friend Eusebius's incarceration, which included "being brought out through the crowd, beaten, having been stripped, strangled [by a collar]" and begging for money, which, when bestowed, was immediately stolen by the guards (*Letter* 1414.3; Schouler 2006, 282).

The frequency with which civic prisons were built directly underneath places of judicial proceedings perhaps sheds light on some summons preserved on papyrus. Over a hundred examples are known from this category of bureaucratic document in Roman Egypt, and while they were originally categorized as "orders for arrest," they have been recategorized as a result of an important observation by Gagos and Sijpesteijn:

> There is one linguistic element [of this category of document] that cannot be ignored: the complete absence of a verb or expression that would translate into the modern notion of "arrest." The documents consistently urge the local police authorities to "send" (*pempō* and a variety of compounds) the accused before the higher authority which issued the order, sometimes accompanied by a guard . . . There is a further element in these orders that does not support the theory that the local authorities are instructed to "arrest": the majority of the orders indicate that the person summoned has been "accused." (1996, 78; Bülow-Jacobsen 1986)

Their proposal, that these ought to be considered "summonses," has been broadly accepted, with further refinements on the Roman period documents and a general understanding that the language could be used widely, including as warrants and orders for arrest (Schubert 2018). We suggest here that some of these documents may in fact be summons for prisoners held in carceral facilities to appear in court, and add the corroborating evidence that common prison architecture seems to have inflected the language—explaining why not only "send" (*pempō*), but "send up" (*anapempō*), and "send *out*" (*ekpempō*) are the common operative verbs in these documents.

To offer two examples out of many: BGU 11.2083 comes from the second or early third century CE and uses language typical to the area around Arsinoites to order three weavers to be "sent up" (Hagedorn 1979, 63). It reads: "To the police chiefs [*archefodois*] and the area leaders of the village of Soknopaiou Nesos. Immediately send up [*anapempsetai*] Abous, a weaver, and Kaieus, a weaver, and the wife of Abous, the one-time area leader, a weaver, and her daughter, who is a weaver, accused by Ammonios" (D225 [second–third centuries CE]) Likewise P. Yale. 1.62 reads, in its entirety: "To the leaders and the chiefs of police of the village of Tebtunis: send out [*ekpempsate*] Onnophris a[nd] . . . having been accused by . . ." (first century CE).

In these rather common judicial orders, it is possible that we see the effect of carceral architecture on the language used to describe prisoner movement—orders to appear before a judge often request that the prisoner literally be "sent up," from a prison that is conceptually—and sometimes physically—beneath places of judgment. The language is not unique to the Roman world: P. Cair. Zen. 4.59626 is a request from a Ptolemaic man named Kallisthenes who appears to have already been in prison or was at least worried that he might be sent to prison if his trial is delayed. As a result, he requests that his case be heard swiftly, specifically using the language of being "called up" (*anakalesamenos*) to attend a hearing (D41 [263–229 BCE]). In this document, the language of "calling up" is explicitly not a warrant for arrest but a call to appear for trial. It is possible that the logic of the prison as underground and beneath the place of trial lurks behind these stock phrases. More certain is this: one essential, ongoing job of the prison staff would have been to transport prisoners under guard from the prisons to trials—often just a floor above.

Regional Movement.   Both exploitation of labor and transferring jurisdiction required prisoners to move within and between regions, and traces of these movements appear frequently in bureaucratic paperwork and visual representations. A late second- or early third-century CE papyrus illuminates the practice of prisoner transfer and the importation of common bureaucratic language to documents ordering long-range transport. P. Bagnall 29 is a report written to the clerk of Thebes, containing a list of prisoners who should be handed over to the regional governor (*epistratēgos*) Julius Julianus. Although the papyrus is fragmentary, it appears to use the term "send up" (*anapempō*) to describe the transfer of prisoners out of a carceral facility under guard. It reads:

> To Antoninus Minor, the royal clerk of Diospolites Thebes, who is acting for the governor, from Ze[. . .] [concerning the prisoners who have been s]ent [up?] to the most excellent regional governor [*epistratēgos*] Julius Julianus, with Dio [. . .] following [the matter] closely. It [i.e. the list of prisoners] in chains is (as follows): Peteësis, son of Tre[. . .], [. . .]psis, mother Aphrodite, [. . .]san[. . .]phis, son of Rhodon [. . .] and also Totoeus. These two are under free guard: Pouoris, son of Pouoris . . . (D101 [ca. 175–225 CE])

Presently, only five names remain on the papyrus, which likely included more when it was written. Interestingly, the five names are both male and female, and the list includes both indigenous Egyptian and Greek names which contrast distinctly with the typically Roman names of the men charged with oversight of these prisoners. The list offers not only the names of prisoners under transport, but also their mode of confinement: some were transported "in chains" (*en desmois*) while others were transported "under free guard" (*eleutherai tērēsei*). Visual sources frequently depict captives in transport, often in chains and led by a soldier or guard, as we discussed above (p. 141–143). This common visual trope might lead one to believe that prisoners were always transported in chains, but P. Bagnall 29 clarifies that stock depictions of prisoners should never be interpreted as direct evidence for uniform practices. There was not a one-size-fits-all approach: in visual sources, chains are clues for viewers about the status of the person bound. In practice, prisoners were transported without chains, at least some of the time.

This raises the question: from where did guards retrieve prisoners, and to where did guards transport them? P. Oxy. 2.259, from 23 CE, is a copy of a bail bond from a Persian man named Theon, addressed to the man in charge of the Prison of Zeus. Theon promises to produce the man he has bailed out of "the public prison" (*politikēs fulakēs*) within thirty days of an official request, and if that he fails, "I shall pay the aforementioned two *minae* of gold immediately and I have no authority to obtain a further period of time nor to transfer myself to another prison [*eis heteran fulakēn*]." (D72). Here we see another avenue for local or regional prisoner transport—prisoners themselves requesting a transfer of facility. A late ancient source speaks to precisely such a request in a later period: in his *Letter to the Monks of Senoun*, the bishop Philoxenus of Mabbug (Manbij, Syria) complained that the conditions of his political exile in a small, guarded room above a kitchen were so awful that he and the men with whom he was imprisoned "repeatedly asked to be transferred to the public prison, where all the wrongdoers and criminals are held" (93–94, L136 [ca. 525 CE]). His request—to be transferred from what Julia Hillner (2013) has called "confined exile" to the public prison—was denied (420–21).

Transport was not solely the concern of prisoners and guards; it was also a concern of the wider public: an inscription from the coast south of Izmir (Turkey) contains an edict commemorating the emperor Hadrian's visit in the spring of 129 CE, and includes a number of laws and a narrative section written in the voice of the emperor. The text begins with an acknowledgement that traveling soldiers were known to wreak havoc while traveling through small coastal towns, including soldiers transporting prisoners. In order to curb some of the army's exploitation of local populations, the emperor directed that soldiers on private business shall not be granted free lodging, but that "if someone is passing through while on duty, or if they are bringing the ruling power's money, or transporting prisoners or wild animals, public lodgings shall be given only to them and provisions at the market price which was effective ten days earlier" (SEG 59.1365, D175; trans. Hauken and Malay 2009, 233). This practice coheres with contemporaneous literary sources, such as a Christian martyr stories from the same period as this inscription confirm the practice—or at least the public impression of it—that soldiers regularly passed through Asia Minor with prisoners in tow (Ignatius of Antioch, *Romans* 5.1, L216 [early second century CE]; *Martyrdom of Polycarp* 6–8, L209 [second century CE]). The edict has at least three key implications: first, the unremarkable nature of prisoner transport overland through Asia Minor over some distance; second, that civic prisoner transport was intended to be a state funded service that occasionally required support from the broader public; and third, that such long-range transports could present a significant burden to the local populations through which the prisoners and guards passed.

In addition to overland transport, visual and literary sources suggest that boats regularly ferried prisoners from place to place. The Roman satirist Petronius imagined a transport ship so full of "guilty men" (*nocentes*) that it was at risk of becoming a kind of floating prison (*Satyricon* 105, L230 [40–66 CE]). A fresco that perhaps belonged to Marcus Agrippa (a close companion of Rome's first emperor) represents naval transport of prisoners of war: a captive is represented as hunched over and hands tied behind the back as he is ushered onto a Roman warship (V41 [first century BCE]; De Souza 2011, 42). A similar story appears in *Third Maccabees*, an account of Jewish martyrs set in the mid-third century BCE, though likely composed in the first century CE (4:1–10, L39). The text describes with rhetorical flair the transport of the elderly, women, and men under the direction of the Ptolemaic king, with prisoners marched quickly and publicly to a ship waiting to transport them under guard. Some are bound in iron chains, others with ropes around the neck, and yet others with their feet in fetters as they descend to the ship's dark lower hold. The *Acts of the Apostles* suggests transport by boat was not reserved solely for prisoners of war, but used also for civic prisoners routed to a different province for trial (27–28, L206 [early second century CE]). Here we find a remarkable story of a Roman centurion leading several prisoners from Caesarea Maritima in Israel to Italy for trial in Rome, paying a fee to travel on other outgoing nonmilitary ships and stopping for winter in Malta, along with the prisoners under his surveillance. All these sources are at least partially legendary and significantly embellished. Nevertheless, the stories were widely repeated and, best as we can tell, believed—both in their miraculous elements and in the more quotidian stage on which the legends play out. It is a matter of debate whether the apostle Paul would have been transported to Rome via commercial ship under military guard in the middle of the first century CE. What later sources about him reveal is clearer, however: in the Roman world of the second century CE, it was reasonable to think that a civic prisoner might have been transported between provinces by ship. And, as we shall see in just a moment, maritime prisoner transports also appear in documents.

Mines.   Condemnation to forced labor in the mines was a typical sentence across the time period of our study—often in royally or imperially controlled facilities far from the cities where the accused became convicts. Overland transport was likely most common, but some evidence suggests that boat travel was also a possibility. For instance, SB 28.16854 is a letter from early May of 225 BCE, containing a report on prisoners transported along the Nile from the civic prison to a mining facility called "Upper Works":

> Amuntas, to Theodotos and Protarchos, greeting. After the letter written to you by Dositheos about the bodies being sent to Upper Works on the order of the king had been sealed, Leonides son of Diod[oros] of the town Asklepieus was left in the prison [*en tēi fulakēi*]. I have written to you in order that you may know and not ask this person from the escort Kyprothemis. (D5; trans. Clarysse)

As Willy Clarysse (2002) suggests, it is likely that this letter is preserved as part of a register of correspondence (99). In it we learn about an order from King

Ptolemy (likely III), directing that prisoners should be transported from a local prison—probably in Alexandria—to a royal mining facility in order to serve as labor for mineral extraction. As a result, an administrator named Dositheos wrote and sealed a letter with names of prisoners to be transported under the care of a military boatman with a Cypriot name: Kyprothemis. Sealed letters are a common technology in the Ptolemaic period and afterward, guarding against prying eyes and, importantly, against editorial changes made after the report was dispatched (fig. 22). In this case, the advantage of such technology is clear: it ensures that any prisoners who disappeared en route could be accounted for. As it turns out, however, the sealed list included a name of a prisoner who was not handed over for transport, rendering the feature a possible bug for the boat captain, should it appear that a prisoner was missing from his transport upon arrival. To deal with this eventuality, Amuntas (perhaps the prison warden or registrar) wrote the letter above: a follow-up to his counterparts in Upper Works informing them that one of the prisoners named in the sealed list was kept in prison and so should not be expected on Kyprothemis's boat. This short letter speaks, then, to a broader bureaucratic state in which prisoner transport was routine, incarcerated people— literally referred to as "bodies" (*sōmata*)—were ferried to and fro at the behest of the king to serve his economic interest, and where bureaucratic paperwork attended and attested to each step of the process.

Long-range prisoner movement continued in the Roman period. In the early third century CE, the jurist Ulpian wrote that "mines are numerous, some provinces possessing them and others not; those that have not [mines] send [their condemned prisoners] to those that have [mines]" (D 48.19.8.4, L120). In the early fourth century CE, the Christian historian Eusebius even reported on the practice of transferring prisoners from Egypt to Palestine and Cilicia, and further evidence suggests movement of prisoners between the provinces of Dalmatia, Upper Moesia, and Dacia (e.g., *Martyrs of Palestine* 8.1 (shorter recension), L207; Dušanić 1977, 74n137).

Convict laborers were transported regularly within mining complexes. Although this sort of movement has not left documentation of the sort that we find in papyrological and literary materials, archaeological evidence can help us think spatially about what such movement involved. The mining town of Simitthus (modern Chemtou, Tunisia) is the single source of the ancient world's famed yellow marble, quarried under Roman imperial monopoly and overseen by the army. A river snakes through the landscape, supplying a small city built on the southwest slope of the marble outcropping, and to the northeast, the enslaved and incarcerated workers quarters discussed above (p. 61–64). A guard tower oversaw the workers' prison, and in its later phases a series of doors allowed secure access from the six cells to a bathing facility built directly adjacent. Nevertheless, it is nearly a half-kilometer walk from the gate of the workers' prison to the mineshafts, necessitating some form of oversight as incarcerated laborers moved between their secure living quarters and the mix of open and closed mineshafts where they extracted marble. If the workers' quarters were operated at anywhere near capacity, the oversight must have been significant; each of the six chambers is capable of holding around 180 people (Rakob 1994, 100).

Likewise, the famous mines in the region of Wadi Faynan appear designed to contain and surveil a large population of laborers with as few guards as possible—in this case, distance and the inhospitable geography of the region aided the aim (Mattingly 2013; Friedman 2009). Unlike at Simitthus where the city and mine were directly adjacent, a still visible Roman road connects one of the main mines of the area at Umm al-Amad with its attendant city, some six kilometers distant (Umm al-Amad, A4). Upon arrival at the mining facility prisoners were further transported underground for labor—often where they were also housed. Transport, in this case, would have involved laborers descending from surface level into the mine shaft by a series of small footholds, perhaps aided by a rope. This mine is but one of dozens in the area that were exploited intermittently from the Chalcolithic period forward. The spatial layout of such mines and mining camps helps us to get a sense of the constant need for the controlled transport of captive bodies to, from, and within these facilities which sometimes comprise entire landscapes.

Transport to Death and Disposal

Many prisoners were released from custody after a time, including those who served limited-term penal sentences (p. 36–37). Many, however, were not so lucky as to leave the prison alive: some were transported under guard to their death, and the bodies of those who died in prison were transported as corpses to sites of disposal. A mass grave south of Athens illustrates the deep history of such acts of organized transportation to death; in the seventh century BCE, seventy-nine males were led to the coast in manacles and buried in three trenches; at least sixteen of them were executed on the spot (Ingvarsson et al. 2019; Chryssoulaki 2020). In this case, it is unclear who these men were, or precisely why they were executed en masse. During the Ptolemaic and Roman periods, on the other hand, much of our data concerning prisoner executions relates to mass entertainment. The scene is repeated most often in Jewish and Christian martyr acts, which themselves present the transportation, trial, and execution of dissidents as a form of popular entertainment, as we see represented in dozens of visual sources that depict convicted criminals transported in chains to their death in the arena.

The Prison for the Condemned in the amphitheater of Roman Carales provides one concrete example of the route traveled from the prison to the arena—through a hundred-meter-long aqueduct, repurposed to serve as a final entrance route for prisoners on their way to meet a gladiator or a *bestiarius*, who controlled their movement while they were attacked and consumed by animal (A24). We may prefer to look away from such violence; ancient interior designers had no such qualms. The second century Mosaic of the Damnati from El Jem, Tunisia, depicts a *bestiarius* holding the condemned man's hands behind his back while a leopard attacks his face, and a Zliten mosaic today housed at the Tripoli Archaeological Museum presents a victim bound to a wheeled platform, pushed by an attendant toward the animal tasked with killing him (Mosaic of the Damnati, V28; Carucci 2018, 212–33; Zliten *damnatio ad bestias*, V46 [first—third centuries CE]; Parrish 1985, 137–58). Reliefs depicting prisoners under transport typically show them led by a guard, often with a placard advertising the crime of which they had been convicted (Vismara 2001, 216).

As a final act of transport, guards often had the duty of disposing of corpses, though this process is not often described in detail. Some literary materials indicate that the common practice at the Tullian Prison in Rome was purposefully spectacular: guards were known to drag the prisoner's body to the riverbank and throw it in the Tiber as an act of purgation, or alternatively to expose the corpse on the Gemonian stairs above the prison (Xiphilinus, *Epitome of Cassius Dio* 146.15–30, L145 [original ca. 230 CE]; Kyle 1998, 213–24). In the fourth century CE, on the other hand, Libanius claimed that many prisoners were dying in the Antiochene prison with comparatively little fanfare, escaping notice beyond the prison walls. "The jailor makes his report; the governor doesn't turn a hair, but merely orders the funeral" (*Oration* 45.11, L52 [386 CE]). It is not clear what such a funeral may have comprised, though one early Christian source suggests that it was customary for the corpses of prisoners to be consumed with fire and the bones disposed of with a studied irreverence—a practice that animates another central theme of many early Christian martyr acts: efforts to locate the remains of the executed Christians and provide them with a proper burial (*Martyrdom of Polycarp* 13, L209 [ca. 200 CE or later]). Other Christian accounts imagine civic authorities combining corpse exposure, cremation, and disbursal in water precisely to preclude the veneration of executed criminals (Eusebius, *Ecclesiastical History* 5.1.62, L283 [account set 177 CE, excerpted early fourth century CE]). Bodily disposal was a pressing issue, especially in the case of condemned prisoners; sources from the Roman imperial period witness to an all-of-the-above approach, well discussed by Donald Kyle (1998, 160–71).

Across antiquity, then, a fundamental duty of prison guards and registrars was to control movement. Officials were tasked with containing prisoners within carceral spaces, to be sure, but the duties that leave the most significant and illuminating data concern prisoner transport, both within the prison and outside it. Some prisoners wasted away in dark cells, shuffled periodically between locations and ultimately to freedom, an alternative punishment, or disposal. As we have suggested, ancient Mediterranean prisons were porous spaces, where city residents could interact in limited ways with the people their society incarcerated. Yet prisoners were most visible on the move, and it is no surprise that images of prisoners often depict them in transit.

SHIFTING PRISON POLICIES

After recovering their island in 322 BCE, the residents of Samos dedicated a statue to a Chalkidian man for his part in freeing Samians, "whom the Athenians, having shut them up in prison [*desmōterion*], sentenced to death" (IG 12.6.1.42, D174 [321–319 BCE]). The inscription dates from just before the temporal boundaries of this study, and gestures toward an important difference between Greek carceral practices immediately prior to the third century BCE and those that came afterward. The inscription provides rare documentary evidence from a previous period and a different location from the earliest sources engaged here, and it evokes the familiar, traditional model of ancient incarceration where prisons serve primarily as place of temporary confinement for public enemies en route to punishment. As we have argued, this is the ideal of the prison that modern historians have envisioned across the premodern world. To be clear: there are examples of such a model, and this inscription is certainly among them. The notion of a prison as a public jail for pretrial detention existed in antiquity, but it was not nearly as common or ubiquitous as has often been claimed.

Thus far we have employed evidence from across the Mediterranean basin to construct a synthetic account of the ideology and experience of ancient incarceration between 300 BCE and 600 CE. We have argued that many of the ideologies and experiences visible as early as the Ptolemaic Zeno papyri remained detectable or traceable, albeit in evolving forms, through the Roman and Byzantine periods, and that such documentary evidence can enlighten literary, visual, and archaeological data from across the Mediterranean. In his article, "Ptolemaic Prisons Reconsidered," John Bauschatz (2007) showed that incarceration was used widely for public and private offenses in the Ptolemaic period, that prison complexes came in a variety of distinct styles, that carceral spaces pertained to different imprisoning authorities rather than distinct prison populations, and that a spectrum is visible in the length of incarceration, with shorter stays having been relatively more common (3–4). Our analysis has shown that each of these facets of Ptolemaic incarceration were in fact widely practiced across the Mediterranean basin through the early Byzantine period at least. They first appear in the documentary record during the Ptolemaic period, but they were not unique to that time and place, and we should not assume that these practices were innovations of the Ptolemies, either. Even so, there are some marked differences to be observed between places and periods within the broad frame of this book. We turn, finally, to some discontinuities visible among our sources.

To begin, a few distinctive patterns are visible in the Ptolemaic material that do not hold in later periods. Most salient perhaps is the location of incarceration:

while the Roman period saw public prisons typically located on the municipal forum, Ptolemaic sources often suggest that prisoners were often held in purpose-built spaces connected to the municipal tax office or the office of the regional governor (*stratēgos*). For instance, in the late third century BCE, a scribe from a village outside Oxyrhynchus complained to the treasurer (*oikonomos*) that he went to the treasury office (*logistērion*) to pay his bill but was interrupted by one of the governor's staffers. "The staffer gave directions to arrest me, and now I am in the lock-up room [*efēmereutērion*]" (P. Petr. 2.10(2), D110 [221–205 BCE]). We see such facilities in use for tax and private debts, and even for crimes that have no obvious connection to debt. As Bauschatz (2013) showed, "debtors were not the only offenders who sometimes found themselves wasting away in Ptolemaic holding cells. The papyri reveal that a broad array of offenses could lead to at least temporary stays in a holding facility: theft, assault, disturbing the peace, poor job performance, and flight (for slaves)" (240). While Cassius Dio is one of a few Roman sources to suggest the use of treasuries as ad hoc carceral spaces, Ptolemaic sources often cast the public carceral regime as part of the tax collection service in much the same way that, in the United States, the Secret Service is part of the Department of the Treasury and not the Department of Justice (quoted in Zonaras *Annales* 8.3 (D), L60 [ca. 230 CE]). One could imagine savings on fiscal outlays—a single set of guards surveilling both the tax office and prison—but the fact that a single royal agency is responsible for tax collection and general carceral implementation suggests, perhaps, a different underlying ideology of carceral oversight than is predominant in Roman sources.

Egyptian tax office prisons remained in use into the Roman period, though not as the central or default location for general public incarceration. In an edict from 68 CE, we see the Roman prefect of Egypt allowing the continued use of tax office prisons, though the source suggests that their use was perhaps marginal and at least distasteful. It reads,

> Whereas some (officials) have had the debts of others transferred to them under cover of the public treasury and have imprisoned in the tax collector's prison [*praktoreion*] or held these debtors in another prison [*fulakas*], I have determined that this practice shall be abolished for this very reason, so that the extraction of debt may be from the property, rather than from the bodies. (OGIS 669, D185)

After a number of other prohibitions, the prefect's edict requires "no one should be confined in the tax collector's prison [*praktoreion*] except for a debtor to the public treasury." Similar to Ulpian's famous statement that governors commonly used prisons for punishment, but that the practice was distasteful, here we see Tiberius Julius Alexander, prefect of Egypt, stating that in the first century CE local administrators often used tax office facilities to hold civic prisoners, as we know was common in Ptolemaic practice, but that they ought not do so any longer. The prefect's logic for disallowing the use of public treasury prisons for private debtors is interesting, as well: prisons, he reasons, extract debts "from the bodies" of the debtors rather than from their property. We cannot say whether the prefect's prohibition was widely followed. But the legal ideal expressed is interesting in and of itself, and it suggests an ideological change between the Ptolemaic and Roman periods. In this Roman's ideal, tax prisons should be solely reserved for public debtors; what is implied is that civic prisons were to be reserved for deviants of other sorts.

There is a continuity of authority in early Roman rule in Alexandria, as seen in BGU 4.1138 from 19 BCE where a scribe of the supraregional governor (*epistratēgos*) approaches a low-level prison guard to request the release of a prisoner, similar to cases in the Ptolemaic Zeno papyri (D107). In Roman sources, however, the location where that guard sat in oversight is consistently inconsistent, and people whom he guarded, too, were likely different from a demographic standpoint: while Romans typically inflicted incarceration primarily on those belonging to a social underclass, while exile and other forms of sanction were reserved for those of noble birth, such class distinctions are harder to glimpse in Ptolemaic practice.

Prison provisioning changed over time as well, so far as we can see. Roman-era sources regularly indicate taxes raised for the support of local police, a continuation of the Ptolemaic *fulaktikon* tax (O. Wilcken 2.422, D149 [68 CE]). It is not until the Roman period, however, that the documentary record indicates taxes levied particularly for the support of prison guards, as discussed above in the section on prison bureaucracy (p. 168–170).

Julia Hillner (2015) argued a decade ago that late Roman legal sources produced a comprehensive legal theory of punishment for the first time, while earlier sources point to a less systematic, more scattered collection of penal ideologies (16). It is hard to say to what extent this insight is dictated by the nature of the sources available from each period: systematic legal compilations only survive from the late Roman period. It is certainly the case that in these late Roman legal codifications we see a comprehensive legal theory of punishment which is not *visible* before—perhaps because the earlier sources are no longer extant, or perhaps because they never were produced in the first place. And, as Andrea Lovato (1994) has argued, late antique legislation witnesses a slow but substantive trajectory in which emperors attempt to wrestle punitive discretion away from judges and even private people, implementing fixed penalties instead (186–93).

What is clearly the case, as Krause (1996) has shown, is that the total number of prisons likely increased in Late Antiquity, even as municipal prisons themselves were increasingly under the direct control of far off, overworked, and often capricious governors rather than local authorities (264–68). More likely, the alleged appearance of a thoroughgoing penology suggested by Hillner is an artifact of increasing prevalence and centralization along with a new form of legal consciousness that found value in producing the great legal codifications of Late Antiquity that survive, while earlier materials, frequently, do not. A similar issue shrouds our view of another major facet of late Roman prisons: reform efforts. Beginning in the fourth century CE, we see sustained social and legal attempts to mitigate some of the worst excesses of the prison, though again the fact that the *Theodosian Code*'s coverage begins with laws of 312 has likely occluded previous reform efforts. But, beginning in the early fourth century and growing through the middle of the fifth, we see a collocation of sources that seem to point to both localized and institutional efforts at reform that are not visible at such scale at any point previously.

A Constantinian law of 320/21 CE presents a comprehensive slate of minimum standards for the treatment of prisoners, though at least some of these are not likely to be reforms, but rather restatements of laws already in force. This law targeted the treatment of prisoners awaiting trial, and it details explicitly the rationale for minimum standards: "the point is to avoid torment, while safeguarding custody" (*CTh* 9.3.1, L133 [320/21 CE]). To that end, the law stipulates, for instance, that defendants "should not be placed in iron fetters that fit close to the bone, but looser chains." Such "shackle poisoning" is well-attested as a cause of convict deaths even in the modern period, and recent archaeological findings suggest that such a concern was not without merit in antiquity—the skeleton of a crucified man discovered in the Roman settlement at Fenstanton, in England, shows abnormal bone growth apparently resulting from long-term shackling (A38; Ingham and Duhig 2022; Oshinsky 1997, 45). The constitution orders, further, that prisoners should generally be allowed access to some sunlight during the day, and that guards who allow prisoners to die of starvation should themselves be subject to capital punishment. As a whole, the law paints prisons as inherently dangerous places, and attempts to deal with some of the eventualities of prison architecture and culture of carceral oversight. Some thirty years later, Libanius praised Constantine's prison legislation in an oration celebrating his sons, reflecting "what seemed to him an improvement in the conditions of incarceration," noting battles won, disbursements made, and the "long-suffering offender in the prisons, set free by the mercy of the ruler" (Pavón Torrejón 2004, 113; Libanius, *Oration* 59.29 [349 CE]). Perhaps their father's example convinced Constantine's sons to attempt further restrictions on the list of offenses for which incarceration was used as punishment. Writing to the governor of Sardinia, they decreed that "provincials must not suffer lashes of leaded whips or the custody of prison on account of unpaid taxes due, since it is recognized that such tortures have not been established for the innocent but for the guilty" (*CTh* 11.7.7, L97 [353 CE?]). A generation later, the emperors Gratian, Valentinian II, and Theodosius I decreed that prisoners should be released on the day of Easter, with the exception of "those person who we know would rather defile the joy and happiness of the community, should they be released"—that is, adulterers and rapists, people who disturb the dead or counterfeit money, murderers, and the like (*CTh* 9.38.8, L29 [385 CE]). Earlier sources, and especially the Severan jurist Ulpian, consider something like the "public good" as dispositive rationale for legal strictures, but this is the first time that we see a law explicitly name the prison as a tool for ensuring general social cohesion.

As discussed in the section on food, a fairly uniform idea of what might constitute prison food rations existed at least as early as the first part of the third century BCE and continued through the Roman imperial period. Nevertheless, the surviving legal corpus suggests that distribution of food to prisoners first became an issue for legislation during the late Roman period. CIL 8.17897 is a fragmentary decree from the *curia* of the Roman colony of Thamugadi from 361 to 363 CE, that seems to give a directive that the local citizenry was responsible for providing food and other provisions for incarcerated people, as well as for prison guards (D171; p. 117–118). The decree in Thamugadi mirrors concerns in a law given decades later at Ravenna by Emperors Honorius and Theodosius II, demanding that judges inspect prisoners each Sunday and that a modest amount of food should be provided to prisoners who have none because Christians are instructed to care for the poor (*CTh* 9.3.7, L44 [409 CE]).

The rhetorician Libanius was so disturbed by the treatment of incarcerated people in Antioch that he declaimed a long list of complaints to the emperor Theodosius I late in 386 CE, complaining that the affluent had hijacked the carceral system, wrongfully accusing people and sending them to rot in prison without trial or access to bail. "In consequence, the prison is packed with bodies. No one comes out—or precious few, at least—though many go in" (*Oration* 45.8, L52). Prisoners of both sexes do not have enough to eat, he complains, and prison wardens hold a monopoly on light, charging inmates exorbitant prices for lamps and oil. Thousands are dying, Libanius reports, and the text of his oration records the emperor's reply: weeping, the emperor expresses an acute concern for the injustice of the carceral system as practiced. At issue were both the material aspects of Antiochene prisons and the legal apparatus that kept people in squalid and exploitative conditions long enough to deny them justice. Responding to an objection that a delay in justice does not render an innocent man guilty, Libanius retorts: "If they are dead, they cannot [clear their name in court]!" (19) Legal reform was impotent without executive action. He complains to the emperor: "I know that you have enacted a law to help people under arrest as regards the length of detention, and that this does serve to protect them. But I also know that the same sort of practices have been current after the passing of the law as would have occurred if it was not in force. When magistrates willing to enforce them are non-existent, laws are mere words, and do not provide assistance to victims . . ." (32). Libanius inveighs against a system in which many are falsely accused, and even those who are guilty are punished by virtue of their incarceration rather than as recompense for their crime; even the laws that are intended to fix the problem are toothless without active enforcement. Libanius's speech points to something like grassroots organizing in the fourth century—attempting to hold the powerful to account for the injustice of the carceral system. It reminds us, too, that laws prescribe an ideal world rather than describing practices on the ground. Previous reform efforts may have existed, but none are as thoroughly documented as those visible in the mid- and late fourth century CE, extending from small peripheral cities like Thamugadi even to the imperial court.

Legislative impotence was not unique to Rome, however. Across the period under discussion private prisons were outlawed variously, and apparently to little effect: P. Tebt. 1.5 is a Ptolemaic royal decree outlawing the use of private prisons in 118 BCE, remarkably similar to a law of Zeno from over half a millennium later attempting to bring about the same result (D7; *CJ* 9.5.1, L134 [486 CE]). Even while the reasons and means of outlawing private incarceration differed, the attestation of such private facilities across and beyond that time frame suggests, again, the gap between prescriptive law and penal practice—perhaps as much as does the central position that private prisons took as a public good in Byzantine Egypt (Fikhman 1970; Torallas Tovar 2003, 221–23; Berkes 2015).

Substitutionary incarceration is a peculiar facet of Byzantine Egyptian carceral practice, especially gendered forms thereof. Sources like PSI 7.824, a Greek letter on papyrus from the late sixth or early seventh century, announce a previously unknown practice, and apparently at scale: the use of women as collateral for men's debts, with wives left to endure the torments of incarceration while husbands remain free to work and earn freedom for their wives (D13 [575–625 CE]; cf. O. Mon. Epiph. 177, D139 [sixth–seventh centuries CE]; Torallas Tovar 2006, 105). While earlier sources like BGU 16.2618, from Herakleopolis in 7 BCE, show incarceration of slaves as debt collateral, it is only in the late antique period that we see wives used as such (D146; Torallas Tovar 2003, 216–17; Krause 1996, 175–76).

One final point of discontinuity warrants mention, though it perhaps speaks equally to the general trend of continuity: prisoner releases are in evidence across our period of analysis, often during a festival or special occasion. The specifics of what occasion, which prisoners, and the process of amnesty differs across our archive and even between locations during the same period. For instance, Ptolemaic amnesties are most common on the occasion of a royal birthday (PSI 4.347, D116 [255–254 BCE]), while late Roman practice tends to prefer religious holidays for the same (*CTh* 9.38.3, L45 [367 CE?]).

We are historians, and when we began this project, our training primed us with an expectation bordering on dogma: we ought to find radical differences in ideology and experiences of incarceration over the roughly nine centuries covered by this book. To be sure, developments are visible, along with a few trajectories and a handful of stark discontinuities. But, by and large, carceral practices remained remarkably, unsettlingly durable across the ancient Mediterranean.

Considered from this broad perspective, we find that remarkably few aspects of even the contemporary US carceral state are truly unique. More often than not, what comes through from a contemporary comparative perspective are resonances or precursors, visible already in various ancient Mediterranean societies. The modern prison is not a new construction but an old and haunted house, full of apparitions of terror and subjugation that linger, whether we choose to recognize them, or whether we hold to the insuperable peculiarity of the premodern world. The explanation of difference is one of the historian's core tasks, but just as important is openness to aspects of human society that have remained surprisingly, disturbingly stable over the *longue durée*. We follow our colleagues in carceral studies in seeing that carceral practices underwent a significant shift in the early modern period. But in most cases those changes were not fundamental; even seemingly novel practices were not generated out of whole cloth. Penal incarceration, limited-term sentencing, solitary confinement, economic drivers behind mass incarceration, the connection between violence, prisoner bodies, and popular entertainment—each of these have clear precursors in the ancient Mediterranean.

The far distant past is beyond the remit of this book, and a global history of incarceration remains unwritten. Nevertheless, so far as we can tell, some aspects of incarceration have appeared in every Mediterranean society for which we have historical data; perhaps incarceration is a facet of every hierarchical, complex society. This may be demoralizing to those committed to abolition of the contemporary prison system and to the end of mass incarceration. Yet it need not be so. A world without prisons is a world we've yet to discover. It is a new, fresh future that could await us, but it is up to us to build it.

THE PRISON'S ANTIQUITY

Wendy Warren

At the heart of this fascinating book lies a rebuttal to the now-famous Foucauldian origin story of incarceration, the narrative that argued for the "birth of the prison" in late eighteenth-century Europe. Michel Foucault's story in *Discipline and Punish* centered Enlightenment thought as a crucial originating force in carceral history and contended that prisons were peripheral to the punishment economy of Europe before the rise of the penitentiary at the eighteenth century's end. Larsen and Letteney dismantle that narrative on nearly every page: no fundamental aspect of imprisonment, their research shows, was birthed in the late eighteenth century. After all, how could something be "born" in the late eighteenth century when it had fully matured already more than one thousand years before? Theirs is certainly not the first book to complicate Foucault's timeline, but perhaps no other work tackles the subject in antiquity with such rigorous attention to detail, and such patient interrogation of taciturn sources ranging from legal documents/papyri, to frescos, to excavations.[1]

This research has daunting ramifications for those interested in solving the problems inherent in modern imprisonment, precisely because it underscores the intractability of imprisonment in the world. Speaking of the prospect of prison reform, Foucault once observed that "it is so difficult to free oneself . . . [from] the impression of the prison's antiquity." He continued by noting that because the prison "appears to be so deeply rooted in our culture," it is viewed with "a historical depth it does not possess." Because, he said, "the prison appears ineradicable, held in a sort of 'obviousness'; in this way it is endlessly

---

1. Examples of scholarship that highlight prisons before their Foucauldian birth include Pugh 1968; Melossi and Pavarini 1977; Pike 1983; Spierenburg 2007; Geltner 2008.

revived."[2] This endless revivification, he meant, can look like continuity, which can be easily confused with necessity. In effect, he thought that the prison's seeming historical ubiquity would make its abolition harder to imagine and enact.

Larsen and Letteney's work makes clear that Foucault quite underestimated the prison's past, and also that the problem is worse than he thought. They show that the prison was alive, functioning, and heavily depended on by authorities already in antiquity; that is, the narrative that Foucault believed to be an impressionistic illusion of the prison's historical depth instead actually offers a realistic depiction of the prison's premodern character.

Interestingly, Larsen and Letteney aren't interested in replacing Foucault's chronology with a new birth story—though this is a common move among historians whose work displaces the late eighteenth century as the prison's originating moment. Rather, Larsen and Letteney portray the ancient Mediterranean world's prisons of from roughly 300 BCE to 600 CE as *already* mature by that era. Imprisonment as a system was *already* established and sophisticated; it was also already diverse in form. Their sources describe people imprisoned in cellars, in civic administrative buildings, on military bases, in temples, and even in cage like spaces under open-air theaters, where spectators could watch condemned prisoners battle both wild animals and professional fighters to the death. The prisons of antiquity were already substantive, bureaucratically organized, and complex. The reader comes to understand quickly that the origin of these institutions lies even further back, in some other age, for some other scholars to uncover.

In short, antiquity was already a sophisticated carceral moment, so sophisticated that the authors offer a typology of eight different kinds of prisons employed in the period— with subcategories further differentiating some of the types. Was imprisonment the main means of punishment in the era? No: the authors make no such claim. But they do insist on its omnipresence and thus importance in the societies they describe.

They also suggest a reason for these prisons: as in so many other places and times, prisons in antiquity existed to solve the problems of people with an abundance of social power. Larsen and Letteney describe an ancient Mediterranean world stratified by a rockhard line between the wealthy and the poor, a world fractured by religious differences and frequently riven by war. In this world, imprisonment served to confine the poor, the heretics, and the vanquished.

If this all sounds familiar, that's because it is: the authors observe that the prisons of the ancient Mediterranean resemble both the prisons of today, around the world, and perhaps the prisons of every other epoch in between. As they note, the infamous hallmarks of modern mass incarnation, the "penal incarceration, limited-term sentencing, solitary confinement, economic drivers of mass incarceration, the connection between violence, prisoner bodies, and popular entertainment," all existed in one form or another in antiquity (p. 195). Prisoners a thousand years ago were surveilled, confined in miserable conditions, differentiated ideologically if not materially from enslaved people, and starved. Prisoners in antiquity labored under the control of authorities, endured family separation, and received social stigma owing to their confinement. Was anything different? Certainly. The sheer numbers of people incarcerated today, for example, cannot be compared to the population described in this book; the *mass* of our own era's "mass incarceration" is certainly historically distinct. The vibrancy of reform, liberation, and abolition movements

---

2. Foucault 2015, 92.

is new, and strongly related to the aforementioned exponential growth of the imprisoned population. The stark racial structure of incarceration in many places today was by no means established or developed in the long-ago past. But, while differences exist, what will strike many readers of this book are the similarities between the prison of antiquity and the prison of today.

But what of in-between? Similarities between then (antiquity) and now (the age of mass incarceration) shouldn't lead us to assume steady continuity. It's conceivable that what Foucault took to be the prison's birth in the late eighteenth century was rather its rebirth—a sort of bleak renaissance of an idea drawn from classical antiquity that disappeared in the centuries between. But what about the era just prior to Foucault's penitentiaries? What of early modernity, the moment before imprisonment became European society's main punishment for most accused, captured, and convicted people (always remembering that this was the same moment in which the Atlantic system of racialized chattel slavery was developed). Did early modernity deviate from the patterns established in antiquity? Oddly, the answer seems to be no, not much. It's an uncomfortable answer for historians, this tale of continuity and growth without any obvious moments of disjuncture, but the academic inclination for ever more epochal fracture and difference must have limits.

Looking at the long history of the prison from the vantage point of early modern Europe, the continuity that stands out the most is also the continuity that is probably the most obvious: the correlation between poverty and incarceration. This has been a constant. As Larsen and Letteney observe, "It was not a crime to be poor, but it was certainly the poor, and people who felt the need to steal food, who most often found themselves sitting in an ancient Mediterranean prison." In antiquity, "the prison was disproportionately inflicted on the poor, manual laborers, and socially vulnerable" (p. 112). People without resources became desperate more easily on behalf of their own needs and that of their families; they turned to "crime" more often as a result; they had fewer resources to protest their imprisonment. The evidence Larsen and Letteney present is striking in and of itself, but perhaps the more so because historians have pieced together evidence suggesting that this same situation persisted into the medieval and early modern period.

For example, the historian Guy Geltner, in his incisive study of medieval imprisonment, noted that throughout the Middle Ages, poverty could lead quickly to prison. Geltner's study of a Florentine prison found that "debts ma[de] up 64 percent of the ground for arrest" of prisoners during a three-year period he analyzed. Similarly, he notes that a strikingly common feature of prisoners throughout medieval Italy was their shared state of poverty.[3]

Geltner's work also lets us think about inconsistent aspects of carceral history. Among the points that Geltner insisted on was the visibility of the imprisoned to the eyes of medieval Florence; Larsen and Letteney describe ancient inmates "carefully hidden from the eye," with facilities "built in such a way that the spaces were accessible, while prisoners themselves were harder to see than to hear, to touch, or to smell" (p. 84). If in fact in medieval Europe prisoners were central and visible, they would not remain so forever. The archive lets us know that in early modern Europe, and also in the colonial Americas, many prisoners would beg, from barred windows, for food from passersby. Authorities worked hard to remove this visibility as the eighteenth century ended.

3. Geltner 2008, 53.

Poverty, though, remained a constant main cause of incarceration in Europe into early modernity. Pieter Spierenburg, in his incisive monograph on the rise of "disciplinary institutions" in early modern Europe, noted of England's fifteenth-century houses of correction that they were, first, intended as a means of controlling the rising population of impoverished people in an increasingly secularized world, and second, that they were certainly intended to be punitive. As in antiquity, imprisonment was not the only means of punishment available to authorities but it was increasingly popular and worked hand-in-hand with the other main institutions of discipline: "the galley, public works, and transportation."[4] Spierenburg noted that the famous workhouses of early modern Europe, despite the implications of their name, rarely turned a profit, or even broke even. Their costs, though, were a small price to pay given how successfully they confined and rendered less visible the new masses of impoverished people that so troubled those with power.

The chain link between poverty and imprisonment persisted into the eighteenth century. In March of 1729, to give just one well-known example, General James Oglethorpe of the British House of Commons led a government committee charged with examining the condition of London's prisons. The group's finding were predictable: marginalized and impoverished people were the most likely to enter prisons, and then also disproportionately the most likely to die inside their walls. Early modern prisons affected impoverished people precisely because they were likeliest to resort to criminalized acts in order to feed themselves, because they were the likeliest to fall afoul of creditors, because they were the least connected to patrons who might help them, and because they had the least ability to pay for services such as attorneys, to pay for court fees, to pay for necessities to make their imprisonment more tolerable, or to pay for bail.[5]

Our authors note that "the fastest track to incarceration across the ancient world was to owe somebody money, especially someone of high social status who had well-established avenues to social and political power and a willingness to grease the wheels of the carceral apparatus to turn in their favor" (p. 156). Not much changed in the succeeding centuries. Oglethorpe underscored the social inequities that fueled the prison system of early modern London. Too many people who ended up in such prisons, he noted, were there not for what he thought of as actual crimes worthy of punishment, but rather for debt. In an early modern catch-22, once an impoverished person was arrested, the chances of paying their debts disappeared, and their situation became extreme.

The situation could be dire in the most basic of ways. Take, for just one example, food in prison, a topic on which Larsen and Letteney offer their readers a fascinating discussion. Not only was food hard to obtain for many incarcerated people during the period under discussion in this book—most notably but not only for the poor—but food-related crimes often *led* people to prison. This was not only a problem of antiquity. Geltner found it to be the case in medieval Italy; Spierenburg found it to be so through northern Europe (and elsewhere); and the problem remained unresolved still in early eighteenth century London, where Oglethorpe's committee report noted that many destitute prisoners starved to death. To pay for food required money, which few prisoners had. Their poverty left them at the mercy of cruel wardens who sometimes resorted to torture to ensure they had fully fleeced

---

4. Spierenburg 2007, 24.

5. James Edward Oglethorpe, Reports (London, 1729), reprinted in Baine 1994, 44–158.

the imprisoned of assets, or just to assert their dominance over the unfortunate prisoners. In the Fleet Prison, for example, one prison keeper put too-tight iron cuffs around the legs of a prisoner for three weeks, leaving the man disabled.[6]

Cui bono? As with later prisons, this is a question we might ask regarding the prisons of antiquity. Were the keepers of antiquity's prisons similarly incentivized to abuse their inmates? The answer to that is, yes, sadly. Larsen and Letteney have found evidence that prisoners were physically abused and chained. In the skeletal remains of a crucified man they observed indentations in the ankle bones that suggest he (too) spent a long time chained by the legs. But they do not claim to understand fully (because the sources simply will not say) who benefited from this sort of abuse. Were wardens benefiting directly from their treatment of prisoners? Did they resort to extortion? We can only say that it seems likely. The authors present ample evidence that people were falsely accused and falsely incarcerated, suggesting some sort of corruption in the system. We learn that even in antiquity, wardens held the right to deny prisoners even light, charging them for lamps and oil, and that some abused the practice in ways that others noticed and protested. In such a system, with such opportunities for personal enrichment, it seems that at least some wardens enriched themselves—the authors note that a third-century jurist recommended that wardens were to be punished if they accepted bribes for better treatment (p. 175). Jurists rarely offer such recommendations as simple hypotheticals.

The poverty of prisoners, though, is far from the only constant of incarceration's long history. Even where we might expect to see difference, it hardly appears. Artistic images of the prison seem to have remained static, for example. The authors describe certain tropes in antiquity's creative representations of prisons and the imprisoned: abased prisoners, dank conditions, hierarchically arranged compositions. Oglethorpe's committee had their portrait painted by no less an artist than William Hogarth (fig. 25). The artist's imagination was drawn to the pathos of the topic; however, what is more interesting to consider in this context is how similar his composition seems to those in antiquity described by the authors. Hogarth puts Oglethorpe into a dimly lit prison cellar, just as does the art of antiquity; Hogarth's prisoner is at the bottom of the composition, in a supplicant position; much of the art described in this book depicts prisoners in a similar fashion. In almost every way, the artistic tropes align: the prisoner is fettered, even though he is within secure walls; the prisoner is naked and emaciated; the prisoner is foreign and a heretic.[7] Even the artistic vision, it seems, saw prisons as having changed little over the course of a millennium; even artists were caught in certain tropes and consistencies; or perhaps even they saw no way to imagine something else.

Such a problem of imagination brings us back to Foucault's difficulty of freeing oneself from faulty impressions. His point, of course, was not that there is anything inherently fatalistic about imagining the prison as something as old as time. He wanted historical knowledge that could contribute to a future without the prison's barbarism. Foucault ended the first chapter of *Discipline and Punish*, with a famous meditation on the purpose of his work. "I would like," he wrote,

6. *Journals of the House of Commons* 21 (1803): 279.
7. William Hogarth, *The Gaols Committee of the House of Commons*, oil on canvas, ca. 1729.

FIGURE 25. William Hogarth, *The Gaols Committee of the House of Commons*. Copyright National Portrait Gallery, London.

to write the history of this prison, with all the political investments of the body that it gathers together in its closed architecture. Why? Simply because I am interested in the past? No, if one means by that writing a history of the past in terms of the present. Yes, if one means writing the history of the present.[8]

It would be a curious thing if the preceding pages, describing a time so long ago, are in fact also a history of our present. But are they also a history of our future? Reckoning with the prison's deeper history might help to prevent that. But if "the impression of the prison's antiquity" is true and the prison has indeed been ubiquitous to human society, then the real reckoning will involve the history of what has gone on *outside* the prison's walls. For millennia, humans outside such walls have locked others within them. What sort of societies have humans made and endured that have come up with nothing better?

8. Foucault 1977, 112–14.

ACKNOWLEDGMENTS

This project has been a collaborative effort from the start, and our long journey benefited enormously from council, critique, and correction from friends and colleagues who read early versions and offered their expertise. Our analysis is clearer and more sophisticated because of their gift of time, and we thank them for joining as collaborators. They include Matthew J. Adams, Adam Bülow-Jacobsen, Elizabeth Castelli, Greta Galeotti, Nicole Giannella, Brandon Green, Simcha Gross, Amit Gvaryahu, Noel Lenski, Rebecca Levitan, Rachel Lilley Love, AnneMarie Luijendijk, Sarah Morris, Candida Moss, Carlos Noreña, Sailakshmi Ramgopal, Brent Shaw, Irene Soto Marín, Rachel Patt, Joel Walker, Caroline Wazer, and Spencer Weinreich. Zachary Herz offered thorough commentary on chapter 1 which rendered the analysis both richer and more precise. Felicity Harley-McGowan carefully read the public transcript section of chapter 4, and her feedback greatly improved our analysis. Roger Ulrich proposed a number of useful architectural parallels that enriched our understanding of the carcer/aerarium at Sufetula, including a suggestion that the room underneath the Capitoline tribunal at Pompeii is an intriguing possible carceral facility. We extend sincere thanks to two reviewers for the press: Tina Shepherdson, who helped us clarify our thinking on several points and guided us toward several Syriac sources that we had missed, and Julia Hillner, who offered the gift of thorough and immensely useful critique and guidance at multiple stages of writing. We are especially thankful that she shared her time and expertise with us.

We are lucky to have received support from a number of generous institutions that saw the value in our endeavor, and supported it financially. We would like to thank the Mellon Foundation, the American Council of Learned Societies, the Carlsberg Foundation, the American School of Classical Studies at Athens, the American Academy in Rome, the Simpson Center for the Humanities, Yale University, Princeton University, the University of Southern California, the Massachusetts Institute of Technology, the University of Copenhagen, and the University of Washington for funding the research underlying this book. This book is open access owing to the generous support of the provost at MIT and the MIT Libraries Department of Scholarly Communications—thanks is due especially to them, and to Katharine Dunn, for making this research freely accessible.

Beyond institutional support, a project of this breadth required an extraordinary amount of administrative magic, for which we would like to thank Amy Braden and Peter Mancall especially. The Ancient Mediterranean Incarceration Database benefited greatly from research assistance of Niels Bargfeldt, Emi Brown, Krysta Fauria, Evan Levine, Naomi Reiss, and its extraordinary digital architect, Hallvard Indgjerd. The University of California Press has been a wonderful partner in our endeavors, and we would especially like to thank Eric Schmidt for believing in a rather unorthodox project from the start, Jyoti Arvey and Margo Irvin for seeing it through to publication, and to Mary Jane Cuyler for compiling the tremendous indices. Titus Kaphar and Gagosian were kind enough to give permission for us to use *Jerome II* as our cover; we extend our sincere thanks to them for their generosity in framing our work.

Much of this research involved traipsing around the Mediterranean basin, and we did so with the aid of a small army of local experts, including Mhamed Gueraini (Algeria), James Herbst, Ioulia Tzonou, Manolis Papadakis, and Paul Scotton (Greece), Aharoni Amitai, Benjamin Arubas, Peter Gendelman, and Yotam Tepper (Israel), Michael Anderson, Caroline Cheung, Mauro Dadea, Andrea De Georgi, and Patrizia Fortini (Italy), Mohammad Najjar (Jordan), Elisabeth Fentress and Mohamed Nabli (Tunisia), and Josep Anton Remolà Vallverdú (Spain).

To all these, and to those we inevitably missed, we offer our sincerest gratitude.

October, 2024
Copenhagen and Seattle

REFERENCES

Abolafia, Jacob. 2021. "Plato's Theory of Incarceration." *Ramus* 50 (1/2): 68–86.

Abolafia, Jacob. 2024. *The Prison before the Panopticon*. Harvard University Press.

Agamben, Giorgio. 1998. *Homo Sacer: Sovereign Power and Bare Life*. Stanford University Press.

Ajootian, Aileen. 2014. "Simulacra Civitatum at Roman Corinth." *Hesperia* 83 (2): 315–77.

Ako-Adounvo, Gifty. 1999. *Studies in the Iconography of Blacks in Roman Art*. PhD Dissertation, McMaster University.

Alexander, Ian J., and Nicole Starosielski. 2023. "Asolarity: Weaponized Sunlight." In *Solarities*, edited by Cymene Howe, Jeff Diamanti, and Amelia Moore, 133–47. punctum books.

Alexander, Michelle. 2012. *The New Jim Crow: Mass Incarceration in the Age of Colorblindness*. New Press.

Allen, Danielle. 1997. "Imprisonment in Classical Athens." *Classical Quarterly* 47 (1): 121–35.

Arendt, Hannah. 1994. *Eichmann in Jerusalem: A Report on the Banality of Evil*. Penguin.

Baine, Rodney M., ed. 1994. *The Publications of James Edward Oglethorpe*. University of Georgia Press.

Bakirtzis, Charalambos. 1988. *The Basilica of St. Demetrius*. Guides of the Institute for Balkan Studies 6. Institute for Balkan Studies.

Ballu, Albert. 1910. *Guide illustré de Timgad (Antique Thamugadi)*. Neurdein Frères.

Ballu, Albert. 1921. *Ruines de Djemila (Antique Cuicul)*. Jules Carbonel.

Ballu, Albert. 1926. *Guide illustré de Djemila (Antique Cuicul)*. Jules Carbonel.

Bastianini, Guido. 1988. "Un ordine di scarcerazione: PBerol. inv. 8997 (ChLA X 421)." In *Proceedings of the XVIII International Congress of Papyrology, Athens 25–31 May 1986*, edited by Basil G. Mandilaras 2:351–56. Greek Papyrological Society.

Bauschatz, John. 2007. "Ptolemaic Prisons Reconsidered." *Classical Bulletin* 83 (1): 3–48.

Bauschatz, John. 2013. *Law and Enforcement in Ptolemaic Egypt*. Cambridge University Press.

Benton, Jared. 2024. "Punitive Labor and Enslavement in the Roman Bakery." *World Archaeology* 55 (1):12–24.

Berkes, Lajos. 2015. "An Estate Prison in Byzantine Egypt: PSI VII 824 Reconsidered." *Zeitschrift für Papyrologie und Epigraphik* 193:241–43.

Bertrand-Dagenbach, Cécile, Alain Chauvot, Michel Matter, and Jean-Marie Salamito, eds. 1999. *Carcer: prison et privation de liberté dans l'Antiquité classique.* De Boccard.

Bertrand-Dagenbach, Cécile, Alain Chauvot, Jean-Marie Salamito, and Denyse Vaillancourt, eds. 2004. *Carcer II: prison et privation de liberté dans l'Empire romain et l'Occident médiéval.* De Boccard.

Besnier, Maurice. 1899. "Les *scholae* de sous-officiers dans le camp romain de Lambese." *Mélanges de l'école française de Rome* 19 (1): 199–258.

Bjornlie, Michael Shane. 2019. *The Variae: The Complete Translation.* University of California Press.

Blackmon, Douglas A. 2008. *Slavery by Another Name: The Re-Enslavement of Black Americans from the Civil War to World War II.* Anchor Books.

Bliss, Frederick Jones, and R. A. Stewart Macalister. 1902. *Excavations in Palestine during the Years 1898–1900.* Palestine Exploration Fund.

Bomgardner, David L. 1989. "The Carthage Amphitheater: A Reappraisal." *American Journal of Archaeology* 93 (1): 85–103.

Bond, Sarah E. 2025. *Strike: Labor, Unions, and Resistance in the Roman Empire.* Yale University Press.

Bonneville, Jean-Noël, Myriam Fincker, Pierre Sillières, Sylvie Dardaine, and Jean-Michel Labarthe. 2000. *Belo VII, le capitole.* Casa de Velázquez.

Bonucci, Carlo. 1827. *Pompei descritta da Carlo Bonucci architetto.* 3rd ed. Raffaele Miranda.

Bowman, Alan K. 1994. *Life and Letters on the Roman Frontier: Vindolanda and Its People.* Routledge.

Bradley, Keith. 2004. "On Captives under the Principate." *Phoenix* 58 (3/4): 298–318.

Brélaz, Cédric. 2020. "Local Understandings of Roman Criminal Law and Procedure in Asia Minor." In *Law in the Roman Provinces*, edited by Kimberley Czajkowski, Benedikt Eckhardt, and Meret Strothmann. Oxford University Press.

Brown, Frank Edward, Emeline Richardson, and Lawrence Richardson, eds. 1993. *Cosa III: The Buildings of the Forum: Colony, Municipium, and Village.* Memoirs of the American Academy in Rome 37. Pennsylvania State University Press.

Bruun, Christer. 1988. "*Caligatus, Tubicen, Optio Carceris,* and the Centurions' Positions; Some Remarks on an Inscription in ZPE 71 (1988)." *Arctos: Acta Philologica Fennica* 22:23–40.

Bryen, Ari Z. *Violence in Roman Egypt: A Study in Legal Interpretation.* University of Pennsylvania Press, 2013.

Bülow-Jacobsen, Adam. 1986. "Orders to Arrest. P.Haun. Inv. 33 and 54 and a Consolidated List." *Zeitschrift für Papyrologie und Epigraphik* 66:93–98.

Bülow-Jacobsen, Adam. 2022. "Callgirls in the Quarries." In *Proceedings of the 29th International Congress of Papyrology: Lecce, 28th July–3rd August 2019*, edited by Mario Capasso, Paola Davoli, and Natascia Pellé, 225–32. Quaderni dell'Istituto Superiore Universitario di Formazione Interdisciplinare 2. Centro di Studi Papirologici dell'Università del Salento.

Cadoux, T. J. 2008. "The Roman *Carcer* and Its Adjuncts." *Greece and Rome* 55 (2): 202–21.

Cagnat, René. 1920. "C. Julius Crescens Didius Crescentianus, fondateur de la basilique Julia, à Djemila (Algérie)." *Revue des Études Anciennes* 22 (2): 97–103.

Canina, Luigi. 1838. *Descrizione di Cere antica*. Canina.

Cardascia, Guillaume. 1950. "L'apparition dans le droit des classes d'honestiores et d'humiliores." *Revue historique de droit français et étranger* 4 (27): 461–85.

Carroll, Maureen. 2020. "Invisible foreigners at Rome? Identities in Dress Behaviour in the Imperial Capital." *Contextus* 41:169–88.

Carucci, Margherita. 2018. "The Spectacle of Justice in the Roman Empire." In *The Impact of Justice on the Roman Empire*, edited by Olivier Hekster and Koenraad Verboven, 212–33. Brill.

Cerrone, Francesca. 2022. "L'iscrizione dedicatoria del Carcer-Tullianum." In *Carcer Tullianum: Il Mamertino al Foro Romano*, edited by Alfonsina Russo and Patrizia Fortini, 1–4. L'Erma di Bretschneider.

Chaniotis, Angelos. 2009. "Ritual Performances of Divine Justice: The Epigraphy of Confession, Atonement, and Exaltation in Roman Asia Minor." In *From Hellenism to Islam: Cultural and Linguistic Change in the Roman Near East*, edited by David J. Wasserstein, Hannah M. Cotton, Jonathan J. Price, and Robert G. Hoyland, 115–53. Cambridge University Press.

Chauvot, Alain. 1999a. "Conclusion." In *Carcer: prison et privation de liberté dans l'Antiquité classique*, edited by Cécile Bertrand-Dagenbach, Alain Chauvot, Michel Matter, and Jean-Marie Salamito, 221–24. De Boccard.

Chauvot, Alain. 1999b. "La détention sous Tibère." In *Carcer: prison et privation de liberté dans l'Antiquité classique*, edited by Cécile Bertrand-Dagenbach, Alain Chauvot, Michel Matter, and Jean-Marie Salamito, 163–76. De Boccard.

Chryssoulaki, Stella. 2019. "The Excavations at Phaleron Cemetery 2012–2017: An Introduction." In *Rethinking Athens before the Persian Wars: Proceedings of the International Workshop at the Ludwig-Maximilians-Universität München (Munich, 23rd–24th February 2017)*, edited by Constanze Graml, Annarita Doronzio, and Vincenzo Capozzoli, 103–14. Münchner Studien zur alten Welt 17. utzverlag.

Clarysse, Willy. 2002. "Three Ptolemaic Papyri on Prisoners." *Archiv für Papyrusforschung* 48 (1): 98–106.

Claytor, W. Graham. 2018. "The Municipalization of Writing in Roman Egypt." In *Literacy in Ancient Everyday Life*, edited by Anne Kolb, 319–34. De Gruyter.

Coarelli, Filippo. 2014. *Rome and Environs: An Archaeological Guide*. Updated ed. University of California Press.

Coleman, K. M. 1990. "Fatal Charades: Roman Executions Staged as Mythological Enactments." *Journal of Roman Studies* 80:44–73.

Corcoran, Lorelei H. 1995. *Portrait Mummies from Roman Egypt, I-IV Centuries A.D: With a Catalog of Portrait Mummies in Egyptian Museums*. Studies in Ancient Oriental Civilization 56. Oriental Institute of the University of Chicago.

Cox, Robynn, and Sally Wallace. 2016. "Identifying the Link Between Food Security and Incarceration: Food Security and Incarceration." *Southern Economic Journal* 82 (4): 1062–77.

Crum, Walter E. 1902. *Coptic Ostraca from the Collections of the Egypt Exploration Fund, the Cairo Museum and Others*. Egypt Exploration Fund.

Crum, Walter E. 1926. *The Monastery of Epiphanius at Thebes Part II: Coptic Ostraca and Papyri*. Vol. 2. Publications of the Metropolitan Museum of Art Egyptian Expedition 4. Metropolitan Museum of Art.

Cummings, Arthur Dickinson, Walter R. Chalmers, and Harold Mattingly. 1956. *A Roman Mining Document*. Electrical Press.

Cupcea, George. 2024. "The Prison in the Fortress of *Apulum* (Alba Iulia)." In *Living and Dying on the Roman Frontier and Beyond*, edited by Harry Van Enckevort, Mark Driessen, Erik Graafstal, Tom Hazenberg, Tatiana Ivleva, and Carol Van Driel-Murray, 179–87. Proceedings of the 25th International Congress of Roman Frontier Studies 3. Sidestone Press.

Curbera, Jaime. 2018. "Lexical Notes on Greek Prisons and Imprisonment." *Revue de philologie, de littérature et d'histoire anciennes* 92 (1): 7–37.

Cuvigny, Hélène. 2010. "Femmes tournantes: remarques sur la prostitution dans les garnisons romaines du désert de Bérénice." *Zeitschrift für Papyrologie und Epigraphik* 172:159–66.

Dadea, Mauro. 2006. *L'anfiteatro romano di Cagliari*. Sardegna archeologica Guide e itinerari 38. Delfino.

David, Jean-Michel. 1983. "Le tribunal dans la basilique: évolution fonctionnelle et symbolique de la République à l'Empire." In *Architecture et société. De l'archaïsme grec à la fin de la République. Actes du Colloque international organisé par le Centre national de la recherche scientifique et l'École française de Rome (Rome 2–4 décembre 1980)*, 219–41. École Française de Rome.

Davis, Angela Y. 2003. *Are Prisons Obsolete?* Seven Story Press.

Davis, Angela Y. 2006. "Racialized Punishment and Prison Abolition." In *A Companion to African-American Philosophy*, edited by Tommy Lee Lott and John P. Pittman, 360–69. Blackwell.

Department of Justice 2021. Press Release 14–1427; NYC Mayor's Office of Criminal Justice Report, October.

De Simoni, Alberto. 2022. "Power to Punish and Authority to Forgive: Imperial State and Imprisonment in 4th Century AD Antioch." PhD Dissertation, University of Florida.

De Souza, Philip. 2011. "War, Slavery, and Empire in Roman Imperial Iconography." *Bulletin of the Institute of Classical Studies* 54 (1): 31–62.

Dreyfus, Hubert L., and Paul Rabinow. 1983. *Michel Foucault: Beyond Structuralism and Hermeneutics*. University of Chicago Press.

Duguid, Stephen. 2000. *Can Prisons Work? The Prisoner as Object and Subject in Modern Corrections*. University of Toronto Press.

Dunbabin, Katherine M. D. 1978. *The Mosaics of Roman North Africa: Studies in Iconography and Patronage*. Oxford University Press.

Durkheim, Émile. 1899. "Deux lois de l'évolution pénale." *L'Année sociologique* 4:65–95.

Dolganov, Anna, Fritz Mitthof, Hannah M. Cotton, and Avner Ecker. 2023. "Forgery and Fiscal Fraud in Iudaea and Arabia on the Eve of the Bar Kokhba Revolt: Memorandum and Minutes of a Trial before a Roman Official (P.Cotton)." *Tyche* 38:37–166.

Donna, Rose Bernard, trans. 1964. *Saint Cyprian: Letters (1–81)*. Fathers of the Church 51. Catholic University of America Press.

Dušanić, Slobodan. 1977. "Aspects of Roman Mining in Noricum, Pannonia, Dalmatia and Moesia Superior." In *Politische Geschichte (Provinzen und Randvölker: Lateinischer*

Donau-Balkanraum), edited by Hildegard Temporini, 6:52–94. Aufstieg und Niedergang der römischen Welt 2. De Gruyter.

Duval, Noël. 1990. "Sufetula: l'histoire d'une ville romaine de la Haute Steppe à la lumière des recherches récentes." In *L'Afrique dans l'Occident romain (Ier siècle av. J.-C.—IVe siècle ap. J.-C.) Actes du colloque de Rome (3–5 décembre 1987)*, 495–536. École française de Rome.

Duval, Noël, and François Baratte. 1973. *Les ruines de Sufetula: Sbeïtla*. Société Tunisienne de Diffusion.

Edgar, Campbell Cowan. 1926. *Zenon Papyri: Catalogue général des antiquités égyptiennes du Musée du Caire*. G. Olms.

Eisenhut, Werner. 1972. "Die römische Gefängnisstrafe." In *Recht, Religion, Sprache und Literatur (bis zum Ende des 2. Jahrhunderts v. Chr.)*, edited by Hildegard Temporini and Wolfgang Haase 2:268–282. Aufstieg und Niedergang der römischen Welt 1. De Gruyter.

Étienne, Robert. 1974. "Recherches sur l'ergastule." In *Actes du Colloque 1972 sur l'esclavage*, 249–66. Annales littéraires de l'Université de Besançon 163. Belles Lettres.

Étienne, Robert, Ioan Piso, and Alexandru Diaconescu. 2002. "Les fouilles du forum vetus de Sarmizegetusa. Rapport Général." *Acta Musei Napocensis* 39–40/I:59–154.

Evans, Trevor V. 2005. "Digital Images of Cairo Papyri and the Writing Hands of the Zeno Archive." *Center for the Study of Ancient Documents Newsletter* 1118/01: 4–5.

Fassin, Didier. 2017. *Prison Worlds: An Ethnography of the Carceral Condition*. Polity.

Ferris, I. M. 2000. *Enemies of Rome: Barbarians through Roman Eyes*. Sutton.

Fikhman, I. F. 1970. "On the Structure of the Egyptian Large Estate in the Sixth Century." In *Proceedings of the Twelfth International Congress of Papyrology*, edited by Deborah H. Samuel. American Studies in Papyrology 12. A. M. Hakkert.

Fink, Robert O. 1971. *Roman Military Records on Papyrus*. Philological Monographs 26. Press of Case Western Reserve University.

Fiorelli, Giuseppe. 1875. *Descrizione di Pompei*. Tipografia Italiana.

Folch, Marcus. 2021a. "Political Prisoners in Democratic Athens, 490–318 BCE Part I: The Athenian Inmate Population." *Classical Philology* 116 (3): 336–68.

Folch, Marcus. 2021b. "Political Prisoners in Democratic Athens, 490–318 BCE Part II: Narrating Incarceration in Athenian Historiography and Oratory." *Classical Philology* 116 (4): 498–514.

Folch, Marcus. 2021c. "Is Red Figure the New Black? The Imprisonment of Women in Classical Athens." *Ramus* 50 (1–2): 45–67.

Folch, Marcus. 2026. *Bondage, Incarceration, and the Prison in Greece and Rome: A Cultural and Literary History*. Oxford University Press.

Foucault, Michel. 1977. *Discipline and Punish: The Birth of the Prison*. Pantheon Books.

Foucault, Michel. 2003. *"Society Must Be Defended" Lectures at the Collège de France, 1975–76*. Edited by Mauro Bertani and Alessandro Fontana. Translated by David Macey. Picador.

Foucault, Michel. 2015. *The Punitive Society: Lectures at the Collège de France, 1972–1973*. Edited by Bernard E. Harcourt. Translated by Graham Burchell. Palgrave Macmillan.

Friedman, Hannah. 2009. "Forced Labour, Mines, and Space: Exploring the Control of Mining Communities." In *TRAC 2008: Proceedings of the Eighteenth Annual Theoretical Roman Archaeology*, edited by Mark Driessen, Stijn Heeren, Joep Hendriks, Fleur Kemmers, and Ronald Visser, 1–12. Oxbow.

Frymer, Tikva Simone. 1977. "The Nungal-Hymn and the Ekur-Prison." *Journal of the Economic and Social History of the Orient* 20 (1): 78–89.

Fuhrmann, Christopher J. 2012. *Policing the Roman Empire: Soldiers, Administration, and Public Order*. Oxford University Press.

Fuhrmann, Christopher J. 2016. "Policing Functions and Public Order." In *The Oxford Handbook of Roman Law and Society*, edited by Paul J. du Plessis, Clifford Ando, and Kaius Tuori, 297–309. Oxford University Press.

Gadamer, Hans-Georg. 2013. *Truth and Method*. 2nd ed. Bloomsbury Academic.

Gagos, Traianos, and Peter J. Sijpesteijn. 1996. "Towards an Explanation of the Typology of the So-Called 'Orders to Arrest.'" *Bulletin of the American Society of Papyrologists* 33 (1/4): 77–97.

Garnsey, Peter. 1968. "Why Penalties Become Harsher: The Roman Case, Late Republic to Fourth Century Empire." *American Journal of Jurisprudence* 13 (1): 141–62.

Garnsey, Peter. 1970. *Social Status and Legal Privilege in the Roman Empire*. Oxford University Press.

Gilmore, Ruth Wilson. 2007. *Golden Gulag: Prisons, Surplus, Crisis, and Opposition in Globalizing California*. University of California Press.

Gordon, Robert W. 1984. "Critical Legal Histories." *Stanford Law Review* 36 (1/2): 57–125.

Gorges, Jean-Gérard. 1979. *Les Villas hispano-romaines: Inventaire et problématique archéologiques*. Publications du Centre Pierre Paris 4. De Boccard.

Hagedorn, Ursula. 1979. "Das Formular der Überstellungebefehle im römischen Ägypten." *Bulletin of the American Society of Papyrologists* 16 (1/2): 61–74.

Harley-McGowan, Felicity. 2015. "From Victim to Victor: Developing an Iconography of Suffering in Early Christian Art." In *The Art of Empire: Christian Art in its Imperial Context*, edited by Lee Jefferson and Robin Jensen, 115–58. Fortress Press.

Harper, Kyle. 2017. *The Fate of Rome: Climate, Disease, and the End of an Empire*. Princeton University Press.

Harries, Jill. 1999. *Law and Empire in Late Antiquity*. Cambridge University Press.

Harries, Jill. 2007. *Law and Crime in the Roman World*. Cambridge University Press.

Hauken, Tor, and Hasan Malay. 2009. "A New Edict of Hadrian from the Province of Asia Setting Regulations for Requisitioned transport." In *Selbstdarstellung und Kommunikation: die Veröffentlichung staatlicher Urkunden auf Stein und Bronze in der römischen Welt: internationales Kolloquium an der Kommission für Alte Geschichte und Epigraphik in München (1. bis 3. Juli 2006)*, edited by Rudolf Haensch and Denis Feissel. Vestigia 61. Beck.

Hauptmann, Andreas. 2007. *The Archaeometallurgy of Copper: Evidence from Faynan, Jordan*. Springer.

Havener, Wolfgang. 2018. "Tropaion. The Battlefield Trophy in Ancient Greece and Rome." In *Societies at War: Proceedings of the tenth Symposium of the Melammu Project held in Kassel September 26–28 2016 & Proceedings of the eight Symposium of the Melammu Project held in Kiel November 11–15 2014*, edited by Kai Ruffing, Kerstin Droß-Krüpe, Sebastian Fink, and Robert Rollinger, 267–92. Austrian Academy of Sciences Press.

Hengstl, Joachim. 1997. "Petita in Petitionen gräko-ägyptischer Papyri." In *Symposion 1995: Vorträge zur griechischen und hellenistischen Rechtsgeschichte (Korfu, 1–5. September 1995)*, edited by Gerhard Thür and I. Velissaropoulou-Karakōsta, 265–89. Akten der Gesellschaft für griechische und hellenistische Rechtsgeschichte 11. Böhlau.

Henning, Meghan R. 2021. *Hell Hath No Fury: Gender, Disability, and the Invention of Damned Bodies in Early Christian Literature*. Yale University Press.

Hillman, Aubrey L., Mark B. Abbott, B. L. Valero-Garcés, Mario Morellon, Fernando Barreiro-Lostres, and Daniel J. Bain. 2017. "Lead Pollution Resulting from Roman Gold Extraction in Northwestern Spain." *Holocene* 27 (10): 1465–74.

Hillner, Julia. 2013. "Confined exiles: an aspect of the late antique prison system." *Millennium* 10:385–434.

Hillner, Julia. 2015. *Prison, Punishment and Penance in Late Antiquity*. Cambridge University Press.

Hillner, Julia. 2020. "Female Crime and Female Confinement in Late Antiquity." In *Social Control in Late Antiquity*, edited by Kate Cooper and Jamie Wood, 15–38. Cambridge University Press.

Hirt, Alfred Michael. 2010. *Imperial Mines and Quarries in the Roman World: Organizational Aspects 27 BC–AD 235*. Oxford University Press.

Hobart, Michelle. 2003. "Ansedonia: The Settlement of the Twelfth through the Fourteenth Cen." In *Cosa V: An Intermittent Town, Excavations 1991–1997*, edited by Elizabeth Fentress, 120–37. Memoirs of the American Academy in Rome. Supplementary vol. 2. University of Michigan Press.

Howley, Joseph A. 2025. "Despotics." In *Writing, Enslavement, and Power in the Roman Mediterranean, 100 BCE–300 CE*, edited by Jeremiah Coogan, Joseph A. Howley, and Candida R. Moss. Oxford University Press.

Humphrey, Caroline. 2005. "Ideology in Infrastructure: Architecture and Soviet imagination." *Journal of the Royal Anthropological Institute* 11 (1): 39–58.

Hunter, Virginia. 1997. "The Prison of Athens: A Comparative Perspective." *Phoenix* 51 (3/4): 296–326.

Huntzinger, Hervé. 2004. "Incarcération et travaux forcés." In *Carcer II. Prison et privation de liberté dans l'Empire romain et l'Occident médiéval*, edited by C. Bertrand-Dagenbach, Alain Chauvot, Jean-Marie Salamito, and Denyse Vaillancourt, 21–32. De Boccard.

Ingham, David, and Corinne Duhig. 2022. "Crucifixion in the Fens: Life & Death in Roman Fenstanton." *British Archaeology* (February): 18–29.

Ingvarsson, A., Y. Bäckström, S. Chryssoulaki, A. Linderholm, A, Kjellström, V. K. Lagerholm, and M. Krzewińska. 2019. "Bioarchaeological Field Analysis of Human Remains from the Mass Graves at Phaleron, Greece." *Opuscula* 12:7–158.

Innes, Joanna. 1980. "The King's Bench Prison in the Later Eighteenth Century: Law, Authority and Order in a London Debtors' Prison." In *An Ungovernable People: The English and Their Law in the Seventeenth and Eighteenth Centuries*, edited by John Brewer and John Styles, 250–98. Rutgers University Press.

Iovino, Gennaro, Alessandra Marchello, Ausilia Trapani, and Gabriel Zuchtriegel. 2023. "La disciplina dell'odiosa baracca: la casa con il panificio di Rustio Vero a Pompei (IX 10,1)." *E-Journal: Scavi di Pompei* 8 (December): 2–16.

Ireland, Richard W. 1987. "Theory and Practice within the Medieval English Prison." *American Journal of Legal History* 31 (1): 56.

Jackson, Ralph. 2005. "Roman Bound Captives: Symbols of Slavery?" In *Image, Craft and the Classical World: Essays in Honour of Donald Bailey and Catherine Johns*, edited by Nina Crummy, 143–56. Monographies Instrumentum 29. Éditions Mergoil.

Jameson, Fredric. 1981. *The Political Unconscious: Narrative as a Socially Symbolic Act*. Cornell University Press.

Joannès, Francis. 2023. "Neo-Babylonian Judicial Texts." In *Judicial Decisions in the Ancient Near East*, edited by Sophie Démare-Lafont and Daniel E. Fleming, 485–574. Writings from the Ancient World 43. SBL Press.

Johnston, Norman. 2000. *Forms of Constraint: A History of Prison Architecture*. University of Illinois Press.

Jones, Michelle Daniel. 2023. "Methodology: 'We're Doing a New Thing.'" In *Who Would Believe a Prisoner? Indiana Women's Carceral Institutions, 1848–1920*, edited by Michelle Daniel Jones and Elizabeth Nelson, xxv–xxxix. New Press.

Joshel, Sandra R. and Lauren Hackworth Petersen. 2014. *The Material Lives of Roman Slaves*. Cambridge University Press.

Jördens, Andrea. 2017. "Entwurf und Reinschrift—oder: Wie bitte ich um Entlassung aus der Untersuchungshaft." *Chiron* 47:271–302.

Journals of the House of Commons. 1803. Vol. 21. London: H. M. Stationery Office.

Kaphar, Titus. 2023. "Titus Kaphar: The Jerome Project." Gagosian. October 13, 2022–January 16, 2023. https://gagosian.com/news/museum-exhibitions/titus-kaphar-the-jerome-project -isabella-stewart-gardner-museum-boston/.

Kelly, Benjamin. 2011. *Petitions, Litigation, and Social Control in Roman Egypt*. Oxford University Press.

Kilpatrick, Jane, Sondra Crosby, and Brock Chisholm. 2023. "'The Darkness': Deprivation of Sunlight as a Form of Torture." *Torture Journal* 33 (1): 79–91.

Knight, K., and P. M. Flynn. 2012. "Clinical Trials Involving Prisoners: A Bioethical Perspective." *Clinical Investigation* 2 (12): 1147–49.

Krause, Jens-Uwe. 1996. *Gefängnisse im römischen Reich*. Heidelberger althistorische Beiträge und epigraphische Studien 23. Franz Steiner Verlag.

Kremer, Gabrielle. 2012. *Götterdarstellungen, Kult- und Weihedenkmäler aus Carnuntum*. Verlag der Österreichischen Akademie der Wissenschaften.

Kyle, Donald G. 1998. *Spectacles of Death in Ancient Rome*. Routledge.

Lapidge, Michael. 2018. *The Roman Martyrs: Introduction, Translations, and Commentary*. Oxford University Press.

Larsen, Matthew D. C. 2019. "Carceral Practices and Geographies in Roman North Africa." *Studies in Late Antiquity* 3 (4): 547–80.

Larsen, Matthew D. C. 2024. "A Prison in Late Antique Corinth." *Hesperia* 93 (2): 337–79.

Last, Richard, and Philip A. Harland. 2020. *Group Survival in the Ancient Mediterranean: Rethinking Material Conditions in the Landscape of Jews and Christians*. T & T Clark.

Lavan, Luke. 2007. "Political Space in Late Antiquity." In *Objects in Context, Objects in Use: Material Spatiality in Late Antiquity*, edited by Luke Lavan, Ellen Swift, and Toon Putzeys, 111–28. Late Antique Archaeology 5. Brill.

Lefebvre, Henri. 1974. *La production de l'espace*. Éditions Anthropos.

Lenski, Noel. 2006. "*Servi Publici* in Late Antiquity." In *Die Stadt in der Spätantike: Niedergang oder Wandel? Akten des internationalen Kolloquiums in München am 30. und 31. Mai 2003*, edited by Jens-Uwe Krause and Christian Witschel, 335–57. Franz Steiner Verlag.

Leschi, Louis. 1953. *Djemila, Antique Cuicul*. 3rd ed. Direction de l'intérieur et des beaux-arts, Service des antiquités.

Letteney, Mark, and Matthew D. C. Larsen. 2021. "A Roman Military Prison at Lambaesis." *Studies in Late Antiquity* 5 (1): 65–102.

Locchi, Maria Chiara, 2021. "Food as Punishment, Food as Dignity: The Legal Treatment of Food in Prison." In *The Language of Law and Food: Metaphors of Recipes and Rules*, edited by Salvatore Mancuso, 127–43. Routledge.

Lovato, Andrea. 1994. *Il carcere nel diritto penale romano: dai Severi a Giustiniano*. Pubblicazioni della Facoltà giuridica dell'Università di Bari 115. Cacucci.

Mackensen, Michael. 2000. "Erster Bericht über neue archäologische Untersuchungen im sog. Arbeits- und Steinbruchlager von Simitthus/Chemtou (Nordwesttunesien)." *Mitteilungen des Deutschen Archäologischen Instituts, Römische Abteilung* 107:487–503.

Malay, Hasan. 1988. "New Confession-Inscriptions in the Manisa and Bergama Museum." *Epigraphica Anatolica* 12:147–54.

Marcone, Arnaldo. 1999. "La privation de liberté dans l'Égypte gréco-romaine." In *Carcer: prison et privation de liberté dans l'Antiquité classique*, edited by Cécile Bertrand-Dagenbach, Alain Chauvot, Michel Matter, and Jean-Marie Salamito, 89–98. De Boccard.

Marek, Christian, and Emanuel Zingg. 2018. *Die Versinschrift des Hyssaldomos und die Inschriften von Uzunyuva (Milas/Mylasa)*. Asia Minor Studien 90. Habelt.

Matter, Michel. 2004. "Libanios et les prisons d'Antioche." In *Carcer II. Prison et privation de liberté dans l'Empire romain et l'Occident médiéval*, edited by C. Bertrand-Dagenbach, Alain Chauvot, Jean-Marie Salamito, and Denyse Vaillancourt, 53–69. De Boccard.

Mattern, Susan P. 2013. *The Prince of Medicine: Galen in the Roman Empire*. Oxford University Press.

Mattingly, David J. 2013. *Imperialism, Power, and Identity: Experiencing the Roman Empire*. Princeton University Press.

Mau, August. 1899. *Pompeii, Its Life and Art*. Translated by Francis W. Kelsey. MacMillan.

Mauer, Mark, and Ryan S. King. 2007. "Uneven Justice: State Rates of Incarceration by Race and Ethnicity." Sentencing Project. July 1. https://search.issuelab.org/resource/uneven-justice-state-rates-of-incarceration-by-race-and-ethnicity.html.

McGowan, Andrew. 2003. "Discipline and Diet: Feeding the Martyrs in Roman Carthage." *Harvard Theological Review* 96 (4): 455–76.

McLennan, Rebecca M. 2018. "Ideal Theory and Historical Complexity." In *The Will to Punish*, edited by Christopher Kutz, 142–53. Oxford University Press.

Meir, Eran. 2012. "Tiberias Basilica as Civic Center in the Talmud Period in Light of the New Excavations" (Hebrew). Master's thesis, Bar Ilan University.

Melossi, Dario, and Massimo Pavarini. 1977. *Carcere e fabbrica: alle origini del sistema penitenziario (XVI-XIX secolo)*. Il Mulino.

Mentzos, Aristotelis. 2005. "Ζητήματα τοπογραφίας των χριστιανικών Φιλίππων." *Egnatia* 9:101–56.

Millar, Fergus. 1984. "Condemnation to Hard Labour in the Roman Empire, from the Julio-Claudians to Constantine." *Papers of the British School at Rome* 52:124–47.

Milnor, Kristina. 2014. *Graffiti and the Literary Landscape in Roman Pompeii*. Oxford University Press.

Mitford, T. B. 1988. "Further Inscriptions from the Cappadocian Limes." *Zeitschrift für Papyrologie und Epigraphik* 71:167–78.

Mommsen, Theodor. 1899. *Römisches Strafrecht*. Systematisches Handbuch der deutschen Rechtswissenschaft 1. Duncker & Humblot.

Moran, Dominique. 2017. *Carceral Geography: Spaces and Practices of Incarceration*. Routledge.

Moran, Dominique, and Karen M. Morin. 2015. *Historical Geographies of Prisons: Unlocking the Usable Carceral Past*. Routledge.

Moran, Dominique, Jennifer Turner, and Helen Arnold. 2019. "Soldiering On? The Prison-Military Complex and Ex-Military Personnel as Prison Officers: Transition, Rehabilitation and Prison Reform." *Howard Journal of Crime and Justice* 58 (2): 220–39.

Morris, Sarah P., and John K. Papadopoulos. 2005. "Greek Towers and Slaves: An Archaeology of Exploitation." *American Journal of Archaeology* 109 (2): 155–225.

Mosser, Martin. 2024. "A *carcer castrensis* in Vindobona?" Lecture given at European Association of Archaeologists 30th Annual Meeting. August 31, 2024. Sapienza Università di Roma. Rome, Italy.

Muhs, Brian. 2018. "Imprisonment, Guarantors, and Release on Bail in the Ptolemaic Fayum." In *Le Fayoum: archéologie, histoire, religion*, edited by Marie-Pierre Chaufray, Ivan Guermeur, Sandra L. Lippert, and Vincent Rondot, 89–99. Harrassowitz Verlag.

Muehlberger, Ellen. 2022. "Perpetual Adjustment: The Passion of Perpetua and Felicity and the Entailments of Authenticity." *Journal of Early Christian Studies* 30 (3): 313–42.

Naddari, Lofti. 2018. "Au coeur de Svfetvla (Sbeïtla, en Tunisie centrale): forum et capitole réparti en trois temples ou bien plutôt *Avgvstevm* pour le culte d'Antonin le Pieux et les siens?" *Comptes rendus des séances de l'Académie des Inscriptions et Belles-Lettres* 162 (3): 1167–1200.

Neudecker, Richard. 2010. "The Forum of Augustus in Rome: Law and Order in Sacred Spaces." In *Spaces of Justice in the Roman World*, edited by Francesco De Angelis, 161–88. Columbia Studies in the Classical Tradition 35. Brill.

Nicklas, Tobias. 2016. "Ancient Christian Care for Prisoners: First and Second Centuries." *Acta Theologica* 23:49–65.

Nielson, Kristina P. 1983. "The 'Tropaion' in the Aeneid." *Vergilius* 29:27–33.

Nogrady, Alexander. 2011. "Zustände wie im alten Rom?! Römisches und heutiges Strafrecht im Vergleich." In *Gefährliches Pflaster: Kriminalität im Römischen Reich*, edited by Marcus Reuter and Romina Schiavone, 385–92. Xantener Berichte 21. Philipp von Zabern.

Notizie degli scavi di antichità. 1910. Rome. Vol. 7. Accademia dei Lincei: U. Hoepli. HathiTrust. Accessed December 31, 2024. https://catalog.hathitrust.org/Record/100184316.

Oglethorpe, James Edward. 1729. *A Report from the Committee appointed to Enquire into the State of the Goals of this Kingdom*. Reprinted in *Publications of James Edward Oglethorpe*, edited by Rodney M. Baine, 44–158. University of Georgia Press, 1994.

Oshinsky, David M. 1996. *Worse Than Slavery: Parchman Farm and the Ordeal of Jim Crow Justice*. Free Press.

Overbeck, Johannes Adolf. 1875. *Pompeji in seinen Gebäuden, Alterthümern und Kunstwerken, für Kunst- und Alterthumsfreunde*. 3rd ed. Engelmann.

Overbeck, Johannes Adolf, and August Mau. 1884. *Pompeji in seinen Gebäuden, Alterthümern und Kunstwerken*. 4th ed. Engelmann.

Pala, Paola. 1994. "Documenti inediti di Doro Levi sull'anfiteatro di Cagliari." In *Omaggio a Doro Levi*, 131–66. Quaderni della Soprintendenza Archeologica di Sassari e Nuoro 19. Sassari.

Parrish, David. 1985. "The Date of the Mosaics from Zliten." *Antiquités africaines* 21 (1): 137–58.

Patrich, Joseph, Eran Meir, and Aharoni Amitai. 2022. "A Provincial Palace (*Praetorium*) in Tiberias? The Archaeological Finds and the Evidence of the Literary Sources." *Scripta Classica Israelica* 41:77–107.

Pavón Torrejón, Pilar. 1999. "Régimen de vida y tratamiento del preso durante los tres primeros siglos del Imperio." In *Carcer: prison et privation de liberté dans l'Antiquité classique*, edited by Cécile Bertrand-Dagenbach, Alain Chauvot, Michel Matter, and Jean-Marie Salamito, 105–13. De Boccard.

Pavón Torrejón, Pilar. 2000. "*Furiosus in Carcerem* (Ulp. 7 *De Off. Proc., D.* 1.18.13.1)." *Habis* 31:261–66.

Pavón Torrejón, Pilar. 2003a. "Las cárceles civiles en el Imperio romano." In *Castigo y reclusión en el mundo antiguo*, edited by Sofía Torallas Tovar and Inmaculada Pérez Martín, 101–14. Manuales y anejos de Emerita 45. Consejo Superior de Investigaciones Científicas.

Pavón Torrejón, Pilar. 2003b. *La cárcel y el encarcelamiento en el mundo romano.* Anejos de Archivo Español de Arqueología 27. Consejo Superior de Investigaciones Científicas, Instituto de Historia, Departamento de Historia Antigua y Arquelogía.

Pavón Torrejón, Pilar. 2004. "Las poenae carceris durante el siglo IV." In *Carcer II. Prison et privation de liberté dans l'Empire romain et l'Occident médiéval*, edited by C. Bertrand-Dagenbach, Alain Chauvot, Jean-Marie Salamito, and Denyse Vaillancourt, 111–22. De Boccard.

Peters, Edward M. 1995. "Prison before the Prison: the Ancient and Medieval Worlds." In *The Oxford History of the Prison*, 3–43. Oxford University Press.

Pike, Ruth. 1983. *Penal Servitude in Early Modern Spain.* University of Wisconsin Press.

Pugh, Ralph B. 1968. *Imprisonment in Medieval England.* Cambridge University Press.

Raber, Paul. 1987. "Early Copper Production in the Polis Region, Western Cyprus." *Journal of Field Archaeology* 14 (3): 297–312.

Rakob, Friedrich. 1994. "Das römische Steinbruchlager (*Praesidium*) in Simitthus." In *Simitthus II: Der Tempelberg und das römische Lager*, edited by Mustapha Khanoussi, 51–140. Philipp von Zabern.

Rakob, Friedrich, and Sebastian Storz. 1974. "Die Principia des römischen Legionslagers in Lambaesis: Vorbericht über Bauaufnahme und Grabungen." *Mitteilungen des Deutschen Archäologischen Instituts, Römische Abteilung* 81: 253–80, plates 135–51.

Raspels, Bernhard. 1991. "Der Einfluß des Christentums auf die Gesetze zum Gefängniswesen und zum Strafvollzug von Konstantin dem Großen bis Justinian." *Zeitschrift für Kirchengeschichte* 102:289–306.

Rea, John R. 1983. "Proceedings before Q. Maecius Laetus, Praef. Aeg., Etc." *Journal of Juristic Papyrology* 19:91–101.

Rebillard, Éric. 2020. *The Early Martyr Narratives: Neither Authentic Accounts nor Forgeries.* University of Pennsylvania Press.

Reid, J. Nicholas. 2022. *Prisons in Ancient Mesopotamia: Confinement and Control Until the First Fall of Babylon.* Oxford University Press.

Rein, Wilhelm. 1844. *Das Criminalrecht der Römer von Romulus bis auf Justinianus: ein Hülfsbuch zur Erklärung der Classiker und der Rechtsquellen.* Köhler.

Reiter, Keramet. 2016. *23/7: Pelican Bay Prison and the Rise of Long-Term Solitary Confinement.* Yale University Press.

Relihan, Joel C. 2007. *The Prisoner's Philosophy: Life and Death in Boethius's* Consolation. University of Notre Dame Press.

Riaño Rufilanchas, Daniel. 2003. "Cárcel y encarcelamiento en la Grecia clásica." In *Castigo y reclusión en el mundo antiguo*, edited by Sofía Torallas Tovar and Inmaculada Pérez Martín, 73–94. Manuales y anejos de Emerita 45. Consejo Superior de Investigaciones Científicas.

Richardson, Lawrence. 1980. "The approach to the Temple of Saturn in Rome." *American Journal of Archaeology* 84 (1): 51–62.

Richardson, Rufus B. 1902. "A Series of Colossal Statues at Corinth." *American Journal of Archaeology* 6 (1): 7–22.

Rivière, Yann. 1999. "Détention préventive, mise à l'épreuve et démonstration de la preuve (Ier–IIIe siècles ap. J.-C.)." In *Carcer: prison et privation de liberté dans l'Antiquité classique*, edited by Cécile Bertrand-Dagenbach, Alain Chauvot, Michel Matter, and Jean-Marie Salamito, 57–73. De Boccard.

Rivière, Yann. 2004a. *Le cachot et les fers: détention et coercition à Rome*. Belin.

Rivière, Yann. 2004b. "L'état romain, les chrétiens, la prison." In *Carcer II. Prison et privation de liberté dans l'Empire romain et l'Occident médiéval*, edited by C. Bertrand-Dagenbach, Alain Chauvot, Jean-Marie Salamito, and Denyse Vaillancourt, 201–41. De Boccard.

Rivière, Yann. 2021. *Histoire du droit pénal romain: de Romulus à Justinien*. Roue à livres 92. Les Belles Lettres.

Robinson, Olivia. 1995. *The Criminal Law of Ancient Rome*. Johns Hopkins University Press.

Robinson, Olivia. 2007. *Penal Practice and Penal Policy in Ancient Rome*. Routledge.

Röder, Josef. 1993. "Die Steinbrüche des numidischen Marmors von Chemtou." In *Simitthus I*, edited by Friedrich Rakob, 17–53. Philipp von Zabern.

Rodríguez Martín, José-Domingo. 2003. "La pena de prisión bajo Justiniano: Ulpiano vs. Calístrato." In *Castigo y reclusión en el mundo antiguo*, edited by Sofía Torallas Tovar and Inmaculada Pérez Martín, 175–92. Manuales y anejos de Emerita 45. Consejo Superior de Investigaciones Científicas.

Rohden, Hermann von. 1880. *Die Terracotten von Pompeji*. Spemann.

Rosman, Kevin J. R., Chisholm Warrick, Sungmin Hong, Jean-Pierre Candelone, and Claude F. Boutron. 1997. "Lead from Carthaginian and Roman Spanish Mines Isotopically Identified in Greenland Ice Dated from 600 BC to 300 AD." *Environmental Science and Technology* 31 (12): 3413–16.

Rothenberg, Beno. 1999. "Archaeo-Metallurgical Researches in the Southern Arabah 1959–1990. Part 2: Egyptian New Kingdom (Ramesside) to Early Islam." *Palestine Exploration Quarterly* 131 (2): 149–75.

Rowlandson, Jane, ed. 1998. *Women and Society in Greek and Roman Egypt: a Sourcebook*. Cambridge University Press.

Rubin, Ashley T. 2018. "Prison History." In *Oxford Research Encyclopedia of Criminology and Criminal Justice*. Accessed December 31, 2024. https://oxfordre.com/criminology /view/10.1093/acrefore/9780190264079.001.0001/acrefore-9780190264079-e-455.

Rubin, Ashley T. 2021. *The Deviant Prison: Philadelphia's Eastern State Penitentiary and the Origins of America's Modern Penal System, 1829–1913*. Cambridge University Press.

Russo, Alfonsina. 2022. "Premessa." In *Carcer Tullianum: Il Mamertino al Foro Romano*, edited by Alfonsina Russo and Patrizia Fortini, vii–xvi. Bibliotheca Archaeologica 74. L'Erma di Bretschneider.

Schellenberg, Ryan S. 2021. *Abject Joy: Paul, Prison, and the Art of Making Do*. Oxford University Press.

Schiavone, Romina. 2011. "*Agens at latrunculum*—Strafverfolgung im Römischen Reich." In *Gefährliches Pflaster: Kriminalität im Römischen Reich*, edited by Marcus Reuter and Romina Schiavone, 225–40. Xantener Berichte 21. Verlag Philipp von Zabern.

Schneider, Rolf Michael. 2012. "The Making of Oriental Rome: shaping the Trojan legend." In *Universal Empire: A Comparative Approach to Imperial Culture and Representation in Eurasian History*, edited by Peter Fibiger Bang and Dariusz Kolodziejczyk, 76–129. Cambridge University Press.

Schott, Jeremy M., trans. 2019. *Eusebius of Caesarea: The History of the Church*. University of California Press.

Schouler, Bernard. 2006. "Un enseignant face aux prisons de son temps." *Pallas* 72:279–96.

Schubert, Paul. 2018. "Warrants: Some Further Considerations on their Typology." *Bulletin of the American Society of Papyrologists* 55:253–274.

Schwartz, Jacques. 1971. "Une levée d'écrou en 210 p.C." In *Studi in onore di Edoardo Volterra*, 1:179–83. A. Giuffrè.

Scott, James C. 1990. *Domination and the Arts of Resistance: Hidden Transcripts*. Yale University Press.

Scotton, Paul D., Catherine de Grazia Vanderpool, and Carolynn E. Roncaglia. 2022. *The Julian Basilica: Architecture, Sculpture, Epigraphy*. Corinth 22. American School of Classical Studies at Athens.

Sessa, Kristina. 2018. *Daily Life in Late Antiquity*. Cambridge University Press.

Shaw, Brent D. 1996. "Seasons of Death: Aspects of Mortality in Imperial Rome." *Journal of Roman Studies* 86:100–138.

Shaw, Brent D. 2011. *Sacred Violence: African Christians and Sectarian Hatred in the Age of Augustine*. Cambridge University Press.

Shaw, Brent D. 2013. *Bringing in the Sheaves: Economy and Metaphor in the Roman World*. University of Toronto Press.

Sironen, Erkki, ed. 2016. *Inscriptiones Argolidis. Fasciculus III, Inscriptiones Corinthiae saeculorum IV, V, VI*. Inscriptiones Graecae, IV.2.3. De Gruyter.

Spano, Giovanni. 1868. *Storia e descrizione dell'Anfiteatro romano di Cagliari*. A. Alagna.

Spierenburg, Pieter. 2007. *The Prison Experience: Disciplinary Institutions and Their Inmates in Early Modern Europe*. Amsterdam University Press.

Stillwell, Richard, Robert L. Scranton, and Sarah Elizabeth Freeman. *Corinth: Results of Excavations Conducted by the American School of Classical Studies at Athens*. Vol. 1, part 2, *Architecture*. American School of Classical Studies at Athens, 1941.

Susanna, Fiammetta. 2022a. "Il *Carcer* in epoca Romana. Considerazioni." In *Carcer Tullianum: Il Mamertino al Foro Romano*, edited by Alfonsina Russo and Patrizia Fortini, 59–65. Bibliotheca Archaeologica 74. L'Erma di Bretschneider.

Susanna, Fiammetta. 2022b. "Il deposito votivo del Tullianum." In *Carcer Tullianum: Il Mamertino al Foro Romano*, edited by Alfonsina Russo and Patrizia Fortini, 87–94. Bibliotheca Archaeologica 74. L'Erma di Bretschneider.

Taussig, Michael T. 1999. *Defacement: Public Secrecy and the Labor of the Negative*. Stanford University Press.

Themelis, Petros. 2010. "Die Agora von Messene." In *Neue Forschungen zu griechischen Städten und Heiligtümern*, edited by Heide Frielinghaus and Jutta Stroszeck, 105–25. Bibliopolis.

Themelis, Petros. 2019. *Ancient Messene*. Kapon Editions.

Thompson, Dorothy J. 2024. "Ptolemaic Egypt." In *Slavery and Dependence in Ancient Egypt: Sources in Translation*, edited by Jane L. Rowlandson, Roger S. Bagnall, and Dorothy J. Thompson, 211–73. Cambridge University Press.

Thompson F. H. 2003. *The Archaeology of Greek and Roman Slavery*. Reports of the Research Committee of the Society of Antiquaries of London 66. Duckworth.

Thompson, Hugh. 1993. "Iron Age and Roman slave-shackles." *Archaeological Journal* 150 (1): 57–168.

Torallas Tovar, Sofía. 1999. "Las prisiones en el Egipto Bizantino según los papiros griegos y coptos." *Erytheia. Revista de Estudios Bizantinos y Neogriegos* 20:47–55.

Torallas Tovar, Sofía. 2003. "Arresto y encarcelamiento en el Egipto romano tardío y Bizantino." In *Castigo y reclusión en el mundo antiguo*, edited by Sofía Torallas Tovar and Inmaculada Pérez Martín, 209–23. Manuales y anejos de Emerita 45. Consejo Superior de Investigaciones Científicas.

Torallas Tovar, Sofía. 2006. "Violence in the Process of Arrest and Imprisonment in Late Antique Egypt." In *Violence in Late Antiquity: Perceptions and Practices*, edited by Harold A. Drake, 103–12. Ashgate.

Trout, Dennis E. 2015. *Damasus of Rome: The Epigraphic Poetry Introduction, Texts, Translations, and Commentary*. Oxford University Press.

Turney, Kristin. 2014. "Paternal Incarceration and Children's Food Insecurity: A Consideration of Variation and Mechanisms." *University of Kentucky Center for Poverty Research Discussion Paper Series* DP2014-12:335–67. http://www.ukcpr.org/Publications/DP2014-12.pdf.

Ulrich, Roger B. 1994. *The Roman Orator and the Sacred Stage: The Roman* Templum Rostratum. Collection Latomus 222. Latomus.

Van Buren, Albert William. 1918. "Studies in the Archaeology of the Forum at Pompeii." *Memoirs of the American Academy in Rome* 2:67–76.

van der Veen, Marijke. 1998. "A Life of Luxury in the Desert? The Food and Fodder Supply to Mons Claudianus." *Journal of Roman Archaeology* 2:101–16.

Vanderpool, Eugene. 1980. "The State Prison of Ancient Athens." In *From Athens to Gordion: The Papers of a Memorial Symposium for Rodney S. Young, Held at the University Museum, the Third of May, 1975*, edited by Rodney S. Young, Keith DeVries, 17–31. University Museum Papers 1. University of Pennsylvania Museum of Archaeology and Anthropology.

Vandorpe, Katelijn. 2013. "Zeno Son of Agreophon." Leuven Homepage of Papyrus Collections. Trismegistos. Accessed December 31, 2024. https://www.trismegistos.org/archive/256.

Vismara, Cinzia. 2001. "La giornata di spettacoli." In *Sangue e arena*, edited by Adriano La Regina, 199–221. Electa.

Wacquant, Loïc. 2009. *Punishing the Poor: The Neoliberal Government of Social Insecurity*. Duke University Press.

Walsh, P. G., trans. 2006. *Pliny: Complete Letters*. Oxford University Press.

Weaver, John B. 2004. *Plots of Epiphany: Prison-Escape in Acts of the Apostles*. Zeitschrift für die neutestamentliche Wissenschaft und die Kunde der älteren Kirche 131. De Gruyter.

Weinreich, Spencer J. 2023. "Why Early Modern Mass Incarceration Matters: The Bamberg Malefizhaus, 1627–31." *Journal of Social History* 56 (4): 719–52.

Weitzmann, Kurt. 1979. *Age of Spirituality: Late Antique and Early Christian Art, Third to Seventh Century*. Metropolitan Museum of Art.

Winkler, Andreas. 2018. "Mouchis and its Crocodiles: Topography, Toponymy, and Theonymy." *Bulletin of the American Society of Papyrologists* 55:229–51.

Yardley, J. C., trans. 2018. *Livy: History of Rome, Books 38–40*. Loeb Classical Library 313. Harvard University Press.

Zarrugh, Amina. 2020. "The Development of US Regimes of Disappearance: The War on Terror, Mass Incarceration, and Immigrant Deportation." *Critical Sociology* 46 (2): 257–71.

Zamora Manzano, José Luis. 2015. *La administración penitenciaria en el derecho romano: Gestión, tratamiento de los reclusos y mejora de la custodia carcelaria*. Dykinson.

SOURCE INDEX

Note: Many source citations in this index include a database ID comprising a letter indicating the type of evidence—D (Documentary) or L (Literary)—and a number indicating the specific source within that category; these data are available in an open access database at historyofIncarceration.com. We have indicated sources of translations that are not our own, or in the case of documentary sources, when translations are not included in the critical edition indicated.

Literary Sources

Acts and Martyrdom of Matthew (L205)
    14: 179

Acts of Martinian and Processus (L171)
    1: 142

Acts of Paul and Thecla
    17–20 (L28): 175
    18 (L28): 114, 128
    27 (L277): 104

Acts of Shmona and Gurya (L1; trans. Burkitt)
    27–36: 108–9
    30: 87
    31: 118
    41: 181

Acts of the Abitinian Martyrs (L32)
    20: 118–19

Acts of Thomas (trans. Drijvers)
    57 (L149): 110, 179
    151 (L36): 128

Alexis (poet)
    Men of Tarentum (L183)
        222 (219K): 116

Ambrose of Milan
    Letter
        50: 41

Ammianus Marcellinus
    History
        28.1.47: 100
        29.1.13: 106

Athanaeus
    The Learned Banqueters (L196)
        4.161: 116

Athanasius of Alexandria
    History of the Arians
        60: 70

Augustine
  Commentary on John (L2)
    49.9: 171
  City of God (L258)
    1.16: 104

Bible
  Jeremiah (L43)
    37:11–38:13: 73
  New Testament (canonical order)
    Gospel according to Matthew
      18:34 (L151): 171
      25:35–36 (L213): 115, 129
    Gospel according to Mark (L62)
      15:6–15: 133–34
    Acts of the Apostles
      16:23–24 (L67): 178
      27–28 (L206): 185
    Paul, *Letter to the Philippians* (L66): 129
    Second Letter to Timothy (L21)
      4:13–21: 107
    Paul, *Letter to Philemon* (L80)
      12: 128
    Letter to the Hebrews (L220)
      13:3: 129
    Revelation of John (L13)
      20:1–7: 179

Calpurnius Flaccus (trans. Sussman)
  Declamations (L46)
    4: 12, 86, 96, 107, 117, 176

Cassiodorus
  Variae (trans. Bjornlie)
    5.39.1–4 (L7): 39
    7.1.3: 41
    9.17 (L8): 134

Cassius Dio
  Roman History (trans. LCL 175, 176)
    59.6.1–3 (L126): 97, 133, 157
    68.10.1 (epitome): 144
  Quoted in Zonaras, *Annales* 8.3
    (L60): 74, 190

Celsus
  On Medicine (L195; trans. LCL 292)
    pref. 23–25: 132–33

Cicero
  Against Verres (trans. LCL 293)
    2.5.147 (L203): 160
    5.21–24 (L227): 117

  Letters to Quintus (L210)
    2.14: 121
  On Behalf of Milo
    60: 86
  On Duties (L225; trans. LCL 30)
    3.18: 23

Justinianic Code (CI; trans. Blume)
  9.2.17.0 (L5): 28
  9.4.5 (L63): 160
  9.5.1 (L134): 194

Columella
  On Agriculture (L47; trans. LCL 361)
    1.6.3: 57, 88, 107

Cyprian
  Letters (trans. ANF)
    12 (L23): 100
    76–79 (L141): 72, 115, 147

Demosthenes
  Against Timocrates (L27)
    24.146, 151: 24, 50

  De vitis patrum (L6)
    5.46: 107

  Didascalia Apostolorum (L16)
    7: 117

  Digest of Justinian (D; ordered by authority, trans. Watson)

  Antoninus Pius
    47.9.4.1 (L170): 34
    48.3.3 (L106), 28
    48.19.22–23 (L131): 36

  Callistratus
    48.19.28.14 (L122): 27, 32, 36
    48.20.2 (L33): 42, 105, 149

  Gaius
    48.19.29 (L169): 59

  Hermogenian
    48.19.8.8 (L173): 34
    48.19.36 (L161): 34

  Modestinus
    48.3.14 (L113): 172
    48.19.23 (L131): 36

Paul
   48.19.38.11 (L123): 56

Papinian
   48.19.33 (L41): 26–27

Ulpian
   On the Duty of the Proconsul: 29, 31–32, 192
     1.18.13.1 (L287): 25
     40.5.24.5: 34
     48.3.1 (L105): 27–28
     48.19.8.4 (L120): 186
     48.19.8.7 (L120): 22–23, 34
     48.19.8.9 (L120): 2, 21–22, 32, 127
     48.19.8.12–13(L120): 35
     48.19.9.11: 2848.20.6 (L124): 42, 114, 149
   On the Edict
     11.5.1.4 (L116): 23

Venuleius Saturninus
   48.3.5 (L107): 28, 32

Diodorus Siculus
   Library of History (trans. LCL 240,
     279, 409)
     1.79.1–2 (L65): 56
     5.38 (L168): 37
     31.8.2 (L57): 85, 109–10
     31.9.2–3 (L57): 116–17

Eusebius of Caesarea
   Ecclesiastical History (L283)
     5.1.62: 188
     10.8.11: 130
   Martyrs of Palestine
     7.4 (L54): 23, 72
     8.1 (L207): 186
     11.6 (L77): 130
   Theophania (L154)
     5.28: 23

Eusebius of Vercelli
   Letters (L38)
     2.5–8: 43–44

Festus
   On the Meanings of Words
     17 s.v. Robum: 86

Firmicus Maternus
   Mathesis (L20)
     3.4.26: 171
     4.14.2: 146

Galen of Pergamon
   *On the Usefulness of the
     Parts* (L61)
     10.3: 108
   Simple Remedies (L160)
     9.3.11–34: 64

Gregory of Tours
   Histories (L162)
     6.6: 72

Hesychius of Alexandria
   Lexicon
     α 5831, *apasiton*, 101

Hesiod
   Theogony
     720–820: 82–83

Hyginus
   Fables
     254.3: 139

Hyssaldomos (poet)
   SEG 68.928 (L130): 180

Ignatius of Antioch
   Letter to the Romans (L216)
     5.1: 142, 184

John Chrysostom
   Homilies on John (L158)
     60: 68, 115
   To Stagirius (L289)
     3.13: 109

John Climacus
   Ladder of Divine Ascent: 83

John of Ephesus
   Ecclesiastical History (L92)
     3.2.5: 106

Josephus
   Judaean War (L292)
     7.434: 95

Juvenal
   Satires (L132)
     3.299–314: 46, 65

Justinian
   Nov. Just. 134.9.1 (L3): 104

Libanius
Autobiography
44–45: 111
232: 131
Letters
391: 111
804: 111
1025: 111
1414: 111, 181–82
1428: 111, 130
1526: 111
Oration 9
12: 81
Oration 33
30: 43
Oration 45 (L52; trans LCL 452): 100
4: 111
5: 158
8: 193
9: 103, 117
10: 175
14: 43, 188
28: 134
30: 119

Life of the Sleepless Alexander, 175

Livy
From the Founding of the City
(trans. LCL 114, 355): 4
1.33.8 (L49): 47
25.7.12 (L200): 181
38.5: 12

Lucian of Samosata (trans. LCL 302)
Toxaris (L143)
29: 106, 110
30: 131, 146
Passing of Peregrinus (L197)
12: 129–30

Martyrdom of Demetrios of Thessalonike (L164)
4–7: 74

Martyrdom of Polycarp (L209)
13: 184, 188

Mishnah
Horayot
3.7: 104
Moed Qatan (L144)
3.1: 147–48

Pachomius
Paralipomena (L201; trans. Veilleux)
34: 98

Passion of Montanus and Lucius (L263)
9.2: 171

Passion of Perpetua and Felicity (L15): 56, 175
1: 114
2.2: 149
3: 106, 120, 128, 149
5.2: 149
6: 149
7–9: 141
15.4: 171

Passion of Saints Chrysanthus and Daria (L50)
22: 110

Petronius
Satyricon
26 (L229): 120
103 (L185): 72
105 (L230): 185

Philo of Alexandria
Against Flaccus (L64; trans. LCL 363)
131: 160–61
On Joseph (L12)
15: 95, 105–6

Philoxenus of Mabbug
Letter to the Monks of Senoun (L136; trans. de Halleux)
93–94: 184

Plato
Laws (L18)
907d–910d: 50
907e–908a: 94
908a–909c: 39, 87, 94

Plautus
The Rope (L178)
713–16: 95

Pliny the Elder
Natural History (trans. LCL 294, 352, 394)
7.36 (L150): 95, 139, 171
33.1 (L165): 83
33.70 (L159): 70
36.28: 71

Pliny the Younger
   Letters (trans. LCL 59)
      10.19–20 (L24): 56, 141, 175
      10.31–2 (L40): 120–21, 127, 175

Plutarch
   Life of Cicero (L85)
      20–21: 95
   Life of Marius (L228; trans. LCL 101)
      12.3–4: 106
   Life of Philopoemen (L148)
      19–20: 50
   Life of Publicola
      12: 47

Procopius
   History of the Wars (L157)
      1.5–6: 87, 96, 104, 175, 181

Quintilian
   Orator's Education (L194)
      6.3.72–73: 145–46

Quintus Curtius
   History of Alexander (L188)
      7.1–10: 33

Sallust
   Catiline's War (L48; trans.
      LCL 116)
      55: 48
   Histories (L192; trans. LCL 522)
      3, fr. 15.19: 117

Seneca the Elder
   Controversiae (L198)
      9.4.20: 117

Seneca the Younger
   Library of History (L71)
      3.12–13: 130
   On Anger (L93)
      3.32.2–3: 96
   On Consolation (L94)
      17.4: 26

Sententia Pauli
   5.17.2: 28

Sirmondian Constitutions
   8 (L99): 148–49
   13 (L100): 41

Socrates Scholasticus
   Ecclesiastical History
      5.18: 121

Strabo
   Geography (L167; trans. LCL 211)
      12.3.40: 71, 125

Suetonius
   Life of Tiberius (L19; trans. LCL 31)
      61: 85, 97, 133

Tertullian of Carthage
   Apology (L262): 105
      44–45: 23

Theodosian Code (*CTh*; trans. Pharr)
   1.5.3: 83
   2.1.1 (L34): 30–31
   4.8.8: 83
   6.29.1 (L87): 40, 43
   6.29.8 (L214): 43
   8.4.2: 40
   9.1.7 (L89): 28
   9.1.18 (L290): 28
   9.2.3 (L90): 31
   9.3.1 (L133): 29, 38, 100, 108, 109, 177–78,
      179, 192
   9.3.2 (L172): 30
   9.3.3 (L72): 86
   9.3.6 (L174): 176
   9.3.7 (L44): 116, 134, 176, 193
   9.38.3 (L45): 41, 194
   9.38.7 (L17): 105
   9.38.8 (L29): 41, 192
   9.40.3 (L199): 121
   9.40.5 (L95): 33
   9.40.22 (L96): 31
   11.7.3 (L35): 9, 21, 29
   11.7.7 (L97): 192
   12.1.6: 83
   15.12.1–2: 70

Theodosius II
   Nov. Th. 3.7 (L101): 176

Third Maccabees (L39)
   4:1–10: 185

Thucydides
   Peloponnesian War
      5.18.7: 141

Valerius Maximus
Memorable Doings and Sayings (L14)
5.4.7: 139

Varro
Latin Language (L187)
5.151: 47

Vegetius
Epitome of Military Science
2.20: 56

Vitruvius
On Architecture (L152)
5.2: 47

Xiphilinus
Epitome of Cassius Dio (L145)
146.15–30: 188

Documentary Sources

Inscriptions
AE 1983, 48 (D164): 170
CIL 3.15192 (D277): 174
CIL 3.3484 (D276): 174
CIL 3.433 (D263): 171
CIL 6.1057–58 (D65): 172
CIL 8.17897 (D171): 13, 118, 193
CIL 9.6343 (D265): 171
CIL 13.780 (D169): 171
CIL 13.6739 (D203): 171
CLE 307 (D165): 118
CLE 2048 (D199): 140, 151
IG 4.2.3.1270–94 (D236–60): 66
IG 12.6.1.42 (D174): 189
IGLSyr 13.1.9088 (D178): 171, 173
OGIS 669 (D185): 24, 48, 190
RIU 3.671 (D275): 174
SEG 8.355 (D166): 127
SEG 9.356 (D176): 172
SEG 35.1571 (D168): 86
SEG 38.1237 (D167; trans. Malay): 13, 97
SEG 59.1365 (D175; trans. Hauken and Malay):
142, 184
Temple of Hibis 2.4 (D177): 24, 58

Ostraca
O. Mon. Epiph. 163 (D194): 131, 135
O. Mon. Epiph. 176 (D195): 105
O. Mon. Epiph. 177 (D139): 102, 131–32,
171, 194

O. Petr. Mus. 260 (D151): 169
O. Wilcken 2.422 (D149): 169, 191
Oxford, Ashmolean Museum 1168.B
(D297): 124
UPZ 1.149 (D54): 174

Papyri
BGU 4.1138 (D107): 191
BGU 11.2083 (D225): 182
BGU 16.2618 (D146; trans. Bagnall and
Cribiore): 102, 194
BGU 16.2639 (D212): 158, 160
BKU 1.144 (D210): 100
CIIP 2.1273 (D206): 82, 173, 181
CIIP 4.3.3689 (D170): 13, 87, 93, 156, 171
C. Pap. Lat 112: 127
CPR 15.15 (D131): 163
P. Bagnall 29 (D101): 85, 183
P. Cair. Masp. 1.67005 (D86): 149
P. Cair. Masp. 1.67020 (D112): 102–3
P. Cair. Masp. 1.67057 (D182): 96
P. Cair. Zen. 2.59296 (D33): 36, 174
P. Cair. Zen. 3.59482 (D35): 135
P. Cair. Zen. 3.59492 (D37): 123–24, 165–67,
166*fig*., 167*fig*.
P. Cair. Zen. 3.59495 (D141): 93, 124
P. Cair. Zen. 3.59519 (D134; trans. Edgar): 13,
102, 107, 167
P. Cair. Zen. 3. 59520 (D38): 123–24
P. Cair. Zen. 4.59626 (D41): 183
P. Cair. Zen. 4.59639 (D213): 93, 166
P. Cair. Zen. 4.59707 (D43): 113
P. Col. 8.209 (D69): 124
P. Coll. Youtie 1.12 (D4; trans. APIS): 100,
156, 162
P. Enteux. 83 (D71): 58, 101
P. Fay. 135 (D119): 124
P. Hib. 1.34 (D48): 157
P. Hib. 1.73 (D49): 157, 173
P. Hib. 2.249 (D53): 157–58
P. Lond. 2.354 (D80): 163
P. Lond. 6.1914 (D118): 74, 131
P. Lond. 7.2045 (D81): 165
P. Mich. 1.36 (D214): 158, 160
P. Mich. 1.55 (D87): 157
P. Mich. 1.85 (D120): 131
P. Mich. 1.87 (D50): 124, 165–67, 167*fig*.
P. Mich. 6.383 (D128): 169
P. Mich. 6.421 (D201): 111
P. Mich. Mchl. 5 (D64): 158, 159*fig*., 160
P. Oslo 2.21 (D89): 56, 111, 158
P. Oslo 3.123 (D90; trans. APIS): 155–56

P. Oxy. 2.259 (D72): 168, 171, 184
P. Oxy. 3.580 (D84): 172
P. Oxy. 6.902 (D16): 103
P. Oxy. 6.903 (D85): 75, 105
P. Oxy. 7.1033 (D20): 158–59
P. Oxy. 16.1945 (D12): 114
P. Oxy. 17.2154 (D18): 4, 73, 111
P. Oxy. 43.3104 (D15): 58, 99, 164, 176
P. Oxy. 50.3581 (D279): 104–5
P. Oxy. 74.5004 (D281): 168
P. Oxy. 83.5373 (D217): 157
P. Oxy. 83.5375 (D216): 157
P. Petr. 2.10(2) (D110): 190
P. Petr. 2.19(2) (D108): 102
P. Petr. 3.36 (D3): 100
P. Petr. 3.36r (D147): 102
P. Petr. Kleon 52 (D93; trans. Bauschatz): 180
P. Petr. Kleon 54 (D17): 113, 114, 164
P. Petr. Kleon 58 (D55): 113, 114, 163, 164
P. Polit. Jud. 2 (D272; trans. Kugler): 129
P. Polit. Jud. 17 (D202): 129
P. Princ. 2.44 (D123; trans. APIS): 168–69
P. Ryl. 2.191 (D124): 169
P. Ryl. 2.193 (D126): 169
P. Ryl. 2.194 (D125): 169
PSI 4.419 (D57): 101, 163, 165–66
PSI 4.344: 174

PSI 4.423 (D58; trans. Bauschatz): 36, 37, 64, 115, 126
PSI 5.532 (D59; trans. Emily C. Brown): 112
PSI 7.824 (D13; trans. Berkes): 132, 194
PSI 8.953 (D23): 114
PSI 13.1307: 172
PSI 13.1315 (D83): 114, 174
P. Sorb. 3.135 (D60): 161, 176
P. Tarich. 3 (D156): 129
P. Tarich. 4 a&b (D157): 129
P. Tarich. 5 (D138): 129
P. Tebt. 1.5 (D7): 194
P. Tebt. 2.290 (D78): 161–62, 162*fig.*
P. Tebt. 2.354 (D66): 169
P. Wash. Univ. 1.57 (D61): 173
P. Wisc. 2.48 (D97): 56
P. Yale 1.62: 182
SB 14.11999 (D105): 37
SB 16.12468 (D1): 113
SB 16.12949 (D62; trans. Rea): 100, 130, 159, 161
SB 20.14631 (D106): 36
SB 24.16117 (D99): 180
SB 24.16185 (D68): 13
SB 28.16854 (D5; trans. Clarysse): 126, 180, 185–86
Stud. Pal. 10.252 (D296): 75, 159

Abolafia, Jacob, 8, 10, 15
Agamben, Giorgio, 153
agriculture and husbandry, 93,
    123–24, 158
Alba Fucens, prison of, 85, 109–10, 116
Alexander, Michelle (*The New Jim Crow*), 34
Allen, Danielle, 9, 10
Ancient Mediterranean Incarceration Database
    (historyofIncarceration.com), xi, xii, 204, 221
Ancus Marcius (king), 47
Antioch: prisons of, 55, 188; Yakto Mosaic, 59, 141
Antoninus Pius (emperor), legislation of, 28,
    33–34, 35
Apollonius of Palermo, imprisonment of, 117
apples, a few bad, 43
archaeology, classical, 1–2, 4–5
archive of sources: limits of, x, 154–55 material
    composition of, 155–57. *See also* bureaucracy
    (carceral), documentary sources for carceral
    bureaucracy; prisoner letters, production of
"arrest," modern notion of, 182
Asian men, Roman depictions of ("handsome
    Asian"), 138
associations (professional, religious, civic):
    protection of incarcerated members, 129–30
Athalaric (Ostrogothic king), 134–35
Athanasius (bishop of Alexandria), 74
Athens: incarceration in, 9–10, 24; mass grave,
    187; prison, 50, 83, 94

Baelo Claudia (Strait of Gibraltar), 77–78
bakeries: brothels and, 121; convict and enslaved
    labor in, 33, 121–22
Ballu, Albert, 48, 53, 79–80
Baratte, Françoise, 79
baths: for prisoners, 41, 61, 63, 115, 186; as
    prisons, 74
Bauschatz, John, 98, 101, 111–12, 123, 170, 174,
    189, 190
beekeepers, 123
Benton, Jared, 122
Bjornlie, Shane, 134
Blackmon, Douglas (*Slavery by Another
    Name*), 34
Boethius (philosopher), 15
Bomgardner, David, 59
Bonucci, Carlo, 1
Bradley, Keith, 143
bribery, 43, 87, 104, 113–14, 120, 130, 160–61, 172,
    175, 201. *See also* extortion
brothels: and bakeries, 121; condemnation to, 33
Browder, Kalief, 91
bureaucracy (carceral): arrest procedures,
    158–59; banality of, 154, 169–70, changes
    in prison oversight, 162–63; documentary
    procedures, 155–56, 161; prison personnel,
    170–77; use of seals, 161–62, 162*fig*.
    See also documentary sources of carceral
    bureaucracy; prisoner letters

Cadoux, T.J., 65–66, 86

Caesarea Maritima (Israel), 178, 185; "Good hope" mosaic, 173; Herodian Palace Prison, 73, 82, 181

Caligula/Gaius (emperor): burning of prison records, 133, 157

Carales (Cagliari, Italy): Gladiator Prison, 13, 59–61, 60*fig.*, 68, 109; Prison for the Condemned, 13, 60*fig.*, 68–70, 69*fig.*, 71*fig.*, 73, 107, 109, 147, 179, 187–88

Carcer: Prison et privation de liberté dans l'Antiquité Classique (Bertrand-Dagenbach et al.), x

Carthage: amphitheater prison, 59, 108; weaving establishment, 33

caste system, Roman, 28, 33–34

Castigo y reclusión en el mundo antiguo (Torallas Tovar and Pérez Martín), 8

Celsus (physician): on vivisection of criminals, 132–33

chains and shackles: artistic depictions of, 136–38, 137*fig.*, 141–42, 144–45, 144*fig.*, 151–52, 202*fig.*; as form of incarceration, 3, 22, 27, 31, 32, 73, 75–76; in mines, 33, 72; pretrial use of, 29, 38; in prisoner transport, 85, 141–42 (or not) 183–84; "shackle-poisoning" and debilitation, 109, 112, 192, 201

Chaniotis, Angelos, 97

Chauvot, Alain, 12

child incarceration, 147*fig.*, 149–50

Christ, depictions of, 144

Christians: accounts of incarceration, 56, 87, 106, 107, 114, 120, 128, 129, 130, 133–34, 178, 179; burial of imprisoned, 188; care of the incarcerated, 118–19, 129–30, 193; influence on carceral practice, 40–41; legal penalties, 23; path to martyrdom, 100

Christogram, 70, 71*fig.*, 144

Chrysanthus (martyr), 110

cisterns, 68–70, 75, 173

citizenship: loss of, 59

Clarysse, Willy, 185

cloaks, requests for, 107

Coarelli, Filippo, 66

cognitio process, 25, 26, 29

coin, depicting captives, 144

commentariensis. See registrar

Constantine (emperor): arch of, 152; legislation of, 21, 29–31, 38–39, 109, 121, 177–78, 179, 192

Constantius (emperor), legislation of, 31–32, 43, 86

convict labor, xii, 4, 13; as economic cornerstone, 43, 124–28; as incarceration, 33–38, 127; vs slavery, 34–36, 64. *See also* mines and

quarries; public works, condemnation to

Coptic: terminology for prisons, 11–12

Corinth: Captives' Façade, 152; Julian Basilica, 61–62, 66, 120, 173–74; late Roman prison, 66–68, 67*fig.*, 178; Lechaion Road basilica, 137–38

Cosa, prison of, 48–49, 49*fig.*, 55, 179

crucifixion, 112, 192, 201

Cuicul (Djemila, Algeria), prison of, 48, 52–53, 53*fig*, 82, 83, 178

Curbera, Jaime, 11

curse tablets, 52

Cuvigny, Hélène, 35

Cyprian (bishop of Carthage), 100, 147

Cyprus, 64, 125

damnati, depictions of, 142, 147, 148*fig.*

Daniel Jones, Michelle (*Who Would Believe a Prisoner?*), 15

Davis, Angela, 99

death: awaiting sentencing, 43–44, 99–100, 101; documentary evidence, 99–101; of incarcerated Christians, 100; in mines and quarries, 125; in prisons, 39, 54, 58, 73, 164; spectacular (in amphitheater), 59–60, 68, 187–88; by suicide, 91, 100, 176

debt imprisonment, 24–25, 29, 58–59, 73, 123–24, 131–32, 164, 190, 199

Demetrios of Thessalonike, 74

Department of the Treasury, 190

De Simoni, Alberto, 3, 55, 92

documentary sources for carceral bureaucracy: accusations of forgery and alteration, 158, 160–61, 180, 186; arrest warrants, 156–59, 159*fig.*, 161–62, 162*fig.*, 182–83; bail/bond paperwork, 28, 168; death notices, 164; lists of prisoners, 159–60, 186; petitions for release, 93–94, 102–3, 112–13, 123–24, 129, 131, 134–35, 156, 162–63; 165–68, 166*fig.*; tax receipts, 168–69; transfer of prisoners, 183–84. *See also* archive of sources; bureaucracy (carceral)

dog owners, legal liability of, 26

domestic spaces: for ad hoc incarceration, 73, 75; for military incarceration, 55

Donatist controversy, 119

Dreyfus, Hubert, 42

Duguid, Stephen, 99

Durkheim, Émile, 5

Duval, Noël, 79

Eastern State Penitentiary (Philadelphia), 62–63

economy, ancient: reliance on convict labor, 43, 124–28

Egypt: Ptolemaic prisons, 58, 189; temple of Hibis (Kharga), 58; under Rome, 24, 58–59
Eisenhut, Werner, 24
elites: "public transcript" of, 135–36
England, medieval, 25
Epicurus, intermittent fasting of, 117
ergastula (slave prisons), 57, 75–76, 88
escape, punishment of, 27
Evans, Trevor, 165
execution, 13, 24, 26, 59, 152, 187–88
exile, 31
extortion, 113, 114, 201

Fassin, Didier (*Prison Worlds: An Ethnography of the Carceral Tradition*), 7
Fayum portraits, xiii
fetters. *See* chains and shackles
figurines: of captives (Maresha) 144–45, 146*fig.*, of dwarves in a pillory, 151
filial piety: in Pero and Micon myth, 84, 95, 140, 143
Fleet Prison, 201
Florence, medieval, 114, 199
Folch, Marcus, x, 8, 10
food insecurity, 101–3; and incarceration, 111–13, 200
foreigners, vulnerability to imprisonment, 101–2
forgery and alteration, 160–61, 180; prevention of, 158–59, 159*fig.*, 186
Fortini, Patrizia, 47
Foucault, Michel, 15–16, 42; *Discipline and Punish: The Birth of the Prison*, 5–7, 197–98, 199, 201–2
Friedman, Hannah, 85
Fuhrmann, Christopher J., 81

Gadamer, Hans-Georg, xi
Gagos, Traianos, 154, 156–57, 182
Galen (physician): on light used for torture, 108; on mining camp in Cyprus, 64. *See also in* Index of Sources
game boards, 66
Garnsey, Peter, 11, 24, 25, 28
Geltner, Guy, ix, 15, 81, 199, 200
Gemma Augustea, 143, 147, 149, 150–51
giallo antico (marble), 61
Gilmore, Ruth Wilson (*Golden Gulag*), xiii, 58
Gladiator Prison. *See under* Carales
gladiators, 13, 59, 68
Gordon, Robert, 20
graffiti, 56, 66, 68–70, 69*fig.*, 71*fig.*; as tactic of resistance, 138
Grand camée de France, 143

Gratian (emperor), legislations of: 31, 41, 105, 192–93
Greek, ancient: terms for prison personnel, 170; terms for prisons, 11–12, 87

Hadrian (emperor): legislation of, 27, 32–33, 114–15, 142; visit to Izmir, 184
hair, matted and disheveled, 147–49
handwriting, 165–68, 167*fig.*
hell, descriptions of, 83, 110
Henning, Meghan, 83
Herod (king), prison of, 141
Hibis, temple of (Kharga, Egypt), 58
Hillner, Julia (*Prison, Punishment, and Penance in Late Antiquity*), ix, 4, 6–7, 8, 25, 32, 33, 39–41, 61, 105, 122, 184, 191
Hirt, Alfred Michael, 63, 125
historians, modern: responsibilities of, 14, 194
Hogarth, William (*The Gaols Committee of the House of Commons*), 201, 202*fig.*
Honorius (emperor): legislation of, 31, 38, 116, 118, 134, 176, 193
Hospicius (hermit), 72
Humphrey, Caroline, 80
Huntzinger, Hervé, 27
Hymn to Nungal, 11

incarceration, ideologies of, xii, 88; centrality of prisons, 80–82; punitive variability, 87–88; separation, 85–87; subterranean liminality, 82–84; surveillance, 84–85; as tool of elites, 111, 135–36
incarceration, pretrial and custodial: death during, 43–44; legal aspects, 27–32, 38–39, 91, 189; salutary legislation, 41. *See also* jail
incarceration, punitive: "absence" in ancient world, 2–4; alternative to execution, 24; ancient terminology for, 11–12; vs custodial, 38–39; definition, xii; described as punishment, 26, 29–31, 92–99, 134; economic hardship of, 124; effects on families, 102–3; legal sources for, 19–20, 21, 23–24; limited term, 26, 32; in Middle Ages, 15, 199; modern scholarship on, 2–11, 25; permanent or prolonged, 32–33; and poverty, 102, 112, 199–201; in Ptolemaic period, 189–91, 194; public pressure in, 132–35; role of in Roman period, 123–24, 191–94; of slaves, 27, 35–36; ubiquity of, x–xi, 9, 12–13, 43
incarceration, reformatory or corrective, 6, 21, 25, 39–40, 94–96
inheritance law, 27
insanity, 25
Ireland, Richard, 25

jail, 91; definition of, x, 38, 86; vs prison, x, xii.
See also incarceration, pretrial and custodial
Jerome Project, The (Titus Kaphar), xiii
Jews: community in Herakleopolis, 129;
    martyrs, 185
John (Bishop of Rome), 134
Johnston, Norman, 45, 80
Joseph (biblical figure), prison of, 94–95, 141
Jugurtha (king), 106–7
Julius Alexander, Tiberius (governor), 24, 190
jurisprudence, classical, 2–7
jurists, Roman: role of, 21; on sentencing
    procedures; 27–33
Justinian (emperor), legislation of, 6, 104
Juvenal, 46, 65

Kaphar, Titus (artist, *The Jerome Project*), xiii
Kavad I (king), incarceration of, 104
Krause, Jens-Uwe (*Gefängnisse im römischen
    Reich*), 5, 8, 42, 81–82, 99, 176, 191
Kyle, Donald, 188

labor, carceral. *See* convict labor
Lambaesis (Tazoult, Algeria), military prison
    of, 56–57, 57*fig.*, 74, 83, 88, 107, 178
Latin: terms for prison personnel, 171; terms for
    prisons, 11–12, 86
latrines, 61–63, 174
Lavan, Luke, 4
La Volpe, Nicola, 143
law, Roman, 20, 21; idealized world of, 43; and
    power of judges, 25–26
lawmakers, medieval, 15, 25
laws, rescripts, and reforms: abuse of power,
    43–44; amnesties, 40–41, 192, 194; bakery
    labor, 121; captive labor, 127; exile, 31; food
    provisions, 118, 130, 134, 176, 193; heretics as
    guards, 176; humane treatment of accused,
    29–30, 31, 32, 38–39, 41, 177–78, 179, 192;
    monastic confinement, 6; permanent
    incarceration, 32–33; post-carceral
    manumission, 27, 35; prisons for punishment,
    30–31; public slaves, 175; release from mine
    service, 36; separation of men and women, 86;
    soldiers and prison transport, 142, 184; stealing
    from sinking ships, 33–34; tax debtors, 29
Lefebvre, Henri, xii
Lenski, Noel, 175
Leschi, Louis, 173
Libanius, 55; imprisonment of, 111; on execution,
    134; on false accusations, 193–94; on food

and wine for prisoners, 117, 119. *See also in*
    Index of Sources
Licinius (emperor), legislation of, 130
light deprivation, as torture, 108–9, 201
Lovato, Andrea (*Il carcere nel diritto penale
    romano: dai Severi a Giustiniano*), 3, 25–16,
    29–30, 39, 191
Lucius Scipio, 4
Lucius Verus (emperor), 27

macella (food markets), as prisons, 74
malnourishment, 112
Marcone, Arnaldo, 37
Marcus Aurelius (emperor), 27; Column of, 152
Maresha (Beit Guvrin, Israel): figurines of
    captives, 144–45, 146*fig.*; "The Punishments,"
    13, 93–94
mass incarceration, 63–64, 195, 198–99
Mau, August, 2
Mediterranean basin (term), ix
Messene (Greece): civic prison ("the Treasury"), 5,
    52, 74, 83; Philopoemen's incarceration in, 50
Miletus (Balat, Turkey): relief depicting chained
    prisoner, 142
military outposts, carceral function of, 57–58
Millar, Fergus, 33, 125
miners, appearance of, 72
mines and quarries, 64; as carceral spaces, 33, 36,
    83, 127; condemnation to, 26, 33, 36–37; death
    in, 125; descriptions of, 147; documentary
    sources for, 36–37; food provisions for,
    115–16, 164; historical sources for, 71–72;
    and local economies, 115–16; profitability
    of, 125–26; surveillance in, 85; as torturous
    environments, 37–38, 71–72, 86–87; transport
    to, 185–87. *See also* convict labor; mines
    and quarries, locations of; public works,
    condemnation to
mines and quarries, locations of: Cyprus, 125;
    Dardania, 127; the Lautumiae (Sicily), 26, 45;
    Mons Claudianus (Egypt), 34, 115, 125; Mons
    Porphyrites (Egypt), 115; New Carthage
    (Spain), 125; Phaino/Feynan (Jordan), 37,
    70–72, 85, 187; Simitthus (Chemtou, Tunisia),
    37, 61–64, 62*fig.*, 125, 186–87; Vipasca
    (Portugal), 115; Wadi Amram (Israel), 71–72.
    See also convict labor; mines and quarries;
    public works, condemnation to
Mommsen, Theodor (*Römisches Strafrecht*), 2–4,
    5, 42, 45, 98–99
monastery of Epiphanius (Thebes), 106

monastic confinement, 6–7, 39, 75, 96; for women, 104

monks: as carceral go-betweens, 131; imprisoned, 175

Mont St. Michel (Normandy), prison of, 86

Moran, Dominique, 72

Morris, Sarah, 72

Mosaic of the Captives (Tipasa basilica), 79, 83–84, 136–38, 137*fig.*, 147, 149, 152

Mosaic of the *Damnati* (El Djem, Tunisia), 147, 148*fig.*, 188

Mount Vesuvius, eruption of, 75

Muhs, Brian, 98, 123

mummy wrapping, Ptolemaic, 151

Nemesis (goddess), 61; altars to (Carnuntum), 174

Neudecker, Richard, 81

Nickenich (Germany), limestone relief from, 141, 143

Nika riots, 129

Nogrady, Alexander, 4

no true Scotsman fallacy, 3

Oglethorpe, James (General), 200, 201, 202*fig.*

oil lamps, 60, 71–72, 114, 120, 193, 201

oportet, interpretations of, 22

Ostia, 172

Overbeck, Johannes, 1, 54

Oxford History of the Prison, 7

Oxford Research Encyclopedia of Criminology and Criminal Justice, 7

Oxyrhynchus: prisons of, 12, 100, 106–7, 173

Pachomius (monk), 98

Palace of Justice (Bucharest), 53

Papadopoulos, John, 72

Paul (apostle), 15, 47, 107, 185

Pausanias, 52

Pavón Torrejón, Pilar (*La cárcel y el encarcelamiento en el mundo romano*), 8, 46, 65, 92, 117, 171, 176

penal ideology, Roman, 25–26

penology, modern, 25

Peregrinus (religious freelancer), 129–30

Pérez Martín, Inmaculada, 8

Pero and Micon, myth of: in Latin elegy, 140; in Pliny the Elder, 95, 171; Pompeiian frescoes of, 84, 139–40, 140*fig.*, 176, 179; statue of, 140, 143

Perpetua (martyr), 56, 87, 120

Perseus of Macedon (king), imprisonment of, 85

Peter (apostle), 47; depictions of, 142, 144; in Tullian prison, 141, 142

Philadelphia (Kom el-Kharaba el-Kebir, Egypt), 13, 131

Philip of Macedon (king), imprisonment of, 116

Plato's theory of ideal prisons, 6, 39, 50, 87, 94–95, 96. *See also in* Index of Sources

Pliny the Younger (governor), on elderly prisoners, 120–21, 127; on guarding prisoners, 175; on prison breaks, 180–81. *See also in* Index of Sources

Pompeii: locked bakery, 121–22; Pero and Micon depictions, 84, 139–40, 140*fig.*, 143, 179; proposed prison locations, 1–2, 12, 53–54, 55; Villa of the Mosaic Columns, 75, 109

Pontius Pilate (governor), 133–34

pottery, courseware, 120

poverty, 102–3, 112, 199–201

power, visual language of, 143–44, 201–2

prison: as "the place with no food at all," 101; definitions of, x–xi, xii, 7–8, 38; *dēmosios*, 59; *robus*, 11; *signa*, 12; *tullianum*, 11; *vestibula*, 11. *See also* incarceration, punitive; jail; prisons, ancient; prisons, modern

prison breaks, 179–81

prisoner letters, production of, 164–69. *See also* archive of sources

prisoners, civic: ix, x, xii–xiii, 14–15; depictions of (artistic) 138–40, 140*fig.*, 142, 143, 176, 179; descriptions of (legal sources), 148–49; descriptions of (literary sources), 145–48; economic exploitation of, 43, 124–28; food provisions (private), 113–16, 193; as "foreign other," 152; food provisions (state), 116–19; gruesome bodily experience of, 109, 112, 147–49; health, 60; hunger, 101–3, 114; innocent, 100–101; personal property of, 43–44, 114–15; penalty for escaping, 27, 34; experience of punishment, 92–99; requests for release, 92–94; and sexual violence, 103–6; transport of, 85, 141–42, 183–85; wine for, 114, 119

prisoners of war (captives): artistic depictions of, 136–38, 137*fig.*, 144–45, 145*fig.*, 150–51; foreigness/otherness of, 152; lead figurines, 144–45, 146*fig.*; muscularity of, 150–51

Prison for the Condemned. *See under* Carales

prison guards: artistic depictions of, 140*fig.*, 142–44, 144*fig.*; bribing of, 175, 179, 181; camaraderie, 173; corrupted by prisoners,

105–6; danger of job, 158–59; numbers of, 172, 174; office spaces, 173–74; public slaves as, 175; recipients of wine and food, 114, 174–75; soldiers as, 56, 141–42, 171; stealing from prisoners, 118; taxes for, 55, 168–69, 174

prison rations, 116–19

prison reforms, 38–41, 104, 192. *See also* laws, rescripts, and reforms

prisons, ancient: abuse (use) of, 40, 44, 133–34; architectural features of, 49, 50, 59–63, 65, 68, 80, 177–79; capacities of, 63; centrality of (near forum/agora), 46–47, 50, 52, 53, 65, 79, 81–82, 181, 189–90; coldness of, 106–7; courseware pottery in, 120; darkness of, 107–9, 177; death in, 39, 54, 58, 73, 99–101, 164; diseases in, 109; documentary sources for, 55; gender separation, 86; historical sources for, 9–14; identification in archaeological record, 4–5, 45–46; infestations of, 106; latrines, 61–63; manholes, 48, 49, 52, 55, 179, as mirror to modern, ix, 16, 58, 64, 112, 158, 194–95, 198; movement within, 177–81; permeability of, 115–16; purposes of, 19, 23; segregation in, 62–63, 85–86; as spaces for punishment, 86–87; stench of, 109–10; torturous conditions in, 48, 99, 107; typologies of, 46, 65, 76; ubiquity of, ix, x–xi, 9, 12–13, 20, 55; visiting privileges, 128–32, 179; visual depictions of, 138–41, 140*fig*. *See also* incarceration, punitive; prison; prisons, locations of; prisons, types of

prisons, locations of: Alba Fucens, 85, 109–10, 116; Antioch, 55; Carales (Cagliari), 11, 61, 68–70; Caesarea Maritima, 173; Cosa, 48–49, 49*fig*.; Corinth, 66–68, 67*fig*.; Cuicul, 48, 52–53, 53*fig*., 82, 83; Dara, 73; Egypt, 4; Gerasa "holy detention center," 86; Lambaesis, 56–57, 57*fig*., 74, 83, 107; Messene, 50, 52; Philippi, 73; Pompeii, 1–2; Rome, 46–48, 47*fig*., 65–66; Simitthus (Chemtou, Tunisia), 37, 61–64, 62*fig*.; Sufetula (Tunisia), 76–80, 77*fig*., 78*fig*., 79*fig*., 107; Tiberias, 54–55; Ulpia Traiana Sarmizegetusa, 49–50, 51*fig*. *See also* under individual city/site names

prisons, modern: architectural features of, 62–63; 80–81; carceral practices, xiii, 27, 80–81; in early modern Europe, 5, 6, 86, 199–200; English names for, 12; food as punishment, 119; military and economic ties, 58, 158; mirrored in ancient practice, ix, 16, 58, 64, 112, 158, 194–95, 198; remote locations of, 80–81; search for "origins" of, 5–8

prison studies, xii

prisons, types of: ad hoc, 65, 73–74; in amphitheaters, 46, 59–61; civic (*carcer publicus*), 11, 44, 46–55, 65–68, 81; converted cisterns, 68–70, 73, 75, 173; in hospitals, 106; military (*carcer castrensis*), 11, 46, 55–58; private, 75–76, 194; purpose-built, 48–63; repurposed, 65–72; in temples, 73–74, 77–78, 81; towers, 72; tax office prison (*logistērion*), 164, 190–91; treasury prison (*praktoreion*), 24–25, 46, 58–59, 190; workers' prisons, 46, 61–65. *See also* incarceration, punitive; prison; prisons, ancient; prisons, locations of

prostitution, 34–35, 103; penal, 105

public works (*opus publicum*): condemnation to, 22–23, 33–38; escape from, 34. *See also* convict labor; mines and quarries

punishment: as reformatory or corrective, 6, 21, 25, 94–96

punishment, differential, 33–34

quarries. *See* mines and quarries

Rabinow, Paul, 42

Rakob, Friedrich, 61, 63

Raspels, Bernhard, 39

Rea, John R., 160

registrar (*commentariensis*), 118, 156, 159–61, 164, 168, 171, 176, 188

Reid, J. Nicholas, ix–x, 8

Rein, Wilhelm (*Das Criminalrecht der Römer von Romulus bis auf Justinianus*), 5

Reiter, Keramet, 44

Rikers Island jail (New York City), 91

riots, 129, 159–60, 161

Rivière, Yann, 21, 40, 45, 48–49, 179; *Histoire du droit penal romain: de Romulus à Justinien*, 3–4; *Le cachot et les fers: détention et coercition à Rome*, 3

robbery, 75; in a bath house, 58; of sinking ships, 33–34. *See also* theft

Rome: Arch of Constantine, 152; Arch of Septimius Severus, 144, 152; Catacomb of Domitilla, 144; Column of Trajan, 152; Forum of Julius Caesar, 47; House of Freedom (*atrium libertatis*)/Lautumiae, 48, 65–66; Roman forum, 47; Temple of Saturn, 47, 48, 74; Tullian Prison (Tullianum), 45–46, 47–48, 47*fig*., 65–66, 82–83, 106–7, 110, 141, 188

Rubin, Ashley T., 7, 9

Samos (island), 189

Sarmizegetusa, Ulpia Traiana (Romania): depiction of Dacian prisoners, 138; tribunal and *curia* prisons of, 49–50, 51*fig.*, 181

Schellenberg, Ryan S., 176

Schiavone, Romina, 4

Schneider, Rolf Michael, 138

Scott, James C., 135–36

Scotton, Paul, 173–74

scribes: use by prisoners, 162–63, 167–68

Secret Service, 190

sentences and sentencing: forms of punishment, 26, 28, 96, 97–98; length of, 96–97; life sentences, 95–96; procedures, 27–33

Sessa, Kristina (*Daily Life in Late Antiquity*), 4–5

sewer lines, 62–63

sexual violence, 103–6

shackles. *See* chains and shackles

ships: for prisoner transport, 184–85; robbery of, 33–34

Sijpesteijn, Peter, 154, 156–57, 182

Simitthus Workers' Prison (Chemtou, Tunisia), 26, 37, 61–64, 62*fig.*, 125, 186–87

skylights, 53, 60, 69–70, 108, 122

slaves: as debt collateral, 102, 194; incarceration of, 27, 35–36; runaway, 35–36, 121

slaves of punishment (*servi poenae*), 34, 35–36

slavery: vs convict labor, 34–36, 64

Socrates (philosopher), 15

Sogliano, Antonio, 54

soldiers: as police officers, 158; as prison personnel, 56, 141–42, 171

solitary confinement, 85–86, 91, 97–98, 195, 198

Sousse relief (Tunisia), 143, 150*fig.*, 152

space, material aspects of, 80–81

Spierenburg, Pieter, 200

sports fans, 129

Sufetula (Subaytilah, Tunisia), 76–80, 77*fig.*, 78*fig.*, 79*fig.*, 107

suicide, 91, 100, 176

swineherds, 93, 124

Tarraco (Tarragona, Spain), domestic prison of, 73

tattoos, 72

Taussig, Michael T., 84

tax collector (*praktor*), 58

taxes for prison guards (*desmofulakia*), 55, 168–69, 174

Temple of the Standards, 56, 178

temples as prisons, 73–74, 81

Thamugadi (Timgad, Algeria), 13, 77, 79–80, 118

theft: of a backpack, 91; of a chisel, 164; of clothing, 159; of food, 111–12, 122, 201; of sheep, 159

Themelis, Petros, 52

Theodoric (king), 39, 134

Theodosian Code, 38, 192. *See also in* Index of Sources

Theodosius I (emperor), 134; legislation of, 31, 105, 148, 192; visit to Rome, 121

Theodosius II (emperor), legislation of, 31, 38, 116, 118, 176, 193

Tiberias (Syria Palaestina), prison of, 54–55, 179

Tiberius (emperor): imprisonment of enemies, 97–98, 133

Tipasa (Mauritania), civic basilica of, 136–37. *See also* Mosaic of the Captives

Torallas Tovar, Sofía, 8, 11, 55, 75, 98

torture: en route to trial, 181–82; leaded whips, 192; light deprivation, 108–9, 201; tactics, 171; vivisection, 132–33

Trajan (emperor), Column of, 152; rescripts of, 127, 175

Twelve Tables, 24

Ulpian: on penal incarceration, 2–3, 22–24, 25–26, 32, 127; on pretrial procedures, 27–28; on *servus poenae*, 35. *See also in* Index of Sources

underworld deities, prisons and, 47–48, 65, 82–83

Valentinian II (emperor), legislation of: 31, 40–41, 192–93

Van Buren, Albert, 2

vincula publica, 23, 24, 96

visiting prisons, 128–32

Vitruvius (geographer): on ideal forum, 1, 46–47, 52, 55, 74, 79, 81, 181. *See also in* Index of Sources

vivisection, 132–33

Warren, Wendy, 63

watchtowers, 63, 65

well, sacred, 47–48

windows: Columella's prescriptions on, 57, 88, 107–8; for communication with outside world, 128, 131, 164–65, 200; in Pero and Micon frescoes, 84, 139–40, 140*fig.*, 142–43, 176; in prison architecture, 50, 54, 56–57, 65, 68, 76, 84; for surveillance, 142–43, 179

wine, 114, 119

women: as debt collateral, 102, 124, 131–32, 194; depiction as prisoners (artistic), 149; mine workers, 34–35; monastic confinement, 104; prostitution, 34–35; sexual violence against, 103–6

Yardley, J.C., 4

Zamora Manzano, José Luis (*La administración penitenciaria en el derecho romano*), 8, 25
Zebatus (prisoner), 87, 93–94
Zeno (businessman), archive of, 92–93, 101, 112, 113, 131–32, 157, 165–68, 166*fig.*, 167*fig.*

Founded in 1893,

publishes bold, progressive books and journals
on topics in the arts, humanities, social sciences,
and natural sciences—with a focus on social
justice issues—that inspire thought and action
among readers worldwide.

The UC PRESS FOUNDATION
raises funds to uphold the press's vital role
as an independent, nonprofit publisher, and
receives philanthropic support from a wide
range of individuals and institutions—and from
committed readers like you. To learn more, visit
ucpress.edu/supportus.